DR DOS 6
By Example

William F. Lawrence

DR DOS 6
By Example

FEATURING DOZENS OF TIPS AND SCREEN ILLUSTRATIONS TO HELP YOU MASTER THE POWER OF DR DOS

William F. Lawrence

 M&T Books
A Division of M&T Publishing, Inc.
411 Borel Avenue, Suite 100
San Mateo, CA 94402-3522

© 1991 by M&T Publishing, Inc.

Printed in the United States of America

All rights reserved. No part of this book may be reproduced or transmitted in any form or by any means, electronic or mechanical, including photocopying, recording, or by any information storage and retrieval system, without prior written permission from the Publisher. Contact the Publisher for information on foreign rights.

Limits of Liability and Disclaimer of Warranty
The Author and Publisher of this book have used their best efforts in preparing the book and the programs contained in it. These efforts include the development, research, and testing of the theories and programs to determine their effectiveness.

The Author and Publisher make no warranty of any kind, expressed or implied, with regard to these programs or the documentation contained in this book. The Author and Publisher shall not be liable in any event for incidental or consequential damages in connection with, or arising out of, the furnishing, performance, or use of these programs.

Library of Congress Cataloging-in-Publication Data

Lawrence, William F.
DR DOS 6 By Example / William Lawrence
    p.   cm.
Includes index.
ISBN 1-55851-245-4
1. Operating systems (Computers) 2. DR DOS. I. Title.
II. Title: DR DOS six by example.
QA76. 76. 063L383   1991
005. 4' 46--dc20   91-42485
                                                                CIP

Project Editor: Christine de Chutkowski

Trademarks:
All products, names, and services are trademarks or registered trademarks of their respective companies.

Cover Design: Lauren Smith Design

    94 93 92 91   4 3 2 1

Dedication

To Kathy, Sarah, Andrew, and Stephanie.
Thanks for your help, patience, and support. You mean the world to me.

Contents

WHY THIS BOOK IS FOR YOU 1

CHAPTER 1: INTRODUCING DR DOS 3
Background 3
Anatomy of a Disk 5
      Write-Protecting Your Data 8
Hard Drives 9
Virtual Disks 10
Files and Directories 11
Advanced Disk Features in DR DOS 12
You and Your Display 13
Communications Ports 13
Serial Communications with FileLink 17
Random Access Memory 17
Task Switching 19
Security 20
The Command Line and Beyond 21

CHAPTER 2: INSTALLING DR DOS 25
Using MemoryMAX 25
Using SuperStor 25
Using PC-Kwik 26
Setting up a New Hard Drive 26
Running the DR DOS Installation Program 27
      Arrow keys and Tab key 27
      Escape key 27

vii

F10 27
    Enter 27
Preparing a New Hard Disk 28
Installing DR DOS 30
    Maximum Application Memory at the Expense of Functionality 30
    Balance Application Memory and Functionality 30
    Maximum Performance and Functionality at the Expense of Application
        Memory 31
TaskMAX 34
DiskMAX 36
ViewMAX 37
Country and Keyboard 38
System Parameters 39
Optional Device Drivers and Utilities 44
Security 45
Finishing Up 46

CHAPTER 3: BASIC DOS SKILLS 47
The Command Line 47
Files 51
    Wildcards in File Names 52
    Changing File Names 53
Disks and Directories 54
    Making and Deleting Directories 56
    Renaming Directories 57
About DR DOS Devices 57
How-to Information 58
    Finding Files 58
    Copying and Moving Files 60
    Deleting Files 62
    Looking at a Text File 64
    Changing File Attributes 64

CONTENTS

Searching for Text in Files 66
Printing Files 67
Formatting a Diskette 69
Copying an Entire Floppy Disk 71
Backing Up the System 72
Restoring Files from Backups 73
Checking Available Memory 74
Making Disk Repairs 74

CHAPTER 4: HELP! 77
Running DOSBOOK 77
DR DOS Basics 78
Commands and Utilities 78
Troubleshooting 79
The Table of Contents, Index, and Glossary 82
The Menus 82

CHAPTER 5: FINE-TUNING DR DOS 85
Phase 1: The Initial Setup 88
Phase 2: Placing Drivers in Upper Memory 93
Phase 3: Placing TSRs in Upper Memory 96
Special Capabilities for CONFIG.SYS 97
CONFIG.SYS Control Statements 100
    ? 100
    :label 101
    CHAIN 102
    CLS 103
    CPOS 104
    ECHO 105
    EXIT 106
    GOSUB 107
    GOTO 108

DR DOS 6 BY EXAMPLE

    RETURN 109
    SWITCH 110
    TIMEOUT 111
Configuration Commands 112
    BREAK 112
    BUFFERS 113
    COUNTRY 114
    DEVICE 116
    DRIVPARM 117
    FASTOPEN 119
    FCBS 120
    FILES 121
    HIBUFFERS 122
    HIDEVICE 123
    HIDOS 125
    HIINSTALL 126
    HISTORY 127
    INSTALL 128
    LASTDRIVE 129
    REM 130
    SHELL 131
DR DOS Installable Device Drivers 132
    ANSI.SYS 132
    DEVSWAP.SYS 133
    DISPLAY.SYS 134
    DRIVER.SYS 136
    EMM386.SYS 138
    EMMXMA.SYS 142
    HIDOS.SYS 143
    PRINTER.SYS 147
    SSTORDRV.SYS 148
    VDISK.SYS 149

CONTENTS

Third-Party Memory Managers 151
The AUTOEXEC.BAT File 152
Configuring for Microsoft Windows 154
DR DOS and Novell 155
DR DOS and PC/NFS 156

CHAPTER 6: THE TASKMAX TASK SWITCHER 157
Things to Consider 158
    Configuring TaskMAX 158
    TaskMAX Shift and Hot Keys 159
    Extended Memory Reserved for Swapping 161
    Expanded (EMS) Memory Reserved for Swapping 161
    Expanded (EMS) Memory Allocated to Each Task 162
    Running TaskMAX 163
    Adding a Task 165
    Switching Tasks 165
    Deleting a Task 166
    Copying Text 166
    Shutting Down TaskMAX 169
    Running TaskMAX from the Command Line 170
    Controlling TaskMAX's Access to Memory 170
    Allocating Expanded Memory for Each Task 171
    Changing the Swap Directory 172
    Adding a New Task 172
    Changing a Task's Name 173
    Deleting a Task From the Command Line 173
    More Things to Consider 174
    The TASKMAX.INI File 174

CHAPTER 7: USING EDITOR 175
Cranking Up 176
The Cursor Control Diamond 178

xi

Moving Further 180
The Accelerator Key 180
Deleting Text 180
Saving and Exiting 181
Moving Text 181
Moving Around 184
Placing Special Characters 185
Repeating Your Last Entry 185

CHAPTER 8: AUTOMATING OPERATIONS WITH BATCH FILES 187
Example 1: A Rudimentary Batch File 187
Example 2: Adding Variables 188
Example 3: Controlling the Display 190
Example 4: Branching and Looping 191
Batch-File Command Reference 193
@ 194
:label 195
CALL 196
ECHO 197
FOR 198
GOSUB 199
GOTO 200
IF 201
PAUSE 203
REM 204
RETURN 205
SHIFT 206
SWITCH 208

CONTENTS

CHAPTER 9: TAKING CHARGE OF YOUR DISK 209
Kicking the Drive Into Gear with PC-Kwik 209
    Configuring PC-Kwik 214
    PC-Kwik Parameters 214
    Notes on Using PC-Kwik 220
Compressing Data with SuperStor 221
    Before Running SuperStor 222
    Installing SuperStor 223
    Working with Compressed Drives 227
Cleaning Up Files with DISKOPT 228
Bringing Files Back With UNDELETE 230

CHAPTER 10: SECURING YOUR DATA 233
System Security 234
Directory Security 236
File Security 238
Locking Your Screen 240
Removing Security 241
Things to Watch Out For 241

CHAPTER 11: USING VIEWMAX 243
ViewMAX, the Graphical User Interface 243
A Brief History Lesson 243
Mousing Around 245
Running ViewMAX 246
Checking Out the Neighborhood 248
Operating Your Windows 249
    To See the Rest of a Window 249
    Filling the Screen with a Window 251
Climbing the Directory Tree 251
The Title Bar Tells All 254
Using the Menu Bar 254

DR DOS 6 BY EXAMPLE

Having it Your Way 256
Copying Files 258
Deleting Files 261
Other Things You Can Do with Objects 261
    Renaming and Examining Files, Directories, and Disks 262
    Changing a Password 265
Formatting Diskettes 267
Changing the View From Your Windows 267
Finding Files 269
Undeleting Files and Directories 270
Help! 271
Desk Accessories 271
    Recycling Old Accessories 273
Running Applications 273
    Takes Parameters 275
    Application Type and Documents 276
    A Sample Configuration 280
    Pitfalls in Configuring Applications 281
    Configuring GEM Applications 283
    Problems with Some GEM Applications 283
Escaping to DR DOS 284
ViewMAX and TaskMAX 284
    The TaskMAX Dialog Boxes 285
    Road-Testing the ViewMAX/TaskMAX Combo 288

CHAPTER 12: COMMUNICATION AND FILELINK 291
Parallel Ports 291
    Controlling Your Parallel Port 294
Serial Ports 295
    Plugging In 297
    Controlling the Serial Port 298

Sending Data Through Your Ports 299
        When Communication Doesn't Work 302
Using FILELINK to Transfer Files Between Computers 304
        Moving FILELINK to Another Computer 305
Setting Up FILELINK 306
Getting Directories From the Slave 307
Transferring Files 308

CHAPTER 13: ADVANCED FUNCTIONS 311

Redirection and Piping 311
        Redirection 311
        Piping 313
Configuring the Display and Keyboard with ANSI.SYS 314
        Color Escape Sequences 315
        Screen-Attribute Escape Sequences 316
        Video-Mode Escape Sequences 316
        Keyboard Escape Sequences 317
Code Pages 318
        How Code Pages Work 318
        Installing Code Pages Through SETUP 319
        Available Code Pages 322
        Installing Code Pages Manually 323
        Checking and Refreshing Code Pages 324
The Symbolic Interactive Debugger 325
        Conventions 325
        Command Summary 326

APPENDIX A: DR DOS COMMAND REFERENCE 329

COMMAND 329
APPEND 331
ASSIGN 334
ATTRIB 336

DR DOS 6 BY EXAMPLE

BACKUP	338
BREAK	340
CHCP	342
CHDIR or CD	343
CHKDSK	346
CLS	348
COMMAND	349
COMP	351
COPY	353
CTTY	357
CURSOR	359
DATE	361
DEL	363
DELPURGE	365
DELQ	367
DELWATCH	368
DIR	371
DISKCOMP	373
DISKCOPY	375
DISKMAP	377
DISKOPT	379
DOSBOOK	381
ERAQ	383
ERASE or ERA	384
EXE2BIN	386
EXIT	388
FASTOPEN	389
FC	390
FDISK	393
FIND	398
FORMAT	400
GRAFTABL	404
GRAPHICS	406

CONTENTS

HILOAD	408
JOIN	410
KEYB	412
LABEL	415
LOCK	417
MEM	419
MEMMAX	421
MKDIR or MD	423
MODE	425
MORE	437
MOVE	439
NLSFUNC	442
PASSWORD	443
PATH	446
PRINT	448
PROMPT	451
RECOVER	454
RENAME or REN	456
RENDIR	458
REPLACE	459
RESTORE	461
RMDIR or RD	464
SCRIPT	465
SET	467
SETUP	469
SHARE	470
SORT	472
SSTOR	474
SUBST	475
SUPERPCK	477
SYS	478
TASKMAX	479
TIME	483

TOUCH 485
TREE 487
TYPE 489
UNDELETE 490
UNFORMAT 493
UNINSTAL 494
VER 495
VERIFY 496
VOL 497
XCOPY 498
XDEL 501
XDIR 503

APPENDIX B: EDITOR COMMAND REFERENCE 507

APPENDIX C: THE VIEWMAX COMMAND REFERENCE 511
The File Menu 512
The Options Menu 513
The View Menu 514
The Help Menu 516
The Information Menu 516
But I Don't Have a Mouse 516
     Navigating Without Benefit of Mouse 517

GLOSSARY 519

INDEX 529

Why This Book is for You

DR DOS 6.0 from Digital Research is one of the most important products for personal computers to emerge in years. Besides greatly expanding the power and capabilities of your system, it shows that excellence still sells and that the software market hasn't become the sole province of huge companies.

This book was written for the average computer user who would like to get the most out of this advanced operating system. This isn't a highly technical discussion, but it does cover things in sufficient detail to be immediately useful. Examples and tips from my own experience are included.

If you're new to personal computers, "Introduction to DR DOS" will give you a crash course in computer literacy. In it, you'll learn about disks, directories, devices, and some of the remarkable features of DR DOS 6.0. Chapter 3, "Basic DOS Skills," covers the most commonly used commands and will give you the skills you need for day-to-day operation of your computer.

If you're an old hand at using personal computers, refer to Chapter 5, "Fine-Tuning DR DOS." You'll learn how loading DR DOS into high memory and device drivers into upper memory will leave a phenomenal amount of conventional memory for your applications.

No matter what your skill level, you should read the chapters on ViewMAX, TaskMAX, and EDITOR.

- ViewMAX (Chapter 11) is a convenient graphical user interface. With its roots in Digital Research's GEM system, ViewMAX is a blend of Macintosh desktop functionality and Microsoft Windows-like menus. If you're not firmly committed to the Windows environment, you may find that ViewMAX is the GUI for you.

- Chapter 6 tells you how to put TaskMAX to work. You'll learn how to load multiple programs simultaneously, switch between them at the touch of a key, and even copy data between two active applications. You'll also see how to combine TaskMAX and ViewMAX to create a powerful task-switching desktop environment.

- If you've ever struggled with the wretched EDLIN, you'll appreciate EDITOR. This convenient, powerful, easy-to-use tool lets you modify your CONFIG.SYS, AUTOEXEC.BAT, and other files. Chapter 7 covers this program's commands and shows you how the cursor diamond works.

If you have a laptop, Chapter 12 will show you how to wire your computers together and install and use the FILELINK utility, which is the fastest way I've seen to shuffle files between two computers.

Also be sure to explore the "Help!" chapter (Chapter 4); it will introduce you to DOSBOOK, a hypertext-like, on-line help facility for DR DOS. You'll also find a quick reference to commands, step-by-step instructions for basic DOS tasks, and a complete reference to DR DOS error messages.

CHAPTER 1

Introducing DR DOS

This chapter explains the fundamentals of DR DOS, what it does, how it organizes information, and what some of the advanced features such as ViewMAX, TaskMAX, SuperStor and PC-Kwik are all about. The chapter covers version 5.0 and 6.0 of Digital Research's DR DOS. If you're an experienced computer user and are familiar with a disk operating system (DOS), you can skip much of this information. If you're feeling a bit overwhelmed by your computer, sit back, take a deep breath, grab a cup of coffee, and read on. Don't think that you need to remember all of this. Just read through it to get a general idea of what's going on.

While you're getting started, don't feel intimidated by your computer or DR DOS. Remember that DR DOS is a great tool for running your computer, and your computer can be the best helper you've ever had. Besides, unless you take a sledgehammer to the thing, you can't really hurt the computer. The worst thing that can happen is that you'll lose some information, and even if that happens DR DOS will probably be able to recover it.

Background

A disk operating system (DOS) is the one, absolutely fundamental software package you must have. It enables you to:

- Store information (which I'll usually just call "data") on floppy and hard disks.
- Access information from these storage devices when you need it.
- Run programs such as spreadsheets, databases, and word processors.
- Control the flow of information from the computer through connections to the outside world, such as printers and modems.

You can think of DOS as your computer's manager, overseeing the operation of:

- Floppy disks.
- Hard disks.
- The video display.
- Serial communications ports (which connect a mouse, a printer, or other computers to your computer).
- Parallel communications ports (which connect a printer to your computer).
- Random Access Memory (usually just called memory or RAM).
- The application programs you run.

DR DOS is an enhanced, MS-DOS-compatible operating system that gives you additional capabilities over MS-DOS or PC-DOS. You may not fully appreciate just how good DR DOS is at this point, but by the end of the book you'll be glad you have DR DOS.

DR DOS also maintains your data in an organizational mechanism called the *file system*, which manages information storage on your computer's floppy and hard disk drives. The file system works very much like files you might have in a filing cabinet. Each file holds a particular kind of information in electronic form. This information can be an application program, a balance sheet, a piece of artwork, a letter to the editor, or almost anything else that you can imagine. Files are named and organized into electronic file drawers called *directories*. Unlike physical file drawers, directories can expand to hold as many files as your disk drive can accommodate. Directories can have sub-directories (file drawers within file drawers if you will), allowing you to further categorize where you store your data.

That's about all you need to know about the file system to understand the rest of this chapter. Later in the book, I'll discuss the file system in detail and show you how to create directories, make copies of files, and delete files that you no longer need. DR DOS essentially makes file management easier and safer, and I'll discuss the how's and why's later.

INTRODUCING DR DOS

Anatomy of a Disk

Disks hold your information and your programs. Disks come in several flavors, the most common of which are *floppy disks*, *hard disks,* and *virtual disks.* As a general rule, floppy disks — or "diskettes" as they are often called — are removable, while hard disks remain in your computer (although hard disks mounted in removable cartridges are available). Virtual disks work like hard disks — you can store and retrieve files from them—but are temporary structures made from computer memory.

In the early days of PCs, there was just one kind of floppy disk. Now there are two types: the flexible 5 1/4-inch diskettes, which are bulky and easily damaged, and the newer 3 1/2-inch diskettes in hard plastic cases. To make matters more interesting, each type of disk comes in low- and high- density varieties, and now there are super-high-density diskettes as well.

The amount of information that a disk can store—its capacity— is measured in "bytes." You can think of a byte as a character, such as a letter or a digit. Low-density 5 1/4-inch disks hold about 360,000 bytes, or 360 kilobytes (KB), which is very little by today's conventions. These types of disks were the standard for older machines such as the original IBM PC and XT types, and as such are becoming rather rare. Such disks may be labeled as DS-DD (double-sided, double-density) on the package, or they may not be labeled at all. Because DR DOS was designed to run on any IBM-compatible PC—including the old ones—the DR DOS 5 1/4-inch distribution disks are low-density.

High-density 5 1/4-inch disks hold about 1,200 KB or 1.2 megabytes (MB) of data. These disks were introduced on the IBM AT-type machines in 1985, and are the most common 5 1/4-inch disks that you'll encounter. Again, they can be marked HD, or not marked at all. Fortunately, you can use DR DOS commands to tell the density of the disk.

Low-density 3 1/2-inch disks hold about 720,000 bytes, or 720 KB. These are most commonly found in the less powerful laptop machines. You can tell a low-density 3 1/2-inch disk because it isn't labeled. (Your DR DOS 3 1/2-inch distribution disks are low-density.) High-density 3 1/2-inch disks hold 1.44 MB, and are almost always marked HD. Super-high-density diskettes hold 4.00 MB. These are still extremely rare, but will be more popular soon.

Figure 1-1 shows a cut-away view of a typical 3 1/2-inch diskette. Note that the diskette is divided into electronic "tracks," and it is within these tracks that data is actually stored. DR DOS divides the tracks into smaller units called "sectors," and a file can be made up of data in multiple sectors. By increasing the number of tracks, or the number of sectors per track (or both), you get more capacity to store data on the disk. This is exactly how a high-density diskette can hold more than a low-density diskette.

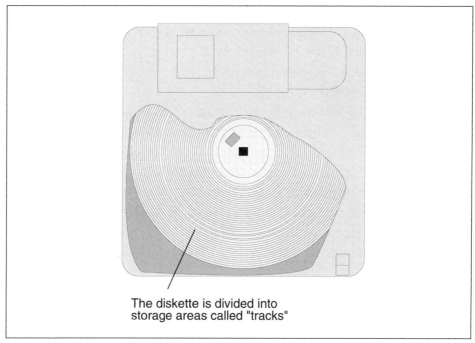

Figure 1-1. A cutaway view of a typical 3 1/2 inch disk.

How does DOS keep track of where the data is stored? It sets aside a part of the diskette for a map, which is updated each time you change the size of a file, or add or delete files on the disk. The map area consists of a "boot record," a "directory table," and a "file allocation table." While the details of these map components aren't important to our discussion, you now know what these terms are about.

If your diskette is *bootable*, then it has an additional number of tracks and sectors set aside to hold DR DOS. This also means that a bootable diskette has less room for your files. When a bootable diskette is inserted into the primary or "A:" disk drive, the computer will automatically read the operating system information from this disk when the system is first turned on or "re-booted." By the way, computer engineers are not shoe fanatics — the term "booting" comes from the expression "to pull yourself up by your bootstraps," which is exactly what the computer does when it loads the operating system, just after you turn on or reset the machine.

Although the 3 1/2-inch diskette is a bit more sophisticated — with its nifty little sliding door — than its older 5 1/4-inch cousin, both work the same way. Once inserted into the drive, the drive mechanism engages the center of the diskette. The diskette then whirls around at high speed. A read/write magnetic head, similar to the kind in a tape recorder, zips in and out propelled by a motor-driven arm. The head pauses over the destination track and waits for the proper sector to come into position. It then reads or writes the data and goes on its merry way.

It's amazing how reliable such a system is, unless of course the diskette becomes damaged or the drive mechanism breaks. Drive mechanisms rarely break, so that's not a worry. You can prevent damage to your disks by using a little common sense:

- Don't leave your diskettes lying around outside of their jackets. Dust, coffee, and other substances can get on them, and once the surface of the disk is coated with gook it doesn't work very well.

- Keep your diskettes away from extremes of heat or cold, such as the inside of your car. Your car's interior can get surprisingly hot in the summer.

- Don't touch the actual magnetic media — the brown surface of the diskette. Oil from your fingers can coat the surface of the diskette.

- Use a felt-tip pen to write on floppy diskette labels, especially on the 5 1/4-inch variety. Sharp points from mechanical pencils or ball point pens can deform or gouge the surface of the diskette.

- Keep your diskettes away from magnetic fields. This includes kitchen magnets, screwdrivers (which may have magnetic tips), magnetic paper clip holders, and electric motors such as those used in household appliances. Magnetic fields will scramble your data.

- Store your diskettes in floppy disk cases or boxes. This further protects them against dust, the klutz who spills Pepsi on your desk, and little children's curious fingers.

There are a few additional little things you can do to make your life with diskettes a lot easier.

- Label your diskettes. You'll eventually accumulate a pile of these things and you will want to be able to find something that you need.

- Always make a "back-up" copy of important diskettes. This includes original software distribution diskettes and important data. Diskettes do eventually get damaged or lose data. It's also a good idea to store back-ups in a different location from your working copies.

- Don't fill your diskettes to the brim with data. You may need to add something to the disk later.

- Write-protect your diskettes if you want to further protect the data. The following section explains write protection.

Write-Protecting Your Data

Write protection does just what it says: it prevents new data from overwriting the old data. You can think of a disk as a VCR tape that you can record over as often as you like. But if you want to protect something on the tape from being erased or overwritten, break off the write protect tab. Diskettes are quite similar to VCR tapes in this way.

To write-protect a 5 1/4-inch diskette, put a tape tab over the little notch on the side of the diskette (shown in Figure 1-2). Tape tabs are shipped with your diskettes, and are usually black or silver. The figure also shows the location of the built-in write-protect tab on 3 1/2-inch diskettes, which slides between read/write and write-protect positions.

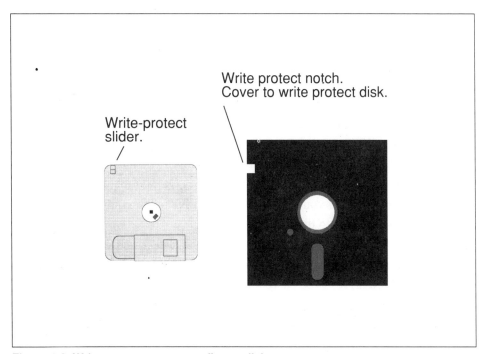

Figure 1-2. Write-protect areas on a floppy diskette.

Hard Drives

Almost all computers have hard drives these days. My venerable Bullet 286 computer has an 80 MB hard drive, although much larger hard drives are becoming common. Hard drives have several advantages over floppy diskettes:

- **Hard drives hold lots and lots of data.** This is important because most of today's application programs — such as word processors, data base managers, spreadsheets, drawing, and painting packages—take up several megabytes of disk space. More recent versions of popular programs cannot run on a floppy-based system at all, while others will run only with a great deal of tedious disk swapping.

- **Hard drives are blazingly fast.** Ranging from 65 milliseconds to less than 10 milliseconds to access a sector of data, they are many times faster than floppy drives.

- **Hard drives are quite reliable.** In fact, they may be too reliable because you'll be tempted to not worry about making back-up copies of important data to floppy diskettes. That's when you'll discover hard disks are not completely reliable.

Hard disks also come in a variety of flavors, which refer to the way they connect to your computer. While you don't need to know exactly what a hard drive controller does, you should know the type of hard drive controller you have. Older computers generally have MFM or RLL hard disk controllers. Newer machines have SCSI, ESDI, or IDE interfaces. If you add another hard drive to the system, you'll need to match the controller type to the drive type.

Because you had either the good fortune or good taste to acquire DR DOS, your hard disk can be a seamless expanse of storage space. Older versions of MS- or PC-DOS required hard drives to be carved into *partitions* that couldn't exceed 32 MB.

Hard disks require very little care. Just remember one thing: never, never, never drop them or the computers that house them. Impact can cause those marvelous little read/write heads within the hard drive to smash into the media platters, irreparably damaging both heads and platters.

It's also not wise to move or jostle your computer while the hard drive is on, and thus spinning. Most modern hard drives have automatic head retraction. This simply means that when you turn the computer off, the read/write heads lock into a safe position. Some hard drives, especially older ones, require that you run a program that retracts the drive heads. This is called *parking* the hard drive (some clone manufacturers may call it something different — check your computer documentation for more information). Make sure that the drive heads are retracted and power is turned off before moving the computer. Otherwise, you'll discover that hard drives are also expensive.

Virtual Disks

Virtual disks aren't really disks at all, but are a large chunk of RAM that is made to look like a hard drive to the disk operating system. Using virtual disks is akin to using a table saw — everything will be fine as long as you think about what you're doing. When the power goes away, everything in the virtual disk also goes away.

INTRODUCING DR DOS

Forever. Always remember to copy new data from the virtual disk to a floppy diskette or hard drive before turning off the power.

A second consideration is that virtual disks gobble up precious computer memory. DR DOS is a lot more intelligent about handling this than other operating systems, but you still must give up memory. *Nada por nada.*

So, with all of these caveats, why use a virtual disk at all? Unlike a real hard drive, there are no moving parts to slow down the virtual disk. There is no faster type of disk available. If you need to perform time-consuming data access, such as manipulating databases or accessing spelling checker dictionaries, you'll want a virtual disk. The chapter on installation (Chapter 2), describes how you can use some of your computer memory as a virtual disk.

Another type of virtual disk you might encounter is the "ROM card." Some of the original notebook or mini-laptop machines didn't have room for a floppy disk drive. Instead, they relied on tiny plug-in circuit cards with programs stored in read-only memory or ROM chips (so named because their contents could not be changed). This was a solution, but not a very good one.

Files and Directories

Now that you know all about drives, I'll cover how your information is stored in the computer. As mentioned earlier, DR DOS manages the "file system." Files hold data. For example, the text for this chapter is held in a file called intro.DOC. The name of the file is "intro," and "DOC" is referred to as the file extension. The file name identifies the file, while the extension is used to identify the type of file. DOC is used to identify my text files, which in this case happen to be generated in Microsoft Word. Applications may use specific file extensions to identify certain types of files, but this is a usage convention and is not strictly enforced — you can use unconventional file extensions with these applications without trouble.

Collections of files are kept in directories. Directories are much like the file drawers used to hold files. DR DOS includes commands that allow you to move between directories, or between disk drives. Unfortunately, you can't do both at the same time.

Directories are organized in a "tree" structure, as shown in Figure 1-3. If you think of the main or top-level directory on a disk to be the trunk of the tree, then you can see how directories branch out from the main directory. Each directory branch can have smaller branches or subdirectories. DR DOS includes a command that will reveal the entire directory tree to you, allowing you to easily navigate the directory structure.

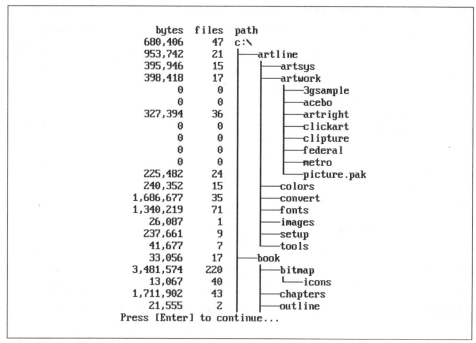

Figure 1-3. Directory Tree.

Advanced Disk Features in DR DOS

DR DOS gives you more control over your disk drives than other versions of DOS. Using DR DOS's SuperStor facility, you can actually increase the amount of data you can store on your disk drives. SuperStor uses *data compression* to "squeeze" your data when its written to a SuperStor hard disk or hard disk partition. When data is read from a SuperStor disk, it is decompressed. All compression and decompression happens automatically as data is read and written; you won't be aware that it's taking place.

INTRODUCING DR DOS

DR DOS can also recover files that have been erased, directories that have been deleted, and disks that have been formatted. It also has the capability to build detailed disk maps to help in these retrieval operations, or protect deleted files in case you want to later undelete that information.

The PC-Kwik facility that comes with DR DOS speeds your disk operations by keeping the most recently or often used information in RAM as well as on disk. When you or a program you're using wants to use this information, it can be grabbed quickly from memory instead of read slowly from the disk. PC-Kwik can also increase the efficiency of writing information by first saving all of the information in RAM and then writing it to disk in a single operation.

You and Your Display

For the most part, DR DOS doesn't really need to know anything about the kind of monitor and display adapter you have. However, monitors and display adapters must be compatible or they simply won't work at all. If you have a VGA display adapter card installed in your computer, you need a VGA monitor to connect to the card. Otherwise, you won't see what's going on. In some cases, connecting a monitor to an incompatible adapter can damage the monitor. Also, there are more modern monitors — called "multi-sync" — that can automatically configure themselves to work with your adapter.

While DR DOS doesn't need to know what you have, it does have facilities for controlling many aspects of the display. This includes colors, cursor size, and something called "video mode." By changing video modes — if you have the right kind of graphics adapter and monitor — you can change the number of characters shown on the screen.

Communications Ports

To connect your printer, external modem, mouse, and other peripherals to your computer, you must plug it into something. Those "somethings" are called *ports*, and like almost everything else we've discussed these come in two flavors: *serial* and *parallel*. Serial ports are generally used to connect your computer to a mouse, a modem, or another computer. They are occasionally used to connect to a printer which, by the way, can be a real hassle. Unless you are technically inclined, don't use

13

the serial port to connect a printer. Wiring for serial connections is somewhat nonstandard. Parallel ports provide a high-speed and trouble-free connection to most printers.

A serial port allows two-way communication between devices. Unfortunately, this type of connection comes in many different variations on the "standard" way of connecting the wires or transmitting the signal, leading to all kinds of headaches for the unwary. Parallel ports allow for fast communication between a computer and a peripheral device, largely in one direction only.

You can use parallel cables that are 10 to 15 feet long without experiencing data transmission errors. Fifteen feet is usually more than enough cable needed to reach a printer. Remember that your cable is also an antenna, and you can pick up a number of random signals, or "noise," from other electrical devices.

Serial cables are less susceptible to noise, and can be as long as 50 feet without significant problems. If your serial device is a long distance from your computer, you can use special shielded serial cables to reach beyond 50 feet.

Like everything else I've discussed, there are two types of serial connectors and two types of parallel connectors. The older IBM PCs and XTs, as well as many of the new 80386 PCs, have 25-pin serial connectors. Figure 1-4 shows this type of connector, as well as the 9-pin serial connector. Since the introduction of the AT-type machines, most computers have 9-pin serial connectors. To bridge the gap, you can buy a 25-pin-to-9-pin converter, also shown in Figure 1-4.

Because serial and parallel ports can look the same, how do you tell the difference? Many computer manufacturers put labels on the computer cases to help you. If your ports aren't labeled, the male connector (the one with the pins sticking out) is usually a serial port.

Figure 1-5 shows the two types of parallel connectors. The first type looks much like the 25-pin serial connector, but is usually female. The second type of parallel connector has more than 25 pins, and is quite distinctive (thank goodness).

INTRODUCING DR DOS

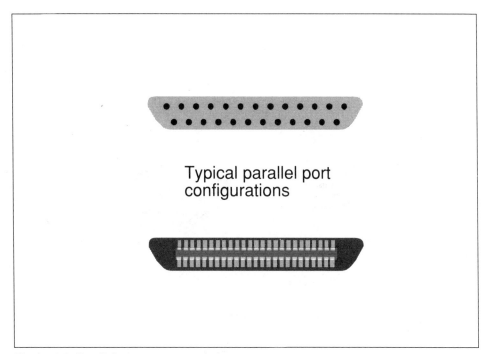

Figure 1-4. Parallel connectors, end view.

15

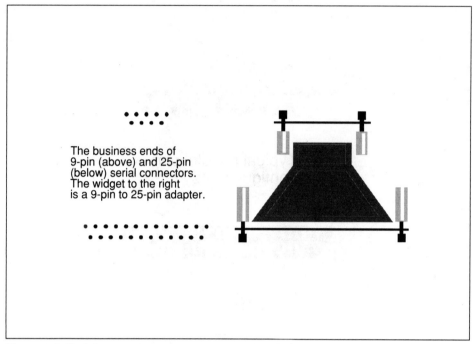

Figure 1-5. Serial connectors.

INTRODUCING DR DOS

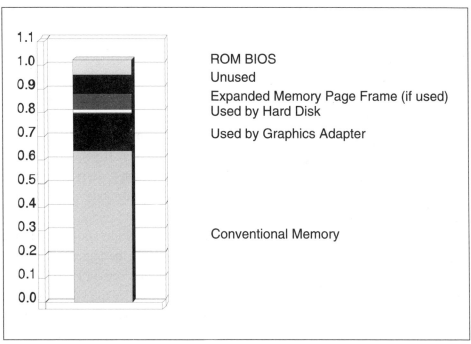

Figure 1-6. PC and XT memory map.

Serial Communications with FileLink

If you need to connect two computers together to quickly move large amounts of information between them, such as between a laptop computer and a desktop machine, the FileLink facility in DR DOS can solve your problems. FileLink can increase the speed of file transfers through the serial ports to rival the speed of a hard drive when copying files. To do this, FileLink runs one machine to start, and makes a duplicate of itself on the other machine using the serial cable to load the program there.

FileLink will also let you look at a list of files on the other computer, and allow you to pick the files on the remote system that you want to transfer.

Random Access Memory

Random access memory, or RAM, is usually referred to as memory. Due to constraints imposed on DR DOS by the design of the original DOS for PCs and XTs, base memory is limited to 640 KB. Base memory is the area that contains the operating system and whatever program you are running. This is a genuine limitation of PCs, because it limits the size of the programs you can run. An although 640,000 bytes sounds like a lot, it's actually not very much memory given the large size of today's application programs. While most of us don't use the older PCs and XTs, we're still stuck with this convention.

Programmers have come up with a variety of ways to get around the 640 KB problem, and most of them considerably slow the computer. If your computer is equipped with an 80286, 80386 or an 80486 processor (don't worry if you don't know which it is), then the computer can run special "protected-mode" programs that get around the 640 KB limit.

Like everything else in life, the few protected-mode programs you can find have their own sets of problems. These include fussiness regarding the degree of true IBM compatibility a machine offers (in fact, some won't run on certain PS/2 models). Protected-mode programs usually conform to something called the *VCPI* standard, and this is fully supported by DR DOS. A competing standard, *DPMI*, is not yet supported by DR DOS.

Memory above the 640 KB barrier becomes another sticky issue. Figures 1-6 and 1-7 show how the first 1024 KB of memory in your computer is used. PCs and XTs are configured slightly differently than later machines. As you can see, everything up to 1024 KB is pretty well stuffed. Memory added above 1024 KB on PCs and XTs is used as "expanded memory." You can't run programs in expanded memory — you can only store data. However, the DR DOS TaskMAX application switcher, which allows you to jump from one program to another, can use expanded memory. ATs and 80386-equipped computers can also have expanded memory, or they can have "extended memory." Extended memory is a bit more useful, but it still can't be used to run most programs (except for very small ones that will fit within 64 KB areas).

So who cares? Well, if you have DR DOS then you care very much. DR DOS can move some special kinds of programs, plus parts of itself, into extended memory. Its ability to do this was further enhanced in version 6.0. This opens nearly all of the base 640 KB of memory where you run your programs — a very nice feature indeed considering how memory-hungry programs have become. I'll go over this in detail and include many examples in Chapter 2.

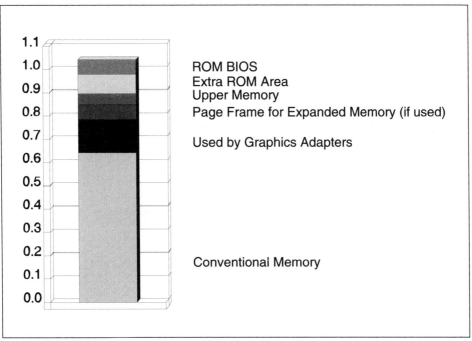

Figure 1-7. 80286 memory map.

Task Switching

DR DOS version 6.0 introduced TaskMAX, the task-switching utility. With TaskMAX, you can effortlessly shift from your word processor to your spreadsheet, and from there to an operating system command line. TaskMAX can divide the computer's memory between itself and the programs running as tasks. Figure 1-8 shows the TaskMAX command window with two tasks running: a command line "DOS" task and Microsoft Word.

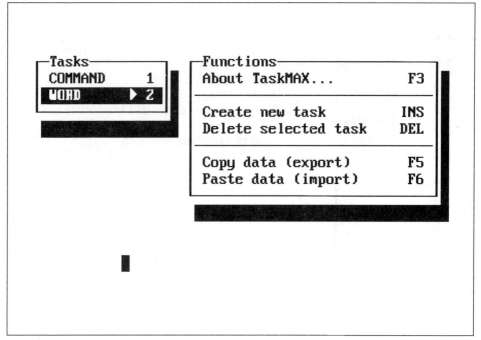

Figure 1-8. TaskMAX main screen.

TaskMAX can also cut and paste data from one application to another. For example, if you want to copy an address from a database into your word processor, TaskMAX will let you do it.

Unlike true multitasking environments such as Quarterdeck's DESQview, TaskMAX can't allow more than one program to run at the same time. When you switch from one program to the other, all tasks but the program currently in use temporarily stop and wait for you to switch back. Still, for most work that you do on the computer, task switching is very handy.

Security

Large computers — mainframes, minicomputers, and to some extent, workstations—accommodate various levels of *security* features offered by software programs or operating systems. Security features protect your data, your programs, and even your computer from being used by someone who shouldn't. If you are in a

INTRODUCING DR DOS

business or research environment, security can be vital to your operation. You don't want just anyone gaining access to payroll records or technical reports.

MS- and PC-DOS have almost no security capabilities at all. You can protect a file from being inadvertently erased or password-protect a "group" in the rather wimpy MS-DOS 5.0 shell, but that's about it. DR DOS, however, allows you to protect files and directories from being erased, copied, or even used at all. Starting with DR DOS version 6.0, you can also prevent access to any hard drive on the system. The only people who can access the secure drive, file, or directory are those who know that password.

You can also lock your keyboard to achieve a degree of security. Suppose that you are currently working with sensitive information, and you want to leave your computer unattended; or perhaps you want to protect what you are doing from your young, curious children. By running the LOCK program, no one can use your computer until the proper password is entered.

If you're worried about such things, DR DOS security is pretty tough to crack. A dedicated soul with a disk sector editor, such as the Mace Muse utility, could gain access to password-protected files or directories. However, it requires quite a bit more to crack the hard drive security.

The Command Line and Beyond

Normally, your interaction with DR DOS will be through the DOS command line. The command line is what you see whenever you start up your computer, provided you are not automatically invoking a more sophisticated shell (such as ViewMAX or Microsoft Windows). The command line looks something like this:

```
C:>
```

If you accept the DR DOS Setup program's defaults for the prompts, you'll see something that looks more like this:

```
[DR DOS] C:\>
```

Later in the book, we'll go over how to make other command line prompts. Regardless of the appearance of the prompt, you enter all of the DR DOS commands

DR DOS 6 BY EXAMPLE

on the command line. For example, to see a directory listing (or list of files) for the current directory, you'd type the following and then press the Enter key:

    XDIR

You'd run a program the same way. To run Microsoft Windows for example, you type this and press Enter:

    WIN

That's the way DR DOS — as well as any other version of DOS — works. You enter a command, the command is executed, and eventually you wind up at the command line prompt again — unless, of course you resort to using a *graphical user interface* (*GUI*).

The DR DOS graphical user interface, ViewMAX, makes running the computer much more like doing other office tasks. It shows you the contents of a directory as a set of files (they actually look much like the pieces of paper). Directories appear as file folders, and disk drives look like either floppy disks or the front face plate of a hard drive. Special-purpose files, such as word processing programs or database programs, have identifying pictures. For example, word processors are shown as typewriters and database programs are shown as file cabinets.

ViewMAX provides more intuitive ways of doing things with files as well. For example, to produce a copy of a file from a floppy drive on a hard disk drive, you might issue this command at the command line:

    COPY A:JUNQUE.DAT C:\DOODLE

This command copies the file JUNQUE.DAT from the A: floppy disk drive to the DOODLE directory on the C: hard drive. To make this work, you must remember the command and how to use it, the exact name of the file, and the exact location where you want the copy of the file to reside. To do the same thing in ViewMAX, you would follow these steps:

INTRODUCING DR DOS

1. Select the file you want on drive A: by clicking on it with the mouse pointer. You can easily tell that it's the file that you want because you can see all of the files in the directory.

2. Use the mouse to drag the file to the DOODLE file folder in the window showing the C: drive. Again, you can see the area where the copy will reside, so you know it's correct.

3. Release the mouse button to complete the copying task.

Pretty cute, huh? Some computers, like the Apple Macintosh series, don't have a command line and all tasks are accomplished using the GUI. On the PC, you normally need to spend extra money, and invest in pretty fast computer equipment, to run a sophisticated GUI such as Microsoft Windows.

But ViewMAX comes as a standard part of DR DOS. And at the risk of becoming repetitious, I'll go over ViewMAX in detail in a later chapter. Figure 1-9 shows a sample ViewMAX screen from DR DOS version 6.0. Note that, like Windows and the Macintosh desktop, ViewMAX sports such niceties as a clock and a calculator.

We'll also touch on the most sophisticated GUI available for PCs: the ubiquitous Microsoft Windows. DR DOS fully supports this, and we'll discuss how to configure it to run efficiently under DR DOS.

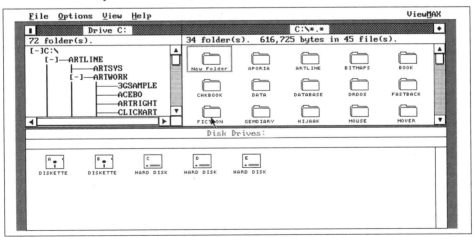

Figure 1-9. ViewMAX, the DR DOS graphical user interface.

DR DOS 6 BY EXAMPLE

OK, that's the 20-minute tour of PCs in general as well as the capabilities of DR DOS. If you are new to computers, consider yourself computer literate. If you take the time to read through the entire book, you can graduate to being a *power user*.

Much of this book is for giving examples of how things are done. Throughout this reference material you'll see sections marked SYNTAX. These tell you the basic structure of the DR DOS command, statement, or device driver. Syntax is always shown with the following conventions.

- Things that you are to type exactly as shown are in standard Roman type. For instance:

CHKDSK

would be typed exactly as shown above.

- Variables or arguments, that is, things that change, such as file specifications, strings of text, and numeric values are shown in italics.

XDIR*files*

In this case, files is a file specification. It could be a single file name and extension, or it could include wildcard characters, a directory path, and a disk-drive designation letter. Optional parameters for a command are enclosed in brackets, like this:

CHKDSK [/F]

If a particular parameter has more than one entry they are separated by a vertical bar;

XCOPY [/H|?]

In this case, you can get help from DR DOS about the XCOPY command by entering either XCOPY /H or XCOPY /?.

CHAPTER 2

Installing DR DOS

DR DOS practically installs itself, and it guides you through all the steps. However, you still have to make some decisions. In fact, DR DOS provides so many options that you'll need to think seriously about which ones to use.

Using MemoryMAX

With the right hardware, MemoryMAX (the DR DOS memory manager and utilities; for more on this see Chapter 5) provides an unprecedented amount of base memory for applications. It works with all computers equipped with 80386 microprocessors, most systems equipped with 80286 processors, and some computers equipped with the older 8088 or 8086 processors. MemoryMAX requires extended memory with an 80286 processor, and certain chip sets (the main components on the computer motherboard) are also directly supported to provide slightly more conventional memory. Both 8088 and 8086 processors will need LIM 4.0 expanded memory.

Using SuperStor

SuperStor is a software component that provides on-the-fly data compression, which greatly increases the number of programs and amount of data that will fit on a hard disk. But be forewarned: SuperStor takes up memory and slows down disk operations. On my 80286-based system, SuperStor chews up 40 KB of base memory—at a minimum it requires 28 KB. That's not a huge amount of memory, but if you also load network drivers, the additional memory consumed by SuperStor can make a big difference for your applications.

Using PC-Kwik

PC-Kwik (the DR DOS disk cacheing program) can be loaded into either extended or expanded memory, so it takes up a minimum amount of space in base memory. It also speeds up software that is disk-intensive. However, it uses up extended or expanded memory, which you may need for applications.

Don't agonize over these decisions. DR DOS is flexible and changeable. You can modify its settings easily when installing the operating system, or anytime later with the SETUP program (see Chapter 5 for more on the SETUP program).

Setting up a New Hard Drive

Before attempting to install DR DOS on a new hard drive, you need to complete a low-level format of the drive. Some kinds of drives (those using IDE controllers) are preformatted by the manufacturer. Consult the documentation that came with your drive or computer to determine whether this has been done. If not, find instructions on how to format the drive. If you need to access DEBUG to run the low-level format program in the controller card, follow these steps:

1. Install DR DOS for floppies only.

2. Run the SID program (instead of DEBUG), and follow the instructions for accessing the formatting firmware.

3. Complete the low-level formatting procedure.

When finished, go on to the installation procedures in the next section.

INSTALLING DR DOS

Running the DR DOS Installation Program

Insert the STARTUP disk (disk 1 of 4) into the A: drive. Reboot the computer. After the usual whirring and buzzing (and perhaps some messages about reading certain files), an opening screen will appear that looks similar to Figure 2-1. This screen explains how to run the installation menus. The controls throughout the installation process are:

Arrow keys and Tab key

These allow you to move up and down the list of items in a menu.

Escape key

This backs up one screen in the process.

F10

This stops the installation process. You'll be asked if you want to quit and exit to DR DOS (running from the floppy).

Enter

This means that you are happy with all settings, want them to be saved, and are ready to go on to the next step in the process.

Now you can press Enter.

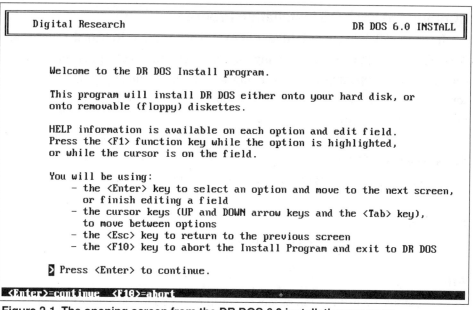

Figure 2-1. The opening screen from the DR DOS 6.0 installation program.

Preparing a New Hard Disk

If the hard drive is already prepared (formatted and partitioned), go on to the next section. If it isn't, the installation program will ask if you want to use FDISK to prepare and partition the drive. (Refer to the FDISK command in the Appendix A for a detailed discussion of partitions and FDISK.) Choose Yes.

At this point it's necessary to create at least a single bootable partition (a segment of your disk, referenced by a drive letter) for the computer to boot directly from the hard drive. The bootable partition holds DR DOS and is the one your computer will seek when you turn the system on or reboot. Usually, you select partition 1 as the bootable partition. When you make a partition bootable, it will display an A-Status in the partition status table. To create a bootable partition, select 1 (Create DOS Primary Partition).

Next, the installation program will ask whether the entire hard drive is to be used by that partition. Normally this is the most convenient configuration. However, you may want to set aside a partition for SuperStor. Doing this allows you to compress only the data stored on that partition. This provides some additional storage but

INSTALLING DR DOS

doesn't slow down the computer's access to files on any uncompressed partitions.

If you do want the entire disk to be used by the partition, enter Y at the following prompt:

```
Use cylinders 0 - ??? for DOS (???? MB) (Y/N).
```

Enter N if you don't want to use the entire disk. Set the starting cylinder to 0 and the ending cylinder to a number less than the total shown for the disk. For instance, a 40-MB drive will have about 1,226 cylinders. To devote about 30 MB to the primary partition, set the ending cylinder to 920. Press Enter. You can now get a cup of coffee, because it's going to take a while to prepare the disk.

As FDISK prepares the disk, it displays the total number of blocks and how far it has progressed. This gives a good indication of how long it will take to finish preparing the drive. Of course, the bigger the partition, the longer this will take. During this process, FDISK will "lock out" any bad blocks it finds, to prevent data from being corrupted.

Once FDISK has finished its task, an on-screen message asks you to name the disk, using up to 11 characters. At this point, you can prepare additional partitions.

After creating all partitions and selecting a bootable partition, press Escape to go on to the next installation step. An on-screen message will say that the operating system needs to be reloaded and that you need to insert a system disk into the A: drive. The installation disk is already in the A: drive, so just press Enter.

After the system reboots, the installation software begins the process of installing DR DOS on the hard drive. After a few seconds, an on-screen message will announce that the system is reading the various initialization files (the .INI files). When it has finished this, the "Welcome to the DR DOS Install Program" screen appears once again.

Installing DR DOS

An on-screen message asks where to install the operating system and displays a list of available drives, both hard and floppy. The installation procedure for floppies is similar to that for the hard drive, but it does take longer. When installing DR DOS onto floppies, the installation program uses the DISKCOPY utility to create a number of disks. Be prepared to do quite a bit of disk swapping: it takes four 720-KB floppies to complete the installation process. The bootable floppy has DR DOS and the most commonly used utilities, without much room for anything else. The other disks have the remaining utilities and the ViewMAX graphical user interface. To create more bootable disks at this point, use the Format-S command.

The configuration steps are the same whether you install DR DOS onto a hard drive or floppies. Use the arrow keys to highlight the drive you want to use (it's probably already highlighted) and press Enter. You'll be rewarded with another "Please wait..." message, but this time it won't be on the screen for very long.

Figure 2-2 shows the next screen that appears, where you get to make some real choices:

Maximum Application Memory at the Expense of Functionality

This means that DR DOS will insert none of the niceties—such as command-line editing, disk compression, and disk cacheing—to provide the most base memory for applications. If your system doesn't have extended or expanded memory, such as a PC or XT, select this choice.

Balance Application Memory and Functionality

This is the default choice and provides what Digital Research calls "a balance between application memory and operating system performance." It's a pretty safe choice if you are unsure about how much memory you'll need. Remember that with most hardware, DR DOS frees more base memory than you've probably ever seen before.

INSTALLING DR DOS

Maximum Performance and Functionality at the Expense of Application Memory

This option installs all the DR DOS features.

These are really only default settings. By going through the configuration screens, you can change each parameter. Use the up and down arrow keys to position the highlight bar over your choice, then press Enter.

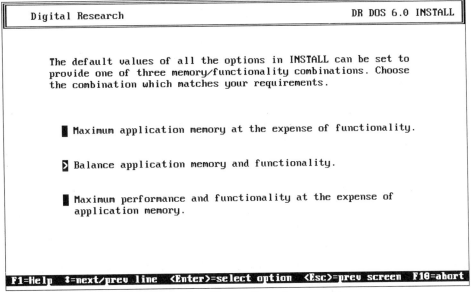

Figure 2-2. The memory and functionality configuration screen.

Next, a screen appears in which you can change the country and keyboard settings. These are the code-page settings (code pages are covered in detail in Chapter 13). If you select the country settings, the list of countries will appear (along with the code page numbers), as shown in Figure 2-3. Once you make a selection, a similar list of keyboard configurations will appear, from which you may choose a keyboard type.

31

DR DOS 6 BY EXAMPLE

```
┌─────────────────────────────────────────────────────────────────────┐
│ Digital Research                                    DR DOS 6.0 SETUP │
├─────────────────────────────────────────────────────────────────────┤
│   Select country:                                                    │
│                                                                      │
│     ▌ Australia         (061)    ▌ Korea             (082)           │
│     ▌ Austria           (043)    ▌ Latin America     (003)           │
│     ▌ Belgium           (032)    ▌ Middle East       (785)           │
│     ▌ Canada (English)  (002)    ▌ Netherlands       (031)           │
│     ▌ Canada (French)   (002)    ▌ Norway            (047)           │
│     ▌ Denmark           (045)    ▌ Portugal          (351)           │
│     ▌ Finland           (358)    ▌ Russia            (007)           │
│     ▌ France            (033)    ▌ Spain             (034)           │
│     ▌ Germany           (049)    ▌ Sweden            (046)           │
│     ▌ Hungary           (036)    ▌ Switzerland       (041)           │
│     ▌ Israel            (972)    ▌ Turkey            (090)           │
│     ▌ Italy             (039)    ▌ United Kingdom    (044)           │
│     ▌ Japan             (081)  ▷ ▌ United States     (001)           │
│                                                                      │
├─────────────────────────────────────────────────────────────────────┤
│ F1=Help  ↕=next/prev line  <Enter>=select option  <Esc>=prev screen  F10=abort │
└─────────────────────────────────────────────────────────────────────┘
```

Figure 2-3. The country code selection screen.

After the country and keyboard settings are chosen, an on-screen message asks where the DR DOS operating system utilities (the external commands) should reside. The default is C:\DRDOS. Unless there's an overriding reason to put these files elsewhere, opt for the default.

The next screen asks whether to replace all DOS files found in the destination drive. This will help avoid problems caused by external commands from a previous version of DOS.

Next, an on-screen message offers the option to proceed with configuration or skip it and let DR DOS make these decisions. Actually, you selected a configuration setup when you chose how DR DOS would balance application memory and functionality. If you are familiar with configuring DOS machines, by all means elect to continue with configuration. If you aren't comfortable with such technical matters, proceed with installation.

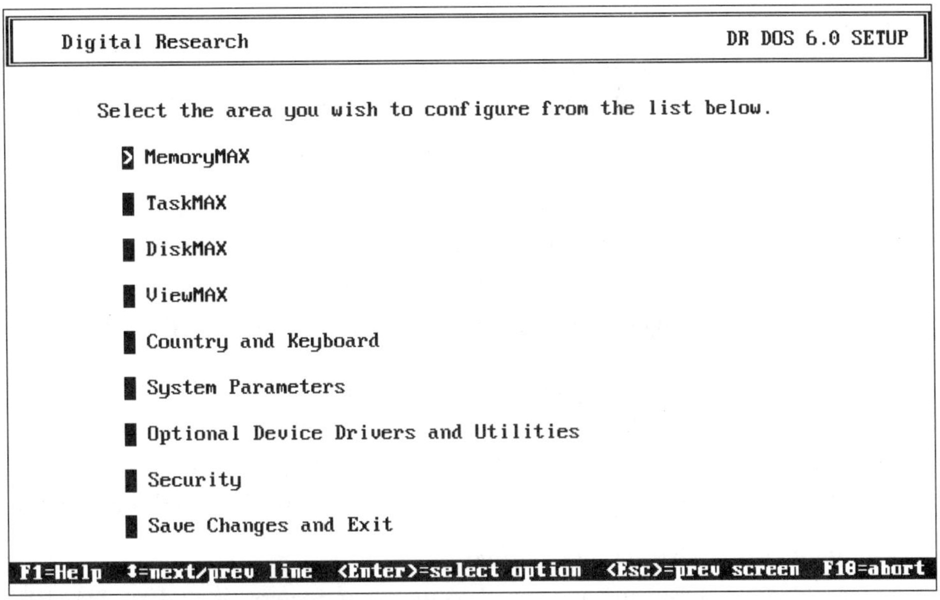

INSTALLING DR DOS

```
┌─────────────────────────────────────────────────────────────────┐
│ Digital Research                              DR DOS 6.0 SETUP  │
├─────────────────────────────────────────────────────────────────┤
│                                                                 │
│    Select the area you wish to configure from the list below.   │
│                                                                 │
│       ▶ MemoryMAX                                               │
│                                                                 │
│       ▮ TaskMAX                                                 │
│                                                                 │
│       ▮ DiskMAX                                                 │
│                                                                 │
│       ▮ ViewMAX                                                 │
│                                                                 │
│       ▮ Country and Keyboard                                    │
│                                                                 │
│       ▮ System Parameters                                       │
│                                                                 │
│       ▮ Optional Device Drivers and Utilities                   │
│                                                                 │
│       ▮ Security                                                │
│                                                                 │
│       ▮ Save Changes and Exit                                   │
│                                                                 │
├─────────────────────────────────────────────────────────────────┤
│ F1=Help  ↕=next/prev line  <Enter>=select option  <Esc>=prev screen  F10=abort │
└─────────────────────────────────────────────────────────────────┘
```

Figure 2-4. The main configuration menu.

For those who chose to continue with configuration, Figure 2-4 shows the main configuration list. The entries are:

TaskMAX This sets up the parameters that concern the TaskMAX task switcher. These parameters include how much extended and/or expanded memory TaskMAX can use, how much expanded memory is allocated to each task, and what the TaskMAX hot keys are. These are explained in detail in Chapter 6.

DiskMAX This configuration screen lets you select whether to use a RAM disk (virtual disk), the PC-Kwik disk cache, the SuperStor utility, or the DELWATCH and DISKMAP file-undeletion utilities.

ViewMAX This configures the ViewMAX graphical user interface. MS-DOS has a primitive version of such a tool—the DOS SHELL. (To use ViewMAX, you'll need to provide some information about your hardware.)

Country and Keyboard

> You've seen this before. It lets you select the display and keyboard code pages for international languages.

System Parameters

> This sets the PATH and APPEND paths for executable and data files. Include all subdirectories for applications typically used in the PATH. Of course, if you just formatted your hard drive, it won't have any subdirectories other than the DR DOS directory.
>
> This also lets you set some nitty-gritty DOS machine configuration values, such as BREAK, LASTDRIVE, FILES, and BUFFERS. Also, HISTORY can be turned on or off (HISTORY allows you to review, edit, and reinvoke previously issued commands).

Optional Device Drivers and Utilities

> These are additional system parameters, including SHARE, FASTOPEN, and code-page switching. You must activate SHARE in order to use ViewMAX. SHARE is selected by default only when "maximum performance and functionality at the expense of application memory" is chosen.

Security

> DR DOS provides real system security. No one will be able to use your system (including you) without the password. This is inactive by default, so this is where you should go to activate it.

All of these options are covered in detail in the following sections.

TaskMAX

Figure 2-5 shows the TaskMAX configuration screen. TaskMAX configuration consists of adjusting key settings to switch between tasks and designating the amount of memory available to TaskMAX. Read Chapter 6 to get a better understanding of these settings.

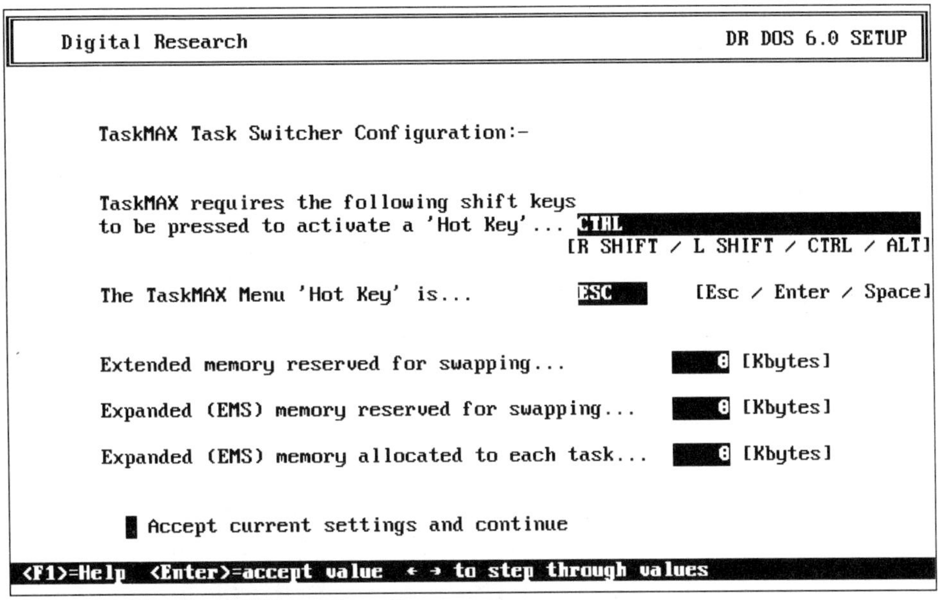

INSTALLING DR DOS

```
┌─────────────────────────────────────────────────────────────────┐
│ │ Digital Research │                          DR DOS 6.0 SETUP │
│ └─────────────────┘                                             │
│                                                                 │
│    TaskMAX Task Switcher Configuration:-                        │
│                                                                 │
│    TaskMAX requires the following shift keys                    │
│    to be pressed to activate a 'Hot Key'... [CTRL        ]      │
│                                             [R SHIFT / L SHIFT / CTRL / ALT] │
│                                                                 │
│    The TaskMAX Menu 'Hot Key' is...         [ESC ]   [Esc / Enter / Space]   │
│                                                                 │
│    Extended memory reserved for swapping...       [ 0] [Kbytes] │
│                                                                 │
│    Expanded (EMS) memory reserved for swapping... [ 0] [Kbytes] │
│                                                                 │
│    Expanded (EMS) memory allocated to each task... [ 0] [Kbytes]│
│                                                                 │
│    ■ Accept current settings and continue                       │
│ ┌───────────────────────────────────────────────────────────────┤
│ │<F1>=Help  <Enter>=accept value   ← → to step through values   │
└─────────────────────────────────────────────────────────────────┘
```

Figure 2-5. The TaskMAX configuration screen.

The Shift Keys are used in combination with the hot key to switch to the TaskMAX main menu or with the task number to switch directly to a task. The list of possible keys to be used in specifying the key combinations appears under the Shift Key and Hot Key fields.

"Extended memory reserved for swapping" is the amount of extended memory allocated specifically for use by TaskMAX. This memory is unavailable to applications. "Expanded (EMS) memory reserved for swapping" is the amount of expanded memory allocated for use by TaskMAX. "Expanded (EMS) memory allocated to each task" is the amount of expanded memory, from the pool of available expanded memory, that each task can access. Extended memory is memory from 1024 to 16 MB. You need at least an 80286 microprocessor to have this. 8088 and 8086 microprocessors can't directly access more than 1024 KB of memory, and must therefore use a trick to reach memory above 1024 KB. Such memory is called expanded memory, and is accessed by being addressed through a page-frame area set up in high memory (the area of memory between 640 KB and 1024 KB). Expanded memory can also be made available in any PC system, regardless of the type of microprocessor.

35

DiskMAX

Figure 2-6 shows the DiskMAX screen. DiskMAX is a set of utilities that allows you to optimize your hard disk. "Virtual disk support" simply places the VDISK.SYS driver in your CONFIG.SYS file. This driver allocates memory (either base, extended, or expanded) as a virtual disk. A virtual disk is many times faster than a hard drive, but its contents vanish when you reboot or when power is removed.

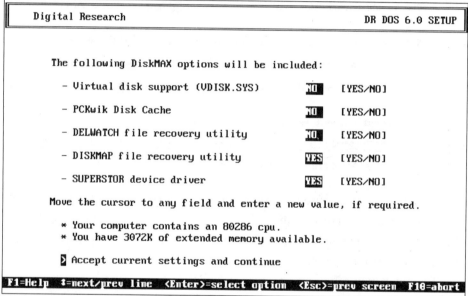

Figure 2-6. The DiskMAX configuration screen.

"PCKwik Disk Cache" uses extended or expanded memory to hold frequently used information from the disk. Since memory access is many times faster than disk access, this provides a tremendous performance boost. Selecting this option allows the installation program to add the appropriate PCKwik files to the CONFIG.SYS and AUTOEXEC.BAT files.

DELWATCH provides foolproof file undeletion. It marks deleted files, then hides them from other programs. You can recover these with UNDELETE or delete them with DELPURGE.

DISKMAP is a more passive method program to aid in file recovery. It makes a file copy of the disk allocation table so that UNDELETE can easily find all the sectors belonging to a deleted file. Of course, if you don't update the DISKMAP file frequently or if the sectors belonging to a deleted file are overwritten with new data, then having an outdated copy of the disk allocation table won't be of much help.

"SUPERSTOR device driver" allows you to use the SuperStor program. It compresses data as it is written to disk and decompresses data when it is read. On average, SuperStor doubles the available storage space. It also slows disk access and uses at least 28 KB of memory.

ViewMAX

Figure 2-7 shows the opening ViewMAX configuration screen. DR DOS makes some initial guesses about your system hardware, and you use the configuration screen to confirm these guesses. If the guesses aren't correct, select "Change the above combination" to display lists of the supported hardware and color combinations. ViewMAX needs to know about your display adapter and mouse and offers a choice of predefined color combinations for the ViewMAX desktop. These values can also be changed in the VIEWMAX.INI file, but it's much easier to change them in the SETUP program.

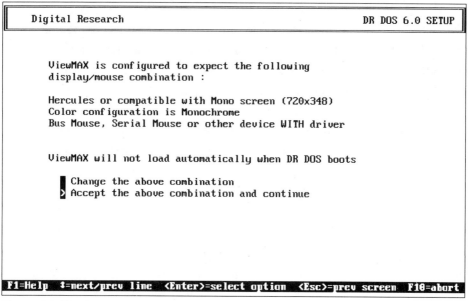

Figure 2-7. The first ViewMAX configuration screen.

Country and Keyboard

Figure 2-8 shows the country and keyboard option screen. This is where you can change the display and keyboard to a language other than American English. Selecting "Change the country and/or keyboard" brings up screens that list the available code pages for the display and keyboard. The keyboard type can also be set. Refer to Chapter 13 for an additional discussion of code pages.

INSTALLING DR DOS

```
┌─────────────────────────────────────────────────────────────────────┐
│ Digital Research                                     DR DOS 6.0 SETUP│
├─────────────────────────────────────────────────────────────────────┤
│                                                                     │
│     The currently selected country, keyboard and keyboard type are: │
│                                                                     │
│         Country   : United States         (001)                     │
│         Keyboard  : United States English (US)                      │
│                    Enhanced keyboard (101/102 keys)                 │
│                                                                     │
│     Do you want to:                                                 │
│                                                                     │
│    ▌ Change the country and/or keyboard                             │
│    ▷ Accept current selection                                       │
│                                                                     │
│                                                                     │
│                                                                     │
│                                                                     │
├─────────────────────────────────────────────────────────────────────┤
│ F1=Help  ↕=next/prev line  <Enter>=select option  <Esc>=prev screen  F10=abort │
└─────────────────────────────────────────────────────────────────────┘
```

Figure 2-8. The country and keyboard configuration screen.

System Parameters

This is one of two miscellaneous catch-all categories for setting various general parameters that affect the system. Figure 2-9 sets the PATH and APPEND paths. PATH points to directories that DR DOS will search for executable files. Executable files are programs ending with .BAT, .COM, or .EXE extensions. When the EDITOR command is issued from a DR DOS prompt, DR DOS will search each of the specified PATH directories for EDITOR.EXE and will run EDITOR when it is found. If it doesn't find the specified executable program, it will complain with an error message.

DR DOS 6 BY EXAMPLE

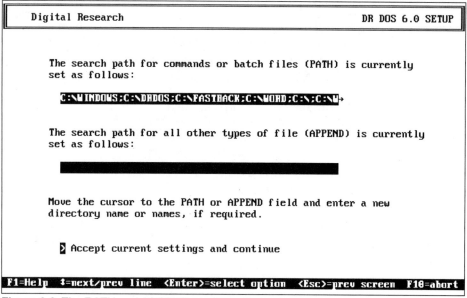

Figure 2-9. The PATH and APPEND configuration screen.

The APPEND path allows programs to find data files in much the same way as PATH finds executable files. However, most modern programs actually bypass this.

Figure 2-10 shows the next system parameters screen. When BREAK is set, it allows you to interrupt a program with the Ctrl-Break key combination. Most programs turn this off internally. LASTDRIVE specifies the last logical drive-designation letter that the system can use. This becomes important with networks or if you are using SUBST and ASSIGN. VERIFY means that DR DOS will check all file-copy operations by verifying the copy against the original. This really isn't necessary with modern systems and greatly slows down your disk operations. HISTORY refers to the DR DOS command-line history capability. With HISTORY on, DR DOS keeps a list of commands as you enter them in case you want to use them again later. Scroll through the set of stored commands by using Ctrl-E to scroll back and Ctrl-X to scroll forward. Coupled with the command-line editing features of DR DOS, this is a very powerful capability. ENVIRONMENT SIZE specifies the DR DOS environment size in bytes. Some of these choices bring up their own configuration sub-screens.

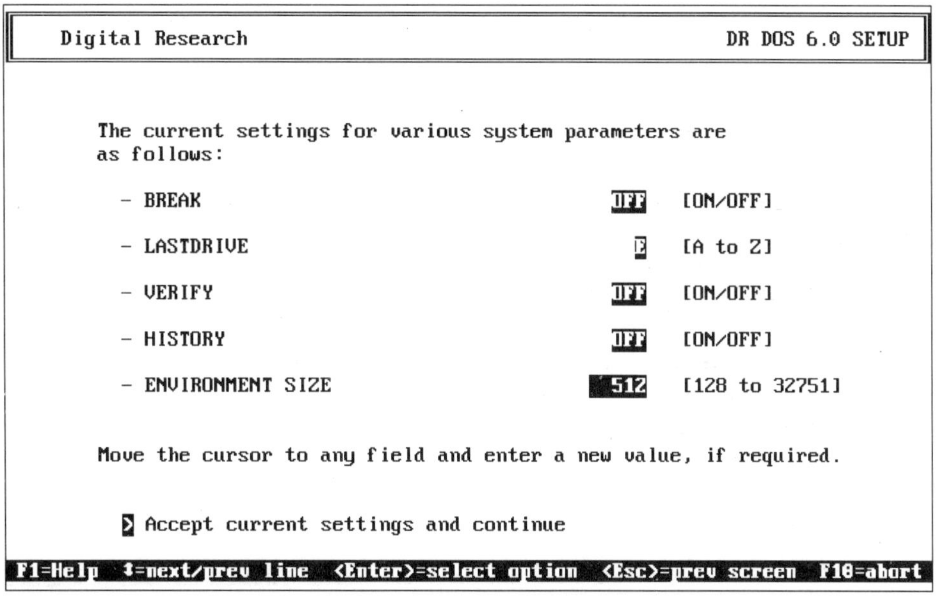

INSTALLING DR DOS

```
┌─────────────────────────────────────────────────────────────────┐
│ Digital Research                              DR DOS 6.0 SETUP  │
├─────────────────────────────────────────────────────────────────┤
│                                                                 │
│    The current settings for various system parameters are       │
│    as follows:                                                  │
│                                                                 │
│       - BREAK                              OFF    [ON/OFF]      │
│                                                                 │
│       - LASTDRIVE                           E     [A to Z]      │
│                                                                 │
│       - VERIFY                             OFF    [ON/OFF]      │
│                                                                 │
│       - HISTORY                            OFF    [ON/OFF]      │
│                                                                 │
│       - ENVIRONMENT SIZE                   512   [128 to 32751] │
│                                                                 │
│    Move the cursor to any field and enter a new value, if required. │
│                                                                 │
│    ▶ Accept current settings and continue                       │
├─────────────────────────────────────────────────────────────────┤
│ F1=Help  ↕=next/prev line  <Enter>=select option  <Esc>=prev screen  F10=abort │
└─────────────────────────────────────────────────────────────────┘
```

Figure 2-10. One of the system parameters configuration screens.

The next system parameters screen, shown in Figure 2-11, is where the number of buffers, files, and file control blocks (FCBs) can be set. Many large application programs require a certain number of files and buffers to be available. Your application program manuals should specify these numbers. In some cases, when applications are installed, they will modify the FILES and BUFFERS statement in the CONFIG.SYS file. When using TaskMAX, set the number of files to equal the total number of files required by all the tasks you normally run. FCBs is an older parameter setting and is not required for modern applications.

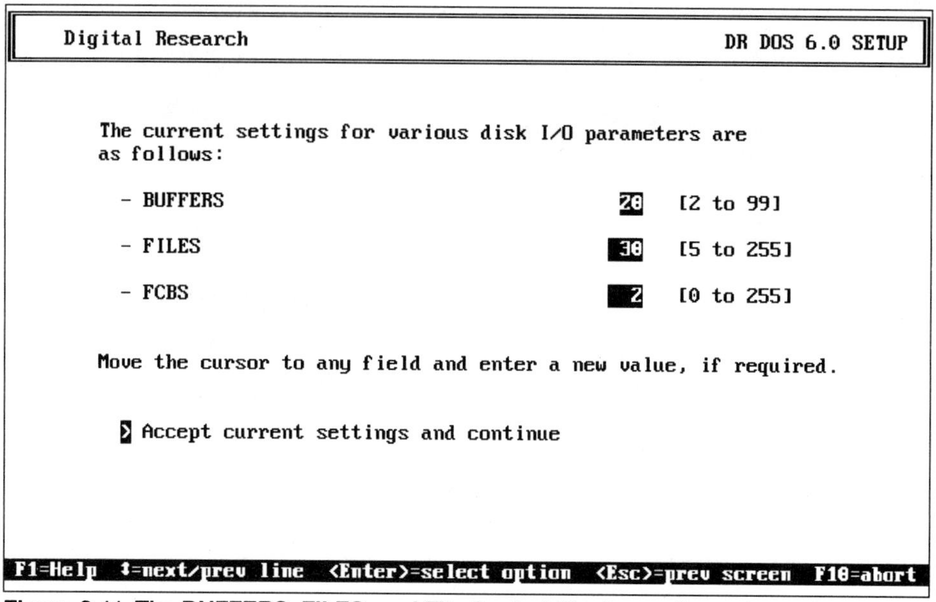

DR DOS 6 BY EXAMPLE

```
┌─────────────────────────────────────────────────────────────────┐
│ Digital Research                                DR DOS 6.0 SETUP │
├─────────────────────────────────────────────────────────────────┤
│                                                                 │
│    The current settings for various disk I/O parameters are     │
│    as follows:                                                  │
│                                                                 │
│      - BUFFERS                              20   [2 to 99]      │
│                                                                 │
│      - FILES                                30   [5 to 255]     │
│                                                                 │
│      - FCBS                                  2   [0 to 255]     │
│                                                                 │
│    Move the cursor to any field and enter a new value, if required. │
│                                                                 │
│      ▶ Accept current settings and continue                     │
│                                                                 │
│                                                                 │
│                                                                 │
├─────────────────────────────────────────────────────────────────┤
│ F1=Help  ↕=next/prev line  <Enter>=select option  <Esc>=prev screen  F10=abort │
└─────────────────────────────────────────────────────────────────┘
```

Figure 2-11. The BUFFERS, FILES, and File Control Blocks configuration screen.

The next screen (Figure 2-12) brings up a prompt configuration menu, where such things as date and time can be added to the DR DOS prompt. This screen is followed by subdirectory locations for temporary and configuration files. Don't change these unless you have a good reason to do so. The last screen (Figure 2-13) presents options for picking the color schemes for DR DOS utility programs such as DISKOPT and UNDELETE. For a color display, Trad and Pasture are nice middle-of-the-road choices.

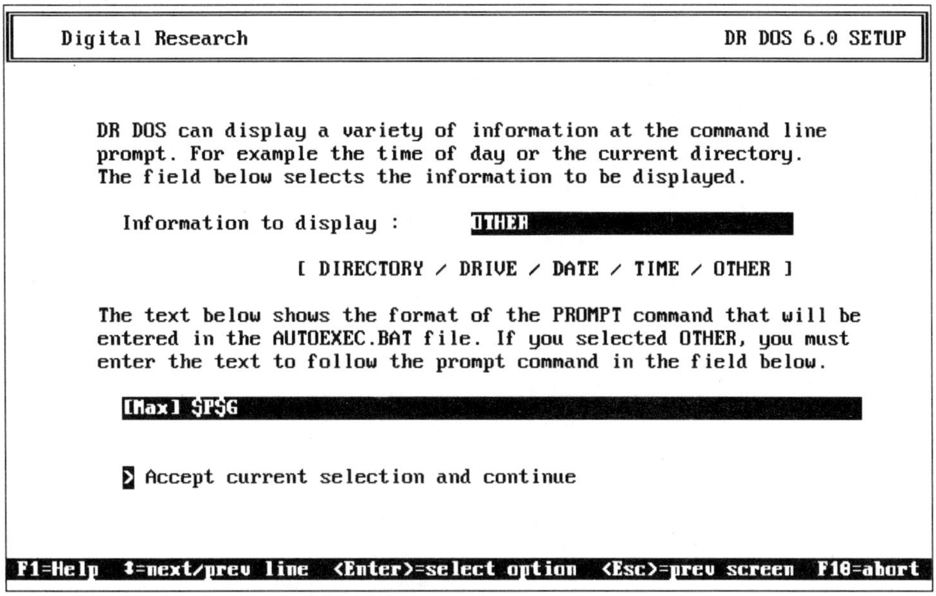

INSTALLING DR DOS

```
┌──────────────────────────────────────────────────────────────────┐
│ Digital Research                              DR DOS 6.0 SETUP   │
├──────────────────────────────────────────────────────────────────┤
│                                                                  │
│    DR DOS can display a variety of information at the command line
│    prompt. For example the time of day or the current directory.
│    The field below selects the information to be displayed.      │
│                                                                  │
│       Information to display :    OTHER                          │
│                                                                  │
│                  [ DIRECTORY / DRIVE / DATE / TIME / OTHER ]     │
│                                                                  │
│    The text below shows the format of the PROMPT command that will be
│    entered in the AUTOEXEC.BAT file. If you selected OTHER, you must
│    enter the text to follow the prompt command in the field below.
│                                                                  │
│    [Max] $P$G                                                    │
│                                                                  │
│                                                                  │
│       ▶ Accept current selection and continue                    │
│                                                                  │
│                                                                  │
│ F1=Help  ↕=next/prev line  <Enter>=select option  <Esc>=prev screen  F10=abort │
└──────────────────────────────────────────────────────────────────┘
```

Figure 2-12. The PROMPT configuration screen.

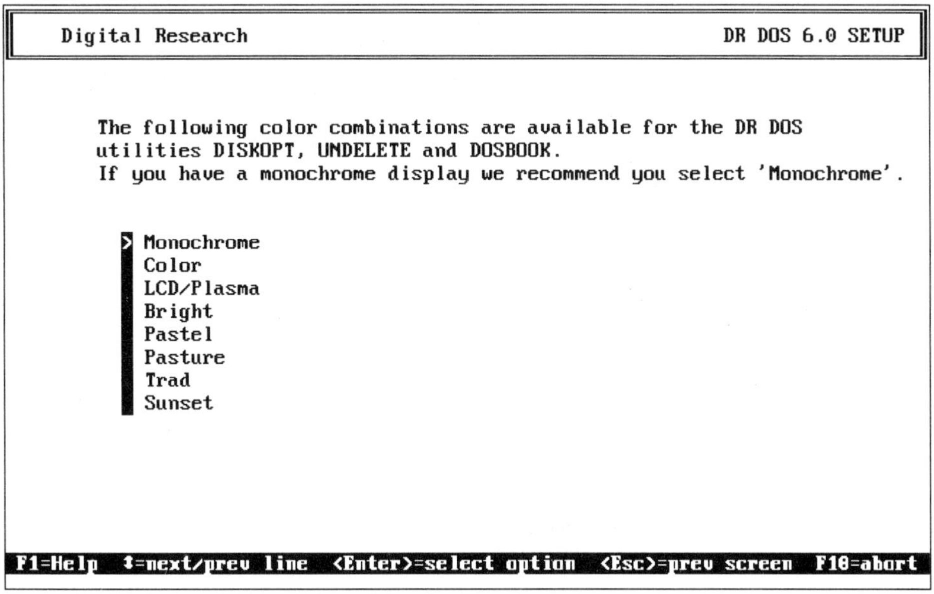

```
┌──────────────────────────────────────────────────────────────────┐
│ Digital Research                              DR DOS 6.0 SETUP   │
├──────────────────────────────────────────────────────────────────┤
│                                                                  │
│    The following color combinations are available for the DR DOS │
│    utilities DISKOPT, UNDELETE and DOSBOOK.                      │
│    If you have a monochrome display we recommend you select 'Monochrome'.
│                                                                  │
│       ▶ Monochrome                                               │
│         Color                                                    │
│         LCD/Plasma                                               │
│         Bright                                                   │
│         Pastel                                                   │
│         Pasture                                                  │
│         Trad                                                     │
│         Sunset                                                   │
│                                                                  │
│                                                                  │
│                                                                  │
│ F1=Help  ↕=next/prev line  <Enter>=select option  <Esc>=prev screen  F10=abort │
└──────────────────────────────────────────────────────────────────┘
```

Figure 2-13. The screen color combination menu.

Optional Device Drivers and Utilities

This is yet another catch-all for system parameter settings. The opening screen is shown in Figure 2-14. The extended display (ANSI.SYS) driver is required by some programs and also provides a neat way of setting screen colors. GRAFTABL display support is specifically for CGA systems and offers a very abridged list of international character sets. "File Fastopen support" allows DR DOS to use a small amount of memory to keep a table of the locations of often-used files, speeding disk access. "File sharing support (SHARE.EXE)" enables file locking. This protects data when using a multitasking system (such as DESQView or Microsoft Windows) or a task switcher (such as ViewMAX). In essence, it prevents multiple applications from writing to the same file, which could corrupt the file or result in lost data. You will need this if you intend to use ViewMAX. Figure 2-15 shows the screen for setting the number of file locks. "Code page switching" lets you change international screen and printer character sets. Refer to Chapter 13 for more on this.

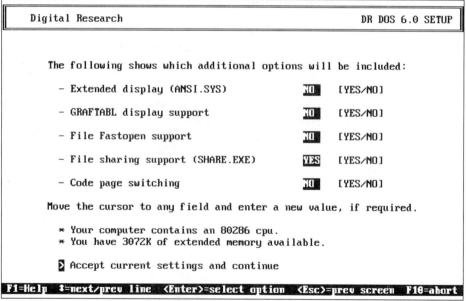

Figure 2-14. The device driver selection screen.

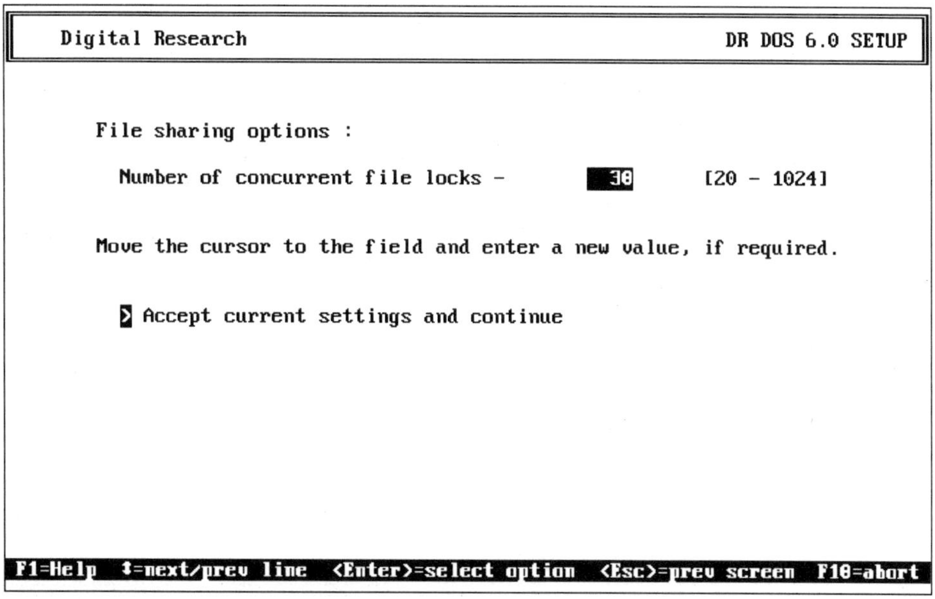

INSTALLING DR DOS

```
┌──────────────────────────────────────────────────────────────────┐
│ Digital Research                              DR DOS 6.0 SETUP   │
├──────────────────────────────────────────────────────────────────┤
│                                                                  │
│    File sharing options :                                        │
│                                                                  │
│       Number of concurrent file locks -    [ 30]   [20 - 1024]   │
│                                                                  │
│    Move the cursor to the field and enter a new value, if required. │
│                                                                  │
│       ▶ Accept current settings and continue                     │
│                                                                  │
│                                                                  │
│                                                                  │
│                                                                  │
│                                                                  │
├──────────────────────────────────────────────────────────────────┤
│ F1=Help  ↕=next/prev line  <Enter>=select option  <Esc>=prev screen  F10=abort │
└──────────────────────────────────────────────────────────────────┘
```

Figure 2-15. The SHARE configuration screen.

Security

Figure 2-16 shows the opening security screen. DR DOS allows you to implement system security. When system security is active, no one can access the computer's hard drives without the password. The system is quite difficult to beat and resists such work-arounds as booting from a floppy drive or attempting to use a sector editor. When this feature is enabled, you'll be prompted to enter and verify two passwords. The master password is required to disable security or change the system password. The user password is required to unlock the hard drive.

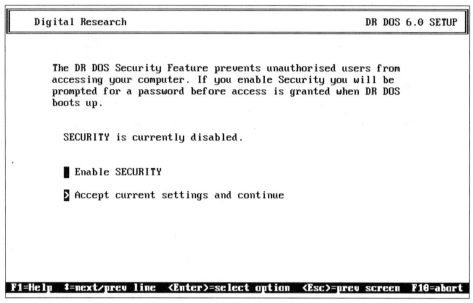

Figure 2-16. The main SECURITY screen.

Finishing Up

After the system is configured, an on-screen message will offer the choice of saving the previous operating system or deleting it. If you save it, you can use the Uninstall command to remove DR DOS version 6 and reload the previous operating system. If you choose to save the old operating system, you'll need to specify a subdirectory for it.

Finally, DR DOS begins the process of transferring itself to the hard drive. While copying, it provides various messages about what it is doing, including the file it is currently copying. Basically, it's coffee time again. Don't stay away too long, though, because the installation program will begin asking for diskettes. After everything is copied, the final screen appears, asking whether to exit to DR DOS or reboot the computer. Remove the disk from the floppy drive, then choose reboot.

If all went well, you'll see a prompt that looks like this:

[DR DOS] C:\>

You might need to answer time and date questions before the prompt appears. And there you have it—DR DOS is installed on your system.

CHAPTER 3

Basic DOS Skills

This chapter covers the basics of command lines, command-line editing, files, directories, and performing everyday tasks. These discussions are limited to what you need to get the job done. However, each of the DR DOS commands discussed has additional capabilities. To find out more about these commands, see Appendix A.

In an age of graphical user interfaces such as Microsoft Windows, Quarterdeck's DesqView, and the DR DOS ViewMAX program, you might ask, why bother with the command line? A friend of mine, a longtime programmer and UNIX guru, takes the opposite approach by pointing out how much mouse waggling and menu clicking it takes to do anything from a desktop environment. And to some extent, he's right. Operating system commands are more convenient for performing certain actions. Still, I must confess that both my home and work systems boot up into Windows. I also have a window devoted to the DR DOS command-line prompt because most file operations are easier using the power inherent in DR DOS.

The Command Line

OK, on to DR DOS and its command line. (Readers who find this a bit too basic may skip this discussion.) The command line consists of a prompt and a space in which to type commands. The prompt can display all sorts of things, including the time and date, but by default the DR DOS prompt looks something like this:

```
[DR DOS] C:\>
```

The drive designation may be something other than C:, but if it's a hard drive it is likely to be C:. The \ designates the current directory, and a backslash by itself indicates the root directory. We'll talk about directories in a moment, but for now let's concentrate on the command line itself.

A command is typed into the command line like this:

```
DIR
```

You enter the command into the command processor by pressing the Enter key. The DIR command displays a list of the files contained in the current directory. No matter what drive and directory you're in, DIR always works because it's built into the command processor. Such commands are called *internal*. DR DOS also has lots of external commands; in fact, this is where much of its power lies. External commands are actually utility programs, much like tools in a toolkit. By default, these are placed in a directory called \DRDOS on the C: drive (if it's a hard drive). In a floppy-drive setup, they're scattered over multiple disks.

External commands, and indeed all other executable programs, end in either .EXE (which stands for *executable*) or .COM (which stands for *command*). External commands are run the same way as internal commands. For example, to run the XDIR command, which is like DIR but shows much more information, type the following at the command line:

```
XDIR
```

and then press Enter. The only gotcha is that DR DOS needs to know where to look for external commands and other programs. If they're in the current directory, DR DOS can find them instantly. If they're in some other directory, that directory must be listed in the PATH statement. The PATH statement, covered in Chapter 5, lists all the directories through which DR DOS will search for a command. During installation, DR DOS puts the \DRDOS directory into the PATH statement. If this hasn't changed, DR DOS will find the XDIR command.

DR DOS doesn't expect perfection. Let's face it, we all make mistakes. On Monday mornings I can barely type at all, let alone type commands correctly. Fortunately, we have command-line editing. This wonderful function allows you to change the typed command before pressing the Enter key. To move the cursor to the left through the command text, press the left arrow key or Ctrl-S. (Throughout this book, control-key combinations are abbreviated as Ctrl- and the letter; for example,

Control and S is written Ctrl-S.) To move to the right through the command text, use the right arrow key or Ctrl-D.

If the command has multiple words, such as a command with an argument or a parameter, you can move to the left one word at a time by pressing Ctrl-left arrow or Ctrl-A. Move to the right a word at a time with Ctrl-right arrow or Ctrl-F. By *word* I mean any set of characters separated from another set by a space. These commands also stop at the periods used to separate file names from file extensions. By the way, those familiar with the WordStar command set will discover that the DR DOS command-line editor uses many of those commands.

Two not-quite-WordStar commands are Ctrl-Q and Ctrl-W. Ctrl-Q and Home move the cursor to the beginning of the command line; Ctrl-W and End jump to the end of the command line.

To add or change the command, move the cursor to the appropriate point in the command text. In overwrite mode, typing replaces whatever is under the cursor. In insert mode, typing pushes the remaining text in the command line over to the right. Switch between overwrite and insert modes with the Insert key or Ctrl-V. Overwrite mode uses the small cursor, which looks like a character underline. A larger, square cursor appears in insert mode.

Characters can also be deleted in the command line. Press the Delete key or Ctrl-G to remove the character under the cursor. Press the Backspace key to remove the character to the left of the cursor.

Try these functions a few times to get the hang of them. For example, type this erroneous command:

```
QDIR 8.*
```

What we really want is

```
XDIR *.*
```

To fix the error, use the right arrow key to position the cursor over the Q. Press Delete to remove the Q. If the cursor isn't a square block, press the Insert key. Now type the letter X. Use the right arrow to position the cursor over the 8. Press Delete, then type an asterisk. Command-line editing is as easy as that.

Several other commands make life even easier. To eliminate all text from the cursor position to the next word in the command, use Ctrl-T. For example, assume we have the following command line:

```
EDITOR C:\AUTOEXEC.BAT
```

Placing the cursor on the E in EDITOR and pressing Ctrl-T results in:

```
C:\AUTOEXEC.BAT
```

Pressing Ctrl-T again results in:

```
AUTOEXEC.BAT
```

And pressing Ctrl-T a final time leaves only:

```
BAT
```

Other delete keys are Ctrl-Y, which destroys the entire line; Ctrl-B, which deletes everything to the left of the cursor; and Ctrl-K, which deletes everything from the cursor to the right.

Command-line editing is a useful feature, but combined with command history it becomes truly powerful. With HISTORY turned on in the CONFIG.SYS file (covered in Chapter 5), you can access previously typed commands. These recycled commands can be used as is, or modified with command-line editing. Figure 3-1 shows how this works. DR DOS adds each of the commands to a list, which it keeps in memory. The length of the list is limited by the amount of memory allocated to HISTORY.

Scroll back up the list one command at a time with Ctrl-E. Scroll forward with Ctrl-X. You can also search through the list. For example, let's say you had typed

```
XDIR *.BAT
```

and now you'd like to issue that command again. To recall it, type XD and press Ctrl-R. The command-line editor will find a command beginning with XD, which in this case is XDIR *.BAT, and place it in the command line. Pressing Ctrl-R again brings up the next previously used command beginning with XD, and so on.

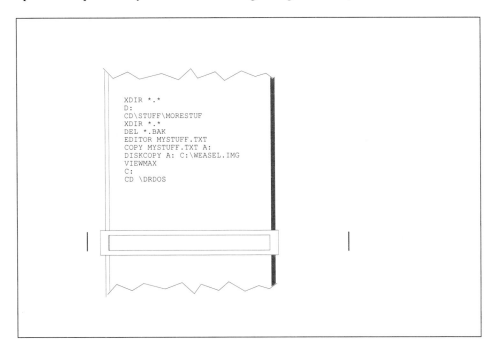

Figure 3-1. Modifying a command with command-line editing.

A slicker version of command-history searching is switched on and off with the Ctrl-_ command. Switch it on and type XD in the command line. The command-line editor will watch each character you type and supply a matching previously used command (XDIR *.BAT, in this case) when you type enough to provide a match.

Files

It's important to understand how DR DOS organizes a hard disk. We touched on this briefly in Chapter 1, and now it's time to go into detail. A set of information—such as the text that makes up a letter, or the lines, shapes, and patterns that make up a drawing, or the machine code that makes up a program—is stored in discrete units called *files*. Files are referenced by name. For example, to modify a text file in the

DR DOS EDITOR program, you must tell EDITOR what file to load. This is done by adding an *argument*—the name of the text file—to the EDITOR command line. If the file is called MYTEXT.TXT, use this command:

```
EDITOR MYTEXT.TXT
```

Complete DR DOS file names are divided into two parts, the name and the extension. In the above example, MYTEXT is the name. A name can have up to eight characters and can't have any spaces or any of the following characters: .:;,*?=\/ <>[].+|. It's also a good idea to avoid the following characters because they could be used as part of a command for a program: (){ }~!.

The file name is followed by the file extension, and the two are divided by a period. The file extension tells us what kind of file this is. Some file extensions have specific meanings in DR DOS. If the extension is .EXE or .COM, it's a machine-code file that the computer can execute. A .BAT extension indicates a *batch file*, which is a series of DR DOS commands that are executed one after another. If the extension is .APP, it's a GEM program that can be run by the GEM desktop. A .SYS extension denotes a device driver. A .CPI extension indicates a code-page information file.

All other file extensions are up for grabs. For example, Microsoft Word and later versions of WordStar use .DOC as extensions for their text files. .DOC can be used as an extension for practically any file, making its meaning entirely relative. Most programs create backup files with a .BAK extension. Source-code files for a computer language have particular extensions as well, such as .C for C files and .BAS for BASIC files.

Understand that file extensions, since they are changeable, are only an indication of what the file might be. Nothing prevents you from changing the extension of a Microsoft Word file to .CDR and loading it into CorelDraw as a graphics file. However, CorelDraw (and most other programs) will immediately detect the incorrect file format and complain to you about it.

Wildcards In File Names

Wildcards can be used to reference a set of files in DR DOS commands. There are two wildcard characters: * and ?. An asterisk (normally referred to in commands

BASIC DOS SKILLS

as a *star*) matches anything. For example, *.* means *all* files. NOVE*.TXT refers to all text files beginning with NOVE and ending with a .TXT extension. The question mark matches any single character in that position in a file name. For example, NOVE?.TXT matches NOVE1.TXT but not NOVEMBR.TXT.

Most DR DOS commands that affect files can accept wildcards. If you aren't sure, check Appendix A. For example, to copy all .TXT files in the current directory to the A: drive, use this command:

```
COPY *.TXT A:
```

To list all the files starting with QED and ending with XT, use this command:

```
DIR QED*.?XT
```

One other point: DR DOS refers to communications ports, the keyboard and screen, the real-time clock, and certain other things as *devices*. I'll cover these in detail later. For now, you should know that each device has a specific name that you shouldn't use in a file name. These names are AUX, CON, COM1, COM2, COM3, PRN, LPT1, LPT2, LPT3, NUL, and CLOCK$.

Changing File Names

RENAME (or REN for short) changes the names of existing files. For example, to change WEASLWRD.TXT to OBFUSCAT.ASC, use this command:

```
REN WEASLWRD.TXT OBFUSCAT.ASC
```

A set of files can be renamed using wildcards, although this is a bit trickier. For example, to rename all files starting with JUNE and ending with .WKS (such as JUNE1.WKS or JUNEA.WKS) so that they begin with JULY, enter:

```
REN JUNE*.WKS JULY*.WKS
```

Oddly enough, a file's location can also be changed with REN. Say a file called MYJUNK.STF is in the C:\WORK directory. To move it to the C:\PLAY directory, use this command:

```
REN C:\WORK\MYJUNK.STF C:\PLAY\MYJUNK.STF
```

There's something vaguely disturbing about being able to move files with the RENAME command, but it does work.

Disks and Directories

Overview time. Consider the disk an expanse of space in which to store things. If it's a large hard disk (80 MB or more), this space is quite expansive. Tossing everything into this big open area will tend to clutter the disk and will make finding files quite difficult. The solution: Divide the space into territories called *directories*. By default, each disk already has at least one directory (called the *root directory*). All other directories branch from the root.

Directories are like file drawers—they are used to organize your files. For example, the chapters of this book reside in the \CHAPTERS directory on my computer. Directories are created with the MKDIR command (or MD for short). For example, to create a directory called STUFF, use this command:

```
MD STUFF
```

This will create the directory STUFF as a branch from the current directory. Directories that branch from other directories are called *subdirectories*. To make a subdirectory of STUFF called JUNQUE, issue this command:

```
MD STUFF\JUNQUE
```

To change to the STUFF directory first, use CHDIR (or CD for short):

```
CD STUFF
```

and then create the \JUNQUE directory from within \STUFF with this command:

```
MD JUNQUE
```

BASIC DOS SKILLS

Directories have exactly the same naming restrictions as files. To get a listing of your current directories, use the TREE command. If this is unfamiliar territory, issue the TREE command using the graphic display parameter:

```
TREE /G
```

The resulting display should look something like Figure 3-2. Note how subdirectories are shown to branch from the directories and how all directories branch from the root. Use the CD command to jump from directory to directory until you are comfortable with this. Remember, the backslash character (\) must normally precede directory names in commands. For example, to jump to the \STUFF\JUNQUE directory, use this command:

```
CD \STUFF\JUNQUE
```

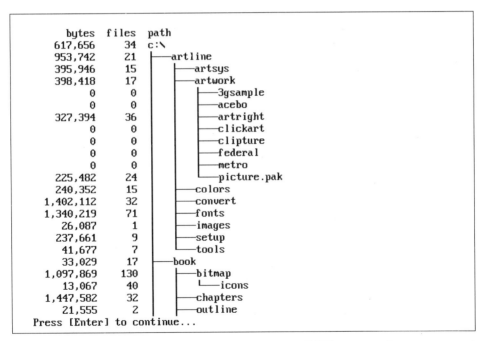

Figure 3-2. A typical directory structure shown by the TREE command.

The only time the backslash can be omitted is when you're jumping directly to a subdirectory of the current directory. However, since the backslash never hurts in a command where the pathname is fully specified, you might as well get into the habit of using it. By the way, CD jumps only to directories on the current drive. To go to a directory on another drive, first log on to that drive, then use CD to jump to the directory. To log on to a drive, type its letter followed by a colon and press Enter. For example, to log on to the D: drive, issue this command:

```
D:
```

Two special directory symbols—"." and ".."—appear in each subdirectory. The single period stands for the current directory, and the double period stands for the parent directory. For example, to go back up the directory structure by one directory, use this command:

```
CD ..
```

Making and Deleting Directories

Directories can be created with the MD command, as illustrated in the preceding examples. You can also create a directory on another drive without first logging on to that drive. For example, to make a \MORESTUF directory on the E: drive, issue the command

```
MD E:\MORESTUF
```

To delete directories, use the REMDIR command (or RD for short). Note: A directory or subdirectory can't be deleted with RD if it contains files or other directories. You can only delete a directory with RD after first deleting all the files and directories within it. As going from subdirectory to subdirectory to do this is a bit tedious, DR DOS allows you to delete all the files in a directory, delete all files in subdirectories, and remove empty subdirectories with a single command:

```
XDEL *.* /S /D
```

BASIC DOS SKILLS

Don't issue this command from the root directory, or it will delete everything on your hard drive partition. Once the files and subdirectories have been removed, you can delete the directory with the RD command:

```
RD MORESTUFF
```

or

```
REMDIR MORESTUFF
```

Renaming Directories

Files can be renamed, so it seems logical that directories can be renamed as well. This is done with the RENDIR command. It works much like the REN command for files. For example, to change C:\WORK\TEDIUM to C:\WORK\CHALLNGE, use this command:

```
RENDIR C:\WORK\TEDIUM C:\WORK\CHALLNGE
```

RENDIR cannot be used to move a directory or to make it branch from another directory.

About DR DOS Devices

DR DOS uses names that refer to devices in a computer system. The usual devices on a computer include serial ports, parallel ports, the keyboard and monitor, and a NUL device. Some DR DOS commands, such as COPY and PRINT, allow these devices to be designated as sources or destinations for data. The MODE command actually configures these devices. The designations for parallel ports are LPT1, LPT2, and LPT3. LPT1 is usually the printer port and can also be referred to as PRN. Serial ports are COM1, COM2, and COM3. COM1 is usually assigned to a mouse or serial printer and can also be called AUX. CON refers to the display and keyboard. The NUL device is a place for output that you would like to disappear. A common use is to redirect output that you don't want to appear on the screen into the NUL device.

DR DOS 6 BY EXAMPLE

How-to Information

The following sections provide quick help with commonly used DOS tasks, listed by function. If you want to look up a specific command, check Appendix A.

Finding Files

The basic way to find files is to use DIR to list the files contained in a directory. DIR lists a number of important things (see Figure 3-3). In addition to the names and extensions of the files, the list displays the size of each file and the time and date each was last modified. The numbers at the end show the total number of files in the directory as well as the amount of space left on the disk. To avoid filling up the disk, delete unnecessary files. Files with a .BAK extension can usually be deleted safely (using the DEL command) because they're backups.

Knowing the size of the file is important. It's good to know which files use up the most disk space, or whether a set of files will fit on a floppy disk. The time and date allow you to keep track of what work was done at what time.

```
ARTLINE   BAT      251   9-04-91   9:56p
AUTOEXEC  BAK      528  11-03-91   8:35a
AUTOEXEC  OLD      509  10-29-91   8:12p
CHECK     TXT      291   9-09-91   9:39p
COMMAND   COM    50456   8-23-91   6:00a
CONFIG    OLD      359  11-03-91   8:28a
AUTOEXEC  BAT      532  11-03-91   8:37a
DEVSWAP   COM     1583   8-23-91   6:00a
DIAMOND   WMF    50854   9-25-91   9:59p
DISKMAP   DAT    62192  11-03-91   9:22p
EMM       SYS    13010   1-01-80  12:03a
FILE0000  CHK     4096  11-02-91   1:06p
FISHLIB   DLL     5372  12-18-90   2:35a
HDCLIB    DLL   208784   3-18-91  11:19a
HIMEM     SYS    11304   5-01-90   3:00a
HT12EMS1  SYS    11392   9-20-90   7:11p
MOUSE     SYS    15526  12-09-88  10:10a
PBRUSH    DLL     7724   5-01-90   3:00a
RECORDER  DLL    11774   5-01-90   3:00a
SEA       BMP    18550   9-06-90   1:15p
SFINSTAL  DIR      430   2-07-91  12:00p
SI        EXE    14946   5-15-87   4:00p
SSTORDRV  SYS    35327   8-23-91   6:00a
SYSTAT    EXE    24228  12-15-89  12:00p
Strike a key when ready . . .
```

Figure 3-3. The DIR command lists all the files in a directory.

BASIC DOS SKILLS

The DIR command has a number of useful parameters, as outlined in Appendix A. The handiest is /P, which pauses the directory listing at each screenful of information. To look at files in another directory or on another drive, give the file and directory path in the command. For example, this DIR command lists all files ending in .DOC in the \SPOOKY directory on the B: drive and pauses (until a key is pressed) to display one screenful at a time:

```
DIR B:\SPOOKY\*.DOC /P
```

DR DOS also features a more powerful directory listing command: XDIR. A typical XDIR display is shown in Figure 3-4. Note that the file attributes appear along with the information provided by DIR. File attributes allow files to be protected or hidden. (I'll talk about this in detail later in this section.) As with DIR, the /P parameter makes XDIR pause at each screenful of information.

```
[Max] C:\>xdir /p
--a---         157   9-04-91   9:56p  c:alsetup.bat
DIRECTORY            1-01-80  12:16a  c:artline
--a---         251   9-04-91   9:56p  c:artline.bat
--a---         528  11-03-91   8:35a  c:autoexec.bak
--a---         532  11-03-91   8:37a  c:autoexec.bat
--a---         509  10-29-91   8:12p  c:autoexec.old
DIRECTORY           11-03-91   8:30a  c:bitmaps
DIRECTORY            1-01-80  12:14a  c:book
--a---         291   9-09-91   9:39p  c:check.txt
--a---      50,456   8-23-91   6:00a  c:command.com
--a---         400  11-03-91   8:35a  c:config.bak
--a---         359  11-03-91   8:28a  c:config.old
--a---         291  11-03-91   8:37a  c:config.sys
--a---       1,583   8-23-91   6:00a  c:devswap.com
--a---      50,854   9-25-91   9:59p  c:diamond.wmf
r-a---      62,192  11-03-91   9:22p  c:diskmap.dat
DIRECTORY            1-01-80  12:08a  c:drdos
--a---      13,010   1-01-80  12:03a  c:emm.sys
DIRECTORY            1-01-80  12:04a  c:fastback
DIRECTORY            9-14-91   1:59p  c:fiction
------       4,096  11-02-91   1:06p  c:file0000.chk
--a---       5,372  12-18-90   2:35a  c:fishlib.dll
--a---     208,784   3-18-91  11:19a  c:hdclib.dll
Press [Enter] to continue...
```

Figure 3-4. A typical set of file information displayed by XDIR.

Perhaps the most powerful use for XDIR is searching through a series of subdirectories, or even an entire drive, for specified files. Use the /S parameter to scan all subdirectories of the current (or specified) directory. For example, the following XDIR command lists every .EPS file on the C: drive and pauses at each screenful of information:

```
XDIR C:\*.EPS /S /P
```

Appendix A lists all of XDIR's powerful capabilities.

Copying and Moving Files

DR DOS gives you four ways to move files:

COPY   Makes duplicates of the specified files. You must specify where the duplicate will reside, and you can't place a duplicate in the same directory as the original file.

XCOPY   A turbocharged version of COPY. XCOPY copies more efficiently by making better use of memory. It can also copy files in subdirectories of the specified directory and even replicate an entire directory structure.

MOVE   Literally moves files from one directory and/or drive to another.

REPLACE   Also makes duplicate files but has a couple of interesting capabilities. It can be used to copy all files to a directory without overwriting any existing files. It can also copy only more recent versions of files than those in the target directory.

To copy a file or set of files, use COPY or XCOPY. For most file copying, either command will do nicely; however, XCOPY is faster when you're copying a set of files. For example, to copy all the files on the A: floppy disk to the C:\WORK directory, use XCOPY:

```
XCOPY A: C:\WORK
```

Note that I didn't need to add the wildcard file designation to copy all files (*.*) because, if no file designation is entered, the XCOPY command assumes you want to copy all the files. However, if you wanted to copy only the files with a .DOC extension, you would need to use this version of the command:

```
XCOPY A:\*.DOC C:\WORK
```

In addition to being more efficient than COPY, XCOPY can copy files from all subdirectories of the designated directory. Copying from subdirectories is done with the /S parameter. For example, to copy all files beginning with JUNE and ending with .WKS that reside anywhere on the C: disk, then place the copies on the A: drive, use this command:

```
XCOPY C:\JUNE*.WKS A: /S
```

Another interesting thing to do with XCOPY (and a number of other commands) is to copy only those files specified in a list of files. To do this, first make a file that lists the files to be copied. Use EDITOR (or any other editing program that can create a standard ASCII text file) to do this. For example, you could create a C:\COPIER.TXT file made up of the following lines:

```
C:\AUTOEXEC.BAT
C:\CONFIG.SYS
```

Now these files can be copied anywhere—in this case, to D:\TEMP—with a command like this (the key is the @ symbol preceding the list file):

```
XCOPY @C:\COPIER.TXT D:\TEMP
```

MOVE is useful for literally moving files. It also uses the /S parameter. For example, suppose you want to move all .GEM files on C: to the D: drive (a SuperStor drive used for archiving). If you're archiving the files, remove them from the C: drive using the following command:

```
MOVE *.GEM D: /S
```

REPLACE is more specialized than the other commands for moving and copying files. It is primarily useful for copying files into a directory without overwriting existing files. This capability is available through the /A parameter. For example, to copy all *.DOC files from the A: drive that didn't already exist in the C:\WORK directory, use this command:

```
REPLACE A:*.DOC C:\WORK /A
```

These commands are described in detail in Appendix A.

Deleting Files

DR DOS also has several commands for deleting files:

DEL   The generic DOS delete command. This removes the specified files from the current directory.

DELQ   Much like DEL but lets you change your mind before deleting the files. This is a safer way to delete files and is also useful for choosing which files in the list to delete.

XDEL   A supercharged version of DEL. It can delete files in branching subdirectories as well and should therefore be used with caution.

For example, to delete the MYSTUFF.TXT file, issue the command

```
DEL MYSTUFF.TXT
```

If the file is on another drive or in a directory, add that information to the file description:

```
DEL E:\PAPERS\MYSTUFF.TXT
```

To delete all the files in the current directory, use this command:

```
DEL *.*
```

BASIC DOS SKILLS

When this command is issued, DEL will ask if you really want to delete all the files before it proceeds. This safety feature keeps you from deleting more than you bargained for (not that deleting is necessarily permanent in DR DOS, as we'll see a bit later).

DELQ asks about each file before deleting it. This can be quite handy for deleting a number of files with different extensions or names from a directory. To pick which files to delete from the current directory, issue this command:

```
DELQ *.*
```

DELQ displays the name of the first file on the list and pauses before deleting it. Press Y to delete or N to skip to the next file on the list.

XDEL is most useful for deleting a particular type of file from branching subdirectories. As with the other commands we've covered, this is done with the /S parameter. For example, most programs create backup files that are merely previous versions. These files are handy, but they become a nuisance when they begin to fill up your disk. Fortunately, most backup files end in .BAK. To delete them from the C: disk, use this command:

```
XDEL *.BAK /S
```

One other useful variation of XDEL involves the /O parameter. Normally, files can be undeleted (as covered in Chapter 9). However, this may not be desirable in every case. For example, a file may contain sensitive or confidential information, and as a security precaution you may want it permanently removed. The /O parameter overwrites the contents of the file, permanently removing the data belonging to that file. For example, to remove the file SALARY.WKS, use this command:

```
XDEL SALARY.WKS /O
```

Before permanently removing files, XDEL will ask if you really want to do so.

DR DOS 6 BY EXAMPLE

Looking at a Text File

Sometimes you'll just want to read through the contents of a file onscreen. That's where TYPE comes in. This command simply lists the contents of the file on your screen. In any version of DOS, TYPE can be paused and started again by pressing the Ctrl-S key. In DR DOS, the /P parameter can be added to the TYPE command to make it pause at each screenful of information until another key is pressed. You'll almost always want to use TYPE with the /P parameter.

To display the README.DOC file that comes with the word processor WeaselWord, use this command:

```
TYPE README.DOC /P
```

Be aware that TYPE is designed to work with files that contain only ASCII text, along with any formatting codes. If your WeaselWord file contains non-ASCII codes, they'll show up as strange-looking characters on the display screen (for example, the happy-face character). Although this will clutter the screen display, it won't hurt anything and may even allow you to discern the text embedded within formatting commands.

You can display more than one file by using wildcards. To look at the contents of all the batch files in the C:\ directory, use this command:

```
TYPE C:\*.BAT /P
```

Changing File Attributes

Earlier I mentioned that files have attributes that can offer limited protection and can hide files from DIR (but not XDIR). Any file can have some or all of these attributes:

Hidden   Hides the file from DIR and COPY, although XDIR can find it. MOVE and XCOPY can move or copy such files when used with the /H parameter (see Appendix A). DEL, DELQ, and XDEL can't touch hidden files.

BASIC DOS SKILLS

System   Generally reserved for operating system files, such as IBMBIO.COM and IBMDOS.COM. The DELWATCH file @DLWATCH.DAT is also set with this attribute. DIR displays such files only if you use the /S parameter.

Archive   Set whenever a file is modified. Certain programs, such as XCOPY, BACKUP, REPLACE, and FILELINK, reset this attribute. When used with the /A parameter, XCOPY and MOVE affect only those files with the archive attribute set.

Read-only   Provides limited protection against accidental deletion. DEL won't delete files with this attribute, but XDEL will when the /R parameter is specified. The only sure way to make sure no one erases a file is to use the PASSWORD command. For more on passwords, see Chapter 10.

File attributes are shown in the leftmost column of the XDIR file listing (see Figure 3-5). File attributes can be assigned or removed with the ATTRIB command. Type ATTRIB alone to see a list of the files and their attributes, though not with the other useful information provided by XDIR. To remove an attribute, use the following form of the command:

```
ATTRIB -[H|S|A|R] files
```

This command is followed by optional single-letter attributes, which are listed within brackets and separated by vertical bars. You do not type in the brackets or the vertical bars; these characters are a shorthand way of representing the syntax of a command. In this command, H stands for *hidden*, S stands for *system*, A stands for *archive*, and R stands for *read-only*. For example, to remove the archive attribute from the file MYSTUFF.TXT, enter this command:

```
ATTRIB -A MYSTUFF.TXT
```

```
[Max] C:\>xdir /p
--a---         157    9-04-91   9:56p   c:alsetup.bat
DIRECTORY             1-01-80  12:16a   c:artline
--a---         251    9-04-91   9:56p   c:artline.bat
--a---         528   11-03-91   8:35a   c:autoexec.bak
--a---         532   11-03-91   8:37a   c:autoexec.bat
--a---         509   10-29-91   8:12p   c:autoexec.old
DIRECTORY            11-03-91   8:30a   c:bitmaps
DIRECTORY             1-01-80  12:14a   c:book
--a---         291    9-09-91   9:39p   c:check.txt
--a---      50,456    8-23-91   6:00a   c:command.com
--a---         400   11-03-91   8:35a   c:config.bak
--a---         359   11-03-91   8:28a   c:config.old
--a---         291   11-03-91   8:37a   c:config.sys
--a---       1,583    8-23-91   6:00a   c:devswap.com
--a---      50,854    9-25-91   9:59p   c:diamond.wmf
r-a---      62,192   11-03-91   9:22p   c:diskmap.dat
DIRECTORY             1-01-80  12:08a   c:drdos
--a---      13,010    1-01-80  12:03a   c:emm.sys
DIRECTORY             1-01-80  12:04a   c:fastback
DIRECTORY             9-14-91   1:59p   c:fiction
------       4,096   11-02-91   1:06p   c:file0000.chk
--a---       5,372   12-18-90   2:35a   c:fishlib.dll
--a---     208,784    3-18-91  11:19a   c:hdclib.dll
Press [Enter] to continue...
```

Figure 3-5. The attributes shown along the right side of the screen in an XDIR file listing.

To remove the hidden and system attributes from all files in the current directory, use this command:

ATTRIB -HS *.*

Setting attributes is quite similar except that a + is used instead of a - (which is logical). For example, to set the read-only attribute for all the .DBF files in the C:\MAILLIST directory, use this ATTRIB command:

ATTRIB +R C:\MAILLIST*.DBF

Searching for Text in Files

Have you ever been faced with a mass of word processor files, only one of which contains the passage you need? No problem: DR DOS has a utility that quickly scans a set of ASCII text files (or nearly-ASCII files from any word processor). This little gem is FIND.

BASIC DOS SKILLS

Suppose a set of .DOC files resides in the current directory. To find the one that references the ACME Giant Rubber Band Company, enter this command:

```
FIND "acme giant rubber band company" *.DOC
```

FIND will display a list of the files containing that bit of text. Notice the quotes around the search string and the fact that the string isn't capitalized. To find text that begins and ends with quotes, put another set of quotes around it: ""It was a dark and stormy night."''

FIND has several useful parameters. The /N parameter displays the line number at which FIND encounters the search string in a file. When you open the file with a text editor that supports access by line number, jump directly to this line to find the text string. The /U parameter makes FIND sensitive to case so that uppercase letters are distinguished from lowercase. The /V parameter does an inverted search, listing only those files that do not contain the search string.

Printing Files

Two DR DOS utilities print text files: PRINT and SCRIPT. PRINT works with everything but PostScript printers. SCRIPT transforms a text file into PostScript and can be used instead of PRINT or in conjunction with it. First we'll look at PRINT.

PRINT is actually a TSR program—once run, it stays in memory and continues to function until you reboot or shut off the system. It makes sense, then, that certain setup parameters can be issued only when PRINT is first run. Some of these parameters can improve performance (see the PRINT section in Appendix A). The most important initial parameter is /D:, which specifies the printer port. For example, if the printer is on LPT2, use the following command:

```
PRINT /D:LPT2
```

This loads PRINT and sets it to work with the LPT2 parallel port. If you don't explicitly define a printer port when you initialize PRINT, it asks you to specify one:

```
LIST DEVICE? [PRN]
```

This indicates that if a port isn't specified, PRINT will assume the printer is attached to PRN (which is the same as LPT1).

To print something with PRINT, specify the file or files as the argument to the command. For example, to print MYSTUFF.TXT, use this command:

```
PRINT MYSTUFF.TXT
```

To print multiple files, use this command:

```
PRINT D:\LETTERS\*.TXT
```

PRINT will allow files to be stacked up in a print queue. These files will print, one at a time, until the queue is empty. If a program is run while files are printing, PRINT will pause until you exit from the program and resume printing where it left off.

To see what's in the queue, type the PRINT command by itself. To remove a file from the queue, use the /C parameter. To remove D:\WEASEL\README.DOC from the queue, for example, use this command:

```
PRINT D:\WEASEL\README.DOC /C
```

To clear the queue completely, use this command:

```
PRINT /T
```

A drawback of using PostScript printers is their inability to print standard text files. Before a text file can be printed, a program must translate the text to PostScript. Some application programs can handle this, but PRINT can't. SCRIPT solves this problem.

SCRIPT can be used as both a command-line program and a TSR. As a command-line program, it's easy to use; it just needs a source file and an output. For example, to print the README.DOC file on a PostScript printer attached to LPT1, use this command:

```
SCRIPT README LPT1
```

BASIC DOS SKILLS

To install SCRIPT as a TSR, specify an input port and an output port. Suppose the PostScript printer is attached to parallel port LPT1 and nothing is attached to LPT3. Set LPT3 as the input and LPT1 as the output, and SCRIPT will intercept everything sent to LPT3, translate it to PostScript if the file is text, and send the PostScript out through LPT1:

```
SCRIPT LPT3 LPT1
```

Now load PRINT and set it to print to LPT3. This still allows for a print queue, but every text file queued through PRINT will be translated to PostScript and printed on LPT1. Again, refer to Appendix A for more information.

Formatting a Diskette

Information can't be stored on a new floppy disk until the disk has been formatted (unless you use a utility such as Fifth Generation Systems' FastBack, which formats and writes information track by track). Formatting is the process of preparing a disk to receive data. It is roughly analogous to painting lane markers on a highway. Information is recorded that marks the positions of the magnetic tracks on the diskette. This information is used by the computer's system software whenever the diskette is accessed.

FORMAT, like the other commands, has several command-line parameters. I'll cover the absolute basics first. To format a disk using the drive's default format type, type FORMAT followed by the drive designator. For example, to format a disk in the B: drive, use the following command:

```
FORMAT B:
```

FORMAT will tell you to put a disk in the drive and then press Enter. If the disk has a different format from the default for that drive, FORMAT will tell you that the formats are different and ask if you wish to proceed. Press Y to format the disk; press N to cancel the program.

The default format capacity for a high-density, 5.25-inch drive is 1.2 MB; for a high-density, 3.5-inch drive, it's 1.44 MB. Some super-high-density drives are available with even more capacity. XT and PC systems have low-density, 5.25-inch drives that format 360-KB disks. Some systems, usually laptops and portables, have 720-KB, 3.5-inch drives. The default capacity of the drive can't be exceeded; that is, high-density disks can't be formatted or read on a low-density drive. Low-density disks can, however, be formatted on a high-density drive. This doesn't usually work very well with high-density, 5.25-inch drives. You can always read a low-density disk in a high-density drive.

On a PC or XT system with a processor clock speed faster than 4.77 MHz, you may have trouble using DR DOS to format disks. There are two ways around this: turn the speed down to 4.77 MHz (if possible) or load the PC-Kwik disk-caching software that comes with DR DOS 6.0. PC-Kwik can correct the formatting problem.

The easiest way to format a low-density disk in a high-density drive is with the /F parameter. /F allows a format to be specified in kilobytes. For example, to format a 720-KB, 3.5-inch disk in a 1.44-MB drive designated as A:, use this command:

```
FORMAT A: /F:720
```

To format a 360-KB disk in a high-density, 5.25-inch drive designated as B:, use this command:

```
FORMAT B: /F:360
```

DR DOS has a unique capability called *quick-formatting*. If FORMAT detects that the disk has previously been formatted, it will write the file allocation table information to an unused portion of the disk and then set up a clean file allocation table. All files on the disk remain intact. If no data has been written to the disk, these files can be recovered with the UNFORMAT command. If FORMAT can't find enough unused space on the disk, it reports that it won't be able to save all the file information.

Quick-formatting has a distinct advantage in that it can format a disk in a few seconds. However, it isn't always a good idea to quick-format a disk. If the disk was originally formatted on another system, you should reformat it in your drive using the /U parameter. This tells FORMAT to format the disk track by track.

```
FORMAT A: /U
```

Copying an Entire Floppy Disk

Sometimes it's useful to copy the contents of one floppy disk to another quickly—when making backup copies of original software disks, for example. This can be done with the COPY or XCOPY command, but it isn't exactly a speedy process. However, when copying between two disks of the same type, you can accelerate the task with DISKCOPY. Unlike COPY and XCOPY, which copy file by file, DISKCOPY copies one disk to the other track by track. That's why it's essential that the disks be of the same type—you can't do a track-by-track copy from a 40-track to an 80-track disk. That doesn't mean you must have two drives that are the same type; DISKCOPY loads as much as it can into memory, then instructs you to remove the original disk and place the copy disk in the drive. It repeats this process until the entire disk has been copied. The disk can also be copied to an image file on the hard drive; DISKCOPY can then make duplicate floppies from the image file.

To copy a disk between two identical disk drives, use a command like the following:

```
DISKCOPY A: B:
```

To copy a disk using a single drive, use something like this:

```
DISKCOPY A: A:
```

DISKCOPY will ask you to insert the source disk (the original) into the drive. When memory is full, DISKCOPY will ask you to remove the source disk and insert the destination disk (the copy) in the drive. It will continue this swapping process until the copy is complete. To avoid confusing the source and copy disks, place a write-protect tab on the source disk.

To copy a disk to an image file, specify a destination file on the hard drive. For example, use a command that looks like this:

```
DISKCOPY A: C:\WEASL1.IMG
```

Then, to make a duplicate disk using the image file, use a command like this:

```
DISKCOPY C:\WEASL1.IMG A:
```

Backing Up the System

Even with highly reliable hard drives, making backups of important files is very prudent. I work at a software company, and we back up all working files every day. The frequency with which you back up your work should be calculated in inverse proportion to the time it would take to re-create it.

The DR DOS backup facility, BACKUP, will fill up a disk. If there is more data to archive, it will ask for additional disks. This means that BACKUP can also be used to transport files that are too big for a single disk. BACKUP itself doesn't compress data, so the process may require a great many disks. Using SuperStor to activate compression for a given floppy disk will reduce the required number of floppies.

BACKUP is a bit slow. A number of utilities for making backups are available; some are very fast and compress data as well. I use FastBack, and I find it extremely quick and convenient. However, if you don't have the luxury of being able to purchase a backup utility, the DR DOS BACKUP command is a serviceable alternative.

To some extent, you can be selective about what to back up with BACKUP. Use the /S parameter to back up all subdirectories of the specified directory. The /M parameter backs up only those files that have been modified since the previous backup was made. /D backs up only those files that were modified on or after a user-specified date. Finally, the /F parameter also formats the floppies during the backup process. Additional parameters are listed in Appendix A, but I think these four are the most useful.

For example, to back up the C:\ACCOUNTS directory and all of its subdirectories to the A: drive, use this command:

```
BACKUP C:\ACCOUNTS A: /S
```

After backing up the files, BACKUP will turn off the archive attribute of each file so it will know which files were modified since the last backup. Later, a much

BASIC DOS SKILLS

shorter backup can be made of only those files that were modified since the previous backup. This command for this is:

```
BACKUP C:\ACCOUNTS A: /S /M
```

To back up the files on the D: drive that were created on or after January 1, 1992, using a new box of unformatted floppies, use this command:

```
BACKUP D:\ A: /S /D:01-01-91 /F
```

Note that this example uses the date set by the country code for USA. If your country setting is different, your date format may also be different.

Restoring Files from Backups

Once data is backed up, it may also need to be accessed. Do this with the DR DOS RESTORE command. RESTORE in DR DOS 6.0 is compatible with all previous releases of DOS, so disks made with the MS-DOS 3.1 BACKUP utility should be read easily. RESTORE also has some handy parameters, including /S, /D, and /M, just like BACKUP.

For example, to restore the C:\ACCOUNTS\EXPENSE.WKS file, use this command:

```
RESTORE A: C:\ACCOUNTS\EXPENSE.WKS
```

To restore all files in the C:\ACCOUNTS directory and their branching subdirectories, use this version of the command:

```
RESTORE A: C:\ACCOUNTS /S
```

To restore only those files in C:\ACCOUNTS and its subdirectories that were modified since the last backup, use this command:

```
RESTORE A: C:\ACCOUNTS /S /M
```

To restore all files that were modified on or after January 1, 1992, use this variation:

```
RESTORE A: C:\ACCOUNTS /S /D:01-01-92
```

Checking Available Memory

The MEM command is used to display the amount of memory available and the amount being used. Issuing MEM alone will produce a listing of the total and available conventional (base), extended, expanded, high, and upper memory (see Figure 3-6). Conventional memory is where applications run, so usually the more that's available the better. Extended and expanded memory is used by various applications. Many DOS applications, such as spreadsheets and graphics programs, use expanded memory. Many other applications, such as Windows, use extended memory. High memory can be used by EMM386.SYS or HIDOS.SYS to hold part of the DR DOS operating system, freeing conventional memory for other uses. Upper memory is used by HIDEVICE and HIINSTALL to hold device drivers, also freeing conventional memory.

Users with a technical background who really want to see what's going on can issue the command using the /A and /P parameters. The /A parameter lists the kind of memory used by the various parts of the operating system, where all device drivers are loaded, and the locations of RAM, ROM, and EMS memory. The /P parameter pauses the listing at each screenful to give you time to look at all this information. To use this version of the command, type the following:

```
MEM /A /P
```

Making Disk Repairs

Occasionally, files aren't closed properly by application programs or some other untoward incident (such as a power failure) occurs. This can cause DR DOS to be unsure of which files certain disk clusters are allocated to. Such clusters are called *lost chains*. Clusters can also be allocated to more than one file, creating cross-linked files. The DR DOS CHKDSK utility can fix both problems by straightening out the file allocation table. Lost chains should always be recovered to free disk space. (And you might find something interesting in the chains, especially if you lost data during

BASIC DOS SKILLS

```
[Max] C:\>mem

  Memory Type         Total Bytes ( Kbytes )        Available

  Conventional          655,360 (     640K )      507,856 (   495K )
  High                   65,520 (      64K )        3,218 (     3K )
  Extended            3,145,728 (   3,072K )            0 (    0K )
  Extended via XMS          N/A                 1,507,328 ( 1,472K )

[Max] C:\>
```

Figure 3-6. Use the MEM command to check available memory.

a power outage.) Cross-linked files should be fixed, but data will probably be lost in both files. If one of the cross-linked files is intact, copy the data out of it before proceeding.

CHKDSK has two modes: scan-only and scan-and-fix. It's usually a good idea to scan for problems first. Otherwise, cross-linked files will be fixed before salvageable data can be retrieved. To scan only, run the command with no parameters. For example, to scan the D: drive, use this command:

```
CHKDSK D:
```

An important note: Don't run CHKDSK to fix problems from within Microsoft Windows. This actually does more harm than good to the file allocation table.

To correct errors, use the /F parameter:

```
CHKDSK D: /F
```

CHAPTER 4

Help!

DR DOS has extensive on-line help facilities. Each command has accessible help for its parameters: Type the command followed by /? or /H. DR DOS also has an on-line version of the command reference in the manual, a set of how-to information for basic DR DOS tasks, and even an error-code listing that can help with troubleshooting. Using DOSBOOK is simple because it is menu driven and uses the Common User Access (CUA) interface found in ViewMAX, Microsoft Windows, and practically everything else. Unfortunately, you can't use a mouse with DOSBOOK, but you can't have everything.

Keep DOSBOOK around in a task or window while using TaskMAX, DESQview, or Microsoft Windows so you can refer to it whenever you like.

Running DOSBOOK

To run DOSBOOK, type

```
DOSBOOK
```

and press Enter. This will work as long as the \DRDOS directory is in the PATH. (If it isn't, add the full path to the command or change the directory to \DRDOS.) If you have an LCD display laptop or a monochrome monitor, you can add the /B parameter.

In DOSBOOK, the screen in Figure 4-1 will appear. From here, the following categories of topics can be chosen.

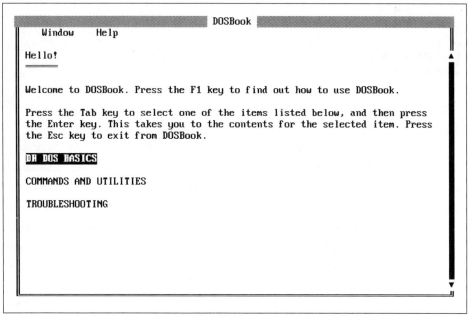

Figure 4-1. DOSBOOK's opening screen.

DR DOS Basics

This covers the basic how-to information for running DOS. Topics include naming files, using wildcards, and the meaning of internal and external commands. If you are unfamiliar with DOS and need to learn quickly how to do a specific task, look it up here.

Commands and Utilities

This is virtually a replica of the DR DOS manual command-reference chapter. Issue a command with /H or /? for a brief summary of the available command parameters. The DOSBOOK command reference provides more detailed information about the parameters. To jump directly to one of these entries from the command line, enter the following:

```
DOSBOOK commandname
```

where *commandname* is the name of the DOS command you'd like to look up. For

HELP!

example, the following provides a reference about the XDIR command:

```
DOSBOOK XDIR
```

Troubleshooting

This is a listing of all the DR DOS error messages and what they mean. These three sections provide a fairly complete quick reference. Press the Tab key to access any of the topic categories. The highlight bar moves from category to category. Press Enter to pick one, and a list of all available topics will appear. Figure 4-2 shows the top screen of the topic list for DR DOS Basics. Navigating the list is reasonably simple. The following table lists the keys used and their functions:

Key(s)	Function
Home	Top of the screen
End	Bottom of the screen
PgUp	Next screenful up
PgDn	Next screenful down
Tab	Next topic down
Down arrow	Next topic down
Shift-Tab	Next topic up
Up arrow	Next topic up
Ctrl-End	Bottom screen in the list
Ctrl-Home	Top screen in the list

Try bouncing around the list using various keys. It won't take long to get the hang of it. One other trick is to press a letter: The highlight will jump to the first entry starting with that letter. The rules for this are a bit odd, though. You can't jump again without moving the highlight bar with one of the keys listed above. Also, it won't jump to the *next* entry with that letter, only to the *first* entry in the list.

DR DOS 6 BY EXAMPLE

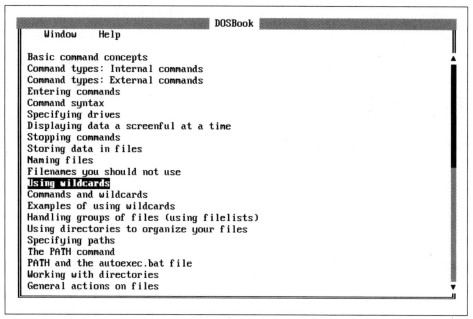

Figure 4-2. Selecting a topic from a DOSBOOK list.

Once you've chosen a topic, place the highlight bar over it and press the Enter key. This brings up the reference material about the topic. A typical example is shown in Figure 4-3. Notice the scroll bar at the right. At first glance it seems a bit silly because you can't use a mouse. However, the scroll bar is useful because it tells you that the reference material takes up more than a single screen. Consider the slider to be equal to one screenful of information. Comparing the size of the slider to the open space in the slide bar gives a pretty good idea of how much information is in the file.

Moving around in the reference information is similar to navigating in the topics list but with fewer options. The following table describes the keys and their functions.

HELP!

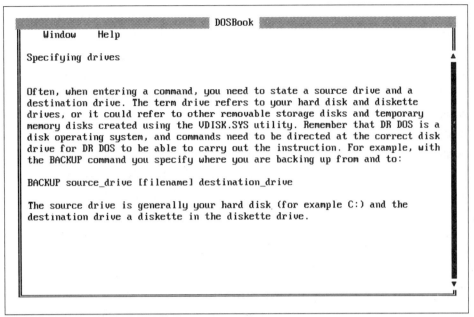

Figure 4-3. A typical DOSBOOK entry for a topic.

Key(s)	Function
PgDn	Down one screenful
PgUp	Up one screenful
Down arrow	Down one line
Up arrow	Up one line
Home	Cursor to the top of the screen
End	Cursor to the bottom of the screen
Ctrl-Home	Top of the reference listing
Ctrl-End	Bottom of the reference listing
Tab	Next key word down
Shift-tab	Next key work up

Key words have additional information as an expansion of an important concept. If the key word is both underlined and bold, it has a rather lengthy listing of its own. If the key word is just underlined, there is only a short note attached. Pressing Enter opens up the key-word reference listing. If it's a short note, it remains on-screen only while Enter is held down. Navigating a key-word reference is the same as in a topic listing.

To get back from a key word to the topic you want to read about, press Alt-B. To jump all the way back to the opening DOSBOOK menu, use Escape.

The Previous and Next Section commands are a bit confusing. Next Section, Alt-N, takes you to the next item in the previous list. Let's say you're in the command listing reading about CHKDSK. Pressing Alt-N brings up the CLS reference material. That's because CLS is the next command in the list of commands. Pressing Alt-P, Previous Section, takes you back to the CHKDSK reference. Got that? Now, if you're looking at the command list itself and you press Alt-N, the list of troubleshooting error messages appears. (Remember that Troubleshooting was one of the three major categories of information available in the DOSBOOK opening menu.) Press Alt-P here, and you're back at the command list.

The Table of Contents, Index, and Glossary

Any good reference book has a table of contents, an extensive index, and a glossary of terms. So does DOSBOOK. Press Alt-C to access the table of contents. Navigation is similar to that in a list of topics. Alt-I opens the index. Alt-G brings up the glossary list, where you'll find definitions of DR DOS terms.

The Menus

Like almost all programs these days, DOSBOOK has drop-down menus. Press Alt-W to access the Window menu, shown in Figure 4-4. Press the up or down arrow key to move the highlight bar up or down the list of commands. To activate a command, highlight it and press Enter. The "Resize Window" command (accessed in the menu or by typing Alt-F5) shrinks or expands the window. "Print Section" is extremely handy because it allows you to print out a reference listing. This prints to the PRN port (usually LPT1). The print format isn't fancy, so it will print on virtually anything. "Exit, Retain Window" returns to DR DOS with a command prompt at the bottom of the screen. However, the DOSBOOK screen remains visible as you try out the command. "Exit" (also accessed in the menu or by typing Alt-X) does just that and returns to DR DOS.

HELP!

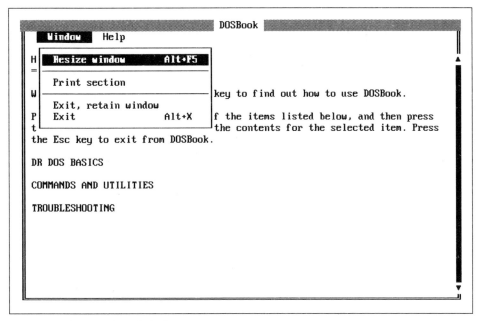

Figure 4-4. The DOSBOOK Window menu.

The Help menu is shown in Figure 4-5, and we've already covered all but two of these commands. "Help for DOSBook" covers how to use DOSBOOK itself. "About" provides the version number for DOSBOOK.

That's about it. Try running DOSBOOK as a task or in a window, and I think you'll agree that it's quite handy.

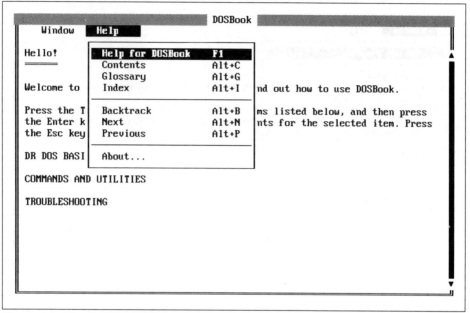

Figure 4-5. The DOSBOOK Help menu.

CHAPTER 5

Fine-Tuning DR DOS

At system start-up, your computer reads the configuration information in the CONFIG.SYS file and runs any programs or commands listed in the AUTOEXEC.BAT file. These two files are always located in the root directory of the boot drive. DR DOS has some special capabilities pertaining to the CONFIG.SYS file; the most important of these is the memory manager, which frees conventional memory.

A wise PC user once referred to memory managers as "memory muddlers." And so they have been. For example, while I was using brand A memory manager, the floppy drives on my Hyundai 80386 wouldn't format floppies. When I switched to brand B, I found that I could look forward each day to one or two mysterious NMI errors that locked up the machine. Since I installed DR DOS 6.0's EMM386 memory manager, the worst problem I've encountered is that I must shut off access to upper memory when installing programs that use the Yoshi compression utility.

This chapter will help you avoid configuration nightmares. Besides discussing the various device drivers and CONFIG.SYS statements DR DOS supports, it shows how I set up my 80286 and 80386 systems. If you'll be using third-party memory managers, you'll be interested in the explanation of how to configure Quarterdeck's QEMM and Qualitas' 386-to-the-Max drivers to work efficiently with DR DOS 6.0.

Before delving into fine-tuning, let's take a moment to go over the various types of memory.

The first 640 KB of memory, called *conventional* or *base memory*, is the area used by DR DOS and your application programs. The first 64 KB is called *lower memory*. This is where DOS is normally loaded. The area from 640 KB to 1,024 KB is called *upper memory*. The DR DOS memory managers can load much of DR DOS and loadable device drivers into this area, freeing conventional memory.

On machines equipped with the 80286, 80386, or 80486 microprocessor, memory above 1,024 KB is called *extended*. Extended memory is used for data storage by most programs. However, because 8088 and 8086 microprocessors can only address 1,024 KB of memory directly, additional memory could only be reached using a trick that involves setting up a 64-KB area in upper memory called a *page frame* (as discussed in the reference section for the EMM886.SYS memory manager later in this chapter). The page frame provides access to this segment (or *pages*) of expanded memory. Expanded memory can, through the use of a memory manager, be made available on 80286, 80386, and 80486 systems as well. Some application programs are set up to use expanded memory for data storage, some can use extended memory, and some can use either memory standard.

One other area of memory that you need to know about is *high memory*, the first 64 KB of extended memory. If you have extended memory, you can use a DR DOS memory manager to load part of DR DOS into high memory, freeing both conventional memory (for your applications) and upper memory (so you can load more device drivers there, freeing additional conventional memory). You can load part of DR DOS into upper memory by specifying to the DR DOS memory manager that the BDOS section should be loaded at starting address FFFF (the hexadecimal starting address for high memory). The BDOS starting-address parameter looks like this in the EMM386.SYS and HIDOS.SYS memory manager statements:

```
/B=FFFF
```

You'll also see a reference to XMA memory in this chapter. This is a special extended memory board found only in PS/2 computers.

This brings us to the subject at hand: MemoryMAX. Digital Research uses this catch-all term to refer to its memory managers and special device drivers. DR DOS 6.0 has three memory managers, each for a different hardware configuration:

 EMM386.SYS The installation program will choose this option if it detects an 80386 or 80486 processor in your computer. You can select it through the MemoryMAX section of the installation or SETUP program.

FINE-TUNING DR DOS

HIDOS.SYS   This memory manager lets you move portions of DR DOS into high memory. You can select this option through MemoryMAX if you have an 80286 processor and extended or upper memory.

EMMXMA.SYS   You can use this only with PS/2-type computers that have XMA memory boards. This driver converts extended memory to expanded memory and can be used in conjunction with the HIDOS.SYS driver.

Regardless of the memory manager you use, you need to provide as much base or conventional memory as possible. That's because most sophisticated programs, such as word processors, spreadsheets, and desktop publishing packages, now run just within the limits of available conventional memory. For instance, Ventura Publisher/GEM 3.0 needs about 560 KB to run. You may also have network drivers competing for precious conventional memory. And then there are the mouse drivers, terminate-and-stay-resident (TSR) programs, and a host of other programs trying to claim a piece of conventional memory for themselves.

To optimize your system, follow these basic steps:

1. Load as much of DR DOS into high and upper memory as possible using the memory manager.

2. Load as many device drivers into high and upper memory as possible using the MemoryMAX device drivers.

3. If any memory is left over, use the MemoryMAX device drivers to move anything else that's gobbling memory (such as TSRs) into upper or high memory.

Think about tackling these steps in phases, using the MEM command to check your progress. You should also take the time to put question marks at the beginning of each CONFIG.SYS statement that loads a new driver; this will allow you to get around a troublesome driver if it locks the computer. (The question mark causes DR DOS to ask if you want to load a driver during boot-up.)

Normally, this sort of precaution is unnecessary. However, if you *don't* take this precaution you'll need to boot from a floppy disk. I'll give you an example from my own experience: My 386 at work runs the PC/NFS network so that it can communicate with UNIX workstations on the network. PC/NFS is notoriously cranky, and you never know what will work with it. For instance, the SuperStor drivers can't coexist with PC/NFS; neither can the Windows RAMDRIVE.SYS driver. I didn't put the question marks in front of these drivers when I first tried to load them, and the system repeatedly locked up on boot-up until I booted from a floppy with a plain-vanilla configuration file.

Phase 1: The Initial Setup

You can install a memory manager in two ways: through the installation/SETUP program or by entering the statements directly with EDITOR, SYSEDIT, or some other ASCII text editor. I find it most convenient to use SETUP initially, then fine-tune and add device drivers with EDITOR.

Figure 5-1 shows the SETUP configuration menu with TaskMAX selected (it's at the top of the menu). If you don't have a TaskMAX option on your menu, that means SETUP has detected an 8088 or 8086 processor and no LIM 4.0 memory (which must be made available through the memory manager that came with the LIM memory board). If it does show a MemoryMAX option, you'll be able to access a menu that looks something like that shown in Figure 5-2. Your menu might look a bit different if you're using an 80386; you'll be able to select the EMM386 memory manager. When you select a memory manager, it's installed with the basic parameters. If you want to gain a few more bytes of conventional memory, or if you run into some problems, refer to the EMM386.SYS, HIDOS.SYS, or EMMXMA.SYS driver reference in the DR DOS Installable Device Drivers section later in this chapter.

In most cases, you'll want to load the memory manager and relocate DR DOS data areas and device drivers.

Two other configuration-menu selections affect the CONFIG.SYS file: System Parameters and Optional Device Drivers and Utilities. These are discussed in Chapter 2, but we'll discuss them here as well because they affect memory use.

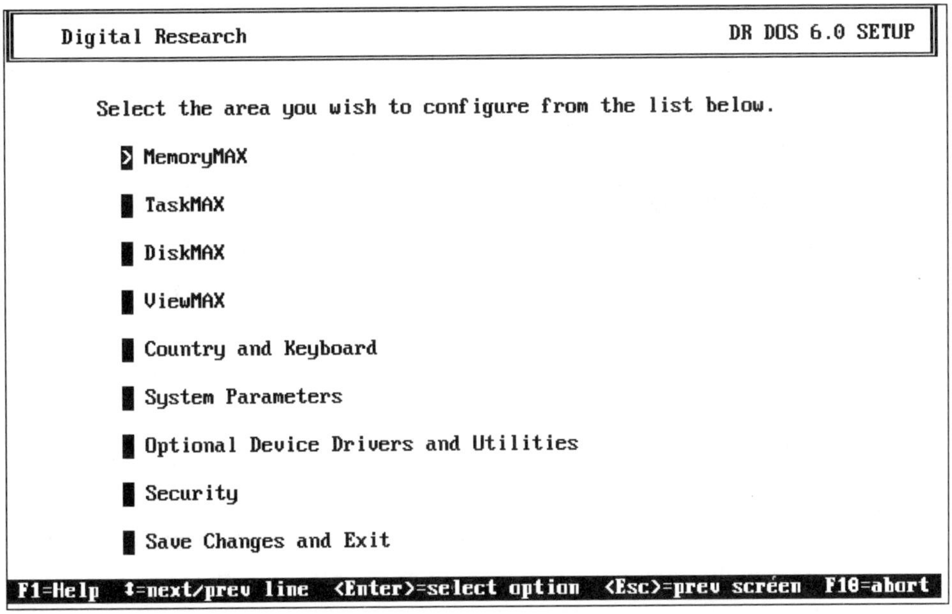

FINE-TUNING DR DOS

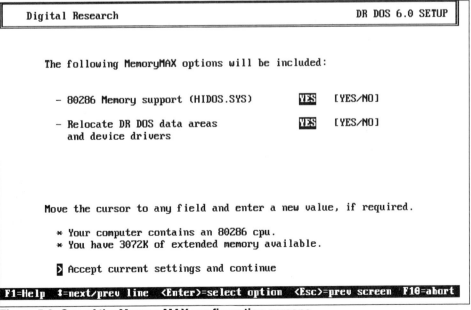

Figure 5-1. The main configuration menu in SETUP or the installation program.

Figure 5-2. One of the MemoryMAX configuration screens.

On the System Parameters menu, you'll find LASTDRIVE, HISTORY, and ENVIRONMENT SIZE (see Figure 5-3). These options have the following features and ramifications:

- LASTDRIVE specifies the last drive letter your computer can use. This becomes an issue when you're working with networks. If some cases, such as with PC/NFS, you'll want to set this to the last drive you'll be using. Otherwise, ViewMAX and Microsoft Windows will become quite confused about what is and isn't a drive, and drives that don't exist will show up on the desktop or in the file manager.

- HISTORY sets whether or not you should enable command-line history. This feature lets you recall and scroll through previously issued commands (as discussed in Chapter 3). It does take up memory, however, so if memory is extremely tight you might want to give up this nicety.

- ENVIRONMENT SIZE sets the DR DOS environment space. I like to have a big environment, so mine is set to 1,024 bytes. If memory is becoming precious, however, you might want to set this to 512 or even 256 bytes. Be careful, though; you may get an "out of environment space" message from DR DOS when you try to run an application program.

Another screen under this option provides settings for BUFFERS, FILES, and FCBS (FCBs are file control blocks), as shown in Figure 5-4. These settings greatly affect performance and, to some extent, memory usage, although both buffers and files can be loaded into high memory. FCBS is an old-fashioned convention, a carry-over from the early DOS days.

- BUFFERS specifies the number of buffers DR DOS uses to cache information from disk. This is similar to but separate from the disk caching done by PC-Kwik. A larger number of buffers affects the speed with which applications can access disk files. The default is 15, though your application documentation may suggest a higher number. If you're using PC-Kwik's cache, you can use as few as three to five buffers because that product does a better job of disk caching.

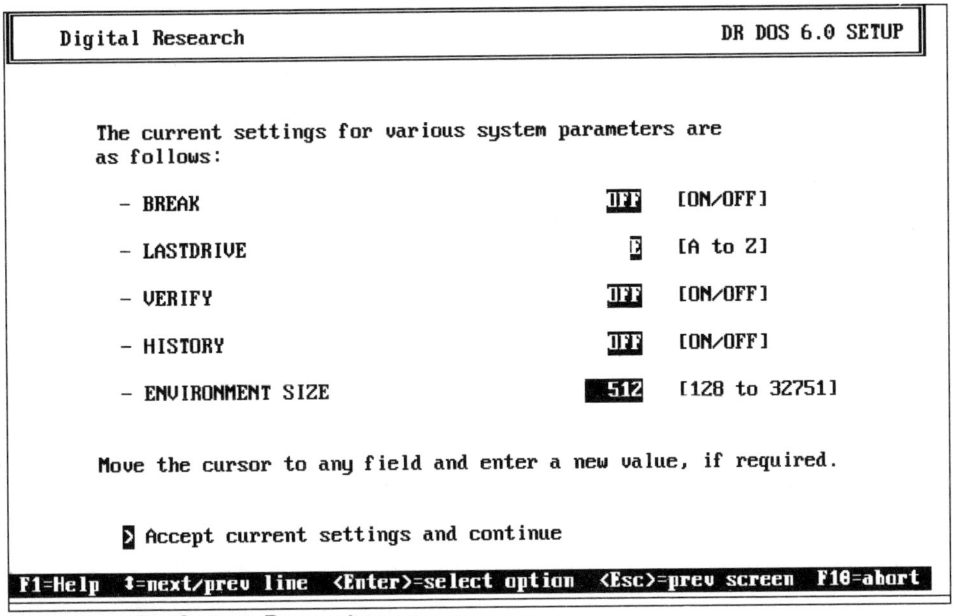

FINE-TUNING DR DOS

```
┌─────────────────────────────────────────────────────────────┐
│ ▌Digital Research                          DR DOS 6.0 SETUP▐│
│ ▔▔▔▔▔▔▔▔▔▔▔▔▔▔▔▔▔▔▔▔▔▔▔▔▔▔▔▔▔▔▔▔▔▔▔▔▔▔▔▔▔▔▔▔▔▔▔▔▔▔▔▔▔▔▔▔▔▔ │
│                                                             │
│    The current settings for various system parameters are   │
│    as follows:                                              │
│                                                             │
│       - BREAK                          OFF    [ON/OFF]      │
│                                                             │
│       - LASTDRIVE                       E     [A to Z]      │
│                                                             │
│       - VERIFY                         OFF    [ON/OFF]      │
│                                                             │
│       - HISTORY                        OFF    [ON/OFF]      │
│                                                             │
│       - ENVIRONMENT SIZE               512    [128 to 32751]│
│                                                             │
│    Move the cursor to any field and enter a new value, if required.│
│                                                             │
│      ▶ Accept current settings and continue                 │
│                                                             │
│ F1=Help  ↕=next/prev line  <Enter>=select option  <Esc>=prev screen  F10=abort │
└─────────────────────────────────────────────────────────────┘
```

Figure 5-3. The System Parameters screen.

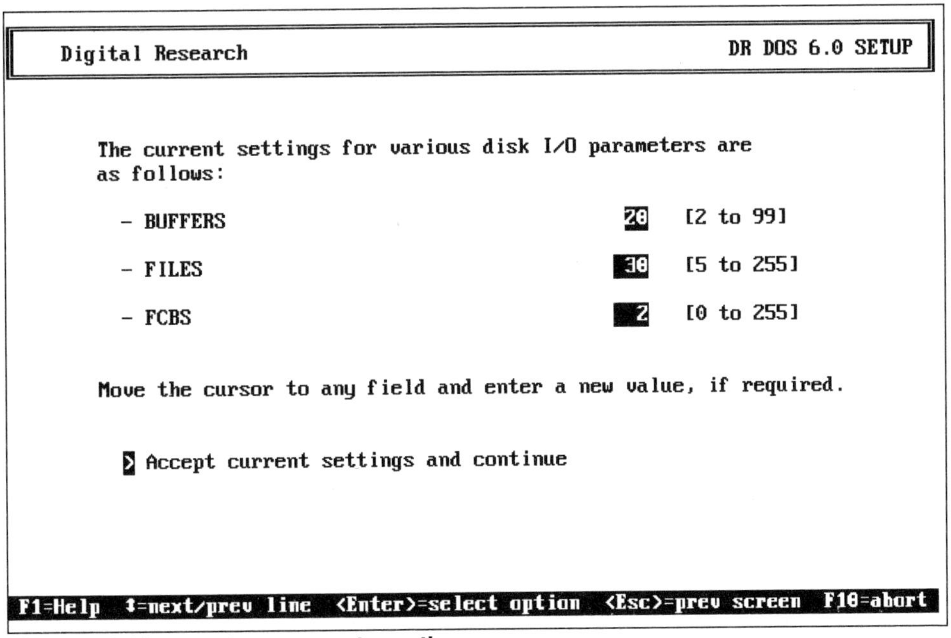

```
┌─────────────────────────────────────────────────────────────┐
│ ▌Digital Research                          DR DOS 6.0 SETUP▐│
│ ▔▔▔▔▔▔▔▔▔▔▔▔▔▔▔▔▔▔▔▔▔▔▔▔▔▔▔▔▔▔▔▔▔▔▔▔▔▔▔▔▔▔▔▔▔▔▔▔▔▔▔▔▔▔▔▔▔▔ │
│                                                             │
│    The current settings for various disk I/O parameters are │
│    as follows:                                              │
│                                                             │
│       - BUFFERS                         20    [2 to 99]     │
│                                                             │
│       - FILES                           30    [5 to 255]    │
│                                                             │
│       - FCBS                             2    [0 to 255]    │
│                                                             │
│    Move the cursor to any field and enter a new value, if required.│
│                                                             │
│      ▶ Accept current settings and continue                 │
│                                                             │
│ F1=Help  ↕=next/prev line  <Enter>=select option  <Esc>=prev screen  F10=abort │
└─────────────────────────────────────────────────────────────┘
```

Figure 5-4. More system parameter options.

- FILES sets aside memory for controlling open files. Some application programs recommend a particular setting (Ventura Publisher/GEM 3.0, for example, recommends a minimum setting of 20). If you don't have enough memory, programs such as ViewMAX and Windows will cause "disk full" errors even though the disk has plenty of space. The default setting is 20.

- FCBS is rarely used; however, some older applications may require it. Check your documentation to make sure.

Under the Optional Device Drivers and Utilities menu, you'll find settings for ANSI.SYS, FASTOPEN, and SHARE.EXE:

- ANSI.SYS is covered in detail in Chapter 13, but basically it provides terminal-like support for controlling the screen and keyboard. Some programs require it to be loaded.

- FASTOPEN cuts the time required to access disk files, but it does use up memory. The default size for the FASTOPEN table is 512 bytes; however, you can set it as high as 32,768 bytes. Don't worry about this if you're using PC-Kwik.

- SHARE.EXE isn't a device driver, but rather a TSR program loaded by the AUTOEXEC.BAT file. It's vitally important if you're using TaskMAX, Windows, or a network. Basically, SHARE prevents you from stepping on your own toes by locking a file once an application has loaded it. This means more than one application won't be trying to write data back to the same open file, a potentially disastrous situation. TaskMAX simply won't load if SHARE isn't active. The default is 20 file locks, but I use 40.

After setting these options, you can continue through the save and exit screens for SETUP. You'll need to reboot the computer for your changes to take effect, so you might as well let SETUP do it for you.

After rebooting, use the MEM command to check available memory. If you told DR DOS that it could relocate itself and you have upper and high memory, you'll be surprised at how much conventional memory is available. Let's go on to phase 2 and see what we can do to further improve available conventional memory.

FINE-TUNING DR DOS

Phase 2: Placing Drivers in Upper Memory

First, use DIR or XDIR and find out how big your drivers are. We'll double-check these numbers against the drivers' actual sizes when they're loaded in the next step.

Second, run MEM and then MEM/D to see what you have to work with. We're primarily interested in four things at this point: available conventional memory, available high memory, available upper memory, and the size of device drivers. Figure 5-5 shows a typical MEM/D display.

```
[Max] C:\>mem /d

  Address       Owner         Size              Type
  70:050B       PRN                             Built-in device driver
  70:051D       LPT1                            Built-in device driver
  70:052F       LPT2                            Built-in device driver
  70:0541       LPT3                            Built-in device driver
  70:0553       AUX                             Built-in device driver
  70:0565       COM1                            Built-in device driver
  70:0577       COM2                            Built-in device driver
  70:0589       COM3                            Built-in device driver
  70:059B       COM4                            Built-in device driver
  70:0602       CLOCK$                          Built-in device driver
  70:0645       CON                             Built-in device driver
  70:0671        A:-D:                          Built-in device driver
 126:0048       NUL                             Built-in device driver
 251:0000       XMSXXXX0      12E0h,    4,832   Loadable device driver
 380:0000          E:          530h,    1,328   Loadable device driver
 3D4:0000       SMARTAAR      55F0h,   22,000   Loadable device driver
 934:0000       $ADDSTOR      9B90h,   39,824   Loadable device driver

[Max] C:\>
```

Figure 5-5. A typical MEM/D display.

MEM/D lets you determine exactly how much memory a driver occupies. It's usually the size of the driver file, but drivers sometimes occupy more memory, so it's a good idea to double-check. Unfortunately, device-driver names in MEM don't always match the device-driver file name. For instance, the SMARTAAR driver shown in Figure 5-5 is actually the SMARTDRV.SYS driver for Windows. Correlating the MEM names and the device-driver file names sometimes takes a bit of deduction.

Write down the available memory sizes and device-driver sizes so you can refer to them later. Also make sure you have enough upper memory to load your device drivers. If not, you'll need to decide which drivers you can fit into the available upper memory.

From here on you'll need to use EDITOR (see Chapter 7) or some other ASCII editor.

Load the CONFIG.SYS file, then load everything you can into upper memory. Typical candidates are:

ANSI.SYS   The ANSI.SYS screen and keyboard driver.

MOUSE.SYS   A mouse driver (which may have a slightly different name).

Network drivers   These are a bit trickier. Most will work when loaded "high," but some won't. A smart way to install these is to preface them with a question mark.

To load a device driver into upper memory, preface it with HIDEVICE= instead of DEVICE=. For instance, the line

```
DEVICE=C:\DRDOS\ANSI.SYS
```

becomes

```
HIDEVICE=C:\DRDOS\ANSI.SYS
```

Device drivers for networks, especially for non-Novell networks, should be prefaced with a question mark. This gives you the option of loading or not loading the driver when its line is reached in the CONFIG.SYS file during boot-up. If the computer locks up, you can experiment to find the culprit. It also allows you to get past a troublesome driver and reach the command-line prompt, then make the appropriate changes to the CONFIG.SYS file. For instance, this line makes loading a hypothetical network driver contingent on your response:

```
?HIDEVICE=C:\WEASLNET\WNSCKT1.DRV
```

By the way, don't try to be too precise about fitting drivers into memory. If DR DOS can't find enough upper memory for a driver, it will load it into conventional memory despite the HIDEVICE command.

FINE-TUNING DR DOS

Once you've made your changes, save the file and exit back to the command line. Reboot and watch what happens. Your drivers should load easily, but if something does go wrong you can try a couple of solutions.

First, try changing the order in which drivers are loaded. If a problem driver, or a set of drivers that must be loaded in sequence, is fairly close to the bottom of the CONFIG.SYS file, place them right underneath the DR DOS memory manager files (they must follow HIDOS=ON). Those files should be near the top of the CONFIG.SYS file. For instance, the CONFIG.SYS file for my 80286-equipped machine looks like this:

```
DEVICE=C:\DRDOS\HIDOS.SYS /B=FFFF
HIDOS=ON
HIDEVICE=C:\WINDOWS\RAMDRIVE.SYS 1024 /E
HIDEVICE=C:\WINDOWS\SMARTDRV.SYS 512 256
SHELL=C:\COMMAND.COM C:\ /P /E:512
BREAK=OFF
HIBUFFERS=20
FILES=40
FCBS=2,2
FASTOPEN=0
LASTDRIVE=E
HISTORY=ON
COUNTRY=001,,C:\DRDOS\COUNTRY.SYS
HIDEVICE=C:\SSTORDRV.SYS
DEVICE=C:\DEVSWAP.COM
```

Notice that the RAMDRIVE and SMARTDRV drivers are loaded right after HIDOS=ON. This allows DR DOS to load itself into upper memory first. Also notice that SSTORDRV.SYS is loaded into upper memory. When I initially loaded RAMDRIVE and SMARTDRV, I had question marks at the beginning of these lines. While I had no problem with RAMDRIVE on my 80286, it collided with the network drivers on the 80386 machine and I was forced to use VDISK instead. The presence of a question mark meant I didn't need to rummage around for a bootable floppy so I could get into the machine.

After successfully loading your drivers, run MEM again and check available conventional, extended, expanded, high, and upper memory. You should have more conventional memory and less upper memory. Extended and expanded memory should be about the same. Make sure any RAM disks you have set up still work. For instance, I've seen the Windows RAMDRIVE driver conflict with SuperStor on an 80486 machine with the Ami BIOS; in this case, VDISK had to be used instead.

If you have any upper memory left, go on to phase 3.

Phase 3: Placing TSRs in Upper Memory

Your network may have a number of TSR programs, such as print utilities, that can be loaded into high memory. You might also want to load such DR DOS TSRs as CURSOR, GRAPHICS, JOIN, and GRAFTABL into upper memory. If you're using MOUSE.COM (or a similar program) instead of MOUSE.SYS, you might want to load it into upper memory as well.

Loading such programs requires the HILOAD command. HILOAD statements are placed in your AUTOEXEC.BAT file. Unlike the CONFIG.SYS file, from which there is no escape, you can interrupt execution of the AUTOEXEC.BAT file with Ctrl-Break or Ctrl-C (it may take several tries to stop the batch file). If something goes wrong, place one of these files in upper memory (99.9% of the time, nothing will go wrong).

Again, you'll need to turn to EDITOR or a similar program. This time you load the AUTOEXEC.BAT file in the root directory of your bootable drive (normally C:). Where you see a statement loading a TSR, such as this one:

```
C:\MOUSE\MOUSE.COM
```

change it to include HILOAD:

```
HILOAD C:\MOUSE\MOUSE.COM
```

After making all the changes, save the file and exit, then reboot. When you return to the DR DOS prompt, run MEM again and see if conventional memory was increased. If not, you didn't have enough upper memory left to HILOAD the program.

At this point, you've done just about all you can do to increase conventional memory. If you still need to squeeze a few more bytes into conventional memory, try the following:

FINE-TUNING DR DOS

- Remove ANSI.SYS. Unless this is required by a specific application, you don't really need it.

- Remove your mouse driver. If you're running Windows, you don't need an external mouse driver anyway. If you're running ViewMAX, Ventura GEM, or other non-Windows applications, see if the program will support your mouse directly without a driver.

- Remove HISTORY. This will save memory at the expense of the wonderful command-line history capability.

- Reduce the number of files and buffers. You need to be careful with the FILES number because your applications may require a minimum number of these. Depending on your application, this may not become apparent until you're well into running it. Check your documentation to make sure.

Special Capabilities for CONFIG.SYS

DR DOS 6.0 has some wonderful commands that apply specifically to the CONFIG.SYS file. These provide programlike capabilities that let you customize your system in a variety of ways. You've already been introduced to the question mark; here's a complete list:

?	Lets you decide whether or not to execute a statement in the CONFIG.SYS file.
:label	Defines a subroutine label within the CONFIG.SYS file. You can jump directly to this label with a GOTO or GOSUB command.
CHAIN	Branches to a different configuration file.
CLS	Clears the screen.
CPOS	Lets you position the cursor anywhere on the screen during CONFIG.SYS execution.
ECHO	Prints a line of text on the screen.

EXIT   Stops CONFIG.SYS execution.

GOTO   Branches to a label.

GOSUB   Branches to a label but returns to the line following the GOSUB when a RETURN is encountered.

SWITCH   Branches to a label, but you can choose from up to nine different labels. You'll be prompted to select one.

TIMEOUT   Sets an amount of time to wait at the CONFIG.SYS prompt, such as from a ? or a SWITCH. If this time elapses, the ? statement is ignored or the first option in the SWITCH is selected.

What can you do with these? Suppose your computer has two network cards requiring different drivers. Further, at times you don't want to be connected to either network. Also suppose that sometimes you want to load a RAM disk and sometimes you don't. Normally, this would require several configuration files, renamed to CONFIG.SYS as required (usually with a batch file). Using DR DOS's unique capabilities, however, you can simply have the CONFIG.SYS file ask you what you want to do, and it will be done.

The following is a sample section of a CONFIG.SYS file that provides these options:

```
ECHO=Select 1 to load the Novell network
ECHO=Select 2 to load the PC/NFS network
SWITCH novell, pcnfs
?"Do you want to load the RAM Disk?"GOTO ramdisk
ECHO=RAM disk is not active
EXIT
:novell
   .
   .
   .
ECHO=Novell selected
RETURN
:pcnfs
   .
   .
   .
```

```
ECHO=PC/NFS selected
RETURN
:ramdisk
DEVICE=C:\DRDOS\VDISK.SYS 1024 /E:8
ECHO=RAM disk active
EXIT
```

The ECHO statements print to the screen; pick 1 for Novell and 2 for PC/NFS. The SWITCH statement then jumps to the appropriate label (either *novell* or *pcnfs*). The three dots following these labels represent lines of text specifying various drivers to be loaded.

After either set of network drivers is loaded, a RETURN statement branches back to the line following the SWITCH. There, a ? statement asks if you want to load the network driver. If you press Y, the GOTO ramdisk is executed and VDISK is loaded. An ECHO statement confirms that the RAM disk is active, and an EXIT terminates the CONFIG.SYS file. If you press N, signifying that you don't want to load the RAM disk, an ECHO tells you the RAM disk isn't active. Again, an EXIT terminates file execution.

The following section discusses the special execution-control statements in DR DOS 6.0. Items within square brackets represent optional constructs in a command. Items separated by a vertical bar are alternatives.

CONFIG.SYS Control Statements

?
SYNTAX

    ?["*text*"]*statement*

    "text"   Any text up to 128 characters long. The text is optional and must be enclosed in double quotes.

    statement   Any CONFIG.SYS statement or command.

FUNCTION

A question mark in the first column of any line in a CONFIG.SYS file causes DR DOS to ask if you want to execute the statement. A Y executes the statement, while an N skips it. If you don't enter anything for *text*, DR DOS prints the statement followed by "(Y/N)?" For example, a ? before the statement that loads a mouse driver would produce something like this on your display:

```
HIDEVICE=C:\MOUSE\MOUSE.SYS (Y/N)?
```

If you do enter *text*, only the *text* is printed. For example, the line

```
?"Should I load the mouse driver?"HIDEVICE=C:\MOUSE\MOUSE.SYS
```

produces this on the display:

```
Should I load the mouse driver?
```

:label
SYNTAX

:label

label   A subroutine name that you can branch to with a GOTO, GOSUB, or SWITCH statement. The label must be preceded by a colon in the first column and can be up to eight characters long.

FUNCTION

Labels are a way of jumping around within a CONFIG.SYS file. Thus, you can have special configuration sections within the file. For example, if

```
GOTO network
```

is encountered in a CONFIG.SYS file, the next line executed will be the one following *:network*.

CHAIN
SYNTAX

CHAIN=*file*

file　　Any valid file on any available drive. *file* must contain the name and extension if the file is in the same directory as CONFIG.SYS ; otherwise, it must also have the complete path (including disk-drive letter if it's on another drive).

FUNCTION

CHAIN tends to be useful only if you have a CONFIG.SYS file in ROM (read-only memory) and is therefore used primarily by manufacturers of portable and laptop computers. It lets the program branch from the ROM file, which can't be changed, to a disk file that you can edit.

Use ? statements to select the configuration file you want to branch to:

```
?"Should I load the DesqView configuration file?"CHAIN DV.SYS
```

SIDE EFFECTS

If you chain to another directory or drive, remember that you can't refer to device drivers in the root directory without their full paths, including drive and directory.

CLS
SYNTAX

    CLS

FUNCTION

CLS works just like the CLS internal command. It clears the screen and repositions the cursor at row one in column one.

CPOS
SYNTAX

CPOS *rr,cc*

rr   Denotes the row in which the cursor will appear. The number of rows depends on the video mode but is usually in the range 1 to 25.

cc   Denotes the column in which the cursor will appear. The number of columns depends on the video mode but is usually in the range 1 to 80.

FUNCTION

CPOS lets you reposition the cursor to any point on the screen. For example, to place the cursor 10 rows down and five columns across, you would use this statement:

```
CPOS 10,5
```

ECHO
SYNTAX

ECHO=*text*

text   Any text you want displayed. This must follow the "=" but can begin with any character, even a space, and doesn't require quotes.

FUNCTION

ECHO is a way to display a line of text. It usually tells the user that an option, such as those offered by a SWITCH statement, is coming up or informs the user that something has happened. For example,

```
ECHO=Select 1 to connect to the network
```

produces this on the screen:

```
Select 1 to connect to the network
```

EXIT
SYNTAX

   EXIT

FUNCTION

   EXIT stops CONFIG.SYS file execution.

GOSUB
SYNTAX

GOSUB *label*

label   Any label set with the *:label* statement.

FUNCTION

A GOSUB statement branches to the specified label. The nice thing about a GOSUB is that you can put a RETURN at the end of the labeled section, and execution will automatically branch back to the line following the GOSUB. For example, these lines, taken from a CONFIG.SYS file, will load a mouse driver and proceed to the next option (for loading a RAM disk):

```
?"Do you want to load the mouse driver?"GOSUB mouse
?"Do you want to load the RAM Disk?"GOSUB ramdisk
    .
    .
    .
:mouse
HIDEVICE=C:\MOUSE\MOUSE.SYS
RETURN
```

GOTO
SYNTAX

GOTO *label*

label   Any label in the CONFIG.SYS file set with the *:label* statement.

FUNCTION

GOTO branches to the specified label. Execution continues from that label until another branching statement is encountered. You can't use RETURN with GOTO. In the following example, a GOTO loads a mouse driver and then exits from the CONFIG.SYS file:

```
?"Should I load the mouse driver?"GOTO mouse
    .
    .
    .
:mouse
HIDEVICE=C:\MOUSE\MOUSE.SYS
EXIT
```

RETURN

SYNTAX
   RETURN

FUNCTION
RETURN branches back to the line following a GOSUB or SWITCH statement. In the following example, a SWITCH statement is used to load a RAM disk; RETURN branches back to the statement following the switch:

```
SWITCH mouse, tablet
?"Shall I load the RAM disk"?GOSUB ramdisk
    .
    .
    .
:mouse
HIDEVICE=C:\MOUSE\MOUSE.SYS
EXIT
```

SWITCH
SYNTAX

SWITCH *label1, label2,* [*labeln*]

label1   A label set by the *:label* statement.

label2   A second label. You must have at least two labels in a SWITCH statement.

labeln   Additional labels that you can branch to. You can have up to nine branches.

FUNCTION

SWITCH is roughly equivalent to a CASE statement. It branches to a subroutine specified by a label, and you choose which label to jump to by entering a number corresponding to that label's position on the list. A subroutine should end with a RETURN so execution can branch back to the line following the SWITCH statement. Pressing Enter is equivalent to pressing 1.

In the following routine, entering a 1 branches to a routine called *mouse* and entering a 2 branches to a routine called *tablet*.

```
ECHO=Enter a 1 to load the mouse driver
ECHO=Enter a 2 to load the graphics tablet driver
SWITCH mouse, tablet
?"Should I also load the RAM disk"GOSUB ramdrive
    .
    .
    .
:mouse
HIDEVICE C:/MOUSE/MOUSE.SYS
ECHO=Mouse driver active
RETURN
    .
    .
    .
:tablet
HIDEVICE C:/TABLET/GRPHCST.SYS
ECHO=Graphics tablet active
RETURN
```

TIMEOUT
SYNTAX

TIMEOUT [=] *seconds*

seconds   Some number of seconds, which may be preceded by an equal sign. Entering 0 specifies an infinite time-out.

FUNCTION

TIMEOUT sets how long DR DOS should wait for a response to a ? or SWITCH statement. If the time-out is exceeded, the ? statement is skipped or the SWITCH statement branches to the first choice. Obviously, TIMEOUT applies only to those ? and SWITCH statements following it in execution.

The following sets a time-out of 20 seconds:

```
TIMEOUT 20
```

Configuration Commands

The following are the DR DOS 6.0 configuration commands. They're listed separately from the CONFIG.SYS control statements because they affect the computer itself and not merely the flow of the CONFIG.SYS file.

BREAK

SYNTAX

    BREAK=ON|OFF

    ON|OFF   Sets BREAK on or off.

CLASS

    CONFIG.SYS statement

FUNCTION

When BREAK is on, pressing Ctrl-Break or Ctrl-C will stop some programs (most commercial applications prevent Ctrl-Break or Ctrl-C from having any effect). If BREAK is off, pressing Ctrl-Break or Ctrl-C will stop the program only when it next scans the keyboard, displays something on the screen, sends data to the printer, or reads or writes data to a disk.

You can override the BREAK statement in the CONFIG.SYS file with the BREAK command issued at the DR DOS command line.

EXAMPLE

```
BREAK=ON
```

BUFFERS
SYNTAX

BUFFERS=*bb*

bb   The number of buffers, between 3 and 99. The default is 15.

CLASS

CONFIG.SYS command

FUNCTION

Buffers are memory blocks that store information read from or being written to a disk. They can increase the performance of disk read and write operations, especially if you aren't using caching software. The downside is that buffers also take up conventional memory. (HIBUFFERS uses high memory instead.)

If you're using caching software, try reducing the number of buffers to between three and five. Otherwise, 15 to 30 should be sufficient. Always check your application program documentation to see how many buffers are recommended.

EXAMPLE

This statement in a CONFIG.SYS file sets 25 buffers:

```
BUFFERS=25
```

OF INTEREST

HIBUFFERS, FILES

COUNTRY
SYNTAX

COUNTRY=*ccc,cp*[*drive*:]*dirpath*\COUNTRY.SYS

ccc   The three-digit country code. Country-code values are listed in the table below.

cp   The code page for the required country information. If it's omitted, the default code page (*ccc*) is used.

drive: The drive on which the COUNTRY.SYS file resides.

dirpath   The directory path pointing to the directory on which COUNTRY.SYS resides.

CLASS

CONFIG.SYS command

FUNCTION

COUNTRY.SYS loads the date format, time format, and currency symbol for the specified country. The code-page information, if specified, is also loaded. You only need to use this if your system's default value isn't what you need. This command affects the entries for DATE, TIME, BACKUP, RESTORE, XDIR, MOVE, and any other commands that can use the time and date formats.

The following are the country codes and corresponding code-page values.

Country	Code Page (first value is default for country)	Definition
061	437, 850	Australia
032	437, 850	Belgium
002	863, 850	Canadian French
045	865, 850	Denmark
358	437, 850	Finland
033	437. 850	France
049	437, 850	Germany
036	852, 850	Hungary

972	862, 850	Israel
039	437, 850	Italy
081	932, 437	Japan
082	934, 437	Korea
003	437, 850	Latin America
785	864, 850	Middle East
031	437, 850	Netherlands
047	865, 850	Norway
351	860, 850	Portugal
007	866, 850	Russia
034	437, 850	Spain
046	437, 850	Sweden
041	437, 850	Swiss French
041	437, 850	Swiss German
090	857, 850	Turkey
044	437, 850	United Kingdom
001	437, 850	United States

(the default)

SIDE EFFECTS

You also need to define the keyboard type using the KEYB command.

EXAMPLE

The following command configures the computer for Latin American time, date, and currency formats:

```
COUNTRY=003,437,C:\DRDOS\COUNTRY.SYS
```

OF INTEREST

KEYB, CHCP, GRAFTABL, MODE

DEVICE
SYNTAX

DEVICE=[*drive*:]*dirpath**driver*[*parameters*]

drive The disk drive where the driver file resides. You only need to specify this if the driver is on a disk other than the boot disk.

dirpath The directory path pointing to the directory where the driver file resides.

driver The loadable device driver.

parameters Parameters that affect the operation of the device driver. These are often unique to each driver.

CLASS

CONFIG.SYS file statement

FUNCTION

DEVICE loads device drivers, which allow your system to operate add-on hardware devices (such as a mouse or network card). Other drivers configure memory (like EMM386.SYS or VDISK.SYS) or control existing or built-in hardware (like ANSI.SYS). Normally, drivers are shipped with the hardware device and have a .SYS file extension. To load the driver, you'll need to copy it onto your hard disk and specify the driver file in a DEVICE (or HIDEVICE) statement in the CONFIG.SYS file.

EXAMPLE

This statement loads a mouse driver:

```
DEVICE=C:\MOUSE\MOUSE.SYS
```

OF INTEREST

HIDEVICE

FINE-TUNING DR DOS

DRIVPARM
SYNTAX

DRIVPARM=/D:d [/C] [/F:t] [/H:h] [/N] [/S:ds] [/T:dt]

/D:d The drive number: 0 is the first drive (A:), 1 is the second drive (B:), and so on.

/C   Add this parameter if the drive can detect when a disk is changed.

/F:t The drive type. The possible types are:

0	360-KB, 5.25-inch drive
1	1.2-MB, 5.25-inch drive
2	720-KB, 3.5-inch drive
7	1.44-MB, 3.5-inch drive

/H:h The number of drive heads (either 1 or 2).

/N   Use this if the drive media cannot be removed.

/S:ds The number of disk sectors supported. You can enter any value between 1 and 63.

/T:ts The number of tracks supported, either 40 or 80.

CLASS

CONFIG.SYS file statement

FUNCTION

DRIVPARM lets you specify the characteristics of a drive DR DOS already knows about (such as drive A:). You can't add a new logical drive (D:, for example) with this command; you must use the DRIVER.SYS device driver.

Typically, this command is used to define a 720-KB, 3.5-inch drive to older equipment, such as a PC or XT. By contrast, 80286, 80386, and 80486 equipment has a CMOS setup, rather than a CONFIG.SYS file, that holds such information.

EXAMPLE

The following command sets drive A: to 720 KB, 3.5 inch. The drive can detect a changed disk.

```
DRIVPARM=/D:0 /C /F:2 /S:9 /T:80
```

OF INTEREST

DRIVER.SYS

FASTOPEN
SYNTAX

FASTOPEN=*ttttt*

ttttt   The number of directory entries the FASTOPEN table can hold. Values range from 128 to 32,768, with 512 as the default. Each table entry requires two bytes of conventional memory.

CLASS

CONFIG.SYS file statement

FUNCTION

FASTOPEN accelerates hard disk file access. It keeps a table of file locations in memory, making the information in files that have previously been opened easier to find.

EXAMPLE

This command sets up a FASTOPEN table with 1,024 entries:

```
FASTOPEN=1024
```

FCBS

SYNTAX

FCBS=*o,c*

o   The number of FCBs that can be open at the same time. Values can range from 1 to 255.

c   The number of files, opened via FCBs, that are protected against automatic closure. Values can range from 1 to 255.

CLASS

CONFIG.SYS file statement

FUNCTION

Back in the days of MS-DOS and PC-DOS 1.0, files were managed with FCBs. Since DOS version 2.0, files have been managed through handles. If you're running a program designed for DOS 1.0, you'll likely need to specify an FCBS value. Check your application documentation to see if it recommends one; otherwise, don't worry about it.

EXAMPLE

The following command sets 10 open files, five of which are protected against closure:

```
FCBS=10,5
```

OF INTEREST

FILES

FILES
SYNTAX

FILES=*fff*

fff   The number of files that can be opened simultaneously. Values range from 20 to 255, with 20 being the default.

CLASS

CONFIG.SYS file statement

FUNCTION

FILES governs the number of files that can be opened at the same time. Check your application literature to see if it recommends a certain number of open files.

SIDE EFFECTS

Programs like TaskMAX allow you to have far more open files than if you were running one application at a time. You can therefore exceed the usual maximum number of open files and need to increase this number. If you're lucky, you may get a message saying you've exceeded the number of allowable open files. With certain applications, you may instead get mysterious "disk full" errors, even though there is plenty of room on your disk.

EXAMPLE

This command sets the number of possible open files to 40:

```
FILES=40
```

HIBUFFERS
SYNTAX

HIBUFFERS=*bb*

bb   The number of buffers, between 3 and 99. The default is 15.

CLASS

CONFIG.SYS file command

FUNCTION

HIBUFFERS, similar to the BUFFERS statement, sets the number of file access buffers. The difference is that HIBUFFERS uses high memory instead of conventional memory for the buffers. Buffers are memory blocks that store information read from or being written to disk. They can increase the performance of disk read and write operations, especially if you aren't using caching software such as PC-Kwik.

If you are using caching software, try reducing the number of buffers to between three and five. Otherwise, between 15 and 30 should be sufficient. Always check your application program documentation to see how many buffers it recommends.

EXAMPLE

This statement in a CONFIG.SYS file sets 25 buffers:

```
HIBUFFERS=25
```

OF INTEREST

BUFFERS, FILES

FINE-TUNING DR DOS

HIDEVICE
SYNTAX

HIDEVICE [SIZE=*mmm*] [*drive*:]*dirpath**driver*[*parameters*]

drive The disk drive where the driver file resides. You only need to specify this if the driver is on a disk other than the boot disk.

dirpath The directory path pointing to the directory where the driver file resides.

driver The loadable device driver.

parameters Parameters that affect the operation of the device driver.

CLASS

CONFIG.SYS file statement

FUNCTION

HIDEVICE works like DEVICE in that it loads device drivers. The difference is that HIDEVICE loads drivers into upper memory instead of conventional memory. Device drivers let your system operate hardware devices, such as a mouse or network card. Other drivers configure memory (VDISK.SYS) or control existing hardware (like ANSI.SYS). Usually, drivers are shipped with the hardware device and have a .SYS file extension. To load the driver, you'll need to copy it onto your hard disk and then specify the driver file in a HIDEVICE statement in the CONFIG.SYS file.

If there isn't enough upper memory to hold the device driver, it's loaded into conventional memory instead. From the command line, you can use MEM to check available upper memory and then check the size of the driver file to see if it will fit.

Some drivers require more memory than the device-driver image occupies. For these, you'll need to use the SIZE option. You can use the MEM /D command to check the actual size of these drivers when they're loaded into conventional memory.

SIDE EFFECTS

You must be using a DR DOS memory manager for this to work. HIDEVICE is not compatible with any third-party memory managers.

EXAMPLE

This statement loads a mouse driver:

```
HIDEVICE=C:\MOUSE\MOUSE.SYS
```

OF INTEREST

DEVICE

FINE-TUNING DR DOS

HIDOS

SYNTAX

HIDOS = ON|OFF

ON|OFF   Sets DR DOS relocation on or off. The default is OFF.

CLASS

CONFIG.SYS file statement

FUNCTION

HIDOS, when on, will load as much of DR DOS as possible into upper memory. You must first load a DR DOS memory manager, such as EMM386.SYS or HIDOS.SYS, before you can use HIDOS.

SIDE EFFECTS

You can't enable HIDOS if you're using a third-party memory manager.

EXAMPLE

This command turns DR DOS relocation on:

```
HIDOS=ON
```

OF INTEREST

EMM386.SYS, HIDOS.SYS, EMMXMA.SYS, MEMMAX

HIINSTALL
SYNTAX

HIINSTALL=*file* [*parameters*]

file A TSR program. If the program isn't in the same directory as the configuration file (usually C:), you'll need to include the directory path. If the program is on another drive, you'll also need to include the drive designation letter.

[*parameters*] Parameters for the TSR program.

CLASS

CONFIG.SYS file statement

FUNCTION

HIINSTALL loads TSR programs into upper memory during CONFIG.SYS execution. If there isn't enough upper memory to hold the TSR program, it's loaded into conventional memory instead. You can check on available upper memory with the MEM command and check on the size of the TSR program with MEM /B.

Before you can use HIINSTALL, you must load one of the DR DOS memory managers (EMM386 or HIDOS.SYS).

SIDE EFFECTS

You can't use HIINSTALL with third-party memory managers.

EXAMPLE

The following command loads GRAPHICS.COM into upper memory and enables color printing:

```
HIINSTALL=C:\DRDOS\GRAPHICS.COM COLOR
```

OF INTEREST

INSTALL, HILOAD

HISTORY
SYNTAX

HISTORY=ON[,*mmmm*[,ON|OFF]]|OFF

ON[,*mmmm*[,ON|OFF]]	Turns command-line history on. You can specify the amount of memory allocated to HISTORY in bytes. The range for memory allocation is 128 to 4,096 bytes, with 512 bytes being the default. (There are actually two memory buffers, one for command-line entries and one for application-command entries.) [,ON|OFF] switches between insert mode (ON) and overtype mode (OFF).
OFF	Switches command-line history off.

CLASS

CONFIG.SYS file command

FUNCTION

Command-line history allows you to recall previously used commands. This is discussed in detail in Chapter 3.

EXAMPLE

The following turns on command-line history, sets a buffer size of 1,024 bytes, and turns on insert mode:

```
HISTORY=ON,1024,ON
```

INSTALL
SYNTAX

INSTALL=*files* [*parameters*]

files   The file name and extension for a TSR program. If the program resides in a directory other than the one with the configuration file (usually C:), you'll need to include the complete directory path. If the file resides on another drive, you'll need to include the letter of that drive as well.

[*parameter*]   Parameters for the TSR program.

CLASS

CONFIG.SYS file command

FUNCTION

INSTALL allows you to load a TSR program during CONFIG.SYS execution. Unlike HIINSTALL, INSTALL uses conventional memory.

EXAMPLE

This statement loads the CURSOR.EXE program:

```
INSTALL=C:\DRDOS\CURSOR.EXE
```

OF INTEREST

HIINSTALL

LASTDRIVE
SYNTAX

LASTDRIVE=*drive*

drive   Any disk-drive designation letter from A to Z.

CLASS

CONFIG.SYS file command

FUNCTION

Normally, DR DOS considers the last drive in your system to be the last valid drive designation. However, you might be connected to a network that sets up additional drives that aren't resident in your computer. In this case, you'll want to set LASTDRIVE to the drive designation of the last logical drive the network created for you. Sometimes setting this value to more than you need for your network will confuse certain applications, such as Windows.

EXAMPLE

This command sets the last allowable drive designation to I:

```
LASTDRIVE=I
```

REM
SYNTAX

REM *statement*

statement   A comment. It can also be any statement or command in your CONFIG.SYS file that you wish to disable.

CLASS

CONFIG.SYS file command

FUNCTION

REM is short for remark and is used to add comments to your CONFIG.SYS file. You can also use it to disable a statement in the CONFIG.SYS file. If you like, you can abbreviate REM as a semicolon.

EXAMPLE

This use of REM (in its semicolon version) adds a comment to the CONFIG.SYS file after the label *:ramdisk*:

```
:ramdisk
;This subroutine loads a RAM drive.
```

This use of REM "removes" a statement from CONFIG.SYS execution:

```
REM HIDEVICE=C:\MOUSE\MOUSE.SYS
```

SHELL
SYNTAX

SHELL=*file* [/E:*mmmmm*] [/P[:*file*]] [/ML|MH|MU].

file   The command processor (COMMAND.COM)

/E:*mmmmm*   The DR DOS environment space, set in bytes. The range is 512 to 32,751 bytes. The default is 512 bytes.

/P:*file*   Makes the copy of the command processor permanent, so EXIT won't work. It also forces the AUTOEXEC.BAT file to be executed after COMMAND.COM runs. If you want to specify another batch file, you can do so with *file*.

/ML|MH|MU   Loads COMMAND.COM into different areas of memory. /ML uses conventional memory, /MH uses high memory, and /MU uses upper memory.

CLASS

CONFIG.SYS file command

FUNCTION

Specifies the command processor, the size of the DR DOS environment, and the automatically executed batch file. If COMMAND.COM resides in any directory other than the root directory of the boot drive, you must point to it with SHELL.

The following is a typical DR DOS shell command from a CONFIG.SYS file:

```
SHELL=C:\COMMAND.COM C:\ /P /E:512
```

OF INTEREST

SET

DR DOS Installable Device Drivers
This section describes in detail the DR DOS 6.0 installable device drivers.

ANSI.SYS
SYNTAX

[HI]DEVICE=[C:\DRDOS\]ANSI.SYS

CLASS

Loadable device driver

FUNCTION

Among the standards defined by the American National Standards Institute (ANSI) is one that governs the "escape sequences" for controlling and configuring a standard terminal. These sequences are implemented in IBM-compatible personal computers through the ANSI.SYS driver. Escape sequences are so named because each control sequence begins with the escape character (decimal 27 and hexadecimal 1B). Some programs require that ANSI.SYS be installed or they won't display things properly on your screen.

ANSI.SYS was often used in the early days of PCs because it was a more stable way of writing text to the screen than IBM's original "snowy" CGA display. It was also the common denominator for screen display for semicompatible DOS machines, such as the Sanyo MBC 550 and the Zenith Z100.

Two useful things you can do with ANSI.SYS are setting up your screen colors and mode and setting function key strings. Understand, however, that your applications will likely override these settings (or your key settings might foul up the application). These settings are covered in Chapter 13.

DEVSWAP.SYS

SYNTAX

[HI]DEVICE=[C:\DRDOS\]DEVSWAP.SYS

CLASS

Loadable device driver

FUNCTION

DEVSWAP is used by SuperStor and swaps the drive designations so your compressed drive can be accessed as "C" and the tiny uncompressed part as "D." If you're using SuperStor, DEVSWAP.SYS must follow SSTORDRV.SYS in your CONFIG.SYS file. It will be placed in the CONFIG.SYS file automatically by SETUP or the installation program. For more information, see Chapter 9.

DISPLAY.SYS
SYNTAX

[HI]DEVICE=[C:\DRDOS\]DISPLAY.SYSCON=(*display*, *intcodepage,a|(a,f)*)

display	The type of graphics adapter. Your type can be MONO (Hercules or MDA), CGA (color graphics adapter), EGA (used for both EGA and VGA displays), or LCD (used for laptops, notebooks, and so on). If you don't specify this parameter, DISPLAY.SYS will interrogate your hardware to discern its type.
intcodepage	The internal or hardware code page. By default, this is 437 in the United States. If you don't know what your internal code page is, you can check it with the MODE CON CP command.
a	Specifies how many additional code pages you are preparing. This can be any number from 1 to 12. All this parameter does is set aside memory for each additional code page; MODE actually prepares the code pages.
f	The number of subfonts. By default, memory is allocated for all subfonts. However, you can reduce memory consumption by limiting this number. By default, three subfonts are supported for VGA and two for EGA.

CLASS
Loadable device driver

FUNCTION
This driver prepares space for additional code pages. If you're using your computer in the U.S. or any other country that uses code page 437, you don't need to worry about this. Otherwise, you'll need to use this driver to prepare memory space for additional code pages.

EXAMPLE

This command sets VGA as the display adapter type and sets aside memory for two additional code pages:

```
DEVICE=C:\DRDOS\DISPLAY.SYS CON=(EGA,437,2)
```

OF INTEREST

MODE, CHCP, GRAFTABL, KEYB

DRIVER.SYS
SYNTAX

[HI]DEVICE=[C:\DRDOS\]DRIVER.SYS /D:*d* [/C] [/F:*t*] [/H:*h*] [/N] [/S:*ds*] [/T:*dt*]

/D:*d*   The drive number: 0 is the first drive (A:), 1 is the second drive (B:), and so on.

/C   Add this parameter if the drive can detect when a disk is changed.

/F:*t*   The drive type. The possible types are:

0	360-KB, 5.25-inch drive
1	1.2-MB, 5.25-inch drive
2	720-KB, 3.5-inch drive
7	1.44-MB, 3.5-inch drive

/H:*h*   The number of drive heads (either 1 or 2).

/N   Use this if the drive media cannot be removed.

/S:*ds*   The number of disk sectors supported. You can enter any value between 1 and 63.

/T:*ts*   The number of tracks supported. Acceptable values are 40 and 80.

CLASS
Loadable device driver

FUNCTION

DRIVER.SYS lets you specify the characteristic of a new drive to an existing DOS system. This command is normally used to define a 720-KB, 3.5-inch drive to older equipment, such as a PC or XT. By contrast, 80286s, 80386s, and 80486s have a CMOS setup, rather than a CONFIG.SYS file, to hold such information.

EXAMPLE

The following command sets the second floppy drive to 720 KB, 3.5 inch. The drive can detect when a disk is changed.

```
DEVICE=DRIVER.SYS /D:1 /C /F:2 /S:9 /T:80
```

OF INTEREST

DRIVPARM

EMM386.SYS
SYNTAX

DEVICE=[C:\DRDOS\]EMM386.SYS [/FRAME=AUTO|NONE|*aaaa*]
[/KB=AUTO|*mmmm*] [/AUTOSCAN=*ssss-eeee*] [/INCLUDE=*ssss-eeee*]
[/EXCLUDE=*ssss-eeee*] [/VIDEO=[*ssss-eeee*] [/BDOS=AUTO|*mmmm*]
[/USE=*ssss-eeee*] [/ROM=AUTO|*ssss-eeee*] [/COMPAQ] [/LOWEMM]
[/XBDA] [/WINSTD]

/FRAME= Manages Lotus-Intel-Microsoft (LIM) 4.0 expanded memory emulation. If this parameter is set to AUTO, EMM386 will scan upper memory for 64 KB of contiguous memory that it can use. A value of NONE will disable LIM memory support. Alternatively, *aaaa* specifies a starting address (in hexadecimal) for the 64-KB section of upper memory. If you pick a starting point that doesn't provide 64 KB of contiguous space, you'll get an error message.

/KB= Sets the amount of LIM expanded memory. AUTO (or 0) sets all memory to extended. You can also specify that the amount of memory (in decimal) be set aside as expanded.

/AUTOSCAN= Scan upper memory in 4-KB blocks to determine whether they're free. You must define the starting address (*ssss*) and ending address (*eeee*) for the scan. If you don't put /AUTOSCAN in the EMM386 statement, it will by default scan upper memory from C000H to FFFFH.

/INCLUDE= A less stringent test of upper memory than /AUTOSCAN. It checks an area of upper memory that /AUTOSCAN might ignore or that you know is free. You must specify the starting address (*ssss*) and ending address (*eeee*) in hexadecimal.

FINE-TUNING DR DOS

/EXCLUDE=   Use this parameter to prevent an area of upper memory from being used. The most common reason to use this is to lock out an area used by a network card. You must specify the starting (*ssss*) and ending (*eeee*) addresses, in hexadecimal, of the areas to be excluded.

/VIDEO=   Increases your conventional memory at the expense of graphics capabilities. You can free about 64 KB on a system equipped with a Hercules card and as much as 96 KB on a CGA-equipped system. Unfortunately, while this space is available as conventional memory, you can't use any applications that run in graphics mode.

If you use this option, you can't access the additional memory until you run the MEMMAX +V command. Just before running graphics-mode applications, you'll need to run MEMMAX -V.

If you specify a starting address (*ssss*), it must be A000H. You can also specify an ending address in hexadecimal.

/BDOS=   Relocates the DR DOS 6.0 kernel into upper memory, providing additional conventional memory for applications. AUTO scans upper memory for a contiguous section that can hold the kernel. If it can't find a free contiguous section in upper memory, high memory (segment base address FFFFH) is used. You can load the kernel at segment FFFFH by specifying FFFF, or you can use any other segment base address. If you specify NONE, the kernel won't be relocated.

/USE=   The manual-override parameter. No testing is done; instead, the specified memory is made available. You must specify a starting (*ssss*) and ending (*ssss*) segment address in hexadecimal. Don't use this parameter unless you know what you're doing.

/ROM=   A "shadow-RAM" parameter that copies information from ROM to RAM. Since RAM is faster, this will improve performance a bit. If you specify AUTO, all ROM information in upper memory is copied to RAM. You can also copy ROM information starting at segment address *ssss* and ending at segment address *eeee*. If you specify NONE, the default, ROM won't be copied to RAM.

/COMPAQ   Strictly for COMPAQ 80386 and 80486 machines. This option will give you an additional 256 KB of extended memory in machines that have more than 1 MB of memory.

/LOWEMM   Forces EMM386 to load itself into conventional memory. Use this if things are becoming a bit crowded in upper memory between EMM386 and the network drivers.

/XBDA   Normally, all extended BIOS data at the top of conventional memory is relocated to the bottom (of the free area). This disables extended BIOS relocation. If you do this and are gaining memory from video RAM, that memory won't be contiguous with conventional memory.

/WINSTD   If you want to run Windows in standard mode, you'll need to use this parameter (otherwise, Windows will quit with an error message when you start it up). Unfortunately, this option also disables upper memory. If you run Windows in 386 enhanced mode, you won't need this parameter.

CLASS
Loadable device driver

FUNCTION
This is the memory manager for computers equipped with an 80386, 80386SX, or 80486 microprocessor. Aside from providing additional conventional memory, the memory manager can divide up memory between extended and expanded. It fully

supports the Virtual Control Program Interface (VCPI) standard used by such protected-mode programs as NeuralWare's NeuralWorks Professional II/PLUS.

The most convenient way to configure EMM386 is through SETUP or the installation program. If you're installing EMM386 by hand, it must be loaded before any other driver that accesses extended memory.

EXAMPLE

The following statement automatically scans memory from C000H to FFFFH, sets up 2 MB of expanded memory, and loads the DR DOS kernel into upper memory:

```
DEVICE=C:\DRDOS\EMM386.SYS /FRAME=AUTO /KB=2048 /BDOS=AUTO
```

EMMXMA.SYS
SYNTAX

DEVICE=[C:\DRDOS\]EMMXMA.SYS [/FRAME=*ssss*] [/KB=*mmmm*]

/FRAME=   Sets the starting segment address (*ssss*) in hexadecimal for the 64-KB memory area used to map expanded memory. If you don't include this parameter, EMMXMA will scan memory between C0000H and DFFFH for a free 64-KB contiguous area.

/KB=   Sets the total amount of expanded memory. If you don't include this option, all available memory will be set up as expanded.

CLASS
Loadable device driver

FUNCTION
You use this driver in addition to EMM386 or HIDOS.SYS if:

- You have an IBM PS/2 or compatible computer.
- You have extended memory on an XMA memory card.
- You want to use that memory as LIM 4.0 expanded memory.

You can't use this driver with third-party memory managers.

EXAMPLE
This statement sets up 2 MB of expanded memory and automatically scans for a free 64-KB area:

```
DEVICE=C:\DRDOS\EMMXMA.SYS /KB=2048
```

FINE-TUNING DR DOS

HIDOS.SYS
SYNTAX

DEVICE=[C:\DRDOS\]HIDOS.SYS [/AUTOSCAN=*ssss-eeee*]
[/INCLUDE=*ssss-eeee*] [/EXCLUDE=*ssss-eeee*] [/VIDEO=[*ssss-eeee*]
[/BDOS=AUTO|*mmmm*] [/USE=*ssss-eeee*] [/ROM=AUTO|*ssss-eeee*]
[/XBDA] [/CHIPSET=AUTO|*settype*|NONE]

/AUTOSCAN=   Scan upper memory in 4-KB blocks to determine if they're free. You must define the starting address (*ssss*) and ending address (*eeee*) for the scan. If you don't put /AUTOSCAN in the EMM386 statement, it will by default scan upper memory from C000H to FFFFH.

/INCLUDE=   A less stringent test of upper memory than /AUTOSCAN. This option checks an area of upper memory that /AUTOSCAN might ignore or that you know is free. You must specify the starting address (*ssss*) and ending address (*eeee*) in hexadecimal.

/EXCLUDE=   Prevents an area of upper memory from being used. The most common reason to use this is to lock out an area used by a network card. You must specify the starting (*ssss*) and ending (*eeee*) addresses in hexadecimal for the areas to be excluded.

/VIDEO=   Increases your conventional memory at the expense of graphics capabilities. You can free about 64 KB on a system equipped with a Hercules card and as much as 96 KB on a CGA-equipped system. Unfortunately, while this is available as conventional memory, you can't use any applications that run in graphics mode.

If you use this, you can't access the additional memory until you execute the MEMMAX +V command. Before running graphics-mode applications, you'll need to run MEMMAX -V.

143

If you specify a starting address (*ssss*), it must be A000H. You can also specify an ending address in hexadecimal.

/BDOS= Moves the DR DOS 6.0 kernel into upper memory, providing additional conventional memory for applications. AUTO scans upper memory for a contiguous section that can hold the kernel. If it can't find a free contiguous section in upper memory, it uses high memory (segment base address FFFFH). You can load the kernel at segment FFFFH by specifying FFFF or use any other segment base address. If you specify NONE, the kernel won't be relocated.

/USE= The manual-override parameter. No testing is done; instead, the specified memory is made available. You must specify a starting (*ssss*) and ending (*ssss*) segment address in hexadecimal. Don't use this unless you know what you're doing.

/ROM= A "shadow-RAM" parameter that copies information from ROM to RAM. Since RAM is faster, this will improve performance a bit. If you specify AUTO, all ROM information in upper memory is copied to RAM. You can also copy ROM information starting at segment address *ssss* and ending at segment address *eeee*. If you specify NONE, the default, ROM won't be copied to RAM.

/XBDA Normally, all extended BIOS data at the top of conventional memory is moved to the bottom of the free area. This disables extended BIOS relocation. If you do this and are gaining memory from video RAM, it won't be contiguous with conventional memory.

/CHIPSET= This parameter, if you can use it, lets you map shadow RAM in upper memory. If you have an expanded memory or EEMS driver loaded, you can also take advantage of this.

The options to this parameter are:

AUTO   Let HIDOS.SYS try to detect the type of chip set. This is the default.

EMSALL   Accesses all EMS upper memory. If you choose this option, your applications won't be able to use expanded memory.

EMSUMB   LIM 4.0 expanded memory or EEMS memory provided through an EMS or EEMS driver.

NEAT   A Chips and Technologies LeAPSet, LeAPSetsx, NEAT, or NEATsx chip set.

NONE   Means you shouldn't use shadow RAM or no shadow RAM is available.

RAM   Accesses any permanent upper RAM. This must be used in conjunction with the /USE parameter.

SCAT   A Chips and Technologies SCAT chip set.

CLASS
Loadable device driver

FUNCTION
This is the memory manager for 80286-equipped computers that have extended memory. At a minimum, HIDOS.SYS will relocate the DR DOS kernel into high memory, clearing additional conventional memory for applications. You'll be able to access additional capabilities if your computer has a Chips and Technologies LeAPSet, LeAPSetsx, NEAT, NEATsx, or SCAT chip set.

HIDOS fully supports LIM 4.0 (or EEMS) upper memory blocks as well as permanent upper RAM. HIDOS may also be used with any XMS-compatible third-party memory manager.

EXAMPLE

The following statement (which is in my CONFIG.SYS file) moves the DR DOS 6.0 kernel to high memory:

```
DEVICE=C:\DRDOS\HIDOS.SYS /BDOS=FFFF
```

FINE-TUNING DR DOS

PRINTER.SYS
SYNTAX

[HI]DEVICE=[C:\DRDOS\]PRINTER.SYS LPTx=(*printer,intcodepage, c*)

- LPTx The parallel port, either LPT1, LPT2, or LPT3. If you wish, you can substitute PRN for LPT1.

- *printer* The specific type of printer. The following are the supported printers and their codes:

Code	Supported Printers
1050	Epson FX 850 and 1050
4201	IBM 4201 and 4202
4208	IBM 4207 and 4208
5202	IBM Quietwriter III

- *intcodepage* The internal hardware code page. For computers produced for the American market, this is 437. This parameter is optional.

- *c* Specifies the number of additional code pages you're preparing. This must be between 1 and 12.

CLASS
Loadable device driver

FUNCTION
Use this driver to enable code pages for your printer. The easiest way to get this into your CONFIG.SYS file is to select code-page switching through the SETUP or installation program. Code-page switching is discussed in detail in Chapter 13.

EXAMPLE
The following statement enables two code pages for an Epson FX 1050 printer on LPT1:

```
DEVICE=C:\DRDOS\PRINTER.SYS LPT1=(1050,437,2)
```

SSTORDRV.SYS
SYNTAX

    [HI]DEVICE=[C:\DRDOS\]SSTORDRV.SYS

CLASS

    Loadable device driver

FUNCTION

This driver is used by SuperStor and is automatically added to your CONFIG.SYS file when you activate SuperStor through SETUP or the installation program. At a minimum, this driver requires 28 KB of memory (this increases by 4 KB for each additional compressed drive).

EXAMPLE

```
DEVICE=C:\DRDOS\SSTORDRV.SYS
```

VDISK.SYS
SYNTAX

[HI]DEVICE=[C:\DRDOS\]VDISK.SYS [*disk*] [*sectors*] [*files*] [/E:*sectrans*] [/X]

disk
: The RAM disk size, in KB. If you're setting this up in conventional memory, the default is 64 KB. The allowable range is 1 KB to 256 KB.

sectors
: The RAM disk sector size. By default, this is 128 bytes; however, you can specify 256 or 512 bytes. Bigger sectors mean faster data transfer, but they're less efficient at storing small files.

files
: Sets a limit for the number of files that can be in the RAM disk's root directory. The default is 64, but you can specify any number of files between 2 and 512. Having a larger directory space takes memory away from file storage.

/E:*sectrans*
: If you're setting up a RAM disk in extended memory, use this parameter. *sectrans* sets the number of sectors that are transferred in a group. The default is 8, and acceptable values are between 1 and 8.

/X
: If you're setting up a RAM disk in expanded memory, use this parameter. The maximum size of an expanded memory RAM disk is 32 MB.

CLASS
Loadable device driver

FUNCTION

This driver sets up a RAM disk, which is a section of memory that is made to appear as a disk drive to your system. RAM disks are very fast but have the considerable drawback of disappearing (with their contents) when you reboot or shut off the computer. An excellent application for a RAM disk is as a place for temporary files. This can increase performance considerably for programs that use many temporary files, such as CorelDraw.

If you use VDISK, place it after the memory manager but before any other drivers that access extended memory. If you use HIDEVICE to load the driver, you can only create an extended-memory RAM disk.

EXAMPLE

The following sets up a RAM disk of 2 MB in extended memory:

```
HIDEVICE=C:\DRDOS\VDISK.SYS 2048 /E:8
```

FINE-TUNING DR DOS

Third-Party Memory Managers

The two most popular third-party 80386 memory managers are QEMM from Quarterdeck and 386-to-the-Max from Qualitas. Qualitas also makes an 80286 memory manager called Move 'em. I've run both QEMM and 386-to-the-Max, and DR DOS's EMM386 seems better behaved. There are only two cases where you might want to use one of these:

- You encounter a program that just won't run with the DR DOS EMM386.SYS memory manager. I've only seen one program that wouldn't run, and it was an i860 accelerator board debugger (hardly something you'd normally use).

- You might want to run the DesqView multitasker from Quarterdeck, in which case you'd want to use QEMM. If you're running DesqView and not really taking advantage of its multitasking capability, why not just run TaskMAX? In many ways, the combination of ViewMAX and TaskMAX is much more convenient than DesqView.

If you find that you must run one of these, you can still use HIDOS.SYS to load much of DR DOS into upper or high memory. The trick is that HIDOS.SYS must directly follow the statement that loads the third-party memory manager. For instance, for QEMM you would place the HIDOS.SYS line like this:

```
DEVICE=C:\QEMM.SYS
DEVICE=C:\DRDOS\HIDOS.SYS
```

For 386-to-the-Max, you would place HIDOS.SYS like this:

```
DEVICE=C:\386MAX.SYS
DEVICE=C:\DRDOS\HIDOS.SYS.
```

Your third-party memory manager will likely be in some directory other than C: (and your memory manager may require additional switches and parameters), but you get the idea. If you want to force HIDOS.SYS to load into high memory, append the /BDOS=FFFF parameter.

When you use a third-party memory manager, you can't use such DR DOS facilities as HIDEVICE and HIINSTALL. However, the memory manager will have similar facilities.

The AUTOEXEC.BAT File

After the CONFIG.SYS file is processed, your system will run AUTOEXEC.BAT. This file loads TSR programs, such as SHARE, and sets environment variables (including PATH and PROMPT). It can also automatically load TaskMAX, ViewMAX, or Windows. The installation program or SETUP will help you build your AUTOEXEC.BAT file, but you can also do that with EDITOR.

The following is my 80286 system's AUTOEXEC.BAT file:

```
@ECHO OFF
REM The DRDOSBEG and DRDOSEND labels tell the SETUP program
REM which statements it should process. Put any additional
statements
REM for DR DOS between these two labels. Any other statements
(e.g.,
REM for other operating systems) should be placed outside the
labels.
:DRDOSBEG
PATH C:\WINDOWS;C:\DRDOS;C:\FASTBACK;C:\WORD;C:\
VERIFY OFF
PROMPT [Max] $P$G
SET TEMP=E:\
DISKMAP C: D:
SET FASTBACK=C:\FASTBACK
SHARE /L:30
:DRDOSEND
WIN
```

A brief explanation of what's happening here will give you an idea what AUTOEXEC.BAT files are all about. However, don't get the idea that this file is an excellent model; it just happens to work for me.

FINE-TUNING DR DOS

- @ECHO OFF prevents a command from being echoed (repeated) during execution so you won't see each command in the AUTOEXEC.BAT file as it's processed. This reduces screen clutter and saves you from having to see the REM statements. The DRDOSBEG and DRDOSEND labels, placed by SETUP or the installation program, show you where to put DR DOS-specific commands.

- The PATH statement defines a search path along which DR DOS searches for executable programs (files with .EXE, .COM, and .BAT extensions). You can also add the APPEND statement to search for other types of files, but I've had unpredictable success with this.

- VERIFY OFF means I trust my drives to write data accurately and spares me the increased time it takes the system to make sure the drives did write the data accurately.

- PROMPT [Max] PG gives me a prompt that begins with Max (my nickname for the 80286 machine) and shows me the current drive and directory (specified by the $P and $G constructs).

- SET TEMP=E:\ specifies a drive and directory for temporary files (in this case, the root directory on drive E:, which is a RAM disk). Programs like Windows use this variable to determine where to place temporary files. This can result in greatly increased performance.

- DISKMAP C: D: creates a file snapshot of the file allocation tables for drives C: and D:. I use this instead of DELWATCH because I usually want deleted files to release their disk space for use by other files.

- SET FASTBACK=C:\FASTBACK is an example of an environmental variable being set. In this case, it points to the directory for FASTBACK PLUS, which I use to back up my hard disk. The variable is specific to the FastBack product.

- SHARE /L:30 sets 30 file locks, which I find to be a convenient number when using TaskMAX.

- WIN is the command to start Windows and is the last line of my batch file.

You may also wish to start a mouse program, load a TSR program such as KEYB, or do a variety of other things from your AUTOEXEC.BAT file.

Configuring for Microsoft Windows

DR DOS 6.0 is 100% Windows-compatible and allows Windows to run in 386 enhanced, standard, and real modes. The following are some things to keep in mind.

If you want to use EMM386 and Windows in standard mode, add the /WINSTD parameter to the DEVICE=EMM386.SYS statement. Otherwise, Windows will quit on start-up and issue an error message to that effect.

You may have trouble using RAMDRIVE.SYS with EMM386. I've been unable to get this to work on two 80386 systems and had to use VDISK instead. RAMDRIVE works just fine on 80286 systems.

If you want to use PC-Kwik instead of SMARTDRV.SYS for disk caching, you'll need to load the PCKWIK.SYS driver in CONFIG.SYS. You'll also need to remove the SMARTDRV.SYS statement from CONFIG.SYS. As to the relative merits of each, I've run both and can't see much difference in Windows execution. PC-Kwik should be the more efficient caching system.

You may need to disable upper memory to install certain Windows programs. Lotus' Ami Pro and a few other programs use a disk-decompression utility called Yoshi when they install themselves. Yoshi gets quite upset about upper memory, so you may need to use MEMMAX to shut off upper or high memory temporarily.

Don't try to run Windows as a task under TaskMAX. I haven't found a way to switch from Windows to TaskMAX.

When you're running Windows in 80386 enhanced mode, one technique for improving performance is to create a permanent swap file. This is a contiguous section of disk that Windows uses as virtual memory. The problem is that Windows can't create or use a swap file on a compressed disk. If you use a permanent swap file, make sure it's in an uncompressed portion of the disk. And *don't* run SuperStor from a DOS window within Windows or you'll have problems with Windows and perhaps the files on your disk.

FINE-TUNING DR DOS

DR DOS and Novell

Digital Research is now owned by Novell, so it's not surprising that DR DOS 6.0 has extensive support for Novell NetWare. In fact, you'll find a /NETWARE directory on one of your DR DOS master diskettes that's full of goodies you'll need. To use them, create a /NETWARE directory on your hard drive and copy all the /NETWARE files from the distribution disk into it. You should have the following files:

EMSNETX.EXE

IPX.OBJ

MAP.EXE

NETX.COM

RPLFIX.COM

TBMI2.COM

TBMI2.DOC

XMSNETX.EXE

EMSNETX.EXE	Replaces your EMSNET3.EXE file (if you're using one).
IPX.OBJ	Updates your IPX.COM file. To do this, you'll need to use either WSGEN or SHGEN. Check your NetWare manuals for instructions on updating IPX.COM.
MAP.EXE	Use this to map your drives before running TaskMAX with Novell.
NETX.COM	Replaces your NET3.COM file (if you're using one).
RPLFIX.COM	Allows your system to load programs remotely with DR DOS 6.0. You run this after the boot image file, such as NET$DOS.SYS, has been created. The boot image file is created with DOSGEN.

To use this file, map a drive to the LOGIN directory on the remote server, then issue a RPLFIX command. The syntax is:

RPLFIX *drive:image.fil*

drive is the drive designation letter for the remote login drive.

image.fil is the name of the image file (NET$DOS.SYS, for example).

TBMI2.COM	Used with TaskMAX to allow switching between peer-to-peer applications (those that make calls to IPX or SPX). A complete, up-to-date description of how to use this is in the file TBMI2.DOC
TBMI2.DOC	Documentation for TBMI12.COM
XMSNETX.EXE	A replacement for XMSNET3.EXE (if you use it).

DR DOS and PC/NFS

The PC/NFS network works just fine with DR DOS 6.0, and you can load the various PC/NFS drivers into upper memory with HIDEVICE. Be aware that PC/NFS doesn't like to coexist with SuperStor. It also gets confused about what drives actually exist if you use VDISK.SYS. You may find that your applications, such as ViewMAX and Windows, think there is an extra drive.

CHAPTER 6

The TaskMAX Task Switcher

Until recently, personal computers were limited to doing one thing at a time. Since I spend most of my time writing and producing printed literature, I'm acutely aware of the frustrations this could cause. I was constantly opening and closing a word processor, two graphics programs, a page-layout program, and various utilities. It would have been so much more convenient to be able to step out of the page-layout program, jump temporarily to a graphics program to fix a drawing, and then jump back into the page-layout program without losing my place. That's exactly what TaskMAX does.

TaskMAX runs each application as a *task*. Each task has its own command processor and, because DR DOS is designed to keep base memory free for your use, has almost as much memory as it would if TaskMAX weren't active. You can even allocate how much extended or expanded memory TaskMAX is allowed to use and how much expanded memory it will allow each task to use. This makes your computer a much more flexible and productive tool.

While TaskMAX provides much of the functionality of environments such as Windows or QuarterDeck's DESQview, it is also quite different. Both Windows and DESQview are *multitasking* environments, which means that with the right hardware, the tasks can actually run simultaneously. TaskMAX takes a slightly different approach. Instead of allowing each program to run separately, TaskMAX allows only one program to run at a time. The other programs are swapped out either to extended or expanded memory (if it's available) or to a disk file. To change to any of the other tasks, TaskMAX swaps the task back and makes it active. If you are swapping to expanded or extended memory, this process is almost instantaneous. Swapping to disk takes a few seconds.

Unlike Windows, where you must run applications designed specifically for Windows to get the full benefit of the environment, TaskMAX will run any DOS program, including protected-mode programs.

Unlike DESQview, TaskMAX can have a graphical user interface. Turn control of TaskMAX over to ViewMAX to provide a very Macintosh-like way of running your computer. This is detailed in Chapter 11.

As I'm writing this book, I use TaskMAX to switch between a task that I use for the command prompt, Microsoft Word, and Artline version 2.0. It's a rather elegant system, especially since I don't really need multitasking.

Things to Consider

Before diving into TaskMAX, consider just what applications you'll run and how much memory they'll require. For example, in my system, I have 4 MB of RAM divided between base memory and extended memory. I allocate 2,048 KB (2 MB) of my extended memory for TaskMAX to use for task swapping. That lets me switch among Ventura, Word, and Artline (if I choose to run all three) without forcing TaskMAX to swap to disk.

Before configuring TaskMAX, take a look at the various programs you're going to run and determine how much of what type of memory each program requires. This will help you decide how to allocate memory between TaskMAX and the application programs.

You can get a bit fancier and allocate expanded memory on a task-by-task basis. You can also specify a general allocation of expanded memory for tasks. We'll go over how to do this as we cover loading and using TaskMAX.

Configuring TaskMAX

TaskMAX configuration is held in the TASKMAX.INI file, and it can be altered using the DR DOS SETUP program. To get to this point, change to the \DRDOS directory and run the SETUP program. (Watch out if Windows is on your system: if you're not in the \DRDOS directory, SETUP will run Windows SETUP instead!)

In DR DOS SETUP, after the first two screens, the DR DOS 6.0 SETUP screen (Figure 6-1) will appear. Select TaskMAX, and the TaskMAX configuration screen (Figure 6-2) appears.

THE TASKMAX TASK SWITCHER

You can set the following TaskMAX options:

TaskMAX Shift and Hot Keys

When pressed together, these keys switch you to the TaskMAX main menu. There is a wide range of key combinations from which to choose. For the Shift key set, use the following keys, either singly or in any combination:

- Right Shift
- Left Shift
- Control (Ctrl)
- Alt

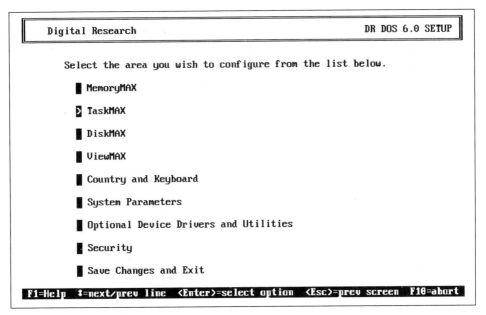

Figure 6-1. The SETUP main configuration menu.

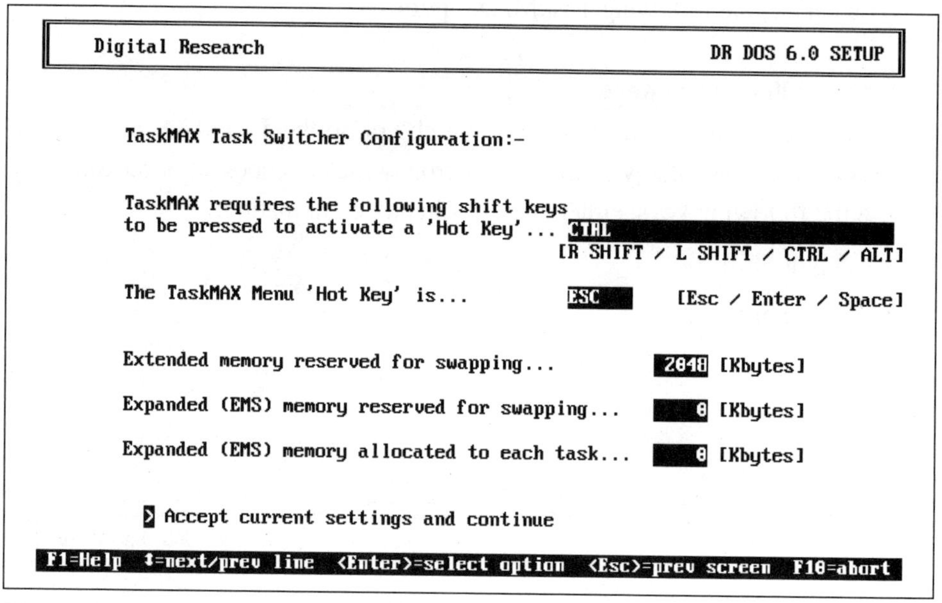

```
┌─────────────────────────────────────────────────────────────────────┐
│ ┌──┐                                                                │
│ │  │ Digital Research                              DR DOS 6.0 SETUP │
│ └──┘                                                                │
│                                                                     │
│       TaskMAX Task Switcher Configuration:-                         │
│                                                                     │
│       TaskMAX requires the following shift keys                     │
│       to be pressed to activate a 'Hot Key'... ██CTRL█████████████  │
│                                            [R SHIFT / L SHIFT / CTRL / ALT] │
│       The TaskMAX Menu 'Hot Key' is...         ██ESC██  [Esc / Enter / Space] │
│                                                                     │
│       Extended memory reserved for swapping...    ██2048█ [Kbytes]  │
│       Expanded (EMS) memory reserved for swapping...  ██0█ [Kbytes] │
│       Expanded (EMS) memory allocated to each task... ██0█ [Kbytes] │
│                                                                     │
│         ▶ Accept current settings and continue                      │
│  ██F1=Help██ ██↕=next/prev line██ ██<Enter>=select option██ ██<Esc>=prev screen██ ██F10=abort██ │
└─────────────────────────────────────────────────────────────────────┘
```

Figure 6-2. The TaskMAX configuration screen.

The hot-key set provides another set of keys from which to choose:

- Escape (Esc)
- Enter
- Space bar

By default, TaskMAX is set to use the Ctrl-Esc sequence to switch to the TaskMAX main menu. The diversity of keys available in the Shift and hot-key sets provides a way to avoid interactions between key sequences meant for TaskMAX and application programs. For example, Ctrl-Esc might mean something to an application program, but because that pair of keys is trapped by TaskMAX, the application program will never see it. It's also possible that the application program has control of the keyboard, intercepting Ctrl-Esc for its own purposes (meaning that you'd have no way of reaching the TaskMAX menu). This is especially true of Windows, from which I find it impossible to reach TaskMAX no matter what key combination I try.

THE TASKMAX TASK SWITCHER

If you encounter problems between an application's use of a key set and TaskMAX's, try other TaskMAX key combinations. If you can't find a combination that works, look for a command in the application that escapes temporarily to the command line. From there, you might be able to switch back to TaskMAX (though this trick doesn't work in Windows either). A disadvantage of this work-around is that (depending on the application program) each time you switch to the command line, you consume base memory for each instance of the command processor. If these instances are not properly terminated (with the Exit command), base memory will be wasted.

Extended Memory Reserved for Swapping

This field allows you to set how much extended memory will be allocated strictly for TaskMAX's use. Switching tasks using extended memory is quite fast, but it also eats up a good deal of extended memory. Most major application programs today occupy most of base memory, and each occupies at least 500 KB of memory. This means 2,048 KB of memory is required to switch four large tasks without having to use the disk.

To determine exactly how much memory you'll need, set this screen so that TaskMAX can't access any expanded or extended memory, and then load all the programs normally run as tasks. Create a new task to supply a command line. At the command line, change directories to the \DRDOS\TMP directory and check the size of the TASKMAX.SWP file. That size is the amount of memory you'll need. For more information on extended and expanded memory, see Chapter 5.

This setting can be overridden by a TaskMAX command-line parameter.

Expanded (EMS) Memory Reserved for Swapping

Like extended memory, expanded memory can be used for swapping. Again, this takes a good deal of memory, and you'll need to decide how much your tasks will require.

This setting can be overridden by a TaskMAX command-line parameter.

Expanded (EMS) Memory Allocated to Each Task

Expanded memory is also used by DOS applications. For example, the GEM version of Ventura 3.0 requires 1,600 KB of expanded memory to load its hyphenation dictionary. Artline version 2.0 can use expanded memory, but only if at least 512 KB is available. This is a general setting that applies to all tasks.

This setting can be overridden at the command line. Expanded memory can also be allocated on a task-by-task basis.

Exiting from this screen brings up a menu of TaskMAX color schemes. Experiment with changing the colors of the TaskMAX menus.

When you exit from SETUP after changing the TaskMAX configuration, SETUP will want to reboot. Let it do so because it may have changed the AUTOEXEC.BAT file, and those changes won't take effect until you reboot. All TaskMAX configuration information is stored in the TASKMAX.INI file, which resides in the /DRDOS directory (or whatever directory you've chosen to house DR DOS).

Before running TaskMAX, set the number of file locks through SHARE. TaskMAX won't run unless you do this. File locks prevent multiple programs from simultaneously accessing the same disk file. Consider this rather ugly scenario: both a word processor and a page-layout program are accessing the same file. In the word processor, you make changes in the file, save, and exit. Then you save and exit from the page-layout package, which overwrites all your changes by saving the old, unedited version of the file that it had in memory.

I've found that the number of file locks needed depends a lot on the application programs. Some programs create only a few files. Ventura Publisher seems to be the worst offender; it creates or opens file after file. Start with the number of SHARE locks set to 20, and work your way up. I currently have 30 locks on my home machine and 60 on my work machine.

Usually, an Out-of-Locks message appears when the barrel of available file locks run dry. I've also gotten erroneous Disk Full errors and the like. These problems can also be caused by an insufficient number of files in the FILES statement.

Make sure there is enough disk space for file swapping. If you're swapping

THE TASKMAX TASK SWITCHER

entirely in memory, this isn't a problem. But if there isn't enough memory to swap all tasks, or if the disk will be used for swapping, you need to ensure that TaskMAX has enough space. TaskMAX normally creates a swap file called TASKMAX.SWP, which resides in the \DRDOS\TMP directory by default. A different path can be specified for the swap file when you load TaskMAX or modify the TASKMAX.INI file. Always run the swap file on the fastest hard drive available.

Running TaskMAX

Here's something to remember before starting TaskMAX: any terminate-and-stay-resident (TSR) program that is run outside of TaskMAX remains accessible within all tasks. Any TSR program run within a task is only accessible within that task. For example, if you run SideKick before starting TaskMAX, you'll be able to access it from any task. If you run SideKick within a task you use for a word processor, you'll only be able to access SideKick when you switch to the word processor task.

For the most part, TaskMAX eliminates the need for TSRs because you can switch to any program desired. However, programs that need to be universally accessible, such as mouse drivers and network drivers, must be loaded before you run TaskMAX.

As for actually running TaskMAX, nothing could be simpler. Enter the command:

```
TASKMAX
```

at the command line. Things will whir and buzz for a few seconds, and then the acknowledgement shown in Figure 6-3 appears, stating that TaskMAX is loaded. Use the MEM command to check available memory; only about 20 KB of main memory is now missing. Press the combination of the Shift and hot keys (for simplicity we'll refer to this by its default, the Ctrl-Esc sequence). Something very similar to the main menu and task list shown in Figure 6-4 appears.

If a mouse driver is loaded, the mouse works in TaskMAX. Click any command in the menu to activate it. If you don't have a mouse and a mouse driver loaded, use the keys designated at the side of the menu to activate the various functions.

```
[Max] C:\>taskmax
TaskMAX R1.00 Application switcher
Copyright (c) 1989,1991 Digital Research Inc. All rights reserved.

The DR DOS application switcher is now loaded.

[Max] C:\>
```

Figure 6-3. You'll see this message when TaskMAX has been loaded.

By the way, the typical mouse-but-no-driver scenario occurs with Windows. Windows uses its own built-in mouse driver, so outside of Windows the user has no mouse driver loaded. This produces the perplexing situation of having a mouse that works in Windows but not in ViewMAX, TaskMAX, or almost any non-Windows program. If you are in this boat, load a driver from the disk or disks that accompanied your mouse.

Once you're actually in TaskMAX, the first function to try is "About TaskMAX." Activate this by clicking on it or by pressing F3. A pop-up box tells you how much free swap space is available, as well as the percentage of the total swap space that has been used. Free swap space is the total amount of the available swapping memory as well as the free space on the hard drive designated for swapping. As tasks are added and deleted, these values will change. Check them from time to time to make sure you don't run out of space.

THE TASKMAX TASK SWITCHER

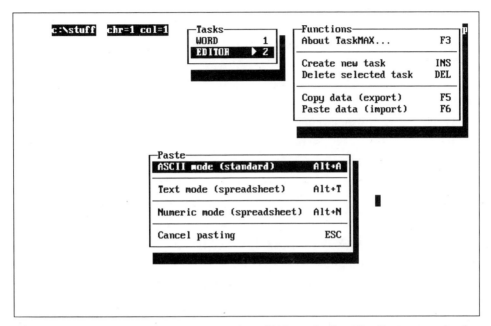

Figure 6-4. The TaskMAX main menu, and available tasks list. The Paste menu is also showing.

Adding a Task

Press the Ins key or click on "Create new task", and a new command prompt appears. This is task 2. Just for fun, run the EDITOR program and return to the TaskMAX main menu with the Ctrl-Esc keys or another hot-key combination. Now the task list has two entries: COMMAND and EDITOR. Select either task by clicking on it with the mouse pointer (the square block) or by moving the highlight bar over the task. Press Enter.

Up to 20 tasks can be added, but that many would be somewhat ridiculous. To maintain both reasonable performance and your sanity, keep the task list down to a half-dozen entries.

Switching Tasks

Of course, you can always return to the TaskMAX main menu to switch tasks. However, once in a task, there is a shortcut: each task has a task number, and that number is the key to bouncing between tasks. Press the Shift key (or keys) and the number of the task, and TaskMAX will switch to the new task. The defaults are Ctrl-1 and Ctrl-2. Try this out.

Deleting a Task

When you've finished running an application, there is no need to keep its task around. Unnecessary tasks gobble up available switching memory and increase the size of the swap file. To exit from a task, first exit from the application and return to the command prompt. Return to the main menu and select the task by moving the highlight bar over it. Press the Del key to remove the task.

To guard against accidentally deleting an active application, if a program is running in the task, TaskMAX will ask if you really want to delete that task. You can stop the whole deletion process by pressing N.

If an application program locks up, as some applications will do, and you can't use the keys to switch back to the TaskMAX main menu, there's still a way out. The Ctrl-Alt-Del combination, usually used to reboot the computer, kills the active task.

Tasks can also be deleted from the command line. This is covered later in this chapter under the heading "Running TaskMAX from the Command Line."

By the way, when a task is deleted, the other tasks below it on the task list are renumbered. Let's say task 2 is called WORD and Task 3 is called COMMAND. When you delete task 2 (WORD), COMMAND becomes the new task 2.

Copying Text

An application can display things in two ways: in text mode or in graphics mode. EDITOR is a text-mode application, as is the TaskMAX main menu. ViewMAX and Windows are graphics-mode applications. Sometimes a program uses graphics mode, even though it looks like text mode. Microsoft Word for DOS is a good example of this because it can use both graphics and text modes, and the two look nearly identical.

TaskMAX can copy up to one screenful of information between text-mode programs. This includes word processors, spreadsheets, and database applications. It does this using the clipboard concept. The clipboard is a scratchpad area onto which a block of text can be copied and then pasted back into as many other text applications as you like. To copy a different block of text, you must cut or copy the new text into the clipboard first.

To experiment with this, open a task and load the EDITOR program. (If you've been following along with the suggested examples, you'll already have an active EDITOR task.) Load any file text—for example, I loaded the ARTLINE.BAT file that starts Artline version 2.0. If you're using a configuration file, make sure you are working on a copy of it so that you don't inadvertently change the settings of one of your application programs!

To copy text, switch back to the TaskMAX main menu and click on "Copy data (export)," or press the F5 key. The dialog box shown in Figure 6-5 appears. This provides the rules of the game and the ability to start or cancel copying. At this point, press Enter.

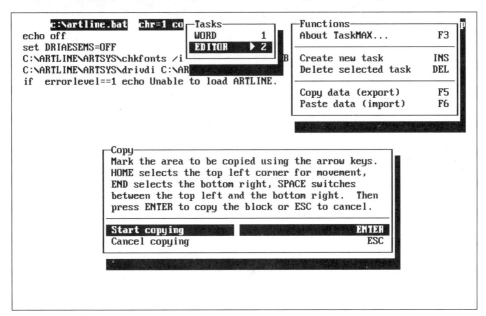

Figure 6-5. The Copy dialog box.

This brings us back to the EDITOR task, and the first line of text is now highlighted. This highlight defines the copy area—only the text within the highlighted area will be copied to the clipboard. Move the right arrow and down arrow keys to redefine the highlighted area. Figure 6-6 shows the results of moving the highlight block down and to the right. To move the left side, press the End key. Now move the left edge of the block with the left arrow key. The End and Home keys toggle between moving the left and right edges of the highlight block. The space bar toggles between moving the top edge of the block and moving the bottom edge.

Try to enclose four or five lines in the highlight area. Once this is done, press the Enter key. The highlighted area is copied to the clipboard, and the main menu reappears on the screen.

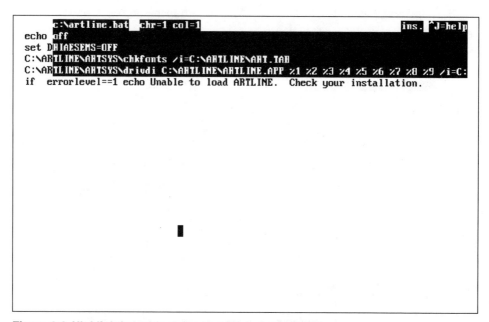

Figure 6-6. Highlighting a block for copying between tasks.

Next, find a place to put the contents of the clipboard. This can be any text application. (Also, there are special modes that allow transfers to spreadsheets.) Since EDITOR serves our purposes, return to the EDITOR task. Once in EDITOR, abandon the current file (Ctrl-KQ) and open a new file with any name you choose (PASTE.TXT, for example).

THE TASKMAX TASK SWITCHER

Press Ctrl-Esc to return to the TaskMAX main menu. This time, click on "Paste data (import)" or press F6. Click "ASCII mode (standard)" or press Alt-A. The clipboard contents will begin to appear, one character at a time, at the cursor position within EDITOR. That's an important point—always remember to place the cursor where you want the clipboard contents before copying them in.

You can paste the clipboard contents again and again, or you can load new text into the clipboard and paste that wherever you like.

In the example above we chose the ASCII mode, which works with word processors, text editors, and most database programs. Each line in ASCII mode ends with a carriage return. There are two other modes:

Numeric Mode This mode was designed specifically for copying numeric information mixed with text to a spreadsheet. The information is usually from a word processor and is typically in a table format. Only numbers, minus signs, and decimal points are copied. All other material vanishes. If a number is enclosed in parentheses, it becomes negative. A down arrow character is placed after every line to force the spreadsheet to paste the next set of numbers in a new cell. Select this mode by pressing Alt-N.

Text Mode This mode is used to copy information to a spreadsheet as text. The text is prefaced with a """ character to indicate to the spreadsheet that what follows is left-justified text. A down arrow character ends each line. Select this mode by pressing Alt-T.

Shutting Down TaskMAX

When finished using TaskMAX, or to turn the computer off, exit by removing all tasks. Press the Del key to delete the last task, and TaskMAX itself will be removed.

I suggest doing this before shutting off the computer. TaskMAX could have a rather large swap file sitting in \DRDOS\TMP. Turning off the computer without removing TaskMAX will leave this file intact to take up a lot of space on your hard drive. The swap file is deleted when you exit in the manner described above.

Running TaskMAX from the Command Line

TaskMAX can be configured and run equally well from the command line itself. About the only things that can't be changed are the colors of the TaskMAX menus and the hot and Shift keys. Also keep in mind that changes made at the command line are temporary and only apply while TaskMAX is active. The next time you run TaskMAX, it will revert to the defaults shown in the TASKMAX.INI files (which have been set either manually by you or by the SETUP program).

Controlling TaskMAX's Access to Memory

The following parameters, added to the TASKMAX command, allow you to control and configure memory use. These parameters can be used only when you initially load TaskMAX—they can't be changed once TaskMAX is active. Note that these parameters override the TASKMAX.INI file defaults during current TaskMAX operation.

/E:[=*eeee*]

This parameter sets the amount of extended memory that TaskMAX can use for task swapping, where *eeee* is the amount of extended memory in KB. If the value is left blank, TaskMAX will use all available extended memory. Setting a value higher than the amount of extended memory available also allocates all extended memory to TaskMAX. Setting the value to 0 prevents TaskMAX from using extended memory. Any remaining extended memory is allocated to application programs within tasks on a first-come, first-served basis.

The following allocates 2,048 KB of extended memory for TaskMAX's use.

```
TASKMAX /E=2048
```

/X:[=*xxxx*]

This parameter sets the amount of expanded memory that TaskMAX can use for task swapping, where *xxxx* is the amount of expanded

THE TASKMAX TASK SWITCHER

memory in KB. If the value is left blank or is higher than the amount of expanded memory available, TaskMAX gets to use all expanded memory. Setting the value to 0 disables TaskMAX's access to expanded memory. Any remaining expanded memory is allocated to application programs on a first-come, first-served basis, *unless* the /L parameter is used. (The /L parameter is described in the next section.) For example, to allocate 1,024 KB of expanded memory for TaskMAX, use the following:

```
TASKMAX /X=1024
```

Allocating Expanded Memory for Each Task

A general allocation of expanded memory can be set for all tasks, or the allocation can be changed on a task-by-task basis. If this parameter isn't used, the setting within the TASKMAX.INI files (which can be set manually or through the SETUP program) will prevail. TaskMAX must already be loaded for this parameter to work.

/L:=*xxxx*

This allocates an amount of expanded memory to each task that follows it, where *xxxx* is the amount of expanded memory in KB. The amount can be changed on a task-by-task basis. Expanded memory will continue to be parcelled out in this amount until it's gone. This parameter only applies to tasks that haven't been created; you can't change the allocation for existing tasks.

Let's assume you're going to run Ventura Publisher 3.0/GEM edition and Artline version 2.0. To load the hyphenation dictionary into memory, you need to have 1,600 KB of expanded memory available to Ventura. Artline requires a minimum of 512 KB of expanded memory if it is going to use expanded memory at all. Before creating the task for Ventura, issue this command:

```
TASKMAX /L=1600
```

After creating the Ventura task, issue this command to change the expanded-memory allocation to 512 KB:

```
TASKMAX /L=512
```

Changing the Swap Directory

As mentioned earlier, TaskMAX will swap tasks to disk by default when it has no more memory available. Disk swapping uses the TASKMAX.SWP file, which resides by default in the \DRDOS\TMP directory. This swap directory can be changed when TaskMAX is loaded. It can't be changed after TaskMAX is active. This parameter overrides the directory location set in the TASKMAX.INI files during the current execution of TaskMAX but doesn't alter the default.

/D=[*drive:*]*path*

> *Drive:* is optional, and *path* is the complete directory path in which the TASKMAX.INI swap file resides.

Adding a New Task

New tasks can be started up from the command line as well. Of course, TaskMAX must be active before you do this. Use this parameter to start a new task.

/C=[[*drive:*]*path*] command

> *Drive:* is optional, but you must specify a program to run and its path. To start a task with a command line, enter COMMAND.COM. If this is entered without the name of a program to run, TaskMAX won't create a new task.

THE TASKMAX TASK SWITCHER

This version of the TaskMAX command starts the Microsoft Word application in the C:\WORD directory:

```
TASKMAX /C C:\WORD\WORD
```

Tasks that run a particular application delete themselves when you exit from that application. In the above example, I created a task to run Word. When I exit from Word, the task is deleted automatically.

Changing a Task's Name

You can change the name of any existing task with this parameter:

/N[:*tt*] [*newname*]   The *tt* designates the task number that will be renamed, while *newname* specifies the name. Get the task number from the TaskMAX menu or issue the TASKMAX command with no parameters. If no task number is entered, the current task will be renamed. The task name can have up to eight characters. Please note that while the DR DOS 6.0 manual says the /N parameter can be used with the /C parameter, I've never been able to make this work.

This version of the command renames task 3 to WEASEL:

```
TASKMAX /N:3 WEASEL
```

Deleting a Task From the Command Line

Finally, tasks can also be deleted with a command-line parameter. When the last task is deleted, TaskMAX itself is removed from memory.

/K:[*tt*]   The /K parameter deletes the task specified by its number, *tt*. Check the task number by switching to the TaskMAX menu and checking the task list or issue the TASKMAX command without any parameters. If no task number is entered, the current task is deleted.

More Things to Consider

There are a number of other things to keep in mind when using TaskMAX.

DISKOPT

Running the DISKOPT utility as a task could be a disaster. It completely rebuilds the locations of files, and none of the other tasks will know about this.

Sector Editors

Don't use programs such as Mace MUSE or Norton NU as tasks. These allow you to change the FAT and the contents of the disk directly and bypass the SHARE locks.

Files

We talked briefly before about the number of file locks. You may need to increase the number of files as well. Check each application's manual to see what the FILES statements should be set to. Add these up and enter this value in the FILES statement in the CONFIG.SYS file.

Temporary Files

These might appear when you run more than one copy of the same application in multiple tasks. Some applications have fixed names for temporary files, and opening a second version of the application can cause file conflicts. Sometimes you can set an environment variable that specifies a directory for these files, and you can set this differently for each version of the application. Check the application manual to see if such an environment variable exists.

The TASKMAX.INI File

More parameters can be changed by editing the TASKMAX.INI file. These include custom color sets, the functions of the various paste modes, and the location of the TaskMAX swap file. Edit the file with EDITOR. Programmers should have very little difficulty modifying the file contents as they are clearly commented. Make a backup copy of the file before beginning to twiddle things (otherwise, you might need to reload it from disk).

CHAPTER 7

Using EDITOR

EDITOR is the DR DOS full-screen text editor. It fulfills some of the same goals as the venerable DOS EDLIN but is much easier to use. A full-screen text editor lets you modify or create ASCII text files with the same ease as a full-screen word processor (although EDITOR has a much more limited set of commands than a commercial word processing program). Thus EDITOR is especially useful for modifying your CONFIG.SYS and AUTOEXEC.BAT files as well as creating new batch files. In fact, EDITOR can be used to modify just about any ASCII file because, unlike many other bundled text editors, it is not limited by file size. EDITOR can handle files as large as the amount of disk space.

EDITOR uses a subset of the WordStar command set, and with the on-screen menu turned on it even looks similar to WordStar. If you've been using computers for long, it's likely that you have been exposed to WordStar (which was once the most popular word processor) or one of the other programs that uses the command set (such as dBASE III). Digital Research has always been enamored with the WordStar command set, and its first word processor, GEM Write, also incorporated these commands.

If you are fond of mousing around, you can leave your mouse behind when using EDITOR. While EDITOR is functionally complete and competent, the program lacks mouse support. Luckily, the WordStar keyboard command orientation is an efficient alternative to the mouse where text editing is concerned.

Before getting too deeply into EDITOR, you should know about Control key sequences. All EDITOR commands consist of either the Control key (Ctrl) plus a letter key or the Control key plus a letter key followed by another letter key. For example, the command to move up one screen is Ctrl-R. Likewise, the command for moving to the top of the document is Ctrl-Q-R. If you type a command but want to cancel the operation before it is completed, type Ctrl-U.

Cranking Up

Start EDITOR by typing

```
EDITOR
```

at the command prompt. This brings you to the EDITOR title or "no-file" screen (see Figure 7-1), where you'll be prompted to enter a file name. You can't go any further without entering a file name, and you can't get a directory from here, so you'll need to remember the exact file name and path of the file you want to edit. If you want to create and edit a new file, simply type a file name for it. EDITOR will then ask if you want to create a new file. If you want to return to the DR DOS command line, press the Escape key.

```
            EDITOR R2.00    Full Screen Text Editor
   Copyright (c) 1988,1989,1990 Digital Research Inc. All rights reserved.




     Please enter the name of the text file you wish to edit.
     If the file does not already exist it will be created.
     Press the Esc key to leave this program.

     File name?
```

Figure 7-1. The title or "no-file" screen.

You can also open a file directly when you open EDITOR by adding its name, extension, and path as a parameter to the command to execute the program. For example:

```
EDITOR C:\STUFF\SWITCHER.BAT
```

opens the file SWITCHER.BAT located in the \STUFF subdirectory on the C: drive.

USING EDITOR

Once in EDITOR, you should see a pretty lonely-looking screen, with just a file name accompanied by row and column counters positioned at the top to indicate the line and column the cursor is on. You can bring up a WordStar-like command menu with the following trick:

- Press Ctrl-J. This will produce the first of a series of help screens listing all of the EDITOR commands.

- Press Enter to move to the next help screen, and repeat this until you see the prompt:

```
Do you wish to have the quick reference display (Y/N)
```

Type Y.

A command menu such as that shown in Figure 7-2 will be displayed. The menu lists the main commands for EDITOR, and if you are unfamiliar with WordStar commands you may want to keep this menu on-screen. Like WordStar, the EDITOR menu shifts to show you the available commands for families of Control-key combinations. For example, if you press Ctrl-K, the menu will change to show all of the command combinations beginning with Ctrl-K. This on-line quick-reference card to EDITOR's commands can be a very good learning tool.

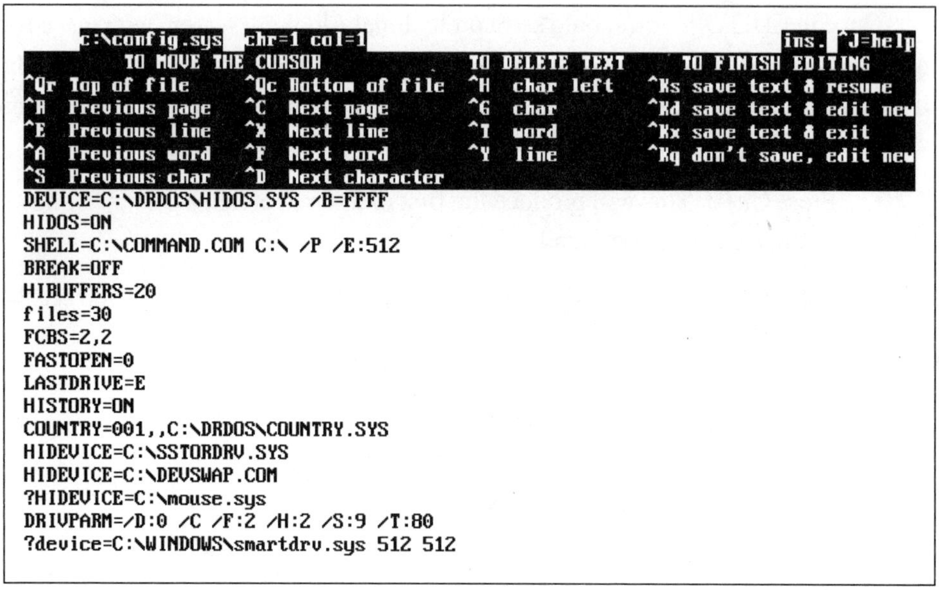

```
      c:\config.sys  chr=1 col=1                                ins. ^J=help
              TO MOVE THE CURSOR            TO DELETE TEXT     TO FINISH EDITING
   ^Qr  Top of file       ^Qc Bottom of file   ^H  char left    ^Ks save text & resume
   ^R   Previous page     ^C  Next page        ^G  char         ^Kd save text & edit new
   ^E   Previous line     ^X  Next line        ^T  word         ^Kx save text & exit
   ^A   Previous word     ^F  Next word        ^Y  line         ^Kq don't save, edit new
   ^S   Previous char     ^D  Next character
DEVICE=C:\DRDOS\HIDOS.SYS /B=FFFF
HIDOS=ON
SHELL=C:\COMMAND.COM C:\ /P /E:512
BREAK=OFF
HIBUFFERS=20
files=30
FCBS=2,2
FASTOPEN=0
LASTDRIVE=E
HISTORY=ON
COUNTRY=001,,C:\DRDOS\COUNTRY.SYS
HIDEVICE=C:\SSTORDRV.SYS
HIDEVICE=C:\DEVSWAP.COM
?HIDEVICE=C:\mouse.sys
DRIVPARM=/D:0 /C /F:2 /H:2 /S:9 /T:80
?device=C:\WINDOWS\smartdrv.sys 512 512
```

Figure 7-2. EDITOR, with the command menu displayed.

The Cursor Control Diamond

Cursor movement in EDITOR is controlled by either the arrow keys or the cursor diamond, a group of character keys that, when used with the Control key, mimic the cursor control of arrow keys. The arrow keys are self-explanatory: the Up key makes the cursor go up, Right makes the cursor go right, and so on. The cursor diamond is located on the left of the keyboard and is shown in Figure 7-3.

Early in the history of the personal computer, a pioneering company named Micropro invented a text editor, called WordMaster, that was very similar to EDITOR, and implemented the cursor-diamond concept because many keyboards didn't have arrow keys. WordMaster evolved into WordStar, and the millions of people who learned WordStar learned to use the cursor diamond. It is just about the only scheme for text editors that has survived more than a decade.

Using the diamond is simple: the combination of Ctrl-D makes the cursor travel one character to the right. Ctrl-S moves the cursor one character to the left. Ctrl-F shifts into a higher gear and moves the cursor one word to the right, while Ctrl-A

USING EDITOR

moves the cursor one word to the left, Ctrl-E moves the cursor one line up, and Ctrl-X moves the cursor one line down.

Figure 7-3. The EDITOR cursor diamond.

Of course, the cursor can't go where there isn't already text. If you want to play around with this, either open a file that you can safely modify with EDITOR or use EDITOR to type some text with which you can experiment. Remember that unlike a sophisticated commercial word processor, EDITOR doesn't wrap around to a new line when you reach the edge of the screen. Instead, it just keeps going on and on. To go to a new line, you'll need to press the Enter key (just as you would on a typewriter). You can shift everything to the right of the cursor down to a new line by pressing Ctrl-N.

After you have a file that you can maneuver about in, try moving the cursor around using the arrow keys and cursor diamond. If you want to insert text, simply position the cursor and type. Pressing Insert or Ctrl-V toggles, or switches, EDITOR between the overtype and insert modes. In insert mode, new text typed at the cursor pushes old text ahead. In overtype mode, new text appears directly over old text, replacing the old text as you type.

Moving Further

The cursor diamond also allows you to scroll the screen up and down. To scroll the screen up one full screen, use Ctrl-R (PageUp does the same thing). You can use Ctrl-C or PageDown to go down a screen. Alternatively, you can scroll up and down one line at a time. As you do this, the cursor does not change position until it hits the top or bottom of the screen, and then it is dragged along as the screen display shifts. To scroll up a line at a time, use Ctrl-W. Scroll down with Ctrl-Z.

The Accelerator Key

You can magnify the functions of some of the EDITOR cursor commands with Ctrl-Q. For example, Ctrl-Q-S moves the cursor to the far left character in the line. Ctrl-Q-D moves the cursor to the far right character, regardless of the length of the line. The combination of Ctrl-Q-R repositions the cursor at the top of the file, while Ctrl-Q-C goes to the bottom of the file. These functions are duplicated by the Home key (top of file) and the End key (bottom of file). Ctrl-Q can be used with E and X as well: Ctrl-Q-E sends the cursor to the top line of the screen, and Ctrl-Q-X sends it to the bottom.

Deleting Text

Because we all make mistakes, it's nice that EDITOR provides a way of erasing them. The easiest way is simply to press the Delete key, which deletes whatever character is currently selected by the cursor. Hold down this key to delete multiple characters. The cursor-diamond equivalent to the Delete key is Ctrl-G. If you want to delete a word at a time, press Ctrl-T. Ctrl-T only deletes text from the current cursor position to the first space, so if the cursor is in the middle of a word, the command won't delete the entire word. To delete an entire line, press Ctrl-Y.

A word of caution here: EDITOR has no undelete capability. Once text is gone, it's really gone. The only way to recover deleted text is to abandon all changes since the last time you saved the file, and this means that editing changes will be lost.

Saving and Exiting

You may be wondering how to get out of EDITOR or how to save your file. EDITOR offers several ways to save and/or exit. If you want to save your file and exit to the command line, use Ctrl-K-X. To save your file and exit to the no-file screen (so that you can load a new file), press Ctrl-K-D. To save your file without exiting to anything, use Ctrl-K-S. Finally, you can abandon everything you've done since the last save and return to the no-file screen with Ctrl-K-Q. If you press this sequence by accident, don't worry; EDITOR will ask you to confirm that you want to abandon the file.

EDITOR creates automatic backups of your files each time you save. When you save a file, EDITOR takes the last version of the file and gives it a .BAK extension. If you save changes that you regret to MYJUNK.TXT, for example, you can recover the previous version, which EDITOR has named MYJUNK.BAK. The only caution is that EDITOR won't directly edit a .BAK file, so you must exit to DR DOS and rename the file extension to something other than .BAK at the command line.

Moving Text

One of the benefits of a full-screen editor is that you can move, delete, or copy sections of your file. EDITOR even allows you to save pieces of your file to separate files or read the contents of other files into your current work. All of these functions are done with additional Ctrl-K commands, and most require that you "block," or select, sections of text you want to manipulate. Figures 7-4a and 7-4b illustrate the text-blocking process.

```
       c:\typeset\techdoc.txt  chr=77 col=9                    ins. ^J=help
@CHAPTER HEAD = PUBLISHING CHAPTER

@HEADING 2 = MENU COMMANDS

Most of <I>Ventura Publisher's functions are controlled through the menus
at the top of the screen. This section describes the operation of
each of these menus and the options within them. These commands are
presented in the order in which they appear on the screen. Use the
index for an alphabetical reference to these commands.

@HEADING 3 = Menu Conventions

Often, a menu option will be shown in gray and cannot be highlighted.
This usually indicates that the proper function has not been selected.
The table below indicates these dependencies.

@HEADING 4 = DESK

@Z_TBL_BEG = COLUMNS(2), DIMENSION(IN), WIDTH(3.8333), INDENT(1.1600),
BELOW(.1667), HGUTTER(.2917), VGUTTER(.0833), BOX(Z_DOUBLE), HGRID(Z_SINGLE),
VGRID(Z_SINGLE), KEEP(OFF)

@Z_TBL_HEAD = TABLE TEXT, TABLE TEXT
```

Figure 7-4a. Marking the start of a block with Ctrl-K-B.

To mark a block:

1. Put your cursor at the beginning of the section of text that you'd like to block, and press Ctrl-K-B. A <B> will appear to indicate that this point begins the block.

2. Move the cursor to the end of the area you want to block, and press Ctrl-K-K. The entire block of text will be highlighted.

If you set the end of the block before setting the beginning, you'll see a <K> in the text denoting the end of the block. In this case, the block is highlighted when you designate its beginning, which must always precede the end, so you'll have to scroll toward the beginning of the text to set the block properly. You can reset beginning and end marks after you've initially set them.

USING EDITOR

```
    c:\typeset\techdoc.txt  chr=167 col=26              ins.  ^J=help
@CHAPTER HEAD = PUBLISHING CHAPTER

@HEADING 2 = MENU COMMANDS

Most of Ventura Publisher's functions are controlled through the menus
at the top of the screen. This section describes the operation of
each of these menus and the options within them. These commands are
presented in the order in which they appear on the screen. Use the
index for an alphabetical reference to these commands.

@HEADING 3 = Menu Conventions

Often, a menu option will be shown in gray and cannot be highlighted.
This usually indicates that the proper function has not been selected.
The table below indicates these dependencies.

@HEADING 4 = DESK

@Z_TBL_BEG = COLUMNS(2), DIMENSION(IN), WIDTH(3.8333), INDENT(1.1600),
BELOW(.1667), HGUTTER(.2917), VGUTTER(.0833), BOX(Z_DOUBLE), HGRID(Z_SINGLE),
VGRID(Z_SINGLE), KEEP(OFF)

@Z_TBL_HEAD = TABLE TEXT, TABLE TEXT
```

Figure 7-4b. Marking the end of the block with a Ctrl-K-K. Note how the blocked area is highlighted.

Now that you know how to make a block, you can:

- **Move it somewhere else**. To do this, place the cursor where you want to move the block and press Ctrl-K-V.

- **Copy it elsewhere**. Copying moves a duplicate of the block, leaving the original undisturbed. Press Ctrl-K-C.

- **Delete it**. Press Ctrl-K-Y to delete the block, but keep in mind that this function is irreversible.

- **Write a copy of it to a new file**. Use Ctrl-K-W for this: enter the path, name, and extension of the file at the prompt.

- **Read in the entire contents of a text file at the cursor location**. Press Ctrl-K-R.

- **Hide it**. Pressing Ctrl-K-H makes the block disappear. Pressing Ctrl-K-H again makes it reappear.

Moving Around

One of WordStar's nicest features is its ability to set markers in the file to which you can move the cursor on command. Digital Research incorporated this feature in EDITOR, providing the ability to set up to 10 separate markers. You can also jump to the beginning or end markers of a block. To set a marker, place your cursor and press Ctrl-K*n*, where *n* is any number from 0 through 9. A marker will appear (see Figure 7-5). This marker isn't actually within your file — it exists in the "mind" of EDITOR. Later, if you read a file back into EDITOR that had previously held markers, they won't be there.

To move the cursor to a marker, press Ctrl-Q*n*, where *n* is the number of the marker. To move to the beginning of a block, press Ctrl-Q-B. Ctrl-Q-K will take you to the end of a block.

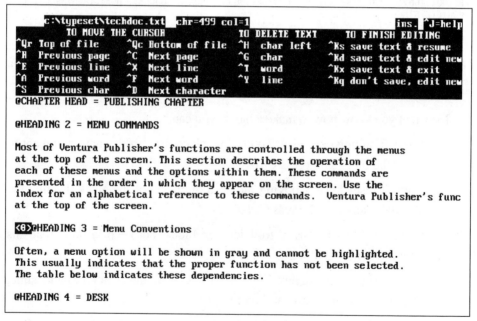

Figure 7-5. Marker <0> set in the text.

Removing a marker is a bit trickier. You must type Ctrl-K*n* again directly at the marker position. Because you may not want to move to a marker to remove it, the easiest way to do it is to type Ctrl-K*n* at your current cursor position (which moves the marker to your cursor). Type Ctrl-K*n* again to remove the marker. Markers can be moved, removed, and reused as often as you like.

Placing Special Characters

EDITOR allows you to insert control characters or any of the extended ASCII characters into a file. Control characters can be used for printer control or may have some special meaning to another program. For example, you might want to insert a Ctrl-L character directly into a file. To many printers, this is a form-feed command. To embed it (or any other control character), use Ctrl-P. In our example, press Ctrl-P followed by Ctrl-L. You'll see a ^L in your file (the ^ is synonymous with "control" in EDITOR, as in "Ctrl-L"). You can place any control character into your file, including a null (Ctrl-P followed by Escape).

To place an extended ASCII character into your file, press Ctrl-Q-N. You'll be prompted to enter either the decimal or hexadecimal equivalent for the ASCII character you want to enter. You may want to use this command to enter a foreign-language character or a graphic character.

When using Ctrl-Q-N to enter an ASCII character in decimal, simply enter the number equivalent at the prompt. If you want to enter the character in hexadecimal, type 0x followed by the hexadecimal equivalent. For example, to enter a cents sign for American currency (¢), type Ctrl-Q followed by the number 155, the decimal equivalent for the character. To enter the same character in hexadecimal, type Ctrl-Q followed by 0x (signifying hexadecimal) and then 9B (the hexadecimal equivalent). Remember, there are no spaces between these entries.

Repeating Your Last Entry

When you are entering the name of a file or writing a block to a file, you can recall the last file name you used simply by pressing Ctrl-R. This is useful if you are writing blocks to file names that are only slightly different, such as BLOCK1.TXT and BLOCK2.TXT, because it is easier to modify a name than to retype it.

CHAPTER 8

Automating Operations with Batch Files

When you interact with DR DOS, you normally issue one command at a time at the command line. However, you can also issue groups of commands from *batch files*. DR DOS 6.0 has special commands that can turn these files into simple yet powerful programs. This chapter lists those commands after giving some examples of useful batch files.

Example 1: A Rudimentary Batch File

The simplest batch files are merely collections of DR DOS commands, with no batch file control commands involved. For instance, suppose you want to clean up your C: and D: disk drives periodically by deleting all the backup files. Such files usually have the extension .BAK or .$?? (the dollar sign is the first character of the file extension, while the question marks are not actual characters but are wildcards that match any character in that particular place).

From the command line, you issue one XDEL /S command to remove the .BAK files and another to remove the .$?? files. You then change drives and repeat the process. However, you can also use EDITOR (or any other ASCII text editor) to create a single file that does all four things. This means you would need to issue only one command to clean up both drives. Such a batch file would look like this:

```
XDEL C:\*.BAK /S /N
XDEL C:\*.$?? /S /N
XDEL D:\*.BAK /S /N
XDEL D:\*.$?? /S /N
```

The /S parameter tells XDEL to search all subdirectories of the specified directory. Since that directory is the root, all subdirectories on the drive will be searched. The /N parameter tells XDEL not to pause and ask if you really want to delete files in subdirectories.

Try using EDITOR to create such a file (call it CLEANUP.BAT) with the letters that represent the drives resident on your system. Make sure no important files have the extensions named in the XDEL commands, and make very sure you enter the file extensions correctly. If you type *.??? instead of *.$??, you'll erase everything and then get plenty of practice using UNDELETE.

The .BAT extension identifies this as a batch file to DR DOS. To run it, just type:

```
CLEANUP
```

and press Enter. When you run the file, you'll see each command execute in turn. Later, we'll talk about how to prevent each command from being displayed as it executes. If you want to stop the batch file, press Ctrl-C or Ctrl-Break. You might need to do this more than once to get the computer's attention. When it does notice you, you'll see a prompt like:

```
Halt Batch Process (Y/N)?
```

A Y at this point will stop the batch file, while an N will tell the system to continue executing each command in the file.

Note that I didn't add the path and drive to the XDEL command. That's because I'm assuming you have the \DRDOS directory (or whichever directory holds DR DOS) in the PATH. If you're referencing commands that aren't in the PATH, you'll need to add the complete directory path and perhaps the drive designation as well.

Example 2: Adding Variables

OK, so much for the absolute basics. Now imagine how much more useful your batch files would be if you could enter arguments as well. For instance, suppose you wanted to search all directories on both drives for a particular type of file, place the

AUTOMATING OPERATIONS WITH BATCH FILES

locations of the files in another file, and see a listing of that file? It would be inconvenient to edit the batch file each time to insert the file extension you're searching for.

Fortunately, batch files let you use variables. Variables take the form %1 through %9 (you can access a greater range with the SWITCH statement) and are entered at the batch-file command line. For example, the following batch file uses variables to search for certain files:

```
XDIR C:\*.%1 /S>LOOK1.TXT
XDIR D:\*.%1 /S>LOOK2.TXT
COPY LOOK1.TXT+LOOK2.TXT %2
DEL LOOK?.TXT
TYPE %2 /P
```

The two XDIR commands search the specified drives for the file extension designated by variable 1 (/S tells them to search all subdirectories of the drives as well). The > is a redirection symbol that tells XDIR to redirect its output to the temporary file LOOK1.TXT or LOOK2.TXT. (The choice of file names is arbitrary and can be changed as long as the temporary file names don't conflict with your valuable permanent files.) Redirection is covered in detail in Chapter 13.

The COPY command concatenates the two .TXT files into a single file with the name specified by variable 2. The .TXT files are then deleted, and the file designated by variable 2 is output to the screen (with the /P parameter added to pause the display at each screenful of information).

The arguments' position in the batch-file command line distinguishes the variables: The first argument from the left is variable 1, the next argument is variable 2, and so on. To use this sample batch file, which we'll call LOOKER.BAT, you would enter something like this:

```
LOOKER TXT MYSTUFF.FIL
```

In this case, TXT is variable 1 and defines the file extension that the batch file will search for. MYSTUFF.FIL is variable 2 and is the file that will hold the information from the file search.

Example 3: Controlling the Display

So far, we've allowed the commands to echo to the screen as they execute. A nice touch would be to hide these command echoes and add instructions or prompts of our own. In this way, we can begin to turn batch files into small programs with a simple user interface.

The following code builds on the previous example and shows the screen-control commands:

```
@ECHO OFF
CLS
ECHO Thanks for using the File Extension Search Utility
ECHO just hang on a minute while I look things over...
XDIR C:\*.%1 /S>look1.txt
XDIR D:\*.%1 /S>look2.txt
COPY look1.txt+look2.txt %2
DEL LOOK?.TXT
@ECHO ON
PAUSE Are you ready to look over the list?
@TYPE %2 /P
```

The @ symbol prevents a command from being displayed on the screen. However, it doesn't prevent any messages from that command from being displayed. ECHO OFF turns off command echoing for all the commands that follow it; since it's preceded by an @, this command doesn't echo either. CLS clears the screen. The next two statements show another way ECHO can be used: If it's followed by a message, that message will be displayed.

Let's jump down to @ECHO ON. This turns command echoing on again, which we need to do for the PAUSE command that follows it. PAUSE will stop the batch file until a key is pressed and will also, as part of its "echo," display the text that follows PAUSE. (If we omitted ECHO or preceded PAUSE with an @, we would never see the message. The @ in front of the TYPE command is there to suppress its echo; it would be a waste of time to turn ECHO off again just for that line.)

The PAUSE line will be followed by the message

```
Strike a key when ready. . .
```

AUTOMATING OPERATIONS WITH BATCH FILES

and then wait until a key is pressed.

By the way, PAUSE lines look a bit messy. Our example looks something like this on the screen:

```
[DR DOS] C:\> PAUSE Are you ready to look over the list?
Strike a key when ready. . .
```

You can get around this in two ways:

1. Don't make the message part of the PAUSE statement; instead, use an ECHO statement.
2. Cheat. You can use EDITOR to embed a number of Ctrl-H (backspace) commands at the beginning of the PAUSE message. This will back up the message. If you enter enough Ctrl-H's, the message will overprint the prompt and PAUSE in the echo. If the message isn't long enough to obscure all of this, you can add spaces to the end of it.

Example 4: Branching and Looping

The following example is a bit contrived, but it does show both branching and looping statements. Branching statements cause a jump to another part of the batch file. (You can make branching, or anything else, conditional by adding an IF statement.) Looping statements repeat a command for a set of files or file specifications containing wildcards.

```
@ECHO OFF
CLS
IF "%1"=="1" GOSUB :killer
IF "%2"=="X" GOSUB :looker
GOTO END
:looker
ECHO Thanks for using the File Extension Search Utility
ECHO just hang on a minute while I look things over...
XDIR C:\*.%3 /S>look1.txt
XDIR D:\*.%3 /S>look2.txt
```

```
COPY look1.txt+look2.txt %4
DEL LOOK?.TXT
@ECHO ON
PAUSE Are you ready to look over the list?
@TYPE %4 /P
RETURN
:killer
ECHO Cleaning up...
FOR %%x IN (*.BAK *.zyx) DO XDEL C:\%%x /S /N
RETURN
:end
```

While you've seen most of these statements before in the preceding examples, this logic is quite a bit more sophisticated. The command line for this batch file takes four arguments. The statement IF "%1"=="1" GOSUB :killer tests argument 1 to see if it's equal to 1. If it is, execution branches to the label :killer; if it isn't, the batch file simply executes the next line in the file.

The commands that follow the label :killer are a variation on the example that deletes files. The statement

```
FOR %%x IN (*.BAK *.zyx) DO XDEL C:\%%x /S /N
```

is a FOR loop. The %%x is a variable that takes the file specifications, one at a time, in the parentheses. The command following the DO is then executed. In this case, C:*.BAK files are deleted, followed by C:*.ZYX files. After both types of files have been deleted, the RETURN takes us back to the line following the GOSUB:

```
IF "%2"=="X" GOSUB :looker
```

This does a GOSUB branch to :looker if the second argument on the batch-file command line is *X*. It's case-sensitive, by the way, so it won't match for *x*. The statements under :looker are from the example we used to scan for files. In this case, the third argument defines the file extension and the fourth defines the file to hold this information.

AUTOMATING OPERATIONS WITH BATCH FILES

Once again, a RETURN bounces us back to the line following the GOSUB, which in this case is a GOTO statement. The GOTO jumps to the label :end. This is an "absolute" jump because RETURN doesn't work with GOTO. After :end, we exit the batch file.

Some very powerful capabilities inherent in IF aren't shown in this example. IF statements can see whether two things are equal, as we just saw. However, they can check three other things as well: the value of ERRORLEVEL, whether a file exists, and whether a directory exists.

- ERRORLEVEL is set when a program error occurs. Your batch file can check this value and branch accordingly. IF ERRORLEVEL will match if the value is equal to or greater than the test value you used. If there is a match, the command on the IF ERRORLEVEL line is executed.

- IF EXIST determines whether or not a file actually exists. If so, the command on the IF EXIST line is executed.

- IF DIREXIST checks (you guessed it) for the existence of a directory. If one exists, the command on the IF DIREXIST line is executed.

These examples show some of the most often-used features of batch files. Now all you need to do is find some procedures to automate.

Batch-File Command Reference

This section lists the DR DOS batch-file commands.

@

SYNTAX

@command

command   Any DR DOS command.

FUNCTION

@, placed at the beginning of a command, hides that command when it is executed. The most common use is to hide the ECHO OFF command, which hides all the other commands in the batch file.

EXAMPLE

```
@ ECHO OFF
```

:*label*

SYNTAX

:*label*

label   The name of a label that defines a subroutine. The name can be up to eight characters long.

FUNCTION

Labels define the beginning of subroutines, which are sections within a batch file designed to perform a specific function. You can branch to subroutines with GOTO, GOSUB, or SWITCH.

EXAMPLE

```
GOTO :doit
     .
     .
     .
:doit
```

CALL

SYNTAX

CALL *batchfile*

batchfile   Another batch file. If it isn't in the same directory, it must be found in the directories listed in the directory path. If it isn't on the same drive as the calling batch file, you must add the drive designation letter to the path.

FUNCTION

You can use CALL much like GOSUB except that CALL runs another complete batch file rather than simply jumping to another subroutine. When the called batch file has executed, execution automatically returns to the original batch file and picks up with the line after the CALL statement.

EXAMPLE

This command calls the batch file CLEANUP.BAT and returns from that file to execute the ECHO statement.

```
CALL CLEANUP.BAT
ECHO Drive swept clean...
```

ECHO

SYNTAX

ECHO [OFF|ON|*text*]

OFF   Turns command echoing off so commands won't display as they're executed within the batch file. This doesn't prevent messages issued by the command from being displayed.

ON   Turns command echoing on and displays each command in the batch file as it executes.

text   A message you wish to display on the screen. It will display without regard to whether ECHO is ON or OFF.

FUNCTION

ECHO is generally used to turn off command echoing so you can't see each command as it executes. It's also used to display messages to the user. If you want to see whether ECHO is ON or OFF, issue the ECHO command with no parameters.

EXAMPLES

The following command turns echoing off. The @ appears before the command to prevent it from echoing as well.

```
@ECHO OFF
```

This command displays a message on the screen:

```
ECHO That's All Folks!
```

FOR

SYNTAX

FOR *%%filevar* IN (*file1*, *file2* [,*filen*]) DO *command*

%%filevar   A variable used to hold each file name, in sequence, in the series of files defined within the parentheses.

file1   The first file in the series of files. You can use wildcards in the file name and extension. If the file isn't in the current directory, you'll need to add the directory path to the file name. If the file doesn't reside on the current drive, you'll need to add that to the directory path.

file2 [,*filen*]   Additional files in the series. The rules just given for *file1* apply to these files as well.

command   Any DR DOS command, with the exception of another FOR command.

FUNCTION

FOR is a looping command: It executes the same command over and over again but with different files or file specifications as arguments. Each file in the series is used as the argument until the series of files is exhausted, at which point execution moves on to the next line.

By the way, you can use a FOR command outside the batch commands (that is, on the command line). The syntax is slightly different, however: Instead of placing a %% before the variable, you can use a single %.

EXAMPLE

This command in a batch file copies a series of files—first all *.EXE files, then all *.OVR files, and finally all *.DRV files—to the specified directory:

```
FOR %%x IN (*.EXE, *.OVR, *.DRV) DO COPY %%x D:\WEASLWRD
```

GOSUB

SYNTAX

GOSUB *:label*

label   An indication of the beginning of a subroutine.

FUNCTION

GOSUB is a branching command that causes execution to branch to the specified label. This lets you force the sequence of lines executed in the batch file to jump to a point that you designate. The nice thing about the GOSUB command is that when a RETURN is encountered in the batch file, execution jumps back to the line following the GOSUB. This allows you to branch to a subroutine to do a specific task, then return to the main part of the batch file when that task is complete.

EXAMPLE

In this example, execution branches to the label :backup. After the commands in :backup are complete, execution branches back to the line following the GOSUB.

```
GOSUB :backup
ECHO Files are now archived
    .
    .
    .
:backup
    .
    .
    .
RETURN
```

GOTO

SYNTAX
GOTO *:label*

label   An indication of the beginning of a subroutine.

FUNCTION

A GOTO statement is a branching command that causes batch-file execution to jump from the GOTO statement to the line with the specified label. Unlike GOSUB, GOTO is an absolute branch, and you can't return to the branching point with a RETURN. Use GOTOs only when you want to jump somewhere, like the end of the batch file, and don't want to return.

EXAMPLE

This command branches to the end of the batch file:

```
GOTO :end
    .
    .
    .
:end
```

IF

SYNTAX

IF [NOT] *qualifier command*

[NOT] Causes the command to execute if the condition isn't met.

qualifier Sets the condition that must be met. Qualifiers come in several flavors:

ERRORLEVEL *errnum* If the previous command in the batch file (such as BACKUP, RESTORE, or XCOPY) generated an error code that equals or is greater than the number specified by *errnum*, this condition has been met.

stringa==stringb If *stringa*, which can be a variable, equals *stringb*, which can also be a variable, the condition has been met. If either string might turn out to be blank, you can put the same character after each string. This prevents a syntax error when a blank string is encountered. An example is %1x==%2x. Note that two blanks will now cause a match.

EXIST *file* If the file specified in *file* exists, this condition has been met. *file* can have a directory path and drive designation.

DIREXIST *directory* If the directory specified in *directory* exists, the condition has been met.

command A DR DOS command.

FUNCTION

The IF statement provides for *conditional* execution—that is, the command is only executed if the conditions set by the qualifier are met. If NOT is added to the statement, the command is executed if the condition is not met.

EXAMPLES

This command tests to see if a RESTORE command executed correctly. If an error is detected, execution branches to the :tellem label.

```
RESTORE A: %1
IF ERRORLEVEL 1 GOSUB :tellem
```

This command checks to see if the variable is equal to OK and, if so, echoes a message:

```
IF %1x==OKx ECHO You Guessed It!
```

This command checks to see if a file exists. If so, execution branches to a label:

```
IF EXIST C:\WEASELWRD\WSLWRD.EXE GOTO :inst1
```

This command checks to see if a directory exists and, if not, makes such a directory:

```
IF NOT DIREXIST C:\TEMP MD C:\TEMP
```

PAUSE

SYNTAX

PAUSE [*message*]

message   A message to be displayed when PAUSE executes. ECHO must be ON for the message to display.

FUNCTION

PAUSE provides a way to stop batch-file execution until a key is pressed. The following always displays after PAUSE executes:

```
Strike a key when ready...
```

The optional message only displays when @ is omitted from the statement and ECHO is ON. If you really want a message to precede the pause, a better method is to use an ECHO statement.

EXAMPLE

The following statements pause the batch program to let the user know that XDEL has wiped the disk clean:

```
ECHO I'm ready for the next disk now
PAUSE
```

REM

SYNTAX
REM [*comment*]

comment   A remark placed in the batch file.

FUNCTION
REM, which can be abbreviated as a semicolon, is used to place comments in batch files. If you place REM at the beginning of another statement, it will prevent that statement from executing. If ECHO is ON, REM will display along with its comment.

EXAMPLES
The following command inserts a comment into the file:

```
:killer
; This label deletes *.BAK files.
```

This command prevents a statement from executing:

```
REM GOTO :killer
```

RETURN

SYNTAX
RETURN

FUNCTION
RETURN is used with GOSUB or SWITCH. When the routine encounters a RETURN after branching to a label with a GOSUB or SWITCH command, execution jumps to the line following the GOSUB or SWITCH.

EXAMPLE
The following RETURN branches back to the line after the GOSUB:

```
GOSUB :cleanup
ECHO All cleaned up...
      .
      .
      .
:cleanup
      .
      .
      .
RETURN
```

SHIFT

SYNTAX
   SHIFT

FUNCTION

Just in case nine variables aren't enough, SHIFT allows you to access more. It also lets you change which value corresponds to which variable.

Suppose you want to enter 11 variables for a batch-file command line. It would look something like this:

```
MYBATCH A B C D E F G H I J K
```

This would map the parameters as follows:

   %1=A
   %2=B
   %3=C
   %4=D
   %5=E
   %6=D
   %7=E
   %8=F
   %9=G

Since you can only have nine variables, you normally can't access the other two. However, SHIFT remaps the variables as follows:

   %1=B
   %2=C
   %3=D
   %4=E
   %5=F
   %6=G

AUTOMATING OPERATIONS WITH BATCH FILES

%7=H
%8=I
%9=J

Another SHIFT command would remap the variables as follows:

%1=C

.

.

.

%9=K

In effect, it allows you to reach all 11 variables.

You can also use SHIFT, along with the :label and GOTO statement, to execute the same command for a set of variables. For instance, the following example shows how a FIND command looks for a series of strings in a set of files. The strings are set by the variables in the batch-file command line, and each variable in turn is SHIFTed to %1.

```
:again
IF %1x=x GOTO END
FIND "%1" *.DOC
ECHO When you have read the list...
PAUSE
SHIFT
GOTO :again
```

SWITCH

SYNTAX
SWITCH *labela*, *labelb*, [*labeli*]

labela	The first label in the series. It corresponds to the number 1, or to Return.
labelb, [*labeli*]	The second and optional subsequent labels in the series. The second label corresponds to 2, the third to 3, and so on. You can have up to nine labels.

FUNCTION
SWITCH lets you enter the value of the label you wish to branch to. You'll need to use ECHO commands to explain what these choices mean. As with a GOSUB, a RETURN statement branches back to the line following the SWITCH statement.

If you enter a number that doesn't correspond to a label on the list, SWITCH will patiently wait for you to enter one that does. If you press Enter, SWITCH will branch to the first label on the list.

EXAMPLE
The following routine allows a user to choose between two functions:

```
ECHO 1 = Make a backup copy of the hard drive.
ECHO 2 = Restore hard disk from previous backup.
SWITCH backup, getback
```

CHAPTER 9

Taking Charge of Your Disk

DR DOS provides a number of advanced tools that help you use your disk drives to their fullest as well as recover from accidents:

PC-Kwik   An advanced disk-caching package that can dramatically improve disk performance.

SuperStor   A disk-compression utility that doubles or triples disk storage capacity.

DISKOPT   A utility that arranges files contiguously, reducing seek time and improving disk performance.

UNDELETE   A utility for recovering deleted files.

Collectively, these tools are known as DiskMAX.

Kicking the Drive Into Gear with PC-Kwik

Disk-caching software keeps information read from the drive in memory. If an application tries to access that information again, the disk cache supplies the information, eliminating the delay of going to the disk again. Since transfers from memory are many times faster than transfers from disk, a disk cache can dramatically improve system performance.

PC-Kwik is a very intelligent disk-caching package because it determines which information is most commonly requested and keeps that in the cache. This further improves system performance. In addition, PC-Kwik speeds up the process of writing information to disk by holding or buffering it. This reduces the cycle of read-from-memory and write-to-disk. The package works with both hard disks and floppy drives; however, it has no effect on RAM drives or remote drives on a network.

PC-Kwik can run in either extended or expanded memory. If these are not available, it can be run from regular memory, but a system upgrade should be considered if possible. Most applications these days either require or can use extended or expanded memory. PC-Kwik is also clever enough to share extended or expanded memory with applications that need it.

PC-Kwik is a terminate-and-stay-resident (TSR) program. You install it through the DR DOS installation or SETUP program by choosing DiskMAX from the configuration menu (Figure 9-1). The DiskMAX screen (Figure 9-2) lists the various disk utility options, including the PC-Kwik disk cache. Selecting this displays the meat of the PC-Kwik configuration (Figure 9-3). The screen asks you four questions; these are discussed in the following sections.

1. "Do You Run Microsoft Windows in Standard or Enhanced Modes?"

If you're running Windows, you're almost certainly running in either standard mode (the usual mode for an 80286-equipped machine) or 386 enhanced mode (typical of 80386 and 80486 configurations). The only other choice is real mode, which is hardly useful and is mostly used with PC- and XT-type machines (or with 286/386 machines that are not fully compatible with Windows).

If you tell the SETUP program you're running Windows, it will load a special driver (PCKWIN.SYS) through the CONFIG.SYS file. This is in addition to the PC-Kwik program itself, SUPERPCK.EXE, which is loaded through the AUTOEXEC.BAT file.

When using PC-Kwik with Windows, you need to disable two drivers that Windows itself has loaded: HIMEM.SYS, which is the Windows extended memory manager, and SMARTDRV.SYS, the Windows disk-caching software.

TAKING CHARGE OF YOUR DISK

```
┌─────────────────────────────────────────────────────────────────┐
│┌──────────────────┐                          ┌────────────────┐│
││ Digital Research │                          │DR DOS 6.0 SETUP││
│└──────────────────┘                          └────────────────┘│
│                                                                 │
│        Select the area you wish to configure from the list below.│
│                                                                 │
│        ▌ MemoryMAX                                              │
│                                                                 │
│        ▌ TaskMAX                                                │
│                                                                 │
│        ▶ DiskMAX                                                │
│                                                                 │
│        ▌ ViewMAX                                                │
│                                                                 │
│        ▌ Country and Keyboard                                   │
│                                                                 │
│        ▌ System Parameters                                      │
│                                                                 │
│        ▌ Optional Device Drivers and Utilities                  │
│                                                                 │
│        ▌ Security                                               │
│                                                                 │
│        ▌ Save Changes and Exit                                  │
│                                                                 │
│ F1=Help  ↕=next/prev line  <Enter>=select option  <Esc>=prev screen  F10=abort │
└─────────────────────────────────────────────────────────────────┘
```

Figure 9-1. The SETUP main menu with DiskMAX selected.

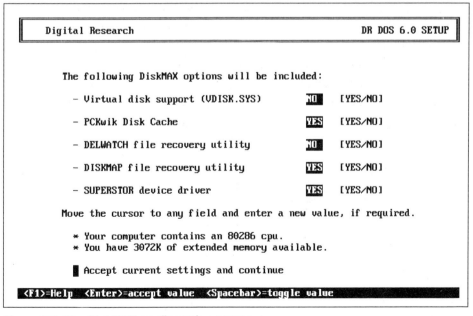

Figure 9-2. The DiskMAX configuration screen.

211

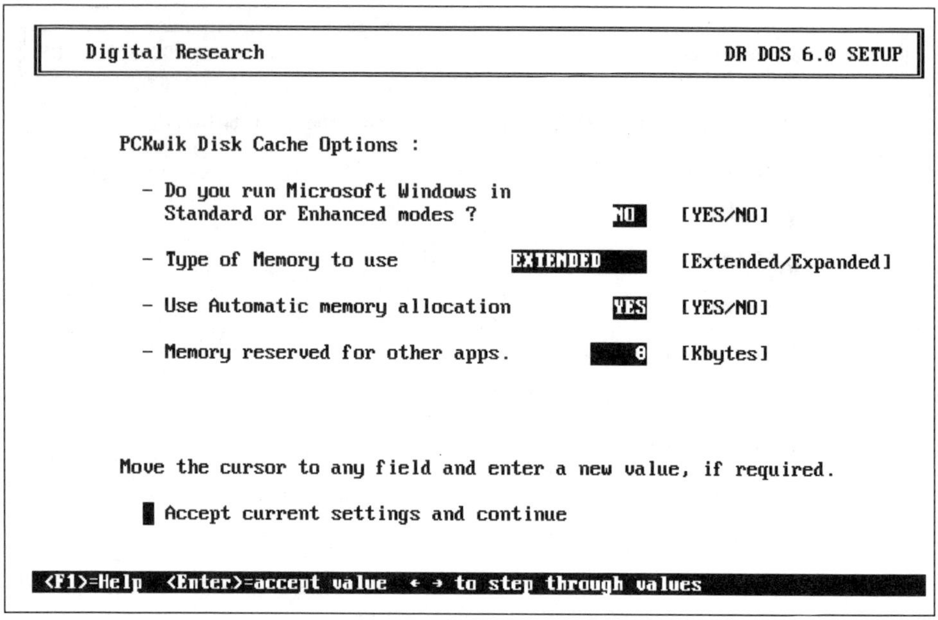

DR DOS BY EXAMPLE

```
┌──────────────────────────────────────────────────────────────────┐
│ ┌──────────────────────┐                                         │
│ │  Digital Research    │                          DR DOS 6.0 SETUP│
│ └──────────────────────┘                                         │
│                                                                  │
│       PCKwik Disk Cache Options :                                │
│                                                                  │
│         - Do you run Microsoft Windows in                        │
│           Standard or Enhanced modes ?        NO     [YES/NO]    │
│                                                                  │
│         - Type of Memory to use             EXTENDED [Extended/Expanded]│
│                                                                  │
│         - Use Automatic memory allocation     YES    [YES/NO]    │
│                                                                  │
│         - Memory reserved for other apps.       0    [Kbytes]    │
│                                                                  │
│                                                                  │
│       Move the cursor to any field and enter a new value, if required.│
│                                                                  │
│       ■ Accept current settings and continue                     │
│                                                                  │
│ ▓<F1>=Help  <Enter>=accept value  ← → to step through values▓    │
└──────────────────────────────────────────────────────────────────┘
```

Figure 9-3. The PC-Kwik configuration screen.

For maximum efficiency, use a DR DOS memory manager (HIDOS.SYS or EMM386.SYS) *and* the PC-Kwik disk cache. For these to work properly, the lines for HIMEM.SYS and SMARTDRV.SYS should be removed from the CONFIG.SYS file. This can be done with the EDITOR utility in DR DOS or with the SYSEDIT utility in Windows 3.0. SYSEDIT.EXE is an undocumented Windows utility that resides in the \WINDOWS\SYS directory. SYSEDIT provides a NOTEPAD-like editor that automatically opens four files: CONFIG.SYS, AUTOEXEC.BAT, WIN.INI, and SYSTEM.INI.

When running Windows in 386 enhanced mode, you need to add a line to the SYSTEM.INI file. (See how useful the SYSEDIT program is?) This line allows PC-Kwik to use its advanced support for diskettes and hard drives. Use SYSEDIT's search capability to find the section marked [386ENH]. At the end of the [386ENH] section, add the following line:

```
VirtualHDIrq=FALSE
```

TAKING CHARGE OF YOUR DISK

Don't worry about upper- and lowercase; Windows doesn't care.

2. "Type of Memory to Use"

PC-Kwik can use either extended or expanded memory. If Windows is running in either standard or enhanced mode, PC-Kwik must be run in extended memory. If you're not running Windows, you can choose between extended and expanded memory. Note that the resident portion of the PC-Kwik TSR consumes less memory if you choose expanded memory.

3. "Use Automatic Memory Allocation"

This feature allows PC-Kwik to share expanded or extended memory (whichever it is using) with other applications that might require such memory. PC-Kwik does this automatically, and you need never notice that it happens. By default, PC-Kwik will lend up to half of its available memory.

If application programs crash while PC-Kwik is running, some memory may need to be reserved specifically for those applications. This can be done here in the configuration menu or with SUPERPCK parameters. In the configuration menu, you'll be asked to specify the cache size and the amount of cache memory available for lending. You'll also need to set the next field in the PC-Kwik configuration menu.

4. "Memory Reserved for Other Apps"

A specific amount of extended or expanded memory for other applications can be allocated here.

After completing these questions, go through the save-and-exit procedure for SETUP or INSTALL. AUTOEXEC.BAT (and CONFIG.SYS, if you're using Windows) will reflect the changes. An onscreen prompt will ask if you want the SETUP or installation program to reboot your computer. Reboot to make PC-Kwik active.

DR DOS BY EXAMPLE

Configuring PC-Kwik

Like most other commands in DR DOS, PC-Kwik can be configured with parameters. However, it's a bit different in that its parameters often end in a plus or minus symbol. The - turns a parameter off, and the + turns it on. Usually, the default is a plus.

To experiment with these parameters without rebooting, first disable PC-Kwik (to reinstall it with the new parameters). To disable PC-Kwik, enter the following command at the DR DOS command line:

```
SUPERPCK /U
```

This removes PC-Kwik from memory. It can be reinstalled from the DR DOS command line.

PC-Kwik Parameters

PC-Kwik has two levels of parameters: standard and advanced. The advanced options are used to adapt PC-Kwik to particular hardware configurations. The syntax for using all options is:

```
SUPERPCK /parameter /parameter+|-
```

The following command lists all available PC-Kwik parameters:

```
SUPERPCK /?
```

Parameters Loaded at Installation Time

This first set of parameters can be issued only when PC-Kwik is installed.

/-drive

Turns caching off for the specified drive. Several commands can be strung together. For example, this command turns caching off for the A: and D: drives:

```
SUPERPCK /-A /-D
```

TAKING CHARGE OF YOUR DISK

/&U-

Prevents part of PC-Kwik from being moved to upper memory. By default, PC-Kwik loads part of itself into upper memory. How much it loads depends on whether extended, expanded, or conventional memory is available. If you're using expanded memory, PC-Kwik will load only a small section of itself into upper memory. If you're using extended memory, the tables, code, and track buffers will be loaded into upper memory. If you're using conventional memory, all of PC-Kwik will be loaded into upper memory. Of course, all these scenarios require that sufficient upper memory exist.

/A+

Loads PC-Kwik into expanded memory. A LIM-compatible expanded memory manager is required for this to work. This is the default parameter when expanded memory is detected but no extended memory is found.

/EM+

Uses extended memory for PK-Kwik caching. It also sets PC-Kwik to use the minimum amount of conventional memory. This is the default if extended memory is detected but no expanded memory is available.

/I+|-

Sets PC-Kwik to display its drive table when it is installed.

/L:*memory*

By default, PC-Kwik will lend half of its available memory to other programs. However, the /L parameter can be used to specify the amount of memory made available. This is important because some programs require more expanded or

215

extended memory than PC-Kwik's default allowance. Specify the memory in kilobytes.

/L-

Disables memory lending.

/P+

Causes PC-Kwik to display a list of parameters that are in effect.

/R:*memory*

Reserves a specified number of kilobytes for exclusive use by other applications. All remaining memory is dedicated to PC-Kwik. If only conventional memory is used, by default, 480 KB is allocated for other programs. With expanded or extended memory, by default, no memory is specifically allocated for applications (it is lent to applications as needed).

Run-Time Parameters

The following parameters can be used while PC-Kwik is running.

/D

Disables disk caching and resets caching measurements (though PC-Kwik remains in memory). These measurements consist of the number of logical transfers (transfer requests), the number of physical transfers (actual transfers), the number of transfers that were saved, and the percentage of transfers that were saved. This gives you some idea of how effective caching is on your system.

/E

Reverses the effects of the /D parameter and reenables caching.

/F

The "flush" parameter. It clears the disk cache and resets measurements to zero.

/M

Displays disk-cache measurements.

/P

Lists all currently active parameters.

/U

Removes PC-Kwik from memory.

Advanced Parameters

Advanced parameters aren't usually necessary, but they can improve performance or adapt PC-Kwik to specific hardware configurations. These parameters can be used only when PC-Kwik is initially run.

/B+

Engages the batch copying capabilities; it's on by default. Batch copying means that PC-Kwik transfers data to and from the disk in batches. This can improve performance, especially when extended memory is in use.

There is a possible glitch here. This option may not work when serial communications, such as modems that run at 2,400 baud or faster, are in use. If you notice trouble with communications programs, use the /B- parameter.

/D+

Turns on advanced support for floppy drives. By default, PC-Kwik tries to determine if your floppy drive controller is 100% IBM compatible. If it is, PC-Kwik enables advanced support. If not, advanced support is disabled. If you experience problems with your floppies, set this option to /D-.

/Ex:*memory*

Sets the lowest extended memory address available for caching. The x option can be either M (which minimizes conventional memory use) or P (which improves performance). You should only need to use this parameter if there is a conflict between PC-Kwik and another program installed in extended memory. The idea is to force PC-Kwik to a higher memory address than the other program.

Before resorting to this, try the /R or /S parameter. The default lowest extended memory address is 1024.

/G+

If PC-Kwik determines that the boot sector information it finds on the drive conflicts with what the BIOS says about the drive, PC-Kwik displays a message to that effect. The /G+ parameter sets PC-Kwik to use the information found on the drive. Conversely, /G- tells PC-Kwik to accept the BIOS information. To ensure you'll have enough time to read the conflict message, use the /K+ parameter.

/H+

Enables advanced caching support for hard drives. This requires a 100% IBM-compatible disk controller, which is available on most systems. The /H- parameter turns off advanced disk caching and uses a less efficient caching scheme. At installation, PC-Kwik tries to determine whether your controller is 100% compatible. Advanced support works with almost all MFM, RLL, IDE, and ESDI control-

TAKING CHARGE OF YOUR DISK

lers. It has been tested with Adaptek, Allways, and Future Domain SCSI controllers and works just fine with my Seagate ST296N SCSI drive.

/K+

Tells PC-Kwik to pause until a key is pressed after displaying a warning. The /K- parameter removes the pause.

/O+

Enables the use of an optional algorithm for advanced hard-drive caching. This algorithm gives priority to disk writes. Use of advanced caching is controlled by the /D+ and /H+ parameters.

/Q+
Enables a faster return to the DR DOS command line when advanced caching is in effect. Commands can be typed as soon as the prompt returns, but don't remove disks from the floppy drives until the light goes out. The /Q+ option works best in conjunction with the /O+ option.

/S:*memory*

Sets aside a specified number of kilobytes of memory for exclusive use by PC-Kwik. Normally, PC-Kwik handles this allocation automatically. When you set aside a cache in extended or expanded memory, it can be any value between 64 and 16,384 KB. If you're using conventional memory, the range is 64 to 512 KB.

/T+

Causes PC-Kwik to read an entire disk track into cache whenever an application attempts to read something from that track. The idea behind this is that if the file is contiguous, the process is streamlined by pulling the whole track into the cache.

However, if the files are segmented (stored a sector here and a block there on different tracks), or when you're reading lots of small files, this option won't help much.

To see how segmented the drive is, run DISKOPT (discussed later in this chapter). If the drive is segmented, DISKOPT can also be used to make the files contiguous.

If you want to reduce memory consumption, if your files are fragmented, or if your disk has many bad sectors that have been locked out, use /T-.

/T has two other variations. If lots of memory is available and the files are contiguous, the /TL option speeds things up by setting PC-Kwik to load the largest track size on the disk. Track size can be specified with /T:*tt*, where *tt* is the number of sectors per track.

/V+

Allows PC-Kwik to use volume-change detection hardware if it exists in the disk drive. This hardware is often built into disk drives (but not 360-KB drives) and provides an internal signal to DOS if the disk is removed. Using it can further improve performance, especially if you're using floppy drives to any great extent.

/W+

Checks the disk to see if it already has the data requested for writing. If the identical data already exists, the write request is ignored.

Notes on Using PC-Kwik

When you use PC-Kwik with TaskMAX, be sure to load PC-Kwik *before* TaskMAX. If not, PC-Kwik may actually read old or erroneous data.

When using PC-Kwik with Bernoulli drives, you must install another driver in the CONFIG.SYS file by adding this line:

```
DEVICE=C:\DRDOS\PCKWIK.SYS
```

Remember to change the C:\DRDOS directory specification if DR DOS was loaded into some other directory. Even if you intend to tell PC-Kwik not to cache the

Bernoulli drive, you must include the PCKWIK.SYS driver after the Bernoulli driver, and the Bernoulli box must be switched on during boot-up. If the IOMCACHE driver is in use with the Bernoulli box, remove it.

The number of buffers can be significantly reduced once PC-Kwik is in place. This can save conventional memory. Try reducing the number of buffers to three or four (10 if you're running Microsoft Windows) and check the system's performance when running applications.

Compressing Data with SuperStor

SuperStor is almost like magic, although it is magic that exacts a price. On my system, I have a partition in which I store graphics files. These usually take up a lot of disk space, so I thought this would be a nice application for SuperStor. The partition has only about 20 MB of space, but SuperStor provides between 2:1 and 4:1 compression of the graphics files. This turns my little 20-MB partition into a huge storage area.

I use SuperStor to compress just a single partition. It can be used to compress an entire hard drive, multiple hard drives, and even floppies. The trade-off is in performance. SuperStor compresses and decompresses the data automatically, slowing down disk activity. Since my home system has only an 80286 processor and I run some pretty intense applications, I don't want to degrade application performance. With a faster computer and faster hard drive than my Seagate SCSI unit, the slower disk access might be negligible.

A second penalty is SuperStor's use of conventional memory. It requires a minimum of 28 KB to run and usually takes a bit more. However, that seems a small price to pay for the tremendous jump in drive storage capacity.

Even when SuperStor can't compress the data in a file, it still saves disk space. Hard drives have rather large block sizes (2,048 to 4,096 bytes). SuperStor uses 512-byte sectors and therefore wastes less space. This is especially helpful when you have lots of small files.

The following table lists compression ratios quoted by Digital Research and, in some cases, compressions that I have tested. This should give you some idea how much data compression to expect from SuperStor.

Before Running SuperStor

There are a number of things to do before running SuperStor. Go through this list *before* installing SuperStor and compressing any data, or you may not like the results.

1. Back up all your data.

If a power failure occurs while you're compressing existing data, that data may very well be lost. Back everything up first using the DOS BACKUP utility, FASTBACK from Fifth Generation Systems, a tape backup unit, or whatever; just make sure you do it.

2. Decide whether to compress the whole disk or just a partition.

If you're compressing the whole disk, no problem. To compress a partition, either let SuperStor create a SuperStor partition, or use FDISK to create a new DOS partition for use by SuperStor. By creating a DOS partition, you can control what gets compressed. When SuperStor creates its partition, it compresses everything it can find and leaves an empty, uncompressed partition.

If you use FDISK to partition your drive, be aware that all data on the drive will be lost. Now you know why you backed up the drive.

3. Determine how Microsoft Windows will be handled.

If Windows is running in 386 enhanced mode, there may be a permanent swap file. Unfortunately, you can't have a permanent swap file on a compressed drive. Either remove the swap file (by running Windows in real mode—WIN /R—and then running the SWAPFILE program) or make sure the drive with the swap file isn't compressed.

4. Remove any copy-protected software.

Some copy-protection schemes, especially those that don't rely on hardware "locks" that attach to a parallel or serial port, won't accept the files after they have been compressed. If you have such software, follow the deinstallation instructions that accompany the product. Reinstall the copy-protected application after SuperStor is fully installed.

5. Make sure your disk is "clean."

Run CHKDSK, reclaim any loose chains, and resolve any cross-linked files before proceeding. Remember that you need the /F option for changes made by CHKDSK to take effect.

6. Make sure you have enough hard drive space.

SuperStor requires a minimum of 1.5 MB of space to compress existing files.

Installing SuperStor

Before installing SuperStor, make sure you're at the DR DOS prompt and that no other environments, such as TaskMAX, Windows, or DesqView, are running. If any of these environments are active, you may corrupt your drive.

Installation consists of two steps. The first step is to install the SuperStor drivers in the CONFIG.SYS file:

```
DEVICE=C:\SSTORDRV.SYS
DEVICE=C:\DEVSWAP.COM
```

This is done by the DR DOS installation or SETUP program. Select SuperStor from the DiskMAX configuration screen (see Figure 9-4). After you go through the save-and-exit process, the installation or SETUP program will want to reboot the computer to load these drivers. You might not want to do this if the PC/NFS network or some other nonstandard network is installed. If the SuperStor drivers and network drivers conflict, the computer will lock up. Normally, that's not such a terrible thing; if the conflict is taking place during CONFIG.SYS execution, however, when you reboot you'll be right back in the same mess.

DR DOS BY EXAMPLE

```
              c:\config.sys  chr=243 col=1                          ins.  ^J=help
DEVICE=C:\DRDOS\HIDOS.SYS /B=FFFF
HIDOS=ON
SHELL=C:\COMMAND.COM C:\ /P /E:512
BREAK=OFF
HIBUFFERS=20
FILES=30
FCBS=2,2
FASTOPEN=0
LASTDRIVE=E
HISTORY=ON
HISTORY=OFF
COUNTRY=001,,C:\DRDOS\COUNTRY.SYS
HIDEVICE=C:\DRDOS\PCKWIN.SYS
HIDEVICE=C:\SSTORDRV.SYS
DEVICE=C:\DEVSWAP.COM
```

Figure 9-4. The DiskMAX configuration screen in SETUP.

When you're using MS-DOS or PC-DOS, such a predicament forces you to boot from a floppy. Fortunately, DR DOS can stop and ask if you want to load a particular driver in the CONFIG.SYS file. To do this, use EDITOR to edit the CONFIG.SYS file, and place a question mark as the first character in the device line. Now SuperStor's device driver lines look something like this:

```
?DEVICE=C:\SSTORDRV.SYS
?DEVICE=C:\DEVSWAP.COM
```

Note that there is no space between the ? and the DEVICE statement. The question mark provides some protection against a lock-up that would prevent you from booting the system. After adding the question marks, reboot. When DR DOS asks if you want to load the SuperStor device drivers, say yes (Y). If all goes well, remove the question marks later with EDITOR.

Now for step 2. When you reach the DOS prompt, run the SuperStor program SSTOR. A screen similar to the one shown in Figure 9-5 appears. Now you can choose to compress the drive. SuperStor can also compress up to eight partitions of no more than 512 MB each. Or you can choose to compress only a section of the drive, leaving a specified amount of drive space free for things that will remain uncompressed. Uncompressed areas can always be compressed later; however, compressed sections can't be decompressed easily. Decompressing a section causes it to lose its data, so do a backup first.

TAKING CHARGE OF YOUR DISK

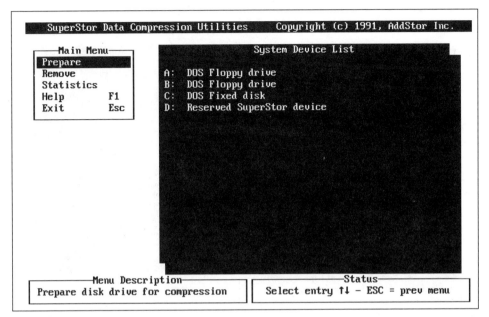

Figure 9-5. The opening SuperStor screen.

Don't worry. Except for being a bit slower, compressed sections and partitions work just about the same as uncompressed sections. Some DR DOS commands, such as XDIR, display how efficient the compression is on each file. Note that you can't UNINSTAL DR DOS from a compressed drive.

Figure 9-6 shows a typical message after Prepare is selected. In this example, SSTOR wants to know whether to compress the C: drive. If there are other drives or partitions, SSTOR asks which one to compress.

After you select the drive or partition to compress, SSTOR asks whether to reserve uncompressed space. If you answer yes, you can specify the amount of space to be left uncompressed. The uncompressed area will be given a new drive letter as if it were an FDISK partition.

Now SSTOR will go about the business of compressing your files. This can take a while, especially with a reasonably large and reasonably full drive. If you care to watch, SSTOR reports its progress as it goes. This is the risky part, by the way: A power outage at this point can destroy your data. (You did make a backup, didn't you?)

DR DOS BY EXAMPLE

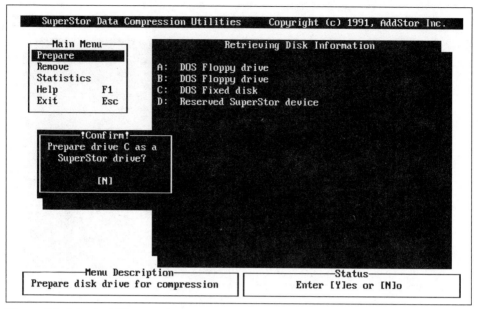

Figure 9-6. A typical "Prepare" message.

After a while, SSTOR completes its task and you can check on how well it did. The Statistics option on the SSTOR menu produces a display like that shown in Figure 9-7, and this can be used to see how much space has been saved. In this instance, the average compression ratio was 1.4:1, for a total space savings of 34%. Not outrageous, but not bad either.

On the subject of statistics, I should explain some of the other things that are reported. "SSTOR Bytes used" is the total number of bytes already used on the compressed drive or partition. "SSTOR Free (est)" is an estimate of the total storage space available and is based on the compression average. DR DOS commands, such as DIR and XDIR, also report the estimate of available space. "SSTOR Total (est)" is another estimate, derived from the sum of the estimated space remaining and the actual space already spoken for. "Actual Bytes Used" is the number of "real" bytes used by SSTOR to store data on the disk. In this case, we crammed 8 MB into 5 MB. "Actual Free" is the total number of "real," uncompressed bytes remaining on the disk. "Actual Total" is the uncompressed size of the hard drive—in this case, 20 MB.

To return to the command line, select Exit.

TAKING CHARGE OF YOUR DISK

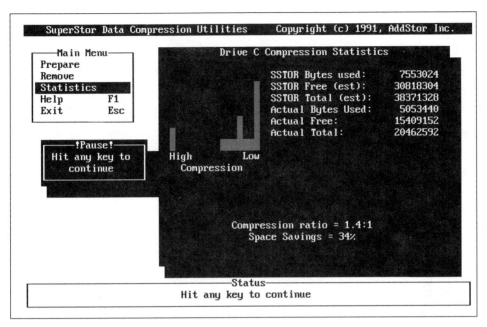

Figure 9-7. Postcompression statistics.

Working with Compressed Drives

There are a few odd things you should know about compressed drives. If the entire bootable drive or partition is compressed, SuperStor creates a small, uncompressed partition for the system files and device drivers. After all, until the SuperStor drivers are loaded, the system doesn't know how to read compressed data. Therefore, the boot-up information must be uncompressed. This means that there are two configuration files: DCONFIG.SYS, which lives in the uncompressed drive, and CONFIG.SYS, which resides in the compressed drive. DCONFIG.SYS has the SSTORDRV.SYS and DEVSWAP.COM drivers, which must be loaded in that order. After these drivers are loaded, DCONFIG.SYS chains to CONFIG.SYS.

Our sample system had only one partition (C:), so the uncompressed partition became D:. If there is already a D: partition or drive, then the uncompressed partition will be somewhere else. To see the uncompressed drive, keep logging on to drives (by cycling through the letters of the alphabet) until you find a drive that has DCONFIG.SYS.

DR DOS BY EXAMPLE

The DCONFIG.SYS file should never be edited, moved, or erased. Doing so will make the system unable to read its compressed areas.

I've already discussed not running SuperStor from Microsoft Windows and not having a permanent Windows swap file in a compressed area. Otherwise, SSTOR is totally Windows-compatible. As for other DOS applications, be aware that some use fixed-length files that can't be compressed. There is nothing wrong with this, except that it will cause a surprising increase in the amount of space used when compared with compressed data.

Cleaning Up Files with DISKOPT

When you start out with a "fresh" hard drive with lots of empty space on it, files are written in sequentially allocated blocks. These are called *contiguous* files, and accessing them is quicker because DR DOS doesn't need to send the drive heads hither and yon to collect data. In fact, the data is often stored on the same track, which makes the track-buffering option in PC-Kwik work that much better.

As files are added and erased over time, bits and pieces of them become scattered over the hard drive. These are called *segmented* files, and access to them is slower because they can't be read in one smooth motion. That's where DISKOPT comes in. DISKOPT goes about the tedious task of shuffling all the data on the hard drive until the files are contiguous again. It also can presort directories, which is nice but unnecessary considering the capabilities of DIR and XDIR.

DISKOPT works on uncompressed and SuperStor-compressed drives and partitions, and I use it every month or two. It really does help performance. Before running DISKOPT, you should do the following:

1. Back up everything on the drive or partition. DISKOPT is relatively safe, but why take the chance?

2. Run CHKDSK with the /F parameter to clean up any loose chains and resolve any cross-linked files before running DISKOPT.

TAKING CHARGE OF YOUR DISK

3. Make sure no multitasking or task-switching environments, such as TaskMAX, Windows, or DesqView, are running. DISKOPT will relocate files and rebuild the file allocation table, which means applications running concurrently with DISKOPT will likely corrupt your disk.

4. Uninstall any copy-protected software. DISKOPT will move things around; the only things it won't touch are files with the system attribute set.

To optimize your disk, type DISKOPT at the command line. The DISKOPT screen looks something like Figure 9-8 and maps the files on your disks graphically. The dots are files, and the blocks are open spaces. Dots scattered about in the area of open space represent fragmented files.

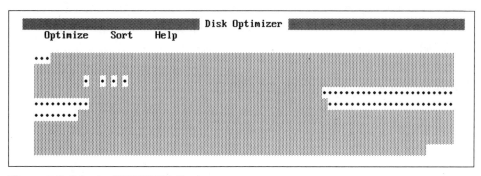

Figure 9-8. A typical DISKOPT display.

To run the program, first press Alt-S to pull down the sorting menu. Now select the way directories will be sorted (if you want them sorted at all). The options are as follows:

Name   Sorts the files alphabetically.

Extension   Does a double sort, by extension and by name.

Date   Sorts the files in date order, oldest to youngest.

Size   Sorts by size, smallest to largest.

Cluster   Sorts by file starting cluster (the first disk cluster used by a file). This is of no use to you but does somewhat reduce the time it takes to optimize the disk.

No sort   Doesn't sort.

After selecting a sort, press Alt-O. If you want to change drives, you can do it from here (Alt-D also selects this command). Otherwise, you can choose to optimize and then go make coffee. Actually, you'll probably have time to make dinner, especially if you have an 80-MB or larger drive.

If you really need to abort the process, press the Esc key. This shouldn't do any damage, but you might want to run CHKDSK just to make sure. Return to the command line with Alt-X.

Bringing Files Back With UNDELETE

UNDELETE rescues deleted files. Actually, when a file is deleted, the operating system doesn't really delete the contents of the file. What happens is that space occupied by the data is made available for the file system. This means that if subsequent operations don't overwrite the data, you'll be able to recover your files. UNDELETE's effectiveness depends on the precautions taken and what has been done since the files were deleted. If you're using DELWATCH, the file can almost certainly be recovered. DELWATCH plays a game with deleted files, marking them for deletion but preserving their file areas so they can't be used by DR DOS. This prevents file space from being recovered until DELPURGE is run, but it does mean that the files will be recovered. See the DELWATCH section in Appendix A for more details.

If you aren't using DELWATCH, be careful not to create, modify, copy, or move any files until the deleted file or files are recovered. Don't do anything that would cause DR DOS to overwrite the data contained in the space that formerly belonged to the deleted file. If you do, the data from the deleted file can't be recovered.

TAKING CHARGE OF YOUR DISK

If the file areas haven't been overwritten, UNDELETE should be able to recover the files without assistance. You can improve UNDELETE's chances a bit by running DISKMAP. (Just don't run it after deleting the files; by then it's too late.) DISKMAP makes a copy of the file allocation table and places it in a file that UNDELETE can access. This gives UNDELETE a good idea where files were located at the time the copy was made. The more often DISKMAP is run, the better. At a minimum, run it from AUTOEXEC.BAT so that it runs daily.

With that bit of preparation out of the way, load UNDELETE. Figure 9-9 shows an UNDELETE screen from my system. Note which files have been erased and their current fate. Most of them have had their file space overwritten and are not recoverable. The AUTOEXEC.BAT file is recoverable, and there is a recent DISKMAP file to help (as noted by the word DISKMAP). If DELWATCH were active, all these files would be recoverable and would be marked "DELWATCH."

```
                              Undelete
   File    Sort    Help
                            c:\stuff

     ..              DIRECTORY  8-31-91    3:18pm
     autoexec bat         508  11-03-91    9:48pm  Diskmap
     in9      pix       2,181  10-19-91    2:56pm  Cannot recover
     ina      pcx      10,250  10-20-91    1:20pm  Cannot recover
     ina      pix       2,501  10-20-91    1:19pm  Cannot recover
     inb      pcx       7,357  10-20-91    1:20pm  Cannot recover
     inb      pix       2,415  10-20-91    1:19pm  Cannot recover
     marker   pcx      13,765   9-26-91    9:20pm  Cannot recover
     marker   pix       2,669   9-26-91    9:19pm  Cannot recover
     mem      pcx       8,678  10-03-91    2:07pm  Cannot recover
     mem1     pix       1,752  10-03-91    2:06pm  Cannot recover
     mem2     pix       2,647  10-03-91    2:07pm  Cannot recover
     memi     pcx       5,524  10-09-91    1:51pm  Cannot recover
     memi2    pcx       9,775  10-09-91    1:53pm  Cannot recover
     menu     pcx      10,167   9-26-91    9:46pm  Cannot recover
     menu     pix       2,252   9-24-91   10:02pm  Cannot recover
     nofile   pcx       4,683   9-26-91    9:46pm  Cannot recover
```

Figure 9-9. Typical UNDELETE display.

If you don't like the way files are displayed when you enter UNDELETE, access the Sort menu with Alt-S and display them any way you like. You can sort by file name, file extension (and file name), file creation date, file size, or recovery method, or not sort at all.

Alt-F brings up the file menu. (The arrow keys can also be used to bounce between menus once a menu is active.) The commands here are:

Undelete   Starts the file recovery process for selected files. This can also be triggered with Alt-U.

Change drive   Lets you pick a different disk drive. To change directories, scroll to the top of the file display until the highlight is over the desired directory (or at least the next directory up the chain) and press Enter.

Select   Selects a file for undeletion. This can also be done by placing the highlight bar over the file and pressing the space bar. Selected files are tagged with a diamond. If you change drives or directories, you'll lose your selections.

Select group   Allows you to use a wildcard mask to select files. For instance, *.BAK selects all files with the .BAK extension.

Deselect group   Lets you change your mind about a group that you previously selected.

Exit   Leaves UNDELETE and returns to the command line. You can also use Alt-X to do this.

To use UNDELETE, select the files to recover and then press Alt-U. As each file is undeleted, it is marked "RECOVERED" in the file display.

UNDELETE can also be used as a command-line application, as discussed in the UNDELETE section of Appendix A.

CHAPTER 10

Securing Your Data

Why secure your data? Well, if you keep sensitive information in your computer, this is pretty obvious. However, you should almost always secure your data. You never know who might be playing around with your system. Potential intruders include your kids, someone working late at the office, someone involved in industrial espionage, or a disgruntled ex-employee. At one job, my boss would often work late, and he felt it was his privilege to use my computer, create new files and directories, reconfigure my application programs, and sometimes make a mess of things. If I'd had DR DOS 6.0 then, I definitely would have set up security. I also know of cases where valuable data was destroyed, either accidentally or intentionally, by people who simply shouldn't have been using those computers.

DR DOS provides security at four levels:

- System
- Directory
- File
- Lock screen

System security requires a password before DR DOS allows access to the hard disk. Without the password, the hard disk is virtually impenetrable. That doesn't mean a dedicated hacker with lots of time won't find a way past the security system, but it does mean most people won't be able to get in. I've tried booting from a floppy equipped with various versions of MS-DOS. I've attempted to find and remove the security system with the Mace MUSE sector editor. I've tried reinstalling DR DOS 6.0. Nothing has worked.

Directory security means that no file in a protected directory can be accessed (or modified, depending on the level of security) without a password.

File security means that individual files can't be accessed (or modified) without a password. Neither file nor directory passwords offer any resistance to sector editor programs such as MUSE. However, they do prevent access through normal DOS channels, such as DR DOS commands and normal application programs.

Lock screen security (the LOCK command) provides a way of locking the mouse and keyboard when you walk away from the system. It secures the computer without turning it off. The computer isn't accessible unless a password is entered. LOCK resists Ctrl-Alt-Delete rebooting, although it can't stop someone from pressing a hardware reset button or powering the system off and then on. However, if it's used with system security, LOCK provides an excellent defense.

System Security

System security can be installed either when you install DR DOS or through the DR DOS SETUP program. Security can be found on the configuration screen, shown in Figure 10-1. Selecting Security from the configuration screen results in a menu in which security can be enabled or disabled (Figure 10-2). Choose to enable security, and you'll be prompted for a master password. Without the master password, security can't be disabled and the user password can't be changed. As the master password is typed, each character is shown on the screen as an asterisk. This prevents anyone who might be looking over your shoulder from reading your password. (Yes, this is paranoid.) After entering the master password, you'll be prompted to enter it again (Figure 10-3). This is to make sure DR DOS got the password you wanted. If the two entries don't match, you'll be asked to press Escape and try again.

If no master password is entered, anyone can change the master and user passwords, or completely disable security, once the system is unlocked.

After entering the master password, enter a user password. This is the password that actually unlocks the computer system when it is powered up. Normally, this should be changed every few weeks just to keep the system secure.

SECURING YOUR DATA

```
┌──────────────────────────────────────────────────────────────────┐
│ ┌─────────────────┐                              ┌──────────────┐│
│ │ Digital Research│                              │DR DOS 6.0 SETUP││
│ └─────────────────┘                              └──────────────┘│
│                                                                  │
│        Select the area you wish to configure from the list below.│
│                                                                  │
│      ■ MemoryMAX                                                 │
│                                                                  │
│      ■ TaskMAX                                                   │
│                                                                  │
│      ■ DiskMAX                                                   │
│                                                                  │
│      ■ ViewMAX                                                   │
│                                                                  │
│      ■ Country and Keyboard                                      │
│                                                                  │
│      ■ System Parameters                                         │
│                                                                  │
│      ■ Optional Device Drivers and Utilities                     │
│                                                                  │
│      ▶ Security                                                  │
│                                                                  │
│      ■ Save Changes and Exit                                     │
│                                                                  │
│ F1=Help  ↕=next/prev line  <Enter>=select option  <Esc>=prev screen  F10=abort │
└──────────────────────────────────────────────────────────────────┘
```

Figure 10-1. The SETUP main menu with Security selected.

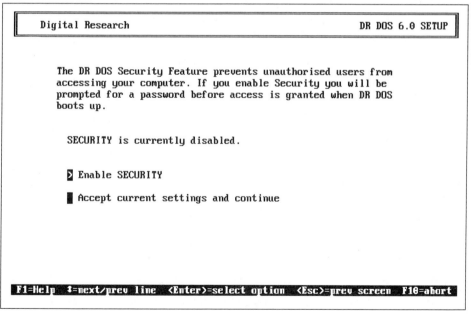

Figure 10-2. The main Security screen in SETUP.

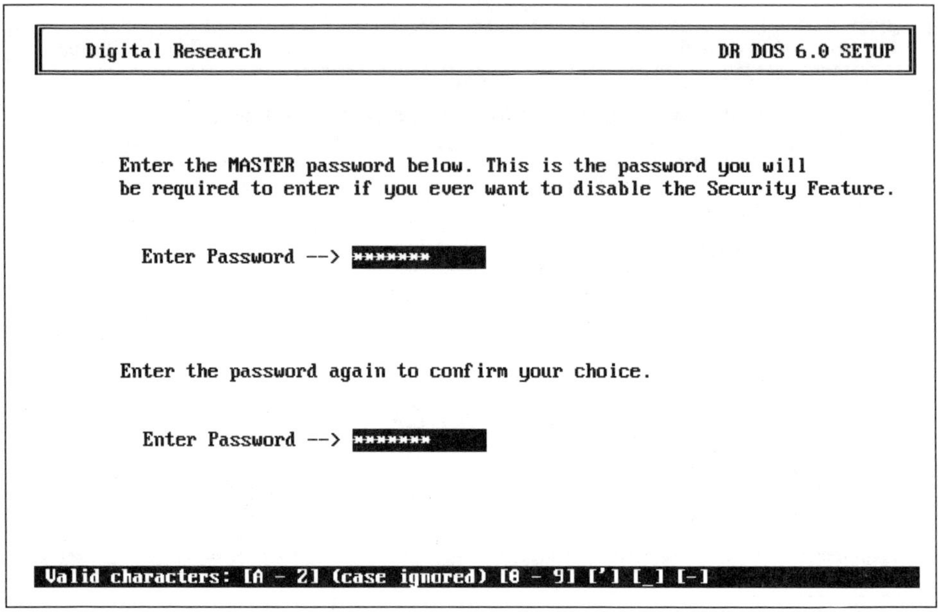

```
┌──────────────────────────────────────────────────────────────────────┐
│  ┌─────────────────────────┐                                         │
│  │ Digital Research        │                     DR DOS 6.0 SETUP    │
│  └─────────────────────────┘                                         │
│                                                                      │
│                                                                      │
│      Enter the MASTER password below. This is the password you will  │
│      be required to enter if you ever want to disable the Security Feature. │
│                                                                      │
│           Enter Password --> ███████                                 │
│                                                                      │
│                                                                      │
│                                                                      │
│      Enter the password again to confirm your choice.                │
│                                                                      │
│           Enter Password --> ███████                                 │
│                                                                      │
│                                                                      │
│                                                                      │
│  ┌────────────────────────────────────────────────────────────────┐  │
│  │ Valid characters: [A - Z] (case ignored) [0 - 9] ['] [_] [-]   │  │
│  └────────────────────────────────────────────────────────────────┘  │
└──────────────────────────────────────────────────────────────────────┘
```

Figure 10-3. The MASTER password screen in SETUP.

That's all there is to installing system security. Just go through the save-and-exit sequence for INSTALL, and it will update the CONFIG.SYS file and modify the boot tracks on the hard drive to work with the security system.

By the way, when system security is installed, the LOCK command uses the user password by default.

Directory Security

Both directory and file security are implemented using the PASSWORD command. Protecting directories and files with PASSWORD is better than using the read-only and hidden file attributes, which are set with ATTRIB. Some DR DOS commands have parameters that allow them to ignore file attributes, but no DR DOS command or standard application program can ignore password protection.

To protect a directory, you must use PASSWORD with the /P: parameter. Directories are protected against entry, and their files are protected against being read, written to, copied, or deleted. You won't even be able to get a listing of the files

SECURING YOUR DATA

in the directory. This is a very handy tool for computers that are shared by a number of people, such as in a classroom. Each person's work can be kept in a separate directory that is only accessible with the directory password.

As an example, the following command protects the C:\WEASEL directory and its subdirectories from unauthorized entry, copying, or use. The password is ROSEBUD.

```
PASSWORD C:\WEASEL /P:ROSEBUD
```

That's all there is to it. To access that directory, either supply the password directly or use the global password. To supply the password directly, append it to the directory name with a semicolon. For example, the CD command to change to the C:\WEASEL directory looks like this:

```
CD C:\WEASEL;ROSEBUD
```

Once you have entered the directory, you can do what you like. However, when you leave, the directory is locked again.

To copy the files from a protected directory, you must supply the password either as part of the command or when prompted. Finding the exact password syntax for any given command is a matter of trial and error. For example, I can't find a way to make COPY work at all for a password-protected directory. However, XCOPY works just fine because it asks for the password. Appending the password to the directory name works for some commands, such as DIR.

To avoid this syntax insanity, unlock the directory with the global password. This is done with the /G: parameter. The following command unlocks all directories protected with the password ROSEBUD:

```
PASSWORD /G:ROSEBUD
```

Note that I said *all* directories protected with that password. A good scheme is to protect all vital directories and files with the same password. Then they can all be unlocked with the global password.

To relock everything, use the /NG parameter:

```
PASSWORD /NG
```

Notice that you don't specify the password when relocking. To remove a directory's password protection permanently, use the /NP parameter:

```
PASSWORD C:\WEASEL /NP
```

You'll be prompted to enter the password. If the correct password isn't entered, the directory will remain protected.

File Security

File security can be assigned with several parameters, each of which provides a different level of security. The PASSWORD parameters that pertain to file security are:

/D:*passwrd*   Protects against file deletion, renaming, or attribute changes unless the password is given. The file can be edited and copied without the password. This is useful for protecting documents, spreadsheets, and databases from unauthorized deletion.

/W:*passwrd*   Provides somewhat stronger protection, preventing modification, deletion, renaming, or attribute changing unless the password is given. The file can still be read without the password. This is useful for protecting style sheets and other files that you don't want changed without authorization.

/R:*passwrd*   Prevents anything from happening unless you provide the password. The file can't even be read. Use this to protect sensitive information.

These passwords can be applied to one file, to a set of files specified by wildcards, or to a set of files specified in a file. They can even be applied to subdirectories.

SECURING YOUR DATA

To provide the highest level of security for a single file, such as the D:\ACCOUNTS\PAYROLL.WKS file, use this command with the /R option. In this example, the password is WHODERE.

```
PASSWORD D:\ACCOUNTS\PAYROLL.WKS /R:WHODERE
```

To provide security against modification or deletion of Ventura Publisher stylesheet files (C:\TYPESET*.STY), use the following command. This time the password is DONTKNOW.

```
PASSWORD C:\TYPESET\*.STY /W:DONTKNOW
```

To prevent unauthorized deletion of all files in the G:\MAILLIST directory, as well as all files in its subdirectories (we'll use the /S parameter), use the following command with the password ROSEBUD:

```
PASSWORD G:\MAILLIST \*.* /D:ROSEBUD /S
```

You can also provide password protection for a set of files listed in an ASCII text file. To create such a file, use EDITOR or any text editor or word processor that can write ASCII files. For example, if the text file consists of the following:

```
C:\TYPESET\*.STY
D:\WINWORD\*.DOT
G:\WEASEL\MYSTLE.TPL
```

security can be assigned to all of these files with one command:

```
PASSWORD C:\@PW.TXT /W:ROSEBUD
```

The file PW.TXT contains the list of files. When it's preceded by an @, PASSWORD knows to look in that file for a list. All the files listed in PW.TXT were given /W-level security and a password of ROSEBUD.

The syntax for password-protected files is a bit odd because the password must be appended to the file specification in the command. For example, suppose you want to delete all .BAK files in the C:\LETTERS directory, but they're protected by /D-level security with a password of HUH. Use this command:

```
DEL C:\LETTERS\*.BAK;HUH
```

Note that the password is appended to the file specification with a semicolon.

Specify the global password to unlock all the files and directories protected with the same password. This is the same as the global password we discussed under "Directory Security." If the global password is ROSEBUD, you can unlock all files and directories it protected using the following command:

```
PASSWORD /G:ROSEBUD
```

Remove the global password with this command (you don't specify the global password when removing it):

```
PASSWORD /NG
```

Locking Your Screen

LOCK provides a way of locking the keyboard and screen while you're away from the computer. When you're using TaskMAX, LOCK is a convenient tool because it can be run as a task. This means you don't need to exit from the applications that are running to lock the screen. If you're using Microsoft Windows, don't use LOCK from a DOS window. Windows allows you to switch away from the DOS task running LOCK, bypassing the requirement for a password.

You can create custom screens for LOCK. The LOCK.TXT file is the screen that's displayed when the screen is locked, and the LOCK.ERR file is the screen that appears if the wrong password is entered. Both files reside in the \DRDOS directory.

Running LOCK is simple: Just type LOCK followed by the password. For example, if the password is ROSEBUD, use this command:

```
LOCK ROSEBUD
```

SECURING YOUR DATA

If system security is enabled and you want LOCK to use the user password, enter the LOCK command alone.

What could be easier?

Removing Security

Removing system security is pretty straightforward: Go into DR DOS SETUP, go to the configuration screen, select security, and then choose to disable it. You will be asked for the master password.

Removing directory and file security requires the /NP (for directories) and /N (for files) parameters. To remove password protection from the C:\ACCOUNTS directory, use this command:

```
PASSWORD C:\ACCOUNTS /NP
```

You'll then be asked to enter the password. If you enter an incorrect password, the directory will continue to be protected.

To remove password protection from the C:\ACCOUNTS\PAYROLL.WKS file, use this command:

```
PASSWORD C:\ACCOUNTS\PAYROLL.WKS /N
```

Again, you'll be asked to specify the password. If the correct password isn't entered, protection will remain. You can also remove protection from a set of files with wildcards or by using a file with a list of files (prefaced with @ in the command). This gets a bit tedious, however, because the password must be entered individually for each file.

Things to Watch Out For

First, if you set up security, be sure to keep a record of the passwords in a safe place. For example, what would happen if you were the keeper of your company's payroll and you decided to chuck it all and become a stand-up comedian? Or worse, what if you forgot your system user password? I haven't a clue as to how to bypass the security system, and you probably won't either. The hard disk that holds all your sensitive data will become an expensive, metal-encased brick without the system user password.

Second, remember that no security system is foolproof. If a person has the motive, time, and technical skill to break into your computer, you can't prevent it. The only comforting thought is that someone having a combination of all three things is pretty unusual.

Third, directory- and file-level security isn't very robust. To keep someone from reading data, depend more on system-level security. The Mace MUSE sector editor, or the Norton Utilities, can bypass file and directory security by reading the file disk sectors directly. They can also modify your secure data.

Finally, don't walk away from your machine after setting file and directory security. The commands you've used, including passwords, will be held in DR DOS's command-line history. Someone can just hit Ctrl-E's and read every password.

CHAPTER 11

Using ViewMAX

ViewMAX, the Graphical User Interface

In this chapter, I'll go over the basics of using ViewMAX, the graphical user interface (GUI) facility in DR DOS. I'll cover how to operate your computer just as efficiently from ViewMAX as you can from DR DOS.

ViewMAX provides a way to control your computer in a more personalized fashion. It uses the metaphors of office desktop, file folders, and pieces of paper to represent the various parts of the computer's file system — disks, directories, and files.

While the DR DOS command line gives you a powerful and flexible way to run your computer, ViewMAX gives you nearly the same capabilities in a more personal environment. In fact, some things are far more convenient to do using ViewMAX, such as copying or deleting selected sets of files.

With DR DOS 6.0, the combination of ViewMAX and the TaskMAX task switcher transforms ViewMAX into a powerful operating environment. From it, you can run all of your DOS applications, switch between them at will, and still do all file management through the convenient ViewMAX Windows. In many ways it rivals Microsoft Windows 3.0 or the Apple Macintosh Multifinder. But unlike Windows, it's fast and handily runs all of your DOS applications.

A Brief History Lesson

Before we dive in, let me give you a little bit of the history of ViewMAX. Back in the days of the original IBM PCs and XTs, Digital Research Inc. introduced the first GUI for PCs. It was called GEM (short for Graphical Environment Manager) and was largely inspired by the Macintosh user interface. GEM was really amazing because it provided a good deal of the functionality of the Macintosh on a sluggish, standard PC.

Apple apparently thought GEM was a significant threat because the company threatened to sue Digital Research, claiming that GEM violated the look and feel of the Macintosh desktop. Digital Research settled out of court and agreed to change the PC product to resemble the Macintosh desktop less closely. However, this Mac-like version of GEM lives on today as the GUI for Atari ST computers.

I don't think the PC version of GEM ever quite recovered from the delay caused by that redesign. Still, in its heyday dozens of excellent applications ran under GEM, including the highly regarded Ventura Publisher. I always thought GEM was a much better GUI than the earlier versions of Windows. However, Microsoft and its prodigious resources eventually overwhelmed GEM.

While the GEM desktop is no longer available from Digital Research, GEM still lives on in a few products. The Ventura Publisher Gold edition is available using a standalone, or "run-time," version of GEM/3. (GEM/3.14 was the last commercially produced version of the GEM Desktop.)

Digital Research currently markets several products that also use a run-time version of a more advanced GEM/4, including Artline version 2.0, which was used to create many of the illustrations for this book. A few other companies still sell GEM applications and even include the GEM desktop. The Migraph Touch-Up paint program, which was also used in producing some of the illustrations, is one example.

Like the phoenix of classical myth, the GEM/3 desktop has risen from its ashes as ViewMAX. ViewMAX was given a facelift to make it comply with the Common User Access (CUA) architecture used by the OS/2 Presentation Manager and Windows. The idea was carried a step further in DR DOS 6.0, where ViewMAX was trimmed with sculptured buttons and slider bars. Similar three-dimensional detail can be found in GUIs such as Windows or the X Window System's Motif environment.

ViewMAX also lost some GEM abilities and can't directly run GEM applications. Instead, it looks for the GEM desktop on your disk and uses it to access the GEM applications. However, if you have any GEM desktop accessories, such as GEM Diary or GEM Snapshot, ViewMAX will run them. (Desktop accessories are tools available throughout the GEM environment.)

USING VIEWMAX

ViewMAX allows you to run standard DOS applications (not the graphically oriented Windows applications, however), copy and delete files, format disks, create and delete directories, and just about anything else you need to do from a rather elegant environment. ViewMAXcan also serve as the control center for the TaskMAX task switcher — not bad, considering you don't need to pay extra for ViewMAX.

Mousing Around

In ViewMAX, the mouse is more important than the keyboard. When I say mouse, I really mean any pointing device such as a trackball, graphics tablet, or whatever. While you can run ViewMAX without a mouse, it's a bit like pounding nails with your bare hand: it's possible, but you won't enjoy it. If you're absolutely determined to do this, you'll find a section entitled "But I Don't Have a Mouse" at the end of the chapter.

While in ViewMAX, you'll use your mouse as a tool for reaching into the display to grab or select objects such as files, directories, and disk drives. As you move the mouse across your desk, a mouse pointer on the screen tracks its movements.

No matter how many buttons your mouse has, you'll only use the left button in ViewMAX. Four mouse techniques require the use of that button:

Clicking Just place the pointer over whatever you want to activate and then quickly push and release the mouse button. If you do this at the right speed, most mice will make a clicking sound. Clicking is used to select or unselect an object or objects in a window. You can tell that something is selected because it will be highlighted onscreen.

If you read books or manuals about the Macintosh, you'll even find *click* used as a verb: *to click on the file.*

Dragging Dragging is like clicking except that you push but don't release the mouse button. While the mouse button is held down, all items you've selected with the mouse pointer will follow the pointer as you move it around. You use dragging to copy files or copy the contents of directories and disks.

You can also create a "rubber rectangle" by dragging. All objects touched by this rubber rectangle are selected when you release the mouse button.

Double-clicking   This is used to activate or run something, such as a program. It's just two clicks in rapid succession. ViewMAX allows you to set the double-click speed it accepts to match your own style.

Shift-clicking   This is used to select more than one object or unselect a single object without unselecting others. Hold down the Shift key while you click.

Running ViewMAX

ViewMAX is also installed during DR DOS installation (recall that you were asked about the type of mouse and display) and resides in the DR DOS directory. As long as the DR DOS directory is within the PATH statement in the AUTOEXEC.BAT file, you can run ViewMAX from any drive and directory.

To run ViewMAX, type the following and press Enter:

```
VIEWMAX
```

After an appropriate amount of disk drive whirring and buzzing, the ViewMAX logo will appear followed closely by the three *windows* shown in Figure 11-1. The top left window (the one marked "drive C:") is the *tree window* and shows the directory tree for the current disk drive. You'll use the tree window to navigate directories and subdirectories quickly. You can also use it as a point for copying, either to copy an entire directory (and its subdirectories) somewhere else or to copy other things into a directory shown on the tree. If you like, you can choose not to display the tree window.

If you are using DR DOS 5.0, forgive the discussion of the tree window. This was added in 6.0 and isn't available to you.

To the right of the tree window is the *top window*. The top window can show you the files and subdirectories within a directory or the set of available disk drives. By default, the top window initially shows the contents of the root directory for the current drive.

USING VIEWMAX

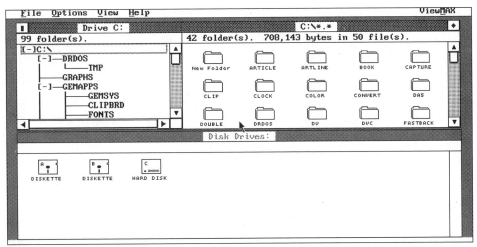

Figure 11-1. The ViewMAX desktop.

The bottom half of the screen is occupied by the *bottom window*. The bottom window initially shows the available disk drives but could also show the contents of directories. Like the top window, it too can be accompanied by a tree window. This is especially handy if you want to look at a different diskette or hard disk partition in the bottom window.

Your screen might show more or fewer floppies and more or fewer hard drives than the example in the figure. You might also have a *network drive*, which is also shown in the figure. Network drives are disk drives (or parts of disk drives) that you can access through a computer *local area network* (LAN). They aren't located within the computer itself, and there are some limitations in dealing with them. If you are connected to a LAN, you'll know it. If you aren't, don't worry about this.

OK, let's stop for a moment and consider what you've got. You now have windows that let you look into the various parts of the directory tree or select any disk drive. Unlike the command line, you can see the contents of a directory and the directory structure at a glance. Moreover, you can look at two directories or disks at the same time.

DR DOS 6 BY EXAMPLE

Checking Out the Neighborhood

Take a look at the top window and tree window (see Figure 11-2). Note that the bar spanning the two along the top is darker or highlighted. This is the visual cue for the *active window*. Also notice that the top, or root, directory in the tree window has a gray rectangle around it. Only the active window can have a gray rectangle. A window becomes active when you click anywhere within it. This is important to understand because you can only manipulate things in the active window.

By the way, you can also use the Tab key to shift the active window. Each time you press Tab, the active window shifts in a clockwise direction.

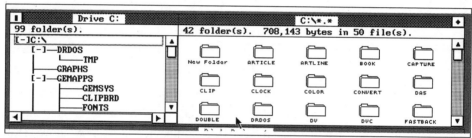

Figure 11-2. The top window (right), and its TREE window (left).

If you are at your computer now and have ViewMAX running, click once on the top window. Notice that the gray rectangle shifts to this window. Click on any file or folder within that window, and notice that it is highlighted. This means that the file is now *selected*. Anything selected in a window will be highlighted like this. (By the way, you've probably determined by now that the "folders" are directories, and the "files" are just that: files.)

Click once on the bottom window, and you'll see that it becomes active. Double-clicking on a drive *icon* in the bottom window opens, or activates, that drive. Before you open a floppy drive, make sure that you really have a floppy in the drive. Nothing serious will happen if you don't, but you'll be obligated to sit and wait until ViewMAX decides there isn't a diskette in the drive and complains about it.

Let's return to the top window for a moment — click on it to make it active. The New Folder icon at the upper left is used to create a new folder or directory. Just double-click on it, and it will ask you for the name of a new folder. You'll find a New

USING VIEWMAX

Folder icon in each directory. Also, note that the terms *folder, directory,* and *subdirectory* are completely interchangeable.

Unless you change the way ViewMAX shows folders and files, folders are always shown on top of the window. To open a folder, simply double-click on it and its contents will be shown in the window. You can also open a directory by clicking on it in the tree window.

Operating Your Windows

Before going on, I'll introduce you to window controls. By the way, when you learn to use these controls you'll also know how to use most of the basic controls for Windows, the Macintosh desktop, and the X Window System environment. Talk about an educational experience!

To See the Rest of a Window

If there are more files than can be shown in the visible portion of a window, you'll see a *scroll bar* along the right side of the window (in the tree window, it appears at the bottom). Figure 11-3 shows a scroll bar. There are three ways to operate a scroll bar: by clicking on the top or bottom arrow, by clicking on the scroll-bar track, and by moving the slider. These techniques are illustrated in Figure 11-4.

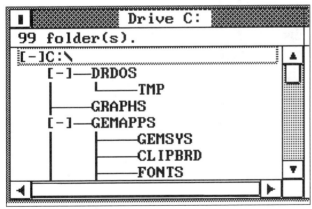

Figure 11-3. Note the scroll bars along the right and bottom of the window.

DR DOS 6 BY EXAMPLE

- To use the arrows:
  Put your mouse pointer over the appropriate arrow.

  Click once to move up, down, or sideways one row of icons, or click and hold to scroll continuously through the icons. Note that the slider, which runs down through the scroll bar, shifts just a little bit.

- To use the scroll-bar track:
  Put your mouse pointer over an empty section of the scroll-bar track (not over the slider).

  Click once. Now the window shifts by one windowful, and the slider jumps by its length.

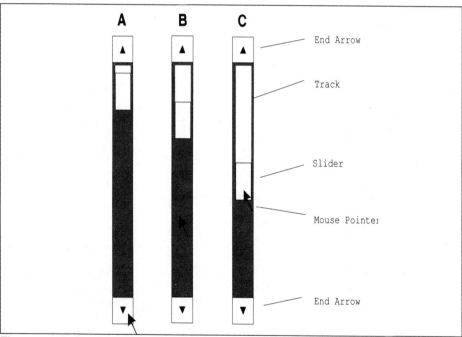

Figure 11-4. Scroll bar methods.

USING VIEWMAX

- To use the slider:
  Put the mouse pointer over the slider, then click and hold.

  As long as you're holding the mouse button down, you can drag the slider up and down in its track. As you drag it, the contents of the window change. For example, to see what's at the bottom of the window, drag the slider to the bottom of its track.

Filling the Screen with a Window

At the upper right of each window you'll see a small diamond in a box, which is actually a tool called the *resizing box*. Click on this and the window will zoom to fill the entire screen. Click on it again and the window will shrink to normal size. Zooming a window to full screen is useful when deleting files because you can see and therefore select a larger number of files in one move.

Notice that if you click the resizing box in either window in a tree window/files window pair, then both will zoom in or out.

Climbing the Directory Tree

As previously mentioned, you double-click on a folder in a file window to open it and display its contents. You can continue until you run out of branching folders. If you want to move the file window back one level, you must click on the *close box* at the upper left of the window (see Figure 11-5). This closes the current "child" directory and displays the "parent" directory where the child resides. For example, let's say you have a directory called STUFF, and within it you have a subdirectory called JUNQUE. JUNQUE is currently displayed in the active window. When you click on the close box, the window will display the contents of the STUFF directory.

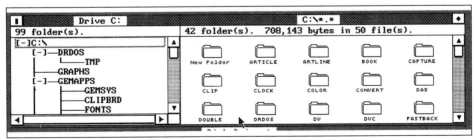

Figure 11-5. The square in the upper left is the close box.

DR DOS 6 BY EXAMPLE

Unlike the DR DOS command line, where you can change to any directory in the drive using the CD command, the file window only lets you change directories one at a time, along the current directory branch. To move more efficiently from directory to directory, use the tree window.

You can use the scroll bar to maneuver around the tree window just as you would the file window. When you find a directory or subdirectory that you want to open, click on it. The contents of the directory will be shown in the adjacent file window (see Figure 11-6).

Notice the [+] and [-] signs beside directories. These allow you to view or hide subdirectories. The [+] or [-] beside the root directory can be used to show or hide all subdirectories. The [+] or [-] beside an individual directory allows you to display or hide subdirectories of that directory.

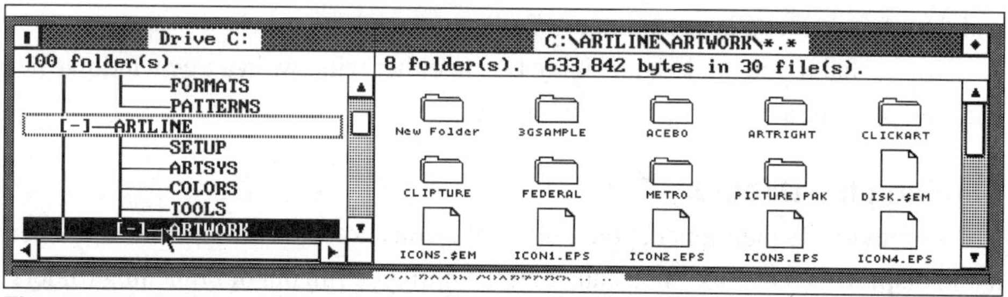

Figure 11-6. The top window (right) shows the contents of the directory selected in the TREE window.

Figure 11-7 shows what happens when you start clicking on these things. "A" shows the effect of clicking on the [-] beside the root directory. "B" shows what happens when you double-click on the same [-]. "C" illustrates the result of double-clicking the [+] that now resides beside the root directory. Finally, "D" shows what happens when you click the [-] beside the GEMAPPS directory.

The plus and minus keys on the numeric keypad mimic the functions of clicking on the [+] and [-] in the tree window. For example, if the gray rectangle is beside the DWEEB directory, pressing the plus key will display the subdirectories of DWEEB. Pressing the minus key will hide those subdirectories. If you move the gray rectangle to the root directory, you can use Alt+ to display all directories and subdirectories in the tree. Alt- will hide all directories in the tree.

USING VIEWMAX

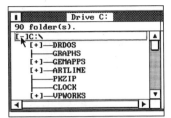

Figure 11-7a. Clicking once on the minus for the root directory hides all sub-directories. Directories marked with a plus have sub-directories.

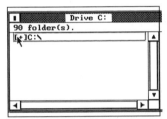

Figure 11-7b. Double-clicking the minus at the root directory hides all directories. The minus changes to a plus to indicate that there are hidden directories.

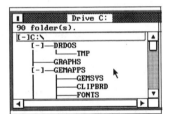

Figure 11-7c. Clicking the plus at the root reveals all directories and sub-directories.

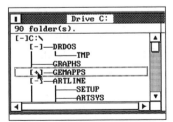

Figure 11-7d. Clicking the minus beside GEMAPPS hides only its sub-directories. The minus turns into a plus to signify that GEMAPPS has hidden sub-directories.

253

The Title Bar Tells All

The *title bar* along the top of each window tells you the name of the drive or drive and directory currently shown in the window. If your window shows only drive icons, the title bar will simply read "Disk Drives."

The *information line* under the title bar gives you a summary of the contents of the directory shown in the window. For example, it might tell you that you have 12 folders and 49 files taking up 3,234,578 bytes.

Using the Menu Bar

The *menu bar* runs along the top of the screen and lists the available menus:

- File
- Options
- View
- Help
- ViewMAX (the accessories menu at the far right)

You can make any of these menus drop down and appear by placing the mouse cursor over the menu title. As you slide the cursor down the menu, each of the commands highlights in turn. Click on a command to activate it. If a command is followed by an ellipsis (three dots), then a *dialog box* will appear when you activate that command. A dialog box will have several types of controls (see Figure 11-8):

Radio buttons   Sets of buttons that offer mutually exclusive choices — you can pick one and only one of the set.

Text-entry fields   These provide a line into which you can type an entry. The Tab, down arrow, and right arrow keys will move to the next field. To go back a field, use the combination of Shift-Tab, up arrow, or left arrow.

USING VIEWMAX

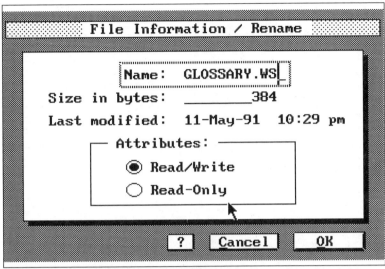

Figure 11-8. A typical dialog box showing radio buttons (round buttons in the lower-middle area), text-entry fields (upper-middle) and exit buttons (bottom).

Exit buttons   These offer a way out of the dialog box. "OK" means that you like what you selected and want something to happen based on those selections. "Cancel" means that you don't want anything to happen and want to get out of the dialog box. If a button has a heavy border, it can also be activated by pressing Enter.

You can also use keyboard shortcuts to execute any of the menu commands. These shortcuts follow the IBM Systems Application Architecture (SAA)/CUA convention. First, press Alt and the first letter of the menu name to pull the menu down—for example, Alt-F pulls down the File menu. Next, press the mnemonic key that corresponds to the command. In many cases, this will be the first letter of that command.

Other environments that comply with the SAA/CUA conventions are Windows, OS/2 Presentation Manager and the X Window System's Motif interface.

You'll see these keyboard shortcuts underlined in the command name. For example, after the File menu is pulled down you can press the X key to exit. For your convenience, a complete set of ViewMAX keyboard shortcuts is listed at the end of this chapter.

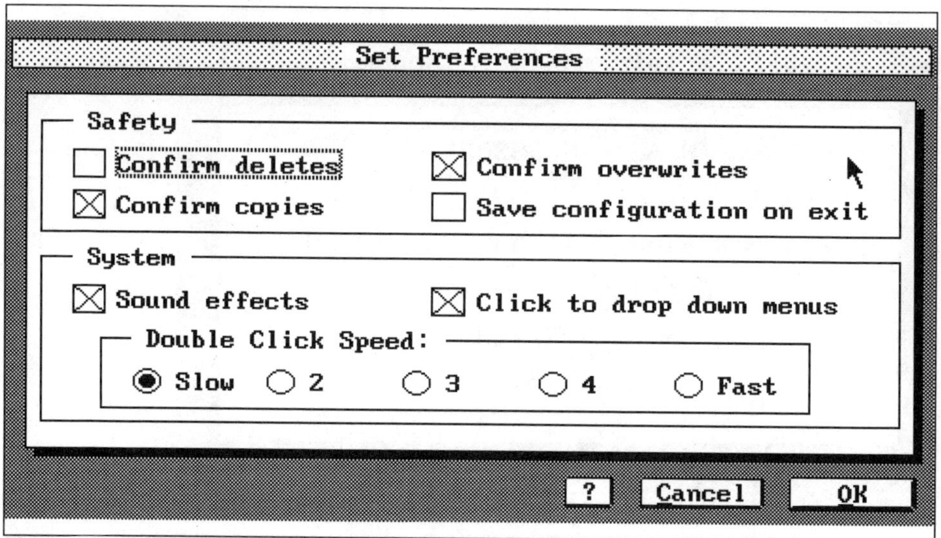

```
┌─────────────────────────────────────────────────────┐
│░░░░░░░░░░░░░░░░░░ Set Preferences ░░░░░░░░░░░░░░░░░│
│ ┌─ Safety ─────────────────────────────────────┐   │
│ │   ☐ Confirm deletes      ☒ Confirm overwrites│ ▲ │
│ │   ☒ Confirm copies       ☐ Save configuration on exit│
│ └──────────────────────────────────────────────┘   │
│ ┌─ System ─────────────────────────────────────┐   │
│ │   ☒ Sound effects       ☒ Click to drop down menus│
│ │   ┌─ Double Click Speed: ───────────────────┐│   │
│ │   │ ⦿ Slow  ○ 2    ○ 3    ○ 4    ○ Fast   ││   │
│ │   └──────────────────────────────────────────┘│   │
│ └──────────────────────────────────────────────┘   │
│                              [ ? ] [ Cancel ] [ OK ]│
└─────────────────────────────────────────────────────┘
```

Figure 11-9. The Preferences Dialog box.

Having it Your Way

ViewMAX can be customized to suit your taste. To do this, you must first click on the Preferences command in the Options menu. The dialog box that appears has several radio buttons, and these allow you to set the options (see Figure 11-9). Click on the button you like for each option.

The "Safety" options affect how many "fail-safe" features you want to use.

> *Confirm Deletes* Setting this to Yes means that ViewMAX won't delete a file, directory, or the entire contents of a disk without first asking if you're sure about this. It will only ask once before blowing away the selected objects. If you set this to No, you won't get a second chance after selecting Delete from the File menu. However, you can likely use Undelete to recover the file.

> *Confirm Copies* Set this to Yes and ViewMAX won't copy a file, a directory, or the disk contents without asking if you really want to copy the selected objects. Set this to No and copies are executed after you drag the objects to their new home.

USING VIEWMAX

Confirm Overwrite

Clicking on Yes gives you a chance to stop ViewMAX from overwriting a file with a copy. For example, if you're copying a file in ViewMAX and a file with the same name will be overwritten, then ViewMAX will warn you and wait for you to acknowledge this. Remember, there is no way to retrieve overwritten data.

Save Configuration on Exit

This is a fail-safe setting to prevent you from losing any changes you've made to ViewMAX. If this is set to No, then any changes you make to preference settings or application configurations will be lost when you exit from ViewMAX *unless* you use the Save Configuration command in the Options menu to save these changes. If you set this to Yes, any changes will be saved when you exit ViewMAX. ViewMAX will also return the directories shown in the windows when you last exited.

The "System" selections affect ViewMAX's general behavior.

Sound Effects Setting this On means that ViewMAX is permitted to beep at you. Setting this Off forces ViewMAX to be seen and not heard.

Double-click Speed

This sets the time delay between clicks that ViewMAX expects for a valid double-click. I like the default, middle-of-the-road setting, but you can increase or decrease the time delay by a couple of steps.

Click to Drop Down Menus

By default, ViewMAX is set to No Click. No Click means that a ViewMAX menu drops down whenever the mouse pointer touches the menu name in the menu bar. This is "GEMish" operation. If you want to make ViewMAX behave more like Windows, set this to Click. Setting to Click means that you must click on the menu name to drop the menu down from the menu bar.

Copying Files

This is one of ViewMAX's handiest features. As flexible as DR DOS is, sometimes it's much easier to decide which files to copy when you can actually see a set of files. I also like to be able to select a set of files at will.

To copy a file, you must first select it. To select a file, you must first make its window active. You can then use one or a combination of these selection techniques (shown in Figure 11-10).

- Selection technique A: Select a single file by clicking on it.

- Selection technique B: Select a group of files by shift-clicking on each in turn.

- Selection technique C: Select a group of files clustered together by dragging a rubber rectangle around the group. To grab a rubber rectangle, position the mouse pointer to the left of and above the group. Click and hold to cause the rubber rectangle to appear onscreen.

  While holding down the mouse button, drag the rubber rectangle down and to the right until its borders at least touch every file you wish to select. All you need to do is touch a file icon with the rubber rectangle border and it will be selected.

USING VIEWMAX

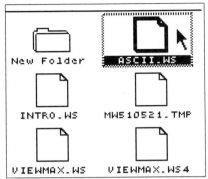

Figure 11-10a. Select a single file by simply clicking on it.

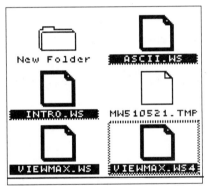

Figure 11-10b. Select multiple files by shift-clicking each in turn.

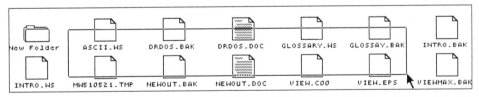

Figure 11-10c. Select multiple files by touching each file you want with a rubber rectangle.

File selection is one of those activities that is best learned through hands-on experience. Go ahead, give it a shot. Try selecting one file, then another. Get a bit fancier and use the shift-click technique to select several. Click on an open area of the window to unselect the files. Finally, try dragging rubber rectangles around.

259

DR DOS 6 BY EXAMPLE

When you've mastered this art, you can try copying files. Figure 11-11 shows how this is done. Basic file copying follows these steps:

1. Get both the source folder (where the files reside) and the destination folder (where you want copies of the files to go) into ViewMAX windows. Remember that the tree window can be a source or destination as well.

2. Select the files you want using any or all of the techniques covered above.

3. When you select the last file, don't release the mouse button. You'll see the mouse pointer change into a little hand to indicate that ViewMAX is ready to copy files.

4. Continue to hold down the mouse button and drag the files to an open spot in the destination window. If you are copying the files into a folder (directory), make sure that target folder is highlighted. If it isn't, ViewMAX hasn't selected it as the destination for your files. This applies if you are copying to either the files window or the tree window.

5. Release the mouse button to drop the files.

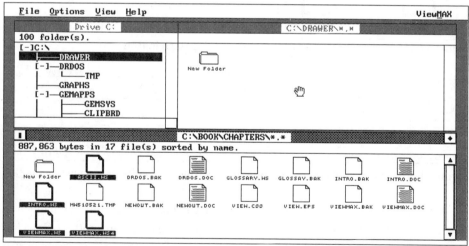

Figure 11-11. To copy files, move the hand to the target window and release the button.

When you copy files, ViewMAX will start by telling you how many files it's about to copy. Depending on how the ViewMAX preferences are set, if there are already versions of some of these files, ViewMAX will ask if you want them overwritten. Remember, once files are overwritten they are gone forever, so make sure that you aren't overwriting the most up-to-date copy or even an older copy of the file that you don't want to change.

As an alternative to dragging the selected files from window to window, you can also use the Copy command. You access this by pressing the Alt-F combination to pull down the File menu, then pressing C for copy.

ViewMAX can also copy folders, including all of the files and subdirectories that they hold. Your destination can also be a folder and need not be an open space on the window. When you copy folders, the subordinate directory structure is also copied. Suppose that you copied the folder called DRUDGE, which has a subfolder called TEDIUM, to the MOREWORK folder. When you open MOREWORK, you'll find a new folder called DRUDGE. If you then open DRUDGE, you'll find a TEDIUM folder.

Deleting Files

You use the same techniques to select files for deletion that you used for copying. Once you've selected the set, you need to use the Delete command. You can access the Delete command by either pulling down the File menu and clicking Delete or pressing Alt-F followed by D.

As in copying, ViewMAX will ask if you've really considered this act and are ready to go through with it. Once deleted, the files are gone but not forgotten, and therefore sometimes recoverable with the right tools.

Other Things You Can Do with Objects

Objects are files, directories, and folders, and there are other commands within ViewMAX that affect them. Unlike the copy and delete functions, these commands deal with only one selected object. If more than one object is selected, you won't be able to access the command (it will be *dimmed* in the menu).

Renaming and Examining Files, Directories, and Disks

ViewMAX allows you to check information about disks, directories, and files. You can also change the names of objects. Moreover, you can look at the contents of any file. These functions are found in the File menu. To check information about an object, select it (remember that for this type of activity, only one object – file, folder, or disk – can be selected at a time). Next, click on the Info/Rename command in the File menu. You can also use Alt-F followed by I.

The information you see depends on the type of object you've selected. Figure 11-12 shows each type of information dialog box. For example, selecting a disk drive will tell you:

- The number of files and directories.

- The total amount of disk space taken by the disk contents.

- The disk label, if any. This is an electronic name that you can assign to any disk drive. You can also change the disk label by using this dialog box.

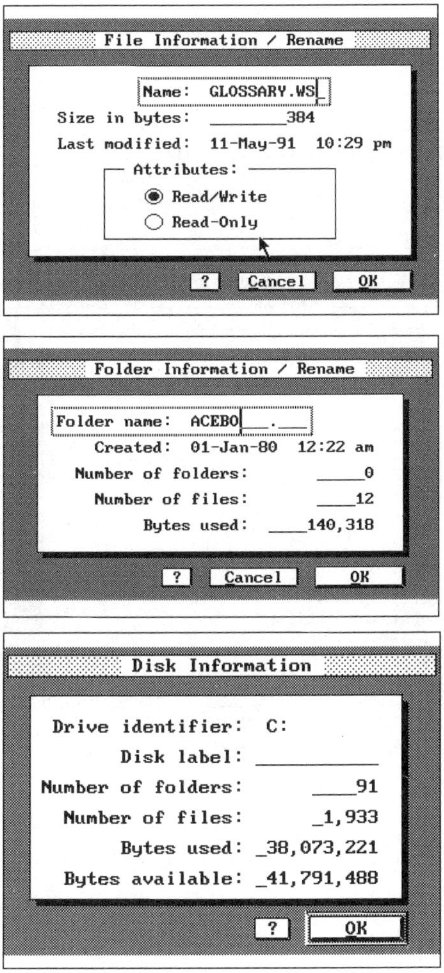

USING VIEWMAX

Figure 11-12. The File, Folder, and Disk Drive Information Dialog boxes.

If you've selected a directory, you'll be able to see:

- The directory name, which you can change if you like.

- How many subdirectories and files reside in the directory.

- How much disk space the directory contents occupy.

DR DOS 6 BY EXAMPLE

If you have selected a file, you'll see:

- The size of the file.

- The read/write status and the file name, which you can change.

- The file name, which you can also change.

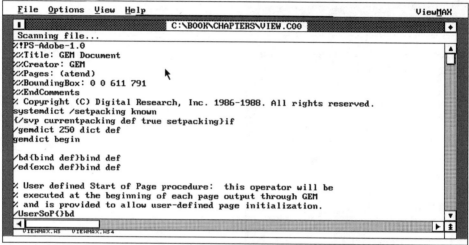

Figure 11-13. A postscript file viewed through "Show Contents."

To view the contents of a file that you've selected, click on the Show Contents command in the File menu (or press Alt-F followed by S). If you've selected a text file, you'll be able to read the text (see Figure 11-13). You can move around through the text using scroll bars. If the file isn't text, and if you're a "techie," you'll love this: ViewMAX will display the file in both hexadecimal and ASCII (see Figure 11-14). The binary file display screen looks a lot like the one you'll find in SID or DEBUG. If you're the type that's interested in looking at binary files, you'll likely be acquainted with the display conventions.

There are three ways to close the file and get back to the ViewMAX window:

- Click the close box at the upper left corner of the window.

- Select the Close command in the View menu, either with your mouse or using Alt-V followed by C.

- Press Alt-F4.

264

USING VIEWMAX

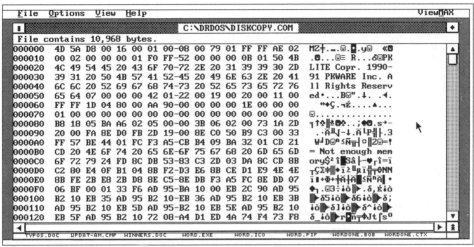

Figure 11-14. A program viewed through "Show Contents."

Changing a Password

Files and folders can have passwords in DR DOS, and you can assign passwords quite easily in ViewMAX. Click the Password command in the File menu to assign a password to a selected object (see Figure 11-15). If it's a file password, you can select whether the password is to protect a file from being deleted, overwritten, or read by someone else.

This is a great way to protect your resume or diary from most people. However, if you look in the advanced tools section in Chapter 13, you'll find that there are sophisticated tools (such as MUSE) that can breeze by the file- and directory-level password protection. If you really want to be secure, you'll need to use the Secure System capabilities made available in DR DOS 6.0. (See Chapter 10, Securing Your Data.)

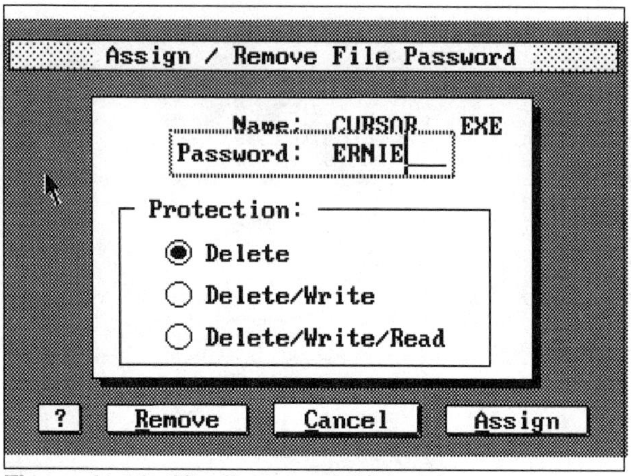

DR DOS 6 BY EXAMPLE

Figure 11-15. File Password Dialog box.

Once you've assigned all of these passwords, you may want to be able to unlock all password-protected files and directories in one pass. To make this work, you must assign the same password to all files and directories you wish to unlock in one operation. You can then unlock them with the Global password command in the Options menu (see Figure 11-16). Enter the password, and click the Assign button.

As long as the global password is assigned, you'll be able to use any file or access any directory protected with that password.

You can also remove the global password, relocking the files and directories. Again, you'll use the Global password command in the Options menu, but this time you'll remove the password.

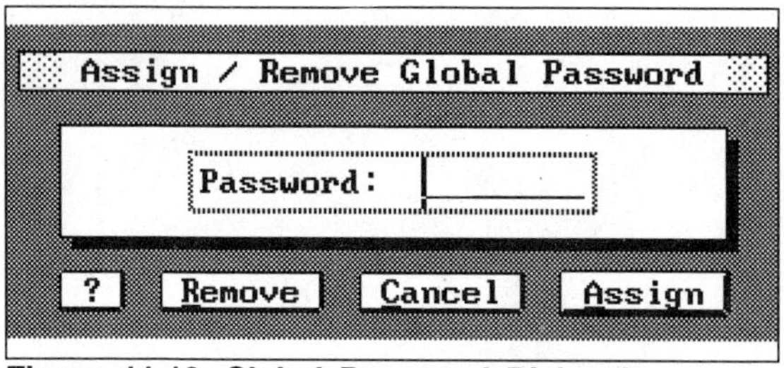

Figure 11-16. Global Password Dialog box.

Formatting Diskettes

The File menu has a limited Format command that you can use to format floppy disks (see Figure 11-17). The keyboard shortcut for accessing this is Alt-F followed by F. The ViewMAX format command won't format a hard disk or disk partition (thank goodness). It doesn't accept any options, so you can't use it to format a low-density disk in a high-density drive. It also can't use the "quick format" capability released in DR DOS 6.0. Its final shortcoming is that it won't allow you to interrupt formatting. If you have a bad disk undergoing a format started this way, you'll just have to be patient until the format program finishes grinding away.

Before you can use the Format command, you must first put a disk in the appropriate drive and then select that drive icon in a ViewMAX file window. Be careful not to open the icon (double-click), or you'll need to wait until ViewMAX decides it really can't read anything from the disk before you can get back to the task of formatting. While formatting, you'll see a window that tells you how much of the disk has been formatted.

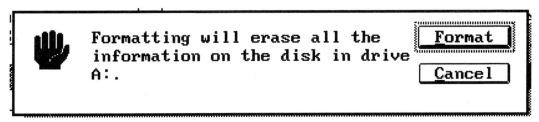

Figure 11-17. Disk format alert box.

Changing the View From Your Windows

ViewMAX will let you change the order in which things are displayed, as well as shift from viewing files as icons to seeing them in text mode. These changes only affect the active window. Each of these display modes is selectable as a command in the View menu. Figure 11-18 shows an example of various window display modes.

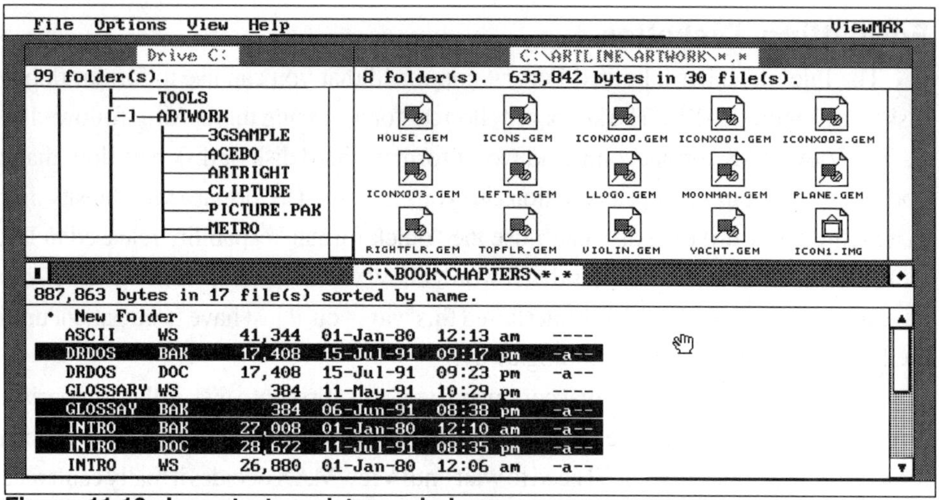

DR DOS 6 BY EXAMPLE

```
 File  Options  View  Help                                          ViewMAX
┌─────────Drive C:─────────┬──────────C:\ARTLINE\ARTWORK\*.*─────────────────┐
│ 99 folder(s).            │ 8 folder(s).   633,842 bytes in 30 file(s).    │
│          ├──TOOLS        │   ▤        ▤        ▤        ▤        ▤        │
│      [-]─ARTWORK         │ HOUSE.GEM ICONS.GEM ICONX000.GEM ICONX001.GEM ICONX002.GEM │
│          ├──3GSAMPLE     │   ▤        ▤        ▤        ▤        ▤        │
│          ├──ACEBO        │ ICONX003.GEM LEFTLR.GEM LLOGO.GEM MOONMAN.GEM PLANE.GEM │
│          ├──ARTRIGHT     │   ▤        ▤        ▤        ▤        ▢        │
│          ├──CLIPTURE     │ RIGHTFLR.GEM TOPFLR.GEM VIOLIN.GEM VACHT.GEM ICON1.IMG │
│          ├──PICTURE.PAK  │                                                │
│          └──METRO        │                                                │
├──────────────────────────┴────C:\BOOK\CHAPTERS\*.*─────────────────────────┤
│ 887,863 bytes in 17 file(s) sorted by name.                                │
│   • New Folder                                                             │
│     ASCII    WS     41,344   01-Jan-80  12:13 am   ----                    │
│     DRDOS    BAK    17,408   15-Jul-91  09:17 pm   -a--                    │
│     DRDOS    DOC    17,408   15-Jul-91  09:23 pm   -a--                    │
│     GLOSSARY WS        384   11-May-91  10:29 pm   ----                    │
│     GLOSSAY  BAK       384   06-Jun-91  08:38 pm   -a--                    │
│     INTRO    BAK    27,008   01-Jan-80  12:10 am   -a--                    │
│     INTRO    DOC    28,672   11-Jul-91  08:35 pm   -a--                    │
│     INTRO    WS     26,880   01-Jan-80  12:06 am   -a--                    │
└────────────────────────────────────────────────────────────────────────────┘
```

Figure 11-18. Icon, text, and tree windows.

If you want to dedicate the entire window space to the file window, just use Hide Tree (Alt-V followed by H). Use the Show Tree command to bring the tree window back (Alt-V followed by T). As with everything else, this applies to the active window only.

You can display files and folders as icons or text entries (similar to what you'd see from DIR or XDIR), or you can opt to display or hide the tree window in DR DOS release 6.0. In DR DOS 5.0, you can display the entire window as a directory tree. When using the icon or text mode, you can change the order in which files and folders are sorted. Your choices are:

Name order   This is alphabetical order by file name, regardless of the file extension. Folders remain at the top of the window and in alphabetical order.

Type order   This is a double sort. First files are sorted in alphabetical order by file type. Then each set of files with the same type is presented in alphabetical order by file name. This is the default method of presenting files, and it leaves folders at the top of the window and in alphabetical order.

USING VIEWMAX

Size order This sorts files by size (it doesn't affect folders, which remain at the top of the window). The largest files are displayed toward the top of the window, just under the folders.

Date order This sorts files and folders by date (however, folders still remain at the top of the window).

Wildcards This affects all of the other display options, but only for files. Normally, ViewMAX displays all possible files, which is equivalent to *.* in the file commands you can issue from the DR DOS command line. However, the Wildcards command lets you change this *file mask*. For example, by setting it to *.GEM, you'd only see the .GEM graphics files. By setting it to FRED*.?GG, you'd only see those files whose names start with FRED and whose extensions end in GG. The question mark (?) character can be used as a wildcard in a command to match a single character, while the asterisk (*) matches any number of characters.

Finding Files

Starting with DR DOS release 6.0, ViewMAX gained the ability to search for a file throughout the current drive and then switch the window to view the directory where the file resides. You'll discover FIND FILE under the File menu (Alt-F followed by N). Figure 11-19 shows the FIND FILE dialog box.

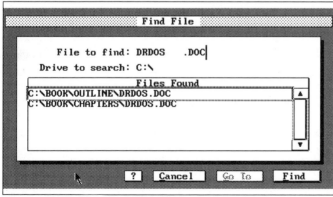

Figure 11-19. The Find File Dialog box.

To use this, just enter the name of the file in the File to Find line. You can use wildcards if you prefer. For example, if you're looking for all of the Artline picture files — which end in .GEM — that might be on a drive, you enter this:

```
*.GEM
```

If you want to limit the search to all of the picture files starting with LOGO, you enter this:

```
LOGO*.GEM
```

Finally, if you want to look for a specific file, you enter its exact name:

```
LOGOTXT.GEM
```

Once you've decided what to look for, just click on Find. After a few seconds of disk whirring and clanking, ViewMAX will report what it found in the scroll box. If you double-click on one of the files shown in the scroll box, ViewMAX will display that file's directory in the file window and highlight that file for you.

Undeleting Files and Directories

DR DOS 6.0 introduced the Undelete utility, and as a consequence ViewMAX was given the capability to call this program. If you select Undelete from the file menu (Alt-F followed by U), ViewMAX will actually load this utility and you'll find yourself using its interface, not ViewMAX's. (Figure 11-20). The Undelete utility is covered in detail in Chapter 13.

A couple of important points relating to Undelete and ViewMAX are:

1. Your mouse doesn't work in Undelete, so don't get concerned if you can't find your mouse cursor.

2. You'll return to ViewMAX when you exit Undelete.

USING VIEWMAX

Help!

Help is reasonably useful and provides memory joggers about how to use windows, menus, and dialog boxes. Just remember that if you get stuck and can't quite remember how to do something, you can check the Help menu.

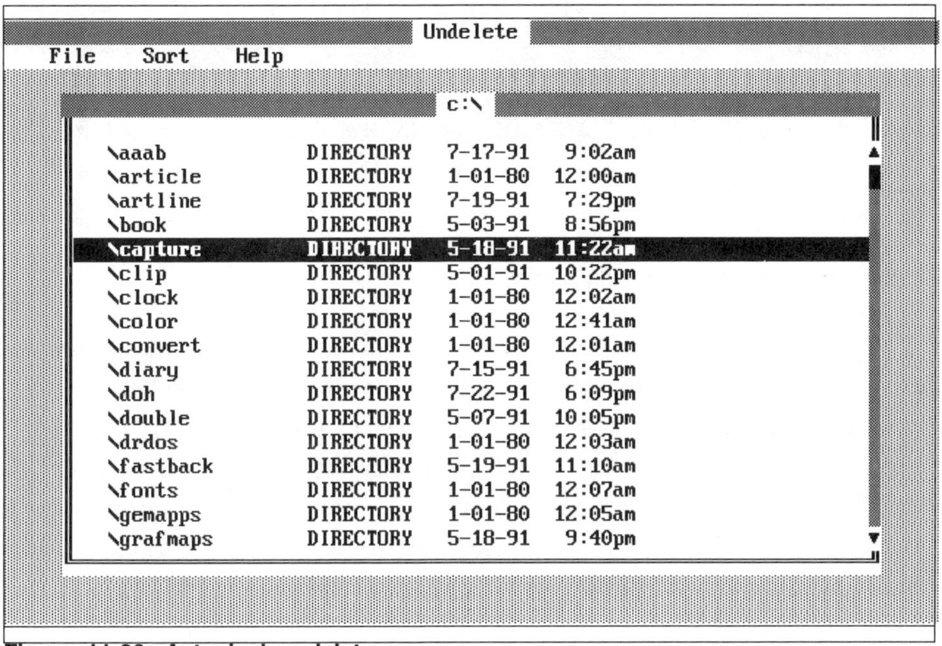

```
                              Undelete
   File     Sort     Help
                              c:\

   \aaab              DIRECTORY    7-17-91    9:02am
   \article           DIRECTORY    1-01-80   12:00am
   \artline           DIRECTORY    7-19-91    7:29pm
   \book              DIRECTORY    5-03-91    8:56pm
   \capture           DIRECTORY    5-18-91   11:22am
   \clip              DIRECTORY    5-01-91   10:22pm
   \clock             DIRECTORY    1-01-80   12:02am
   \color             DIRECTORY    1-01-80   12:41am
   \convert           DIRECTORY    1-01-80   12:01am
   \diary             DIRECTORY    7-15-91    6:45pm
   \doh               DIRECTORY    7-22-91    6:09pm
   \double            DIRECTORY    5-07-91   10:05pm
   \drdos             DIRECTORY    1-01-80   12:03am
   \fastback          DIRECTORY    5-19-91   11:10am
   \fonts             DIRECTORY    1-01-80   12:07am
   \gemapps           DIRECTORY    1-01-80   12:05am
   \grafmaps          DIRECTORY    5-18-91    9:40pm
```

Figure 11-20. A typical undelete screen.

Desk Accessories

ViewMAX comes with two semi-useful desk accessories: a calculator and a clock (see Figure 11-21). The desk accessories can be found under the ViewMAX menu at the right of the menu bar. I call these accessories semi-useful because you must be in ViewMAX to use them. For example, say you're running your favorite word processor — WeaselWord — from ViewMAX, and you want to use the calculator. You'll need to exit WeaselWord and return to the ViewMAX window to get to the calculator. If you're using TaskMAX in conjunction with ViewMAX, reaching your accessories is reasonably convenient. All you need to do is switch back to the ViewMAX task.

DR DOS 6 BY EXAMPLE

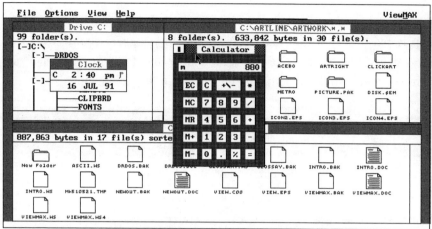

Figure 11-21. Calculator and clock accessories.

These accessories are actually borrowed from the GEM/3 desktop accessories, except that with ViewMAX you don't get a print spooler. The calculator is a fairly typical four-function calculator, with "C" for Clear and "EC" for Clear Entry. You'll also find that the calculator has a single-value memory, which you control with the "M" keys — MC (memory clear), MR (memory recall), M+ (add current value to memory), and M- (subtract current value from memory). Frankly, I find something appealing in the ability to turn a computer worth several thousand dollars into a five-dollar calculator on demand.

The clock accessory displays the day and date. It also has an alarm, but again you must have ViewMAX active and on the screen for the alarm to sound. This is like having an alarm clock that will only go off if you're looking at it. Click on the time and date numbers to turn them into text-entry fields, allowing you to change the time and the date. To bring up the alarm display, click on "C" in the upper left corner of the clock. "C" denotes the clock mode, while "A" stands for alarm mode. Clicking on the letter toggles the clock between modes.

To set the alarm, click the time and date values shown to change them to text-entry fields. To arm the alarm, click the note in the upper right corner. A gray or dimmed note means the alarm in inactive, while a solid note means that the alarm is set.

Recycling Old Accessories

If you have any GEM accessories from GEM/3, you can also load these into ViewMAX. Simply copy the .ACC and .RSC files for that accessory to the /DRDOS directory. For example, the handiest GEM/3 accessory was GEM Diary. It had a calculator, an appointment calendar, and a set of six Rolodex files (one of the Rolodex files is shown in Figure 11-22). There are two things to remember when recycling GEM/3 accessories:

1. The extended character set in ViewMAX is different from GEM/3. For example, an arrow in GEM/3 will be a face in ViewMAX.

2. Some GEM/3 accessories take more memory than the ViewMAX accessories. If you are tight on memory, you might not be able to load them. One way around this is to rename VIEWMAX.ACC (the ViewMAX accessory file in the DR DOS directory) to VIEWMAX.CCA or another unused file extension. This will prevent VIEWMAX.ACC from being loaded into ViewMAX. If you want to use the ViewMAX accessories again at a later date, rename the file extension to .ACC.

Running Applications

Like other GUIs, ViewMAX allows you to assign icons to applications. If the application has related files, you can also assign identifying icons to these. For example, Lotus 1-2-3 can be given a spreadsheet icon, and all .WKS or .WK3 files can be given icons indicating that they are spreadsheet files. Applications are .EXE, .COM, and .BAT files — anything you can run from the command line. You can also run GEM/3 .APP files if the GEM/3 desktop resides on the system. In ViewMAX, you run applications by double-clicking on them. If an application will

DR DOS 6 BY EXAMPLE

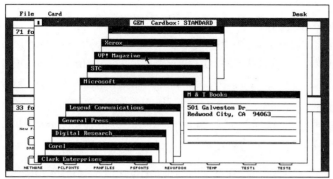

Figure 11-22. GEM diary running as ViewMAX accessory.

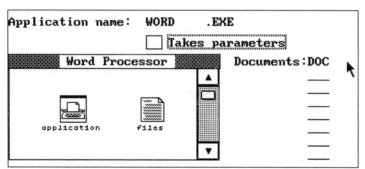

Figure 11-23. The Application Configuration Dialog box.

accept a file name as an argument for a file to be loaded, then you can set ViewMAX to load and run an application by double-clicking on a related file. For example, to run Microsoft Word from the DR DOS command you would type the following and press Enter:

```
WORD
```

If you want to load the file WHATEVER.DOC automatically when you start Word, you use the following command:

```
WORD WHATEVER.DOC
```

USING VIEWMAX

Because Word will take the name of a file as an argument, you can also configure ViewMAX so that when you double-click on any .DOC file Word starts and automatically loads that file.

While you can run any application from DR DOS without configuring it, if it's an application that you use frequently you will want to introduce it properly to DR DOS. To run an unconfigured application, simply double-click on it. DR DOS will ask you for any arguments, such as a file name, that you might want to load. Clicking OK in the dialog box runs the application.

By the way, if it's an application that simply presents information and then returns to the command line, you probably won't get a chance to read the information before ViewMAX reappears. The DR DOS memory usage reporter, MEM.EXE, is a good example of such a program. If you want to run such a program from ViewMAX, your best approach is to create a batch file that pauses after running the application. See Chapter 8 on batch files for an example of this.

To configure an application:

1. Click on an executable file (.BAT, .EXE, .COM, or .APP file extensions point to these) to select the file.

2. Click the Configure Application... command under the Options menu.

3. In the dialog box that appears (see Figure 11-23), you'll need to specify the type of program and whether the program accepts parameters. Here are your parameter choices:

Takes Parameters

Click Yes only if the program normally takes arguments or "switches." An example might be a program that has no menus or dialog boxes, but is run completely from the command line. The DR DOS BACKUP utility is a good example of this kind of program. For example, to run BACKUP and copy the contents of the C:\STUFF directory to floppy disks in the A: drive, you'd use the following command:

```
BACKUP C:\STUFF A:
```

275

Selecting Yes will cause ViewMAX to provide a text-entry dialog box where you can enter command-line arguments. This appears each time you run the program from ViewMAX.

If your program doesn't normally take command-line arguments (except for a file name to load), then click on No.

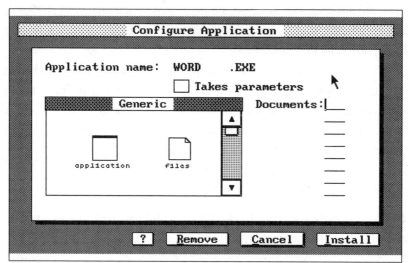

Figure 11-23. The Application Configuration dialog box.

Application Type and Documents

You can select an icon to identify the type of program and can tell ViewMAX what sort of files — the so-called documents — are created by this program. Keep in mind that a document may be any type of file, such as a graphics file, a database, or the source code for a program compiler.

Having the proper icon allows you to pick the application you want at a glance. If the application can load a document file by adding it as an argument to the command used to run the application, then you click on an associated document to run the application and load the document.

To select an icon, simply scroll down through the set available until something applicable appears. Then type the file extensions in the set of text fields to the right of the scroll box. Figure 11-24 shows a configuration for the Microsoft Word word processor. Note that the document type is .DOC.

USING VIEWMAX

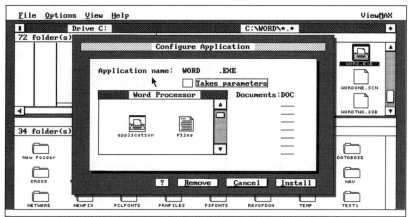

Figure 11-24. Configuration for Microsoft Word.

The possible icon selections are shown in Figure 11-25 and are listed below:

Generic This is a last resort, to be used only if nothing else seems remotely applicable. It's also the default ViewMAX assigns to each executable file it encounters.

Spreadsheet A Lotus 1-2-3-type or SuperCalc-type application.

Word Processor Something like Microsoft Word or WordStar. DR DOS Editor, the full-screen text-editing utility, is assigned one of these by default.

Data Base An application such as dBase IV or SuperBase.

Draw Draw packages are line-oriented graphics applications. Digital Reseach's Draw PLUS is one example, and a computer-aided drafting package is another.

Paint A pixel or "dot-based" graphics application, such as PC Paint or Migraph TouchUp.

Project	A project management or planning application, such as Microsoft Project or InstaPlan.
Graph	A business graphics package, such as Harvard Graphics or Digital Research's Presentation Team.
Outline	An outline creation utility, such as PC Outline.
Accounting	An accounts receivable, accounts payable, payroll, or MRP application. Pacciolli 2000 is one such program.
Multifunction	Integrated packages that attempt to do a number of functions, including word processing, spreadsheet capabilities and database management. Microsoft Works is an example.
Education	Educational packages such as Reader Rabbit fit this description, as do computer-based instruction programs or authoring utilities.
Communications	Telecommunication packages such as ProComm or Kermit. The DR DOS Filelink package gets this icon by default.
Programmer's Tool	This should be used for compilers, linkers, macro assemblers, tool debuggers, and the other tools of the programmer's trade. The DR DOS SID debugging tool is assigned this icon by default. I also use this for any general utility that doesn't have a better match.
Game	Self-explanatory.
Output	A utility that is used to send files to a printer or prepare files for printing. The DR DOS PRINT utility gets one of these.
Desktop Publisher	A page-layout program such as Ventura or Publish-It!
Scan	A scanner front-end program used to select options for scanning or to edit scanned images. Most of these run under Windows now, so you'll be hard pressed to find one that you can run from ViewMAX unless you have GEM Scan.

USING VIEWMAX

Mail If your computer is on a network, you'd assign this to your electronic mail facility.

Artline Artline is for Digital Research's Artline professional illustration package. You could also use it for such programs as Draw Perfect.

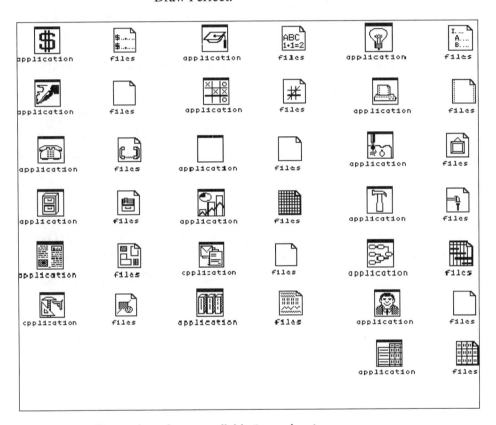

Figure 11-25. The various icons available to assign to programs.

The trick about configuring an application is that ViewMAX won't remember this information unless you use the Save Configuration command in the Options menu (actually, if you used the Set Preferences command in the Option menu to set Save Configuration on Exit to On, ViewMAX will remember). If you forget to save the configuration, the next time you use ViewMAX you'll need to configure the application again.

DR DOS 6 BY EXAMPLE

A Sample Configuration

You need to be at your computer and have ViewMAX up and running to try this easy example of configuring applications and documents. All set? First, to make sure we've actually accomplished something, we'll need to know the date on our example file.

1. From wherever you are in ViewMAX, click your way to the DR DOS directory.

2. When you get to the DR DOS directory, click once on VIEWMAX.ACC to select this file.

3. Look under the File menu for the Info/Rename command. Click this and you'll see a dialog box that provides all sorts of helpful information about VIEWMAX.ACC. Note the date that VIEWMAX.ACC was last modified (such as the June 15, 1990, or whatever your dialog box shows).

4. Click on Cancel.

OK, now we'll configure a DR DOS external command called TOUCH.EXE. TOUCH simply changes the last modification date and time for a file to the current date and time. Let's set up all .ACC files as documents for TOUCH and try it out.

1. Scroll down until you can see the TOUCH.EXE application.

2. Click once on TOUCH.EXE to select it.

3. Select the Configure Application command from the Options menu.

4. Scroll through the icon set until you find the Programmer's Tool icon (the hammer).

5. Click once on the top line in the set of text fields. This will put your cursor (vertical line) in the field.

6. Type ACC, then click OK.

Now, notice that TOUCH.EXE has a hammer icon and that VIEWMAX.ACC has the hammer-and-nail icon. Double-click on VIEWMAX.ACC. ViewMAX will run TOUCH against the VIEWMAX.ACC file. You can verify that this really happened by using Info/Rename (File menu) to check the last modification date for VIEWMAX.ACC. If it worked, the modification date is now the current date.

Pitfalls in Configuring Applications

As a service to its GEM/3 customers, Digital Research preconfigured each of its GEM applications — the GEM FirstWord Plus word processor assigned the extension .DOC to its word processor files, for example. However, Word and later versions of WordStar also used .DOC. Here's what happens:

1. You configure Word properly.

2. You double-click on Word and, sure enough, it loads.

3. Now for the acid test: you exit word and double-click on a Word .DOC file. Instead of seeing your file loaded in Word, you'll find yourself looking at a "can't find related program" error. If you have FirstWord Plus, ViewMAX will try to load the file into FirstWord instead of Word.

To correct this or similar problems, you need to edit the VIEWMAX.INI file in the DR DOS directory. This is not for the faint of heart, because this file holds all of the configuration information for ViewMAX. However, this is a Catch-22 situation. (You can only see the Major if the Major isn't in, remember?) You can only fix this configuration problem by editing the VIEWMAX.INI file, but if the DR DOS Setup configuration program detects tinkering with an .INI file, then Setup won't load it. If this occurs, you'll need to load a fresh copy of VIEWMAX.INI from the DR DOS disks, configure this with Setup, and then modify it again to cure the .DOC problem.

Here's where the problem originates. Note the following section taken from the VIEWMAX.INI file:

```
(G:12,44) DRAW.APP *.GEM
(G:23,55) OUTPUT.APP *.LIS
(G:21,53) INSTALL.APP ~
(G:21,53) GEMSETUP.APP ~
(G:15,47) GRAPH.APP *.GRF
```

```
(G:13,45) PAINT.APP ~
(G:10,42) WORDCHRT.APP *.WCH
(G:10,42) WRITE.APP ~
(G:10,42)   WORDPLUS.APP   *.DOC,*.SUP,*.MRG
(G:21,53) MAPED.APP *.MAP
(G:24,56) PUBLISHR.APP *.GWD
(G:26,58) 1ST_MAIL.APP ~
(G:27,59) ARTLINE.APP ~
(p:23,55) PRINT.COM ~
(p:10,42) EDITOR.EXE *.ME,*.TXT
(p:21,53) SID.EXE ~
(p:20,52) FILELINK.EXE ~
(p:21,53) EXE2BIN.EXE *.BIN
(p:18,50) PT.BAT *.PTP,*.PTS
(D:00,00) ~ ~
(M:00,00) ~ ~
(M:00,00) ~ ~
(p:00,00) ~ ~
(p:00,00) ~ ~
(m:10,42)   WORD.EXE   *.DOC
```

The two lines in bold tell the tale. This part of the .INI file defines all of the configured files and the extensions of their related files. ViewMAX looks for .DOC and first finds it listed with WORDPLUS.APP, so it then tries to load the .DOC file into GEM FirstWord Plus. If you want to use .DOC files with some other word processor, you must delete the *.DOC from the WORDPLUS line. That way, ViewMAX will continue to look for a match to .DOC until it finds WORD.EXE or whatever program you are using.

Note that the other extensions in this list can cause trouble. If any of your applications use these extensions, except of course the GEM and DR DOS applications listed, you'll need to modify the appropriate lines in the VIEWMAX.INI file. If you are going to modify VIEWMAX.INI, any ASCII file editor will work (including the DR DOS EDITOR program).

USING VIEWMAX

Configuring GEM Applications

If you have GEM/3 on your system, you can use ViewMAX to activate these applications. However, keep in mind that it is really calling the GEM/3 desktop to run the applications. If default icons are assigned to these applications, such as with any of the Digital Research applications, you'll see this icon displayed from the ViewMAX window.

For example, to run Migraph's TouchUp professional graphics package, follow these steps.

1. First, locate Migraph and display it in a window. Like most GEM/3 applications, it resides in the GEMAPPS directory.

2. Double-click on TOUCHUP.APP, causing ViewMAX to load the GEM/3 desktop and provide it with the TOUCHUP.APP command line argument. If you are familiar with GEM/3, this is the same as entering GEM TOUCHUP.APP from the command line.

3. GEM/3 then loads TouchUp. You can still switch between tasks if TaskMAX is loaded.

Upon exiting TouchUp, GEM/3 shuts down and ViewMAX redisplays its windows.

Problems with Some GEM Applications

Some GEM applications can't run from within GEM/3, but ViewMAX doesn't know this. For instance, Ventura GEM edition versions 2.0 and 3.0 have their own run-time versions of a modified GEM/3 and don't run properly from within the standard version of GEM/3. Likewise, the new GEM/4-based applications from Digital Research, such as Artline, Presentation Team, and Draw Plus, don't run properly from within GEM/3.

Normally, you run all of these applications from the command line by executing a batch file. You use the same technique in ViewMAX. For example, to use Ventura GEM edition 3.0, you first find the VP.BAT or VPPROF.BAT file in the root directory. Then you configure this file and assign it a desktop publisher icon. You also tell ViewMAX that it takes no arguments. After saving this configuration, you can run Ventura simply by double-clicking on the .BAT file — you don't need to double-click on the .APP file.

Escaping to DR DOS

Occasionally you might want to jump out of ViewMAX temporarily and back to the DR DOS command-line environment. One reason to do this would be to use command-line arguments to format a low-density disk in a high-density drive. Another reason might be to run the LOCK program to lock your keyboard until you return to the computer. One method allows you to escape to DR DOS without losing your place in ViewMAX, which would happen if you merely exited to DR DOS and then restarted ViewMAX.

When you escape to DR DOS, it starts a new shell — a new version of COMMAND.COM that starts a new command-line processor. Just enough of ViewMAX remains in memory for you to recover your position. However, if TaskMAX is active, it simply starts a new task at the command line, and you don't lose additional memory.

To escape to DOS, select Enter DR DOS Commands from the Options menu. To return to DR DOS, type EXIT at the command line and then press Return.

There are a couple of things to remember about escaping to DR DOS. If you aren't running TaskMAX, the DR DOS shell has a bit less memory (about 20 KB less). You've also got to keep in mind that you need to type EXIT to return to ViewMAX instead of running ViewMAX again. If you are using DR DOS 5.0, you'll find that the keyboard command-line memory capability isn't available to you when you are running within a shell.

ViewMAX and TaskMAX

TaskMAX can run ViewMAX as a separate task, or you can use ViewMAX to manage TaskMAX. If you want to know more about TaskMAX, refer to the TaskMAX chapter. Before we get into the particulars, let's look at the advantages of either arrangement.

If you choose to leave control of TaskMAX with TaskMAX itself, pressing the TaskMAX hot-key sequence will take you to the standard TaskMAX menu. From there, you can initiate new tasks, delete tasks, cut and paste, and perform other tasks just as you normally would. ViewMAX is treated just like any other task.

If you choose to use ViewMAX to control TaskMAX, pressing the TaskMAX hot-key sequence returns you to ViewMAX. You'll see the TaskMAX Interface dialog box.

There are a few more key differences: if you start a program through the ViewMAX file window, ViewMAX will automatically take control of TaskMAX and use it to create a new task for that program. You can then switch out of the task directly back to ViewMAX using the switch-to-task keys or the TaskMAX hot-key sequence. For instance, let's say that Control-Esc is the hot-key sequence and that ViewMAX is the first task. If you start Microsoft Word from a ViewMAX window, you can return to ViewMAX by pressing Control-1. If you want to return directly to the TaskMAX interface dialog within ViewMAX, press Control-Esc.

Using ViewMAX to control TaskMAX means giving up the cut-and-paste procedure. These functions are not available from the ViewMAX TaskMAX interface dialog box. And regardless of how you decide to manage TaskMAX, you can't access it at all from ViewMAX unless you activate TaskMAX before starting ViewMAX.

The TaskMAX Dialog Boxes

I mentioned earlier that, if TaskMAX is active, then simply double-clicking on an application in ViewMAX (i.e., starting the application) gives ViewMAX management over TaskMAX. However, you can also control this from the TaskMAX Preferences dialog box. You access this dialog box, shown in Figure 11-26, through the Options menu (Alt-O followed by M). The dialog box has two controls:

- A check box that sets whether TaskMAX is managed through ViewMAX. You can turn this off and on while TaskMAX is active. For example, if you want to access the cut-and-paste function you can turn off ViewMAX management.

- A slider bar that allocates LIM memory (not extended memory). LIM stands for "Lotus-Intel-Microsoft," the names of the companies that created the LIM memory standard. This sort of memory is called *expanded memory*. Providing expanded memory to some applications, such as spreadsheets and word processors, will increase the amount of data you can use or enhance the speed of operation. Other programs, such as Ventura Publisher GEM edition with the Professional Extension, won't run at all without expanded memory.

To use the slider bar, click and hold on the slider and move it right or left. The dialog box will show you how much memory is allocated to ViewMAX. The slider bar spans the total amount of LIM memory available on your system. However, you may already have allocated some expanded memory to other programs, and this won't be reflected in the slider bar. Also, you can change the amount of expanded memory on a task-by-task basis. For instance, you can allocate 512 KB to Artline version 2.0, 1,600 KB to Ventura, and 0 KB to Word.

Setting LIM memory is tricky, and you should check your application program manuals to find out how much they need. Remember that you also use Setup to set how much memory, from the total available memory, is available to applications. For example, Ventura 3.0 Professional needs 1.6 MB to load the dictionary and its Professional Extension features. If either Setup or the slider bar (or both) doesn't allocate this much memory to tasks, you won't be able to run Ventura with all of its features.

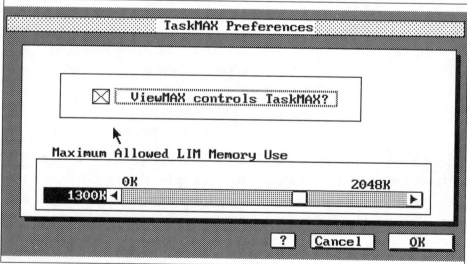

Figure 11-26. The TaskMAX Preferences Dialog box.

By the way, this is a good time to let you know that Artline and Presentation Team both require a minimum of 512 KB of expanded memory if they are going to access expanded memory at all (they don't need expanded memory to run, but it does improve performance). Unfortunately, both programs are a bit confused by TaskMAX and will think 512 KB is available when perhaps there isn't that much expanded memory. If this occurs, Artline and Presentation Team will try to access expanded memory and may lock up, forcing you to delete the task and restart. To avoid this, allocate no expanded memory or at least 512 KB to these programs.

If you set ViewMAX to manage TaskMAX, you'll be able to access the TaskMAX interface dialog box (Control-O followed by T), shown in Figure 11-27. This is the equivalent of the standard TaskMAX menus. From here you can open a new task, delete an existing task, or run a task shown in the scroll window.

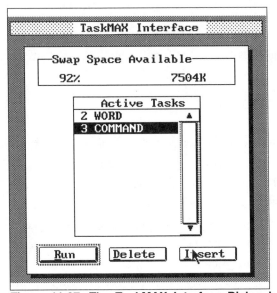

Figure 11-27. The TaskMAX Interface Dialog box.

Here's an interesting thing about creating tasks: if you create a task by clicking on the application in the file window, TaskMAX automatically deletes the task when you exit from the application. If you create a task through the TaskMAX interface dialog box, you will need to delete it through that dialog box.

DR DOS 6 BY EXAMPLE

The reason for this is simple: when you execute an application, your intent is to run only that application. A task opened through the TaskMAX interface dialog box is general-purpose, complete with a command line. You can run a number of application programs from a general-purpose task. As such, ViewMAX doesn't know when to close the task by itself. You need to decide that.

Road-Testing the ViewMAX/TaskMAX Combo

If you desire, you can use your computer as you follow this example. We're about to open a few tasks and switch between these and ViewMAX. I'll make it simple and use programs that are part of DR DOS itself.

First, make sure that TaskMAX is running. To do this, type

```
TASKMAX
```

at the DR DOS command line, then press Enter. After the computer responds that TaskMAX is loaded, you can run ViewMAX by typing the following at the command line and pressing Enter:

```
VIEWMAX
```

Once in ViewMAX, you can start to control TaskMAX. Pull down the Options menu and select the ViewMAX Preferences command. Click on the check box to select ViewMAX Managing TaskMAX. As for the slider bar, the total to the right is all of the expanded memory available to TaskMAX. You can allocate as much as you like to TaskMAX, but remember to save enough for those programs that need it. Also remember that TaskMAX will try to provide each task with the amount of expanded memory selected through Setup. When you're done, click on OK.

Now let's launch a new task. If the DR DOS directory isn't shown in a window, use the tree window or the close boxes and open folder functions to find your way there.

Once the DR DOS directory is visible, scroll the window until you can see the Editor icon.

Select the Editor Icon (click once) and then double-click on Editor to run the program.

USING VIEWMAX

When Editor comes up, enter any silly name you like for the sake of this example. RHINO.TXT is a good name for a test file.

After getting Editor started use Control-1 (or whatever set of keys you use for TaskMAX), to switch back to Task 1 (ViewMAX). The speed that you switch back to ViewMAX is determined by the amount of memory available and the speed of your hard drive. If you have enough memory to hold the tasks, TaskMAX will switch almost instantly. If you don't have enough memory, TaskMAX will need to copy the tasks to your hard drive. While this process is a bit slower, it won't take more than a few seconds to complete the switch.

Once back at ViewMAX, you'll find yourself looking at the TaskMAX interface dialog box. From here you can create new tasks, delete active tasks, or click on Cancel to return to the ViewMAX interface. Remember that all of your TaskMAX hot-key sequences still work as well.

Take a look at the Swap Space Available statistics at the top of the TaskMAX interface dialog box. This feature reports on the amount of memory available as well as the amount of contiguous disk space available to the TaskMAX swap file. As you add tasks, the amount of available space will begin to decrease. If you begin to approach zero percent available, it's time to close some tasks before attempting to start others.

Just for fun, let's launch a task from the TaskMAX interface dialog box. Click the Insert button and TaskMAX will start another task, but this time instead of loading a particular application you'll find yourself with a command-line prompt. Once the task-switching operation is over, switch back with Control-Esc or Control-1 (or whatever).

Now the TaskMAX interface dialog box shows a new task named Command located directly beneath the Editor task. To switch back to Editor, you can use the hot-key sequence or the task scroll box. To use the scroll box, click the Editor task to select it and then click the Run button. You can also simply double-click the Editor task.

Once back in Editor, press Control-K followed by Q. This will abandon the file. If you typed anything, Editor will ask if you really want to leave without saving. If it asks, respond by pressing Y. Finally, press the Escape key to exit from Editor. Now notice what happens: when Editor shuts down, TaskMAX will automatically return to the TaskMAX interface menu and delete the task.

To get rid of the command-line task, you'll need to delete it from the TaskMAX interface dialog box. Click once on Command to select it, then click on Delete. TaskMAX will ask you if you are sure about deleting the task, and you can reassure it by pressing Y.

OK, that's TaskMAX and ViewMAX in action. Just remember that exiting from ViewMAX doesn't automatically remove TaskMAX from memory. You will need to disengage TaskMAX in the usual way:

1. Delete all active tasks. Make sure you close any open files that you might want to save before deleting a task.

2. After exiting from your last task, which is probably ViewMAX, you'll need to enter the TaskMAX menu with the hot-key sequence.

3. Use the Delete key to remove TaskMAX from memory.

CHAPTER 12

Communication and FILELINK

This chapter covers using DR DOS to configure your communication ports, send files through those ports, and use the FILELINK program to quickly transfer files between two computers. If you are connecting a modem, mouse, or printer to your computer, or you wish to use FILELINK, read on.

Parallel Ports

In the introductory chapter, I mentioned that your computer has two kinds of communication ports: serial and parallel. DR DOS has a number of commands and utilities that allow you to control and use these ports. I'll discuss parallel ports first because they are more straightforward and are the common means for connecting to printers.

Parallel ports send information very efficiently by transmitting the bits in each byte in parallel. For example, each letter of the alphabet or numeral you send to your printer is contained in a "byte" of information, and that byte is made up of eight bits of information. A bit is the fundamental unit of information, representing a value that is one of two states: on, or off, expressed mathematically as a one or a zero. When the letter A is sent to your printer, it is actually sent as a series of "on" or "off" electrical pulses representing this set of ones and zeroes: 01000001. This is the standard ASCII code for an A. The parallel port achieves its efficiency by simultaneously sending each bit on a separate wire, allowing it to transmit the entire byte in one shot (see Figure 12-1). When I discuss serial communication later, you'll understand that this type of port sends data one bit at a time, over a single wire, in a series of pulses spread out over a particular period of time.

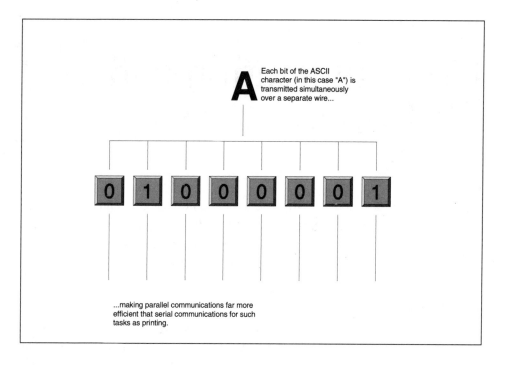

Figure 12-1. Parallel data transmission.

Figure 12-2 shows the end view of two types of parallel ports. Typically, your computer will have a connector like that shown as "A," while your printer may have either an "A" type 25-pin connector or a "B" type connector, also called a Centronics connector. If the connector on your computer isn't labelled, you can tell that it's the parallel port if no pins are sticking out.

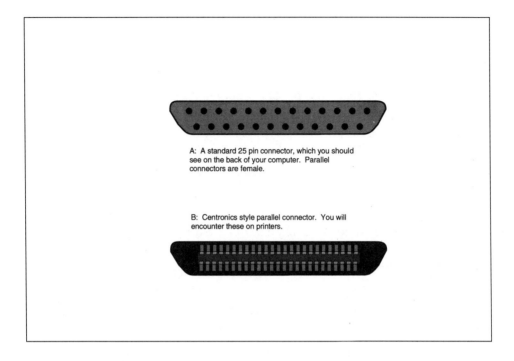

Figure 12-2. Parallel connectors.

You may wonder what the other wires are for, since only eight are needed to send information. These extra wires carry signals for pacing the flow of information, so that the device doesn't receive more than it can handle. Other wires are used for electrical grounding.

The only thing to remember about parallel connections is that you shouldn't try to use long connector cables. A practical maximum length is about 10 to 15 feet, and here's why: the cable acts as an antenna, picking up signals from electrical devices or even radio and television. These signals induce "noise" into the communication, causing errors to occur in the data transmission. Parallel cables are susceptible to noise, so the shorter your cable the less of a problem you'll have. If you keep the cable length under 10 to 15 feet (and almost all commercially available cables are less than this) you shouldn't have any problems.

DR DOS 6 BY EXAMPLE

Controlling Your Parallel Port

While the speed of parallel communication is established by the hardware and is not under software control, there are few things left to adjust:

- the number of characters per line sent to the parallel port,
- the number of lines per inch for the printer,
- whether or not DR DOS should continue trying to transmit data through the parallel port when the device obviously isn't receiving, or indicates it is busy.

These parameters are controlled by the DR DOS utility called MODE. However, the printer control sequences work only with printers that accept IBM/Epson control codes for printers. While there are a few laser printers that respond to this code set, you'll find that the usefulness of these commands is almost entirely restricted to dot matrix printers. You won't be able to use MODE to set the number of lines per inch or the number of characters per line for HP LaserJet or PostScript laser printers. You won't be able to set non-IBM/Epson-compatible dot matrix printers this way either. Check your printer manual to see if it is an IBM graphics printer or Epson dot matrix-compatible. Also, such settings are valid only when you are using COPY or PRINT to send data to the parallel port — modern applications will take control of the printer in their own manner, without assistance from the MODE command.

With these points in mind, the following example sets a printer attached to parallel port 1 to a setting of 132 characters per column, six lines to the inch, and tells DR DOS to continually retry sending data through the port.

```
MODE LPT1:132,6,P
```

In this command, "LPT1:" refers to "line printer port number #1" or parallel port #1. While you'll need to check your computer system to determine the number of parallel ports, DR DOS supports three ports: LPT1 (also called PRN), LPT2, or LPT3.

The 132 parameter sets the printer to 132 characters per line mode (80 and 132 are your only choices for this parameter). This is the normal setting if you have a

FILELINK

wide-carriage printer. If you have a narrow or standard-carriage printer (just wide enough for 8 1/2-by-11-inch paper), the 132 parameter sets it to a condensed print mode. For narrow-carriage printers, the standard value is 80.

The parameter " ,6" sets the number of lines per inch, and your choices here are 6 or 8. Don't forget the comma preceding the 6 or 8 (in fact, don't forget the commas before any of the parameters discussed in this section).

"P" tells DR DOS to keep trying when the printer doesn't respond or is busy. An unresponsive printer may be malfunctioning, or simply out of paper. A busy printer is already processing a print job.

When you use ,P, part of MODE is loaded into memory and will stay there until you reboot the system. Notice that when the ,P parameter is active, DR DOS won't give up trying to send information until you force it to by pressing the Control and Break keys together.

Serial Ports

Unlike parallel ports, serial ports send information in a bit-at-a-time fashion (see Figure 12-3). Serial ports connect two computers together to transfer data, or for connecting a mouse, stand-alone modem, and some types of printers to your computer.

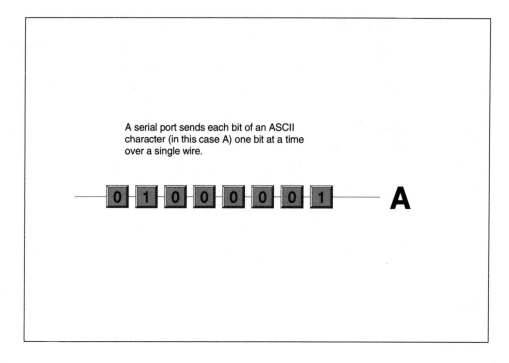

Figure 12-3. Serial data transmission.

Figure 12-4 shows end views of both 9- and 25-pin serial port connectors. If these aren't labeled either "serial" or "RS-232" on your computer, look for the male connector (with pins sticking out). This port is used to plug the serial cable into the computer. And this is also where all of the trouble starts. Usually, serial devices are configured so that a typical serial cable used with a mouse or modem will work without a problem. Things get a bit trickier with printers, and a whole lot trickier when wiring computers together.

FILELINK

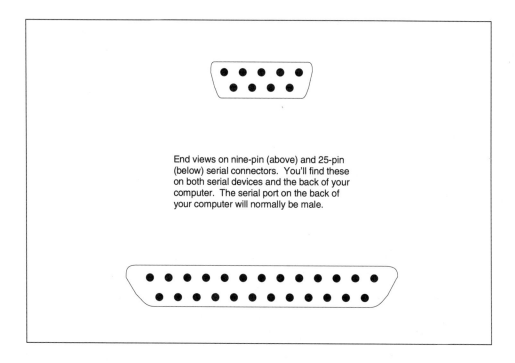

Figure 12-4. Serial connectors.

The trouble is due to the wide variety of connection combinations. While each of the pins on the serial connector has a standard function, there are many possibilities available to product designers for using or not using these pins. Moreover, your serial device and your computer must transmit and receive information at the same speed. Finally, you may find that you are connecting a PC with a 25-pin connector to a device with a 9-pin connector, requiring a special cable or an adapter. Stay with me as I lead you through the RS-232 jungle.

Plugging In

First, make sure that the cable will physically plug into the back of your computer. If your cable has a male connector and the serial port has a male connector, they won't go together. Your local computer or electronics store can sell you an adapter — a plastic block with interconnected female connectors at either end. This is sometimes called a gender changer, because it turns a male connector end into a female connector end, or vice versa. Install this adapter in the serial port, and then plug the male cable into the other end of the adapter. If you must go from a 25-pin serial connector on your computer to a 9-pin connector on the serial device, you must purchase a special cable with both connectors.

On the subject of cables, note that serial communication is less prone to noise than parallel communication. Unless you are running cables through factories or other electrically busy areas, you should be able to use a 50-foot serial cable with no problem. For distances beyond 50 feet, you can buy special serial cable with built-in noise shielding.

Controlling the Serial Port

Serial ports can normally transmit data at varying rates of speed, ranging from 110 to 9600 bits per second (bps), or 19200 on some computers such as the IBM PS/2. FILELINK can use your serial port at much higher speeds, the speed range for normal serial communication. The higher the transmission speed, the faster the data gets to the serial device. However, keep in mind that higher transmission speeds increase the effects of noise on transmissions.

Several parameters affect the way in which data is transmitted by the serial port:

Parity	This can be *odd, even,* or *none*. Parity uses the eighth bit of every byte for error checking.
Data length	Either seven or eight bits. If you are using even or odd parity, this must be set to seven.
Stop bits	This can be set to either one or two, and is used to signal the end of a unit of data. A setting of two is the default for 110 bps.
Time out	Like the parallel mode, you can set your serial port to keep on trying to send information forever. If you set the port for infinite retries, part of MODE is loaded into memory and stays there until you reboot the system. If you use this option, you'll need to use the combination of Control and Break to interrupt communication.

FILELINK

For example, a MODE statement to set serial port COM1: to 9600 bps, no parity, one stop bit, a data length of eight, and infinite retries is as follows:

```
MODE COM1:9600,N,8,1,P
```

This version of MODE sets COM3: for 1200 bps, odd parity, seven data bits, one stop bit.

```
MODE COM3:1200,O,7,1
```

The following table lists valid settings for each of these parameters:

Sending Data Through Your Ports

Aside from the printing capabilities of your application programs, there are three commonly used ways to send data through serial and parallel ports: the COPY command, the PRINT utility and the SCRIPT utility. Just as you can use COPY to make duplicates of files, you can also send duplicates of files to any port. For example, the following sends all .TXT files in the current directory to the PRN: (the LPT1:) device:

```
COPY *.DAT PRN:
```

This version of the command sends the files TEDIOUS.LST and HUGE.DAT to serial port COM2:

```
COPY TEDIOUS.LST+HUGE.DAT COM2:
```

COPY is a reasonably efficient way to send data to a port, although you can't enter additional commands or PRINT entries at the DR DOS command line while PRINT is running. Also, COPY won't work for sending standard text to PostScript printers, which requires the SCRIPT utility. If you want to interrupt the COPY command while it is sending data through a port, simply press the combination of the Control and Break keys.

The PRINT utility is actually a *print spooler*. A print spooler allows you to stack up a number of files to print, and PRINT will see to the rest. Unfortunately, PRINT will run only while no other application programs are running. Thus, if you start your word processor, or use TaskMAX to switch away from the PRINT task, printing will cease until you return to the command line or PRINT task. Suppose you want to print all .TXT files in the C:/MORETEXT directory to your LPT1 printer. Issue this command:

```
PRINT C:/MORECRUD/*.TXT
```

Note that this command doesn't specify a port, and the PRN: device is where PRINT sends things if a device isn't specified. If you want to send the files to some other device, such as COM3:, issue this variation of the command.

```
PRINT C:/MORECRUD/*.TXT COM3:
```

After it is invoked, PRINT will queue the designated files and return you to the DR DOS command prompt. PRINT can do this because it is a terminate-and-stay resident (TSR) program and remains active in memory until you reboot. Once returned to the command line, you can issue DR DOS commands to your heart's content, and PRINT will continue to send the files to the designated port.

To remove a file from the print queue, use this command:

```
PRINT MYFILE.TXT /C
```

You can also delete all files from the queue with this variant:

```
PRINT /T
```

PRINT tends to be slower than COPY. You can adjust the amount of attention DR DOS pays to it, and you can also set the number of files allowed in the PRINT queue. There are several adjustments available with PRINT, and for the most part they only take effect the *first* time that you issue PRINT after booting the computer. If you care to toy with these paramemters, refer to the PRINT entry in Appendix A, the command reference chapter.

That brings us to SCRIPT. If you use a PostScript printer, you'll love this utility. Basically, SCRIPT takes an ordinary ASCII text file and converts it into simple

FILELINK

PostScript so that it will print on your printer. Your text file can also include extended characters from the HP LaserJet II character set. If you are a programmer, this means that you have a utility that will print your source code listings on a PostScript device. You can run SCRIPT in two ways.

- As a stand-alone program for printing designated text files on a PostScript printer (parallel ports only), or converting the text files into PostScript files.

- As a TSR program that automatically intercepts all files that are sent to a particular parallel port and then translates those files to PostScript. Be careful with this, because it will also intercept PostScript files created by application programs and corrupt them: instead of printing what you want, SCRIPT will print out the PostScript code itself for you to admire.

To use SCRIPT to translate a text file to PostScript and send it to the PRN: (LPT1:) port, issue the following command:

```
SCRIPT MYTEXT.TXT
```

To specify any other port, you must add the port designation to the command line. For example, use this command to send the file to LPT3:

```
SCRIPT MYTEXT.TXT LPT3:
```

Finally, to load SCRIPT as a TSR so that it will automatically translate all files sent to a parallel port, omit the file specification from the command. For example, to have SCRIPT automatically translate all text bound for LPT2:, use this command.

```
SCRIPT LPT2:
```

Script also has parameters that allow you to change point size, choose portrait or landscape printing, and implement a variety of other useful features. Refer to the SCRIPT section in the command reference for a complete listing of the utility's capabilities.

When Communication Doesn't Work

There really isn't much that can go wrong with parallel communication. If you are trying to send something to a parallel printer and nothing is happening, make sure that the cables are snug and that the printer is currently using its parallel port. More sophisticated printers, such as laser printers, often have multiple communication ports and you must tell the printer to use the parallel port. Consult your printer manual for more information on this topic.

Another source of parallel communication failure is contention. The parallel port might be using the same I/O address as something else, such as a network card or a second card with a parallel port. This is rare and is quite difficult to track down. Troubleshooting usually means removing suspected cards from the computer to narrow the problem down to a specific component.

Most serial communication problems can be solved by checking and adjusting the settings for the serial ports. If you have tried unsuccessfully to communicate between two serial devices, make sure that the parameters for each device are set for the same data transmission rate, parity, and number of stop bits. If your problem can't be solved this way, you likely have one or both of these problems:

- the transmit and receive lines need to be switched
- the handshaking lines aren't wired correctly

A PC is considered a Data Terminal Equipment (DTE) device, while printers and modems are considered Data Communications Equipment (DCE) devices. A DTE transmits on pin 2 of the serial port, and receives information on pin 2. If you have cabled two PCs together, these lines must be switched in order for the computers to talk. Handshaking is more difficult. For 25-pin serial ports, pins 4, 5, 6, 8, and 20 can all be used to pace serial communication. The following explains the functions of the signals carried by these pins. While this discussion may seem technical, play along and you'll see that it's simple.

Here's how it works: your PC must send a signal on pins 4 and 20 to tell the printer or modem that the PC is present and has something to send. On the other hand, the printer or modem must send a signal on pin 6 to show that it is alive, and a signal

FILELINK

on pin 5 to indicate that it is ready to receive information. To indicate that they are temporarily busy, printers will shut off the signal on pin 5. This causes the PC to pause data transmission until the printer again signals through pin 5 that it is ready. Note that this explanation describes only the general concept of how things should work. In the real world of printers and modems, everyone does things a little differently, using some some signals, and not others.

So why do you care about this? Because it explains why your PC and whatever serial device it's trying to talk to aren't on speaking terms. For example, if you connect your PC to another DTE type device, such as a PC, they both try to transmit on pin 2 and receive on pin 3; they both wait for signals on pins 5 and 6 that never arrive. The solution is to create a special cable called a *null modem*. You can buy null modem cables, or you can easily make one with a little cheater device called a *break-out box*. A break-out box has little sockets for each pin in the connector, allowing you to patch the signal from any input pin to any output pin. More sophisticated break-out boxes have lights that indicate when signals are present on the handshaking and data pins. This allows you to instantly tell the type of device, either DTE or DCE, to which you are connected. And, of course, if you have a techie streak, you can either solder or use crimp pins to construct your own custom cables.

Figure 12-5 shows the wiring for three types of null modems. Type A shows a 25-pin-to-25-pin null modem, which reflects the signals shown in the previous table. Type B shows a 25-pin-to-9-pin null modem, and type C shows a 9-pin-to-9-pin. I know they work, because I had to build several of these when fooling around with FILELINK.

Using FILELINK to Transfer Files Between Computers

DR DOS comes with a dandy utility program that allows you to wire two PCs together through their serial ports and quickly transfer files back and forth. FILELINK is especially useful for moving data between desktop and laptop computers, because it is much faster than using floppies to transfer files. One caveat: if you are trying to move files by modem, use a telecommunication program such as CrossTalk or ProComm instead of FILELINK.

DR DOS 6 BY EXAMPLE

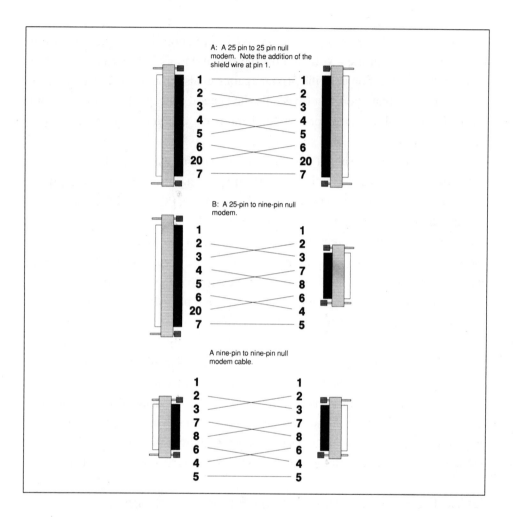

Figure 12-5. Null modem schemes.

Actually, the toughest part in using FILELINK is getting the cabling right. You'll need to use one of the null modem cables outlined in the previous section to connect between your computers. Once the cabling is complete, using FILELINK is a snap. It will even *relocate* itself from your computer to the target computer using the cable connection, so that you only need FILELINK on one computer to start. Once FILELINK is resident on the second computer, you can operate one of the computers in *slave mode* and transfer files to and from that computer.

FILELINK

Moving FILELINK to Another Computer

If you can exchange floppies between the two systems, by all means use a floppy to get FILELINK to the target system. If you can't exchange floppies, relocate FILELINK through the serial connection. First, cable the systems together using a null modem cable. Next, issue this command at the computer that has FILELINK currently resident.

```
FILELINK DUP COM1:9600
```

You can substitute COM2: for COM1: or any of the following data transmission rates for 9600. The baud rate of 9600 is as fast as you can go when starting out, so use that value. After you relocate FILELINK you can experiment with higher bps rates.

After starting the duplication process, you'll be asked what serial port you are using on the target computer. Once you supply that information (COM1:, for example), FILELINK will tell you to type the following commands on the target computer.

```
MODE COM1:9600,N,8,1,P
CTTY COM1:
```

The MODE command sets the serial port for 9600 bps and eight-bit communication. Using eight-bit communication enables you to transfer binary (program) information. The CTTY utility redirects the console to the serial port, allowing FILELINK a primitive though effective way of controlling the target computer. FILELINK will then attempt to connect with the target computer. If it fails to connect after a reasonable time (such as 20 seconds), your cabling isn't correct. If you have a null modem and you can't connect, make sure you specified the right serial port in the MODE command. If you did, then either you need technical help, or you should acquire a break-out box to debug the cable.

Once FILELINK establishes communication, things move fairly quickly. First, FILELINK will transfer the small loader program, and then use that to transfer FILELINK.EXE to the target computer. Once FILELINK is resident in the target computer, it is activated and set to run in slave mode. And that's all there is to it.

Setting-up FILELINK

Once FILELINK is resident on both computers, you can get down to the business of exchanging files. Before I go into detail about this, you need to understand the master/slave relationship. The *master* computer is the system you will use to control file exchanges. The *slave* computer is remotely controlled though FILELINK on the master.

The first order of business is setting up the slave and master computers. On both machines, use this sort of FILELINK command:

```
FILELINK SET COM?:BAUD
```

COM?: is the serial port (either COM1: or COM2:) and *BAUD* (synonymous with bps) is one of the following data transmission rates:

I've found that you can use up to 38,400 bps reliably on even older XT-type computers, and it's certainly a sufficient rate for transferring files. To set up COM2: at 38,400 bps you enter the following:

```
FILELINK SET COM2:38
```

After completing setup of both machines, enter the following command on the slave computer.

```
FILELINK SLA
```

This places the computer into slave mode, so that it can be controlled by the master computer. By adding the /X parameter, like this:

```
FILELINK SLA /X
```

you can prevent files on the slave computer from being overwritten.

To exit from slave mode, either press the Control and Break keys, or release the slave remotely from the master with the command.

```
FILELINK QUI
```

FILELINK

Getting Directories From the Slave

Look at the contents of directories on the slave with the command

```
FILELINK DIR
```

which works in the same manner as the DR DOS command DIR, but has a different set of parameters:

/A   Displays only the files that have their archive bits set.

/D:*mm-dd-yy* Displays only files that have dates on or after the specified date.

/H   Displays only the files that have their hidden or system attribute bits set.

/P   Pauses after each screen of information.

/S   Also displays files in subdirectories.

For example, if you want to get a directory of the root directory of drive D: on the slave, enter this command:

```
FILELINK DIR D:\
```

To find all .WKS files in drive C:\ and pause the listing after each screen, enter this command:

```
FILELINK DIR C:\*.WKS /S /P
```

To see only those files in the C:\BEANCNT directory modified after 2/24/92, enter this command:

```
FILELINK DIR C:\BEANCNT\*.* /D:02-24-92
```

Transferring Files

Once you've found the files you want on the slave computer, or the slave directories that you want to use to receive files from the master, you're ready to begin moving files. To get files from the slave, use the FILELINK RECEIVE command. For example, to receive all *.WKS files from the slave C:\BEANCNT directory and put the files in the MASTER D:\LAPTOP directory, use this command:

```
FILELINK REC C:\BEANCNT\*.WKS D:\LAPTOP
```

Note that this is similar to the DR DOS COPY command. If you omit the file destination, they'll arrive in the master's current directory. As with the other FILELINK commands, there are many available parameters. These parameters also apply to the TRANSMIT command:

/A	Transfers only the files that have their archive bits set.
/D:*mm-dd-yy*	Transfers only files that have dates on or after the specified date.
/H	Transfers files that have their hidden or system attribute bits set.
/M	Transfers only files that have archive bits set and don't already exist on the master computer with archive bits set.
/P	Prompts you to accept or reject each file before it is transferred.
/R	Allows files on the destination computer to be overwritten.
/S	Transfers matching files from subdirectories.
/U	Only transfers files that either don't exist on the destination, or that have a previous date.

For example, to receive all *.DBF files from the slave C:\MAILLIST directory that were updated on or after 01/01/92, use this command:

```
FILELINK REC C:\MAILLIST\*.DBF /D:01-01-92
```

To pick up all files on .DOC files from the slave's C: drive that don't already exist in the master's D:\DOCS directory, use this command:

```
FILELINK REC C:\*.DOC /S
```

To fetch only those *.NND files from the slave's C:\NW2V40 subdirectory, use this variation on the theme:

```
FILELINK REC C:\NW2V40\*.NND /P
```

To send files to the slave, you use the TRANSMIT command. This command has exactly the same syntax as RECEIVE. For example, to send all files in the master's E:\ANTIVRUS directory to the slave's current directory, use this command:

```
FILELINK TRA E:\ANTIVRUS\*.*
```

To send all D:\DRDOS files to the slave's C:\DR DOS directory, and overwrite any read-only files on the slave, use this version:

```
FILELINK TRA D:\DRDOS\*.* C:\DRDOS /R
```

You can release the slave computer from slave mode by entering this command:

```
FILELINK QUI
```

CHAPTER 13

Advanced Functions

This chapter concentrates on the more esoteric functions within DR DOS 6.0. You may not need these functions very often, but they can come in extremely handy. We'll cover:

- Redirection and piping
- The ANSI.SYS driver
- Code pages
- The Symbolic Interactive Debugger (SID)

Redirection and Piping

DR DOS has several commands that make the output of a command or program go somewhere other than where it would normally go. This can be as simple as sending the output that usually shows up on the screen display to a file (*redirection*) or as complex as taking the output of one program and making it the input to another (*piping*).

Redirection

As an example, the output of XDIR normally goes to the screen. With the > symbol, you can place output anywhere you desire. For instance, say you want to use XDIR to search through all the files on a disk and report all the files that end in .SYS. You'd also like a record of this, so you want to preserve XDIR's findings in a file. No problem—just issue the following command:

```
XDIR C:\*.SYS /S > MYSYS.TXT
```

As proof that it works, part of the output from the resulting MYSYS.TXT file follows:

```
 -a-     52,736      3-28-90     3:41p c:\ventura\pd_post5.sys
 -a-     60,994      5-01-90     3:00a c:\windows\emm386.sys
 -a-      5,719      5-01-90     3:00a c:\windows\ramdrive.sys
 -a-      6,866      5-01-90     3:00a c:\windows\smartdrv.sys
total files 39    total bytes 611,639    disk free space 4,020,224
```

Redirection can work with any DR DOS command that outputs to the screen. For instance, to find the occurrence of the word *WeaselWord* in all the .DOC files in the D:\REPORTS directory and record those findings in the file WEASL.TXT, which is in the C:\CHECK\LATER directory, you would use this command:

```
FIND "weaselword" D:\REPORTS\*.DOC > C:\CHECK\LATER\WEASL.TXT
```

You can also take the output of a command and add it to the end of an existing file (that is, append it to that file). In the preceding examples, the output redirected to a file with the > symbol would overwrite any existing file with that name. The following command creates the file CHECK.TXT (or replaces its contents if the file already exists):

```
CHKDSK C: > CHECK.TXT
```

If you use the >> symbol and specify an existing file, the output is simply added to the end of that file. The following command appends to the file CHECK.TXT:

```
CHKDSK D: >> CHECK.TXT
```

You can also redirect output to any valid DR DOS device. (A complete list of devices appears in Chapter 3.) The following command sends the locations of the files found by XDIR to a printer:

```
XDIR *.DOC > LPT1
```

ADVANCED FUNCTIONS

You can also redirect input, but that's a bit trickier because you must specify something that can handle an input. SORT and MORE are two special DR DOS commands, called *filters*, that work strictly with redirection symbols and pipes and can therefore handle inputs. For instance, to display the CHECK.TXT file using MORE, you would type this command:

```
MORE < CHECK.TXT
```

You can also combine input and output redirection symbols. For instance, this command sorts the file CHECK.TXT and outputs the sorted information to a new file called SCHECK.TXT:

```
SORT < CHECK.TXT > SCHECK.TXT
```

Piping

Pipes take the output from one program and feed it to another program as input. They are often used with all three filters: MORE, SORT, and FIND. For example, suppose you want to list all the directories that are part of an application, such as Artline. You could issue this command:

```
TREE | FIND artline
```

You would then see a display that looks like this:

```
953,742         21  c:\artline
395,946         15  c:\artline\artsys
398,418         17  c:\artline\artwork
327,394         36  c:\artline\artwork\artright
225,482         24  c:\artline\artwork\picture.pak
240,352         15  c:\artline\colors
1,686,513       35  c:\artline\convert
1,340,219       71  c:\artline\fonts
26,087           1  c:\artline\images
237,661          9  c:\artline\setup
41,677           7  c:\artline\tools
```

The command took the output of TREE as the input to FIND, then used FIND to display only those directories that contained the word *artline*.

You can play the same kind of game with SORT. For instance, the following command pipes the output of TREE into SORT, which reverses the order of the directories and displays them:

```
TREE | SORT /R
```

If you really want to get carried away, you can combine redirection and piping. This variation on the command takes the reverse sorted output from TREE and places it in a file:

```
TREE | SORT /R > REVSORT.TXT
```

Configuring the Display and Keyboard with ANSI.SYS

The ANSI.SYS driver allows your screen and keyboard to respond as if they were part of a computer terminal. The terminal they emulate is actually the "standard" terminal designated by the American National Standards Institute (ANSI), hence the name ANSI.SYS. Before you can experiment with this driver, you must specify it in your CONFIG.SYS file like this:

```
DEVICE=ANSI.SYS
```

You can also use HIDEVICE if you have enough upper memory. If you don't care to add the line to the CONFIG.SYS file manually, you can do it during installation or with SETUP. Once ANSI.SYS is loaded, you can:

- Change the display colors
- Change the display mode
- Program keys with custom strings
- Position the cursor on the screen

Most terminals are controlled through *escape sequences*. These are sequences of characters preceded by an escape. For instance, the following escape sequence

ADVANCED FUNCTIONS

shifts your display to 40 columns by 25 rows, monochrome mode:

```
Esc [=0h]
```

You can't just type such a sequence at the command prompt and expect something to happen. The command processor traps an escape; in fact, it clears the command line when it sees one.

You can get the system to accept escape sequences in two ways: First, you can make them part of the prompt. (The $e in the prompt stands for *escape*.) Second, you can place them in a file with EDITOR, then TYPE this file to the screen. You must type Ctrl-PQ in EDITOR before you can actually place an escape in the file. If you're using some other ASCII text editor, you may have to consult the documentation to find out how to enter control characters into a file (some editors don't support this feature).

Of course, you can also write a program to do this. In fact, many of the sequences, such as the ones for cursor positioning, are really only useful to programmers and aren't listed here. However, the ones that change screen color or video mode can be useful when issued from a file or a prompt. The following sections describe these escape sequences.

Color Escape Sequences

The following are the escape sequences for changing foreground and background color:

Color	Background Sequence	Foreground Sequence
Black	Esc[30m	Esc[40m
Red	Esc[31m	Esc[41m
Green	Esc[32m	Esc[42m
Yellow	Esc[33m	Esc[43m
Blue	Esc[34m	Esc[44m
Magenta	Esc[35m	Esc[45m
Cyan	Esc[36m	Esc[46m
White	Esc[37m	Esc[47m

You can also group these into pairs to set the foreground and background colors simultaneously. You do this by separating the numbers with a semicolon. For instance, this sequence sets the background to magenta and the foreground to cyan:

```
Esc[35;46m
```

Screen-Attribute Escape Sequences

The following sequences change screen attributes:

Attribute	Escape Sequence
White on black	Esc[0m
Bold	Esc[1m
Underline (works only in monochrome)	Esc[4m
Blink	Esc[5m
Black on white	Esc[7m
Black on black	Esc[8m

Video-Mode Escape Sequences

You can even change the video mode. The following are the escape sequences:

Video Mode	Escape Sequence
40-column x 25-row monochrome	Esc=0h1
40-column x 25-row color	Esc=1h1
80-column x 25-row monochrome	Esc=2h1
80-column x 25-row color	Esc=3h1
320 x 200 (pixels) monochrome	Esc=4h1
320 x 200 (pixels) color	Esc=5h1
640 x 200 (pixels) monochrome	Esc=6h1
Wrap text at end of line	Esc =7h1
Disable end-of-line wrap	Esc=7l

ADVANCED FUNCTIONS

Keyboard Escape Sequences

These sequences allow you to define any key on the keyboard. For the most part, you'll want to leave your "normal" keys alone; however, you may want to define the function keys, including Shift-function key, Ctrl-function key, and Alt-function key.

To redefine a key, issue the following sequence:

```
Esc[0;code;"whatever";13p
```

Entering an escape in EDITOR simply requires that you first type Ctrl-P. The left bracket and zero are straightforward enough, and *code* is the key code for the function key. The *"whatever"* is what you want to map to the key. It could be "XDIR," "CHKDSK," or "Polly-want-a-cracker"; just make sure you enclose it in quotes. The *13* stands for the Return key, which is required to execute any command you map to a key. The *p* is what a key redefinition sequence must end with.

For instance, the following string redefines Ctrl-F10 to execute the XDIR command:

```
Esc[0;103;"XDIR";13p
```

Now all you need to know are the key codes for the various function keys. And here they are:

Function Key	Key Code	Shift Code	Control Code	Alt Code
F1	59	84	94	104
F2	60	85	95	105
F3	61	86	96	106
F4	62	87	97	107
F5	63	88	98	108
F6	64	89	99	109
F7	65	90	100	110
F8	66	91	101	111
F9	67	92	102	112
F10	68	93	103	113

If you want to redefine a large set of these keys, you'll find the most convenient way to do this is to create a file that contains the complete set of redefinition codes. You can put each code on a separate line. If you want to use this file to redefine your function keys each time your computer powers up, simply add a TYPE command to the AUTOEXEC.BAT file and type the key-code file.

Code Pages

Code pages let you load international character sets for your screen, redefine the keyboard for these sets, and even load the sets for your printer. This is a powerful feature, and DR DOS provides a wide array of character sets. If you need to use code pages, pay close attention—they're a bit wacky. (Don't blame their complexity on the folks at Digital Research; they were just implementing what had already become standard in DOS.)

How Code Pages Work

Each key on your keyboard issues a unique scan code that lets DR DOS know which key has been pressed. When you press a key, a scan code is issued (preceded by an interrupt to get the microprocessor's attention) and passed to the device driver responsible for the keyboard. This device driver matches the scan code to the proper character. (That's how you get an "A" when you press the A key.) Since the scan codes are matched to the character sets through the device driver, you can change this scan-code-to-character mapping to accommodate different character sets. You can even accommodate different keyboard layouts this way.

That's fine as long as you only need to handle 256 characters, which is the number of scan codes a keyboard can issue. Some international character sets have larger alphabets than English or must deal with a variety of accent symbols. Such character sets require more than 256 scan codes; these additional characters are handled by key combinations, which are called, oddly enough, *dead keys*.

The various international character-set tables—the code pages—reside in files with .CPI extensions. You'll find these files in your DR DOS directory. You must have an EGA or VGA video system to display these character sets.

ADVANCED FUNCTIONS

To access code-page tables, perform the following steps.

In the CONFIG.SYS file:

1. Use COUNTRY to load the country information.

2. Use DEVICE to load DISPLAY.SYS and PRINTER.SYS and thereby allocate memory for the code pages.

In the AUTOEXEC.BAT file:

3. Use KEYB to specify the keyboard translation table.

4. Use MODE to prepare code pages for display or for your printer.

5. Load NLSFUNC to provide support for extended country information.

6. Execute CHCP to select a code page.

Realizing that the original DOS designers had made a mess of this, Digital Research added support for code-page additions in SETUP and the installation program. That greatly simplified the process of installing code pages because SETUP does most of the work for you.

Installing Code Pages Through SETUP

SETUP only supports two code pages directly: the hardware code page (437 is the default for the USA) and 850, the universal international character-set table from the International Standards Organization (ISO). In its attempt to be all things to all people, 850 ended up with a number of shortcomings. For instance, some of the line-drawing characters have been remapped to accented letters. On the other hand, 850 eliminates the need for code-page switching.

Even if you intend to use a code page other than 850, you should allow SETUP to install 850 for you. This at least puts all the necessary commands and statements in their proper places, simplifying your task to one of editing the code-page numbers in the commands.

DR DOS 6 BY EXAMPLE

To install code pages, select "Optional Device Drivers and Utilities" from the SETUP configuration screen (Figure 13-1). Next, set "Code page switching" to YES (Figure 13-2). After setting this parameter, you'll need to bypass the next screen and get to the one that asks if you want to install code-page switching for your printer (by default, LPT1). If you say yes, you'll be presented with a list of supported printers to choose from (Figure 13-3). Finally, you'll get to pick which code page you want (the hardware code page or 850).

```
┌─────────────────────────────────────────────────────────────────┐
│   Digital Research                            DR DOS 6.0 SETUP  │
├─────────────────────────────────────────────────────────────────┤
│                                                                 │
│         Select the area you wish to configure from the list below. │
│                                                                 │
│            ▌ MemoryMAX                                          │
│                                                                 │
│            ▌ TaskMAX                                            │
│                                                                 │
│            ▌ DiskMAX                                            │
│                                                                 │
│            ▌ ViewMAX                                            │
│                                                                 │
│            ▌ Country and Keyboard                               │
│                                                                 │
│            ▌ System Parameters                                  │
│                                                                 │
│            ▶ Optional Device Drivers and Utilities              │
│                                                                 │
│            ▌ Security                                           │
│                                                                 │
│            ▌ Save Changes and Exit                              │
│                                                                 │
│  F1=Help   ↕=next/prev line   <Enter>=select option   <Esc>=prev screen   F10=abort │
└─────────────────────────────────────────────────────────────────┘
```

Figure 13-1. SETUP main configuration menu.

After you select a code page and go through the save-and-exit sequence, SETUP will modify your CONFIG.SYS and AUTOEXEC.BAT files.

ADVANCED FUNCTIONS

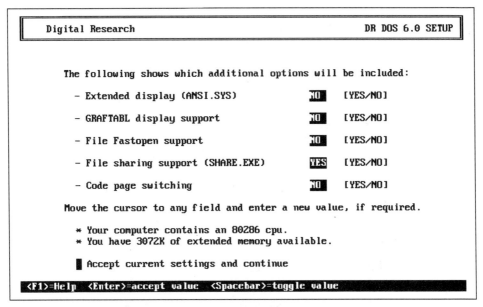

Figure 13-2. The Optional Device Drivers and Utilities screen.

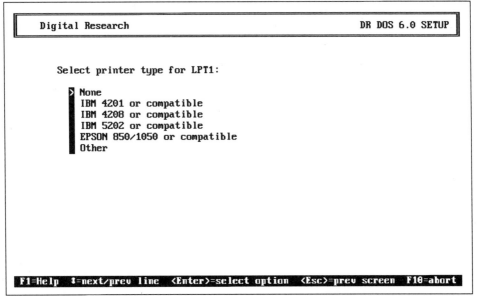

Figure 13-3. Code-page compatible printers.

DR DOS 6 BY EXAMPLE

Available Code Pages

The following table lists the code pages, country codes, and keyboard codes supported by DR DOS 6.0.

Country Code	Keyboard Code	Code Page (1st value is default for country)	Definition
061		437, 850	Australia
032	BE	437, 850	Belgium
002	CF	863, 850	Canadian French
045	DK	865, 850	Denmark
358	SU	437, 850	Finland
033	FR	437. 850	France
049	GR	437, 850	Germany
036	HU	852, 850	Hungary
972		862, 850	Israel
039	IT	437, 850	Italy
081		932, 437	Japan
082		934, 437	Korea
003	LA	437, 850	Latin America
785		864, 850	Middle East
031	NL	437, 850	Netherlands
047	NO	865, 850	Norway
351	PO	860, 850	Portugal
007	RU	866, 850	Russia
034	SP	437, 850	Spain
046	SV	437, 850	Sweden
041	SF	437, 850	Swiss French
041	SG	437, 850	Swiss German
090	TF, TQ	857, 850	Turkey
044	UK	437, 850	United Kingdom
001 (the default)	US (the default)	437, 850	United States

ADVANCED FUNCTIONS

Installing Code Pages Manually

In the CONFIG.SYS file, add the following:

```
COUNTRY=countrycode, codepage,C:\DRDOS\COUNTRY.SYS
```

This line sets the time and date formats for your country and allows the code page to convert uppercase characters to lowercase. For example, to set the country to USA and select the international code page, use the following line:

```
COUNTRY=001,850,C:\DRDOS\CONFIG.SYS
```

Next, add these lines to set the number of code pages (in this case, one) for the display and printer:

```
DEVICE = C:\DRDOS\DISPLAY.SYS CON=(EGA,,1)
DEVICE = C:\DRDPS\PRINTER.SYS LPT1=(1050,,1)
```

You can allocate from one to 12 code pages, but remember that each allocation steals memory from your applications. The PRINTER.SYS driver in this example is set for an Epson 1050. (For more detailed information on the DISPLAY.SYS and PRINTER.SYS drivers, see Chapter 5.)

In the AUTOEXEC.BAT file, add this line:

```
KEYB keycode[+|-], codepage
```

Keycode is the keyboard code, and *codepage* is the code page that maps to the keyboard. The plus and minus symbols select an enhanced keyboard and standard keyboard, respectively. For example, the following selects an enhanced keyboard for the USA and code page 850:

```
KEYB US+,850
```

Next is the MODE command (you may need more than one) that prepares the code page for the display or printer. In the following example, the first MODE command prepares code page 850 for the display, while the second prepares the same code page for the Epson 1050 printer on parallel port LPT1.

```
MODE CON CODEPAGE PREPARE=((850) C:\DRDOS\EGA.CPI)
MODE LPT1 CODEPAGE PREPARE=((850) C:\DRDOS\1050.CPI)
```

You must now load NLSFUNC. This command for national-language support allows DR DOS to use the extended country information. You can't use CHCP, which switches between code pages, without first loading this command. To do that, simply type NLSFUNC.

Finally, you need to select the code page for use with CHCP. You can also use CHCP to switch to any of the loaded code pages. In this case, we'll use the 850 code page:

```
CHCP 850
```

CHCP changes code pages for all devices. If you want to switch code pages for a single device, use MODE SELECT (refer to the MODE command in Appendix A for more information).

Checking and Refreshing Code Pages

If you want to see which code pages are installed for a particular device, use the following command:

```
MODE device CODEPAGE /STATUS
```

For instance, to see which code page is loaded for the display, you would issue this command:

```
MODE CON CODEPAGE /STATUS
```

If you turn your printer off, and therefore lose the code-page information stored in it, don't worry; all you need to do is refresh the printer to reload the code-page fonts. The command to do this is:

```
MODE device CODEPAGE REFRESH
```

ADVANCED FUNCTIONS

For instance, the following command refreshes the printer attached to LPT1:

```
MODE LPT1 CODEPAGE REFRESH
```

The Symbolic Interactive Debugger

This machine-code debugger is generally of interest only to programmers. However, just in case you need to know how it works, herein lies a synopsis of SID conventions and commands.

SID command lines can have up to 64 characters and are parsed after Enter is pressed. The command characters must be entered at the beginning of the line, and no space can appear between those characters and the first argument. You can, however, make the line a comment by entering a semicolon as the first character.

Start SID simply by typing SID. You can also add the program you want to debug as an argument to the command line:

```
SID WEASLWRD.EXE
```

To exit from SID, press Ctrl-C or type Q at the # prompt.

Conventions

SID normally expects hexadecimal entries; however, you can enter decimal numbers if you place a number sign (#) before them. You can enter ASCII characters by enclosing them in single quotes. SID is not case-sensitive.

You can combine numbers and strings using the + and - operators. Blanks aren't allowed in the sequence.

A 20-bit address is entered as a 16-bit segment number (optional) followed by a 16-bit offset. The syntax is:

nnnn:oooo

where *nnnn* is the segment number and *oooo* is the offset.

Command Summary

The following summary of SID commands and their functions should give you an idea of SID's capabilities. For the exact syntax of these commands, issue ?? from the SID # prompt.

Command	Definition
?	Lists commands and their definitions
??	Provides more complete help with commands
A	Assembles 8086 mnemonics into memory at a specified address
B	Compares two specified memory blocks
D	Memory display (you can set the number of bytes to display)
E	Loads a file so that it can be executed; E alone clears memory
F	Fills memory from a start address to an end address with the specified value (byte or word)
G	"Go." Starts program execution. You can optionally set one or two breakpoints.
H	Hexadecimal math capabilities
I*string*	Sets up a "command tail" (command-line argument)
L	Lists memory; does not show symbols
M	Moves a memory block
P	"Passpoint" (breakpoint) control; lets you set, clear, or list breakpoints
Q	Quits
QI, QO	Inputs from (QI) or outputs to (QO) a specified port
QR, QW	Reads (QR) or writes (QW) sectors on a disk

ADVANCED FUNCTIONS

R	Reads a disk file into a contiguous memory block
S	Stores changes in memory or enables/disables the segment register display
SR	Searches through memory
T	Traces specified number of steps
U	Untraces specified number of steps
V	Shows the start and end memory addresses for the last file loaded
W	Writes memory contents from specified blocks to a file
X	Examines or alters the CPU state and registers
Z	Examines the 8087 coprocessor registers

APPENDIX A

DR DOS Command Reference

This chapter is a complete alphabetical reference to all DR DOS commands. (Device drivers and other statements used in CONFIG.SYS files are given in Chapter 5; batch-file statements are listed in Chapter 8.)

The entries are organized as follows:

COMMAND

The name of the command or DR DOS device driver.

SYNTAX

The proper grammar for the command, including all options and parameters. The command and its parameters are shown in Roman type. You must enter this information, including punctuation marks, exactly as shown. Variable parameters appear in italic type. For these, don't type in exactly what's shown; you must substitute your own parameter (such as a file name or disk-drive letter) in place of the variable. Additional syntax conventions are discussed in Chapter 1, "Introducing DR DOS"; wildcards are discussed in Chapter 3, "Basic DOS Skills."

CLASS

A command can be either internal or external. Internal commands are those that are available through the command processor and therefore always accessible. These commands are always in memory, so no disk access is required. External commands are executed through a DR DOS utility program that's stored on disk. To execute such a command, the utility must be in either the current directory or a directory pointed to by the PATH statement. You can also preface the external command with the path of the file or program the command executes. For example, if the extended directory command (XDIR) applies to an executable file in the C:\DRDOS directory, issue the command as:

```
C:\DRDOS\XDIR
```

FUNCTION
A discussion of what the command does and why it's used.

SIDE EFFECTS
Things to watch out for when using the command.

EXAMPLES
Useful examples of the command in action.

OF INTEREST
Commands that have related functions.

APPEND

SYNTAX

APPEND [/?|H] *x:dir*[[;]*x:dir*...] [/X:ON|OFF] [/E:ON|OFF] [/PATH:ON|OFF]

/?|H	Help screen for this command.
x:dir	The drive and directory designation to be appended.
;*x:dir*...	Additional drives and directories to be appended. Each additional drive and directory must be preceded by a semicolon. Don't put a space between the semicolon and the directory designation.
[/X:ON|OFF]	Controls whether APPEND is to search only or search and execute from an appended directory. If it's set to OFF (the default), DR DOS will find and read files in the appended directory. If it's set to ON, DR DOS will find and read files as well as execute programs in the appended directory.
[/E:ON|OFF]	Determines whether the APPEND statement becomes part of the DR DOS environment. (The environment is a section of memory where you can store settings for various commands and programs.) If /E is set to ON, the APPEND statement becomes part of the environment. You can then look at it by typing SET and use SET to change the appended directories. Setting the /E parameter to OFF (the default) prevents APPEND from becoming part of the DR DOS environment.
[/PATH:ON|OFF]	The PATH parameter controls whether DR DOS should check the appended directories if the file it's looking for has a specific path name. For example, suppose DR DOS is looking for /STUFF/JUNQUE/CRUD.TXT. If CRUD.TXT isn't in /STUFF/JUNQUE and the parameter is set to ON (the default), DR DOS will look in the appended directories. If it's set to OFF, DR DOS will limit its search to /STUFF/JUNQUE.

The APPEND command line cannot exceed 128 characters. To cancel APPEND, type:

```
APPEND;
```

CLASS

External: APPEND.EXE

FUNCTION

APPEND extends the DR DOS search path to the directories named in the APPEND command. It is similar to PATH but will find not only executable files (.EXE, .COM, and .BAT) but *all* files. The command is very useful with old programs that don't support the concept of path names. In fact, most current DOS programs will ignore the appended directories when searching for files. For instance, EDITOR and Microsoft Word ignore appended directories, while the DR DOS TYPE command doesn't.

SIDE EFFECTS

Programs that read files from appended directories may write them instead to the current directory.

APPEND can confuse some installation programs.

If you're using ASSIGN with APPEND, use APPEND first.

APPEND can confuse the BACKUP program.

EXAMPLES

To set DR DOS to search for and execute programs in the \MORE\STUFF directory, even if a path is given in the command line, use:

```
APPEND C:\MORE\STUFF /X:ON /PATH:ON
```

To set DR DOS to search for files in (but not execute programs from) the appended D:\JUNQUE directory and enter the APPEND into the DR DOS environment, use:

```
APPEND D:\JUNQUE /E:ON
```

OF INTEREST
   PATH, JOIN, ASSIGN, SUBST

ASSIGN

SYNTAX
ASSIGN [/?|H] *drive1=drive2* [*drive3=drive4*] ... [/A]

/?|H	Help screen for this command.
drive1	The disk-drive letter for the drive whose assignment you want to change. Enter a single letter without the colon.
drive2	The disk-drive letter you want to assign temporarily to this drive. If you're going to have more than one assignment, use spaces to separate them.
/A	Used without other arguments, this parameter shows the current drive assignments.

CLASS
External: ASSIGN.COM

FUNCTION
ASSIGN temporarily changes the disk-drive assignment for a specified drive. You can only ASSIGN one valid drive to another. For example, if you have two floppy drives (A: and B:), you can assign B: to A:.

ASSIGN is useful for fooling installation programs or other programs that expect to execute from a particular drive or expect data to be on a particular drive.

To cancel an assignment, simply enter the command with no arguments:

```
ASSIGN
```

SIDE EFFECTS
You can't use the following commands when ASSIGN is in effect: SUBST, RESTORE, PRINT, LABEL, FORMAT, DISKCOPY, DISKCOMP, and BACKUP. For example, if you assign A: to C: and try to do a DISKCOPY A:=A:, DR DOS will respond with a message indicating that the drive has nonremovable media.

You can paint yourself into a corner with this command. For example, if you issue:

```
ASSIGN C=A
```

you won't be able to access anything on the C: hard drive (including ASSIGN). This means you can't turn ASSIGN off. The only way out is to reboot.

Also, Microsoft Windows is anti-ASSIGN. ASSIGN creates file paths that can later vanish, leading Windows to wonder where the files went.

EXAMPLES

To assign the B: drive to A: so that when A: is accessed you're actually reading the B: drive, use:

```
ASSIGN B=A
```

To assign A: to B: and C: to G:, use:

```
ASSIGN A=B C=G
```

OF INTEREST
APPEND, JOIN, PATH, SUBST

ATTRIB

SYNTAX
ATTRIB [/?|H] [+|-A] [+|-H] [+|-R] [+|-S] *files* [/P] [/S]

[/?|H]   Help screen for this command.

[+|-A]   Turns the archive attribute on (+A) or off (-A).

[+|-H]   Turns the hidden attribute on (+H) or off (-H).

[+|-R]   Turns the read-only attribute on (+R) or off (-R).

[+|-S]   Turns the system attribute on (+S) or off (-S).

files   Specifies the files, including wildcards. If you don't include a *files* specification, ATTRIB will assume you want to work on all files (*.*).

[/P]   Pauses at each screenful.

[/S]   If you want to change files in the subdirectories of the current directory, use this parameter.

CLASS
External: ATTRIB.EXE

FUNCTION
ATTRIB lets you change the attributes of your files. The archive attribute is set when a file is modified. The BACKUP, XCOPY, and MOVE commands can copy only those files with this attribute set, so you can use ATTRIB to pick files to be copied.

The hidden attribute hides files from the DIR command. XDIR displays such files. The system attribute hides the files not only from DIR, but from COPY, REPLACE, TOUCH, and MOVE as well. However, COPY, REPLACE, TOUCH, and MOVE have parameters that allow them to find these files.

The read-only attribute is your first level of defense against accidental erasure of files. Be aware that MOVE, REPLACE, XCOPY, TOUCH, and XDEL have parameters that allow them to handle read-only files. Password protection provides a better defense.

You can use combinations of these parameters to clear and set multiple attributes.

If you want to check the attributes set for a file or set of files, you can issue the ATTRIB command with no parameters; however, XDIR will give you that and other useful information.

SIDE EFFECTS

You can't use this command on files that reside on network drives.

EXAMPLES

To set the archive attribute for all files with an extension of .DOC in the C:/LETTERS directory and its subdirectories, use:

```
ATTRIB +A C:\LETTERS\*.DOC /S
```

To clear the read-only attribute and set the hidden attribute for all files beginning with G and ending with AT in the current directory, use:

```
ATTRIB -R +H G*.?AT
```

OF INTEREST

XDIR, COPY, MOVE, TOUCH, XCOPY, REPLACE

BACKUP

SYNTAX

BACKUP [/?|H] *source destination* [/S] [/M] [/D:*date*] [/T:*time*] [/A] [/L:*logfile*]

[/?|H] Help screen for this command.

source The source drive and optional directory and file specification.

destination The target floppy disk drive.

[/S] Back up all subdirectories of the source.

[/M] Back up files in the source that have the archive attribute set.

[/D:*date*] Back up source files whose archive attribute was set on or after the specified date. The date format is determined by the COUNTRY command set in the CONFIG.SYS file. In the U.S. the date is entered as MM/DD/YY. In Europe it's usually entered as DD/MM/YY, while in Japan it's YY/MM/DD.

[/T:*time*] Back up source files whose archive attribute was set at or after the specified time. This is useful in conjunction with the /D parameter. The time is entered as HH:MM:SS.

[/A] Appends new files to a previous set of backup disks without erasing the previously backed up files. If /A isn't used, BACKUP will overwrite previously backed up files.

[/L:*logfile*] Creates a backup log that lists the files and their disks (by number) and the time and date of the backup. By default, this file is called BACKUP.LOG and is written to the root directory of the source. You can use your own file name for the backup log file if you prefer.

CLASS
External: BACKUP.COM

FUNCTION

BACKUP allows you to copy large amounts of data in numerous files onto multiple floppy diskettes. It's primarily used to provide copies of important files in case something nasty happens to your computer or hard drive. It's also a handy way to send large amounts of data (more than will fit on a single disk) to someone else.

Files copied onto disks with BACKUP are reloaded with the RESTORE command. The BACKUP command in DR DOS version 6.0 is compatible with previous versions of DR DOS and version 3.3 or later of MS-DOS or PC-DOS.

Remember to label and number the disks. If you have a set of 33 backup disks, you won't want to find files by trial and error.

ERRORS

After running, BACKUP returns an ERRORLEVEL code to indicate whether everything went well or a problem was encountered. The following are the possible values for the ERRORLEVEL code:

0	Everything OK.
1	No files matching the source specification were found. Nothing was backed up.
2	File-sharing conflicts prevented some files from being backed up.
3	You aborted the backup by pressing Ctrl-Break.
4	BACKUP quit because it encountered an error.

You can trap and check this error code in a batch file (as discussed in Chapter 8).

SIDE EFFECTS

Don't use BACKUP when JOIN, SUBST, or ASSIGN is in effect; the subsequent RESTORE could alter the directory structure.

BREAK

SYNTAX
BREAK [/?|H] [ON|OFF]

[/?|H] Help screen for this command.

[ON|OFF] ON allows BREAK to interrupt a program whenever it calls a DOS function. OFF prevents BREAK from interrupting the program except when the program is accessing a DOS device, such as the keyboard or printer.

CLASS
Internal

FUNCTION
BREAK makes it easier to interrupt some programs. Normally, DOS only checks for a Ctrl-C or Ctrl-Break when a program is accessing a DOS device (the disk or the keyboard). This mode allows programs to run a bit faster, but they can also get stuck if a problem occurs. Setting BREAK to ON causes DOS to scan more often for a Ctrl-C or Ctrl-Break.

Many programs trap the BREAK command, which prevents you from finding yourself back at the DR DOS prompt instead of editing your monthly progress report. Compilers and similar utilities can often be interrupted with a Ctrl-C or Ctrl-Break.

If you want to play with this command, turn BREAK on and execute the DR DOS UNDELETE program. By pressing a series of Ctrl-Break and Ctrl-C key combinations, you can eventually terminate the program. Turn BREAK off and try this again with UNDELETE, and you won't be able to interrupt the program.

To check the current status of BREAK, simply type the command without any arguments:

```
BREAK
```

SIDE EFFECTS

Programs run a bit slower with BREAK set to ON.

EXAMPLE

To turn on the BREAK function, type:

```
BREAK ON
```

CHCP

SYNTAX

CHCP [/?|H] [*pagenumber*]

[/?|H]   Help screen for this command.

[*pagenumber*] The number of the code page.

CLASS

Internal

FUNCTION

CHange Code Page, CHCP, switches the current active code page. This affects the drivers for all devices that support code pages and DR DOS itself. You can't issue this command without first loading NLSFUNC, which in turn checks the COUNTRY statement in your CONFIG.SYS file. You might also need to load the DISPLAY.SYS and PRINTER.SYS drivers in the CONFIG.SYS file. This is explained in detail in Chapter 13.

SIDE EFFECTS

Aside from the caveats listed above, this command has no effect on a device unless it's on and connected to the system.

EXAMPLES

To load the character set that allows access to Greek characters, type:

```
CHCP 866
```

To see which code page is active, type the command by itself:

```
CHCP
```

OF INTEREST

NLSFUNC, MODE, KEYB

CHDIR or CD

SYNTAX
CD [/?|H] [x:][\directory]

[/?|H]   Help screen for this command.

[x:]   Disk-drive specification letter.

[\directory] Directory path.

CLASS
Internal

FUNCTION

CHDIR, or simply CD, lets you change directories. If you issue the command without a drive letter, you'll change to that directory on the current drive. If you issue the command with a drive specifier for a different drive, you'll change the current directory for that drive. However, you'll still be logged into the current drive and directory.

For example, suppose you've used the PG prompt suggested in SETUP and your command line looks like this:

```
C:\>
```

Now type:

```
CD \WORD
```

You'll be in the WORD directory, if it exists. If it doesn't, CHDIR will display a message to that effect:

```
C:\WORD>
```

343

However, if you type:

    CD D:\JUNQUE

the prompt will still show C:\WORD. If you enter:

    D:

you'll find yourself in D:\JUNQUE.

You can also specify "." as the current directory and ".." as the next directory up in the hierarchy. For example, if you're in D:\JUNQUE and you want to change to D:\JUNQUE\STUFF, type:

    CD .\STUFF

or

    CD STUFF

To switch to the parent directory, type:

    CD ..

You can omit the "\" only when you're changing to a subdirectory of the current directory.

EXAMPLES

To change to the \WEASEL\LEX\DICT directory, enter:

    CD \WEASEL\LEX\DICT

To change to the root directory, enter:

    CD \

To change the directory on drive Q: to \TEDIUM, enter:

```
CD Q:\TEDIUM
```

OF INTEREST
   PROMPT, MKDIR, RMDIR, RENDIR

CHKDSK

SYNTAX

CHKDSK [/?|H] [*x:*][*files*] [/F] [/V]

[/?|H]	Help screen for this command.
[*x:*]	Optional disk-drive specification for the file that will contain the CHKDSK report.
[*files*]	Optional name for the file that will contain the CHKDSK report.
[/F]	Allows CHKDSK to fix problems on the disk. Because CHKDSK can alter the file allocation table (FAT), it's often best to first run CHKDSK without this command to see what, if anything, it proposes to fix.
[/V]	The verbose mode. CHKDSK will give the name of each file it encounters.

CLASS

External: CHKDSK.COM

FUNCTION

CHKDSK is your disk doctor; it scans the specified disk for file-allocation errors. CHKDSK also reports other useful information, such as the number of directories and files, the amount of space used and available, and the amount of memory available. It includes files that are pending deletion (created by DELWATCH) in its tally of files. Pending deletion files have a clover as their identifying mark. When used with specific files, CHKDSK tests these files to see if they are contiguous (if you discover that a number of files aren't contiguous, consider running DISKOPT).

When CHKDSK looks over the FAT, it scans for clusters that aren't allocated to a specific file or clusters that are allocated to more than one file. If the /F parameter is used, it will ask if you want to convert these lost clusters to readable files in case they contain something useful. If you respond with Y, CHKDSK creates one or more files with the .CHK extension; if you respond with N, it frees these clusters so they can be allocated for file storage.

SIDE EFFECTS

You can't run CHKDSK on a network drive or drives set up through the ASSIGN, JOIN, or SUBST command.

EXAMPLES

The following runs a test of the current disk, causes CHKDSK to report on every file it finds, and writes the results to a file on the A: drive:

    CHKDSK A:DISKRPRT.TXT /V

The following allows CHKDSK to fix lost clusters:

    CHKDSK /F

OF INTEREST
DISKMAP

CLS

SYNTAX
CLS [/?|H]

[/?|H]   Help screen for this command.

CLASS
Internal

FUNCTION
Clears the screen and repositions the command line at the top. This command resets the screen colors to either black and white or the colors you selected through the ANSI.SYS driver.

EXAMPLE
To clear the screen, type:

```
CLS
```

COMMAND

SYNTAX
COMMAND [/?|H] [*drive:*][*directory*] [CTTY-*device*] [/E:*xxxxx*] [/P] [/C *program*]

    [/?|H]   Help screen for this command.

    [*drive:*]   The drive on which the copy of COMMAND.COM resides.

    [*directory*]   The directory in which COMMAND.COM resides.

    [CTTY-*device*] Calls the CTTY command to redirect the console (keyboard and display) to the specified device.

    [/E:*xxxxx*]   Sets the environment size. The range is 512 bytes to 32,751 bytes.

    [/P]   Disables EXIT, making the copy of COMMAND.COM permanent (until you reboot). Also runs the AUTOEXEC.BAT file.

    [/C *program*] Runs the specified program or batch file. You must make this argument the last one in the command line.

CLASS
External: COMMAND.COM

FUNCTION
All of your interaction with DR DOS at the command line is through the command processor. Running COMMAND loads a new copy of the command processor on top of the existing copy. You exit from a command processor by typing EXIT and pressing Enter. Programs usually use COMMAND to return temporarily to the DOS command line.

An interesting trick is to place COMMAND in a batch file. This temporarily drops you out of the batch file until you type EXIT, which causes batch-file execution to resume.

When you start a new command processor, it inherits the environment settings and drivers from the original command processor. This includes such niceties as environment variables created through SET, the PATH, and the settings from PROMPT. It will also set the COMSPEC to the referenced copy of COMMAND.COM. (COMSPEC sets the path pointing to the command processors.)

By using the CTTY argument, you can redirect the console to some other device, such as a serial communication port. This would be handy if you wanted to control the computer temporarily through a terminal or another computer. Control would then automatically return to the computer when you typed EXIT on the remote console.

EXAMPLE

To run the command processor, set the environment size to 1,024 bytes and run a program called BUFFALO.BAT:

```
COMMAND /E:1024 /C BUFFALO
```

OF INTEREST
SET

COMP

SYNTAX
COMP [/?|H] [*files files*] [/A] [/M:*x*]

[/?|H] Help screen for this command.

[*files files*] The pair of files to compare or the set of files defined by wildcards. If you don't enter any file names, COMP will ask you for them.

[/A] Displays comparison mismatches in ASCII rather than in hexadecimal format (the default).

[/M:*x*] The number of mismatches allowed before COMP gives up. Entering a 0 allows an infinite number of mismatches. The default is 10.

CLASS:
External: COMP.COM

FUNCTION
COMP does a byte-by-byte comparison of two supposedly identical files or sets of files. If the files or a file pair within a set aren't the same size, it will report this and ask if you want to continue.

Each time COMP finds a pair of bytes that don't match, it displays the mismatch and the byte locations. Normally it displays the mismatches in hexadecimal; however, you can use the /A parameter to have it display ASCII text instead.

COMP is useful for discovering changes in source code or in copies of executable files (which might have been corrupted or infected by a virus). It will also tell you if Ctrl-Z (the DOS end-of-file character) is missing from the end of any of the files.

EXAMPLES

The following compares WEASEL.EXE with D:\SQUID\WORM.EXE and allows an unlimited number of mismatches during the comparison:

```
COMP WEASEL.EXE D:\SQUID\WORM.EXE /M:0
```

To compare a set of .TXT files in D:\NEWSTUFF with a set of .TXT files in O:\OLDSTUFF and show any mismatches as ASCII, type:

```
COMP D:\NEWSTUFF\*.TXT O:\OLDSTUFF\*.TXT /A
```

OF INTEREST

DISKCOMP, FC

COPY

SYNTAX

COPY [/?|H] *sourcefiles\device* [+*morefiles*] [/A] [/B] [/C] [/S] [/V] [/Z] *destfiles\device* [/A] [/B] [/C] [/S] [/V] [/Z]

[/?|H]	Help screen for this command.
sourcefiles\device	The source files or DOS device. File specifications can include wildcards.
[+*morefiles*]	Additional source files you may list if you're combining several files.
[*destfiles\device*]	The destination file or set of files, or the destination DOS device. If you don't enter this field, COPY will use the current directory as the destination.
[/A]	COPY considers the file ASCII or text. It stops copying a source file when it finds an end-of-file character and adds an end-of-file character to the end of the destination file. This command is useful primarily when combining ASCII files.
[/B]	COPY considers the file to be binary and copies the entire file without regard to end-of-file characters. It doesn't add an end-of-file character to the end of the destination file. This command is intended for use when combining binary files.
[/C]	COPY asks you to press Y for yes or N for no before actually copying each file in the designated set of source files. This gives you a chance to choose the files you want to copy.
[/S]	Instructs COPY to copy files with the system or hidden attribute set.
[/V]	Verifies each copied file by comparing it to the original file. This takes longer but ensures that the copies are accurate.

[/Z] WordStar and a few other word processors use the high-order bit to indicate whether a word is within a paragraph or at the end of a paragraph. This option zeros that bit, converting a WordStar file into something more closely resembling an ASCII file. (You can tell just how popular WordStar was by the fact that it has its own COPY parameter.)

CLASS

Internal

FUNCTION

COPY copies a file or set of files to a new destination (either a disk or a directory) or to a DOS device such as a parallel or serial port. You can also use COPY to combine several files into one, a process called *concatenation*.

If you need to create a file, you can use COPY as a text-entry program. Enter the CON: device as the source and a file name as the destination. If you make typing errors, use the Backspace, left and right arrow, and Delete keys to correct them. When you finish a line, press Enter to create a new one. Close the file by typing Ctrl-Z.

Reverse the process to copy a file to the screen for viewing. Press Ctrl-S to pause the scrolling and Ctrl-S again to continue scrolling.

COPY is a reasonably efficient way to send a file or set of files to a printer. To do this, use the DOS device for the printer as the destination. This is almost always PRN, but you can specify the exact parallel or serial port as well.

You can use the following DR DOS device names:

CON The console (the keyboard and monitor).

LPTx A parallel port. x is the port number—1, 2, or 3.

PRN The printer port, usually LPT1.

NUL Nowhere. Sometimes called the *bit bucket*, this is simply a dummy output. Its usefulness is restricted to testing and practical jokes. Try COPY CON NUL on a patient and understanding

DR DOS COMMAND REFERENCE

friend's computer. The computer won't respond until Ctrl-Z is pressed.

COM*x*   A serial port. *x* is the port number; 1 through 4 are the options.

AUX   The auxiliary port, a synonym for COM1.

SIDE EFFECTS

If you overwrite a file with COPY, that file is gone forever. Make sure you don't copy an old version of a file over the new version.

EXAMPLES

To copy the file TEST.DOC to the A: drive:

```
COPY TEST.DOC A:
```

This variation copies all files in the O:\REALLY directory to the G:\WHIZ directory:

```
COPY O:\REALLY\*.* G:\WHIZ
```

This time we'll concatenate TEST1.DAT, TEST2.DAT, and finally TEST3.DAT into ALLTEST.DAT. The file contents will be found in that order within ALLTEST.DAT. Note the use of + to indicate which files will be combined:

```
COPY TEST1.DAT +TEST2.DAT +TEST3.DAT ALLTEST.DAT
```

To copy all files beginning with FRED and ending with NE to the B:\BEDROCK directory and verify each copy, type:

```
COPY FRED*.?NE B:\BEDROCK /V
```

The following command copies the file CHAPTER.C00 to the printer attached to line printer port one (LPT1):

```
COPY CHAPTER.C00 LPT1
```

Finally, this command copies what is typed on the keyboard to the file QUICKY.BAT:

```
COPY CON QUICKY.BAT
```

OF INTEREST
 MOVE, REPLACE, XCOPY, DISKCOPY

CTTY

SYNTAX
CTTY [/?|H] *device*

[/?|H]   Help screen for this command.

device The device where the console will now reside. This can be CON, COM1 (AUX1), or COM2.

CLASS
Internal

FUNCTION
CTTY allows you to redirect your console (keyboard and display) to a serial communications port. This means you can run your computer from a terminal or from another computer using a communication package. Of course, this presumes that the communication parameters you've set through the MODE command agree with those of the terminal or remote computer.

SIDE EFFECTS
Clearly, you can't run graphics programs this way. Also, remember that you're limited to the speed of the serial port, which is far less than the speed at which the computer communicates with its display screen.

EXAMPLES

To redirect the console to the COM1 serial port, type:

```
CTTY COM1
```

The following command, entered from the remote terminal or computer, returns control of the computer to its keyboard and display:

```
CTTY CON
```

OF INTEREST
COPY, MODE, FILELINK

CURSOR

SYNTAX
CURSOR [/?|H] [/S*xx*] [/C] [OFF]

[/?|H]	Help screen for this command.
[/S*xx*]	Sets the cursor flash frequency in increments of 1/20th of a second.
[/C]	"Snow" repellent on old-style CGA displays. Some CGAs will momentarily appear to lose control of the screen when the software cursor is used. This parameter prevents the screen from breaking up.
[OFF]	Turns the software cursor off and returns the default system cursor.

CLASS
External: CURSOR.COM

FUNCTION
Cursors on laptop and notebook computers with liquid crystal or plasma display devices may blink faster than the rate at which the display can respond. In such a situation, the cursor appears as a blur or a solid block. The CURSOR command fixes this by substituting a large block cursor with a variable flash frequency. The default flash rate is 1/5th of a second; however, you'll want to experiment with different rate settings.

CURSOR was designed for EGA, VGA, and CGA displays but also works fine on a Hercules display.

SIDE EFFECTS
Some programs generate their own software cursors and will override your selection through the CURSOR command.

EXAMPLES

This command sets the cursor on and causes it to blink every 1/4th of a second:

    CURSOR /S5

To turn the software cursor off, use:

    CURSOR /OFF

DATE

SYNTAX

DATE [/?|H] [*xx-xx-xx*]

[/?|H]   Help screen for this command.

[*xx-xx-xx*]   The month, day, and year. Each set of digits corresponds to month, day, or year, depending on the country code.

CLASS

Internal

FUNCTION

DATE allows you to check or change the month, day, and year settings in DR DOS's software clock. If your computer has an internal hardware clock, it will run automatically on boot-up. Older XT and PC systems with real-time clock boards must use a program, normally run through the AUTOEXEC.BAT file, to read the time and date from the clock. If your computer doesn't have a hardware clock, you should include both TIME and DATE in your AUTOEXEC.BAT file so that you can set these on boot-up.

The format used to enter the date is set through the COUNTRY= statement in the CONFIG.SYS file. If the country setting is USA, the configuration is mm-dd-yy (*mm* is the month, *dd* is the day, and *yy* is the last two digits of the year). Most European codes cause DATE to accept dd-mm-yy, while Japan shifts the order to yy-mm-dd.

SIDE EFFECTS

DATE can reset the software clock, but it has no effect on the internal hardware clock. Hardware clocks are adjusted either through the system configuration software (common to PCs since the introduction of AT machines) or through a special clock-setting program (shipped with clock boards for XT and PC machines).

EXAMPLES

To check the current date setting, use:

```
DATE
```

To change the date to December 25, 1999, in the United States, use:

```
DATE 12/25/99
```

OF INTEREST
TIME

DEL

SYNTAX
DEL [/?|H] *files* [/C] [/S]

[/?|H] Help screen for this command.

files The file specification. DEL accepts wildcards.

[/C] Makes DEL query whether you want each file deleted as it goes through the set of files designated by *files*.

[/S] Lets DEL also delete files with the system attribute set.

CLASS
Internal

FUNCTION
DEL, a pseudonym for the ERASE command, "removes" the file from the disk. Actually, DEL marks the file as "erased" so that DR DOS can use the sectors it occupied on the disk to store other files. This means that if you don't create or modify any files, you have an excellent chance of recovering an erased file with the UNDELETE command. As you create or modify existing files, however, the chances of successfully recovering the file diminish because DR DOS may overwrite data in the erased file with data from new or modified files.

If you use the DELWATCH command, you can recover as many erased files as DELWATCH is set to preserve. When DELWATCH is active, DEL marks the files for deletion, but DR DOS won't use their sector space until DELPURGE is issued.

If you attempt to erase all files in a directory, DEL will ask you to confirm that you want to perform this task.

XDEL is a more powerful command for deleting files, and QDEL is a safer command for deleting.

EXAMPLES

To delete the file JUNQUE.TXT, type:

```
DEL JUNQUE.TXT
```

To delete all files in C:\STUFF ending with .BAK, type:

```
DEL C:\STUFF\*.BAK
```

To delete all files in the current directory, including system files, type:

```
DEL *.* /S
```

OF INTEREST

XDEL, DELWATCH, DELPURGE, UNDELETE, QDEL

DELPURGE

SYNTAX
DELPURGE [/?|H] *files* [/A] [/D:*date*|-*xx*] [/L] [/P] [/S] [/T:*time*]

[/?|H]	Help screen for this command.
files	The file specification, which can include wildcards. The default is all files (*.*).
[/A]	Purges the files without asking.
[/D:*date*|-*xx*]	Purges only those files deleted on or before the date specified. The date-entry order is set through the country code and is mm-dd-yy for the USA, dd-mm-yy for Europe, and yy-mm-dd for Japan. You can also enter this as -*xx*, where *xx* is the number of days before the current date.
[/L]	Lists files matching the file specification and the /D and /T settings but does not purge the designated files.
[/P]	Prompts you before purging the files. This is the default.
[/S]	Also purges all files matching the file specification and /D and /T settings in all subdirectories of the current directory.
[/T:*time*]	Removes files that were deleted at or before the specified time. This can be used in conjunction with the /D parameter.

CLASS
External: DELPURGE.EXE

FUNCTION
DELPURGE works in conjunction with DELWATCH. The DELWATCH command marks deleted files for erasure but protects their file space from being overwritten. This assures you that you can recover these files with UNDELETE.

When you want to free up the disk space occupied by these deleted files, issue the DELPURGE command.

Even after issuing the DELPURGE command, you can usually recover deleted files with UNDELETE if you haven't created any new files or modified existing files.

SIDE EFFECTS

Keep in mind that DELWATCH isn't a bottomless pit. By default, it will allow for painless recovery of 200 files and can be set to a maximum of 999 files. When the limit is reached, DELWATCH automatically purges the oldest files.

Also keep in mind that files deleted while DELWATCH is active don't give up their storage space. Therefore, if you don't have much room on your disk, don't allow too many files to stack up before issuing this command.

EXAMPLES

To list all the files in the current directory that DELPURGE can purge, type:

```
DELPURGE /L
```

To purge all files that were deleted on or before December 25, 1992, and that may be in any directory on the D: drive, type:

```
DELPURGE D:\*.* /D:12/25/92 /S
```

OF INTEREST

DELWATCH, UNDELETE

DELQ

SYNTAX
DELQ [/?|H] *files* [/S]

  [/?|H]   Help screen for this command.

  files   The file specification. Wildcards are allowed, and a file specification must be entered.

  [/S]   Delete files with the system attribute set and that match the file specification.

CLASS
Internal

FUNCTION
DELQ and its pseudonym, ERAQ, are similar to DEL and ERA command except that they ask before erasing files. They are handy for selecting files to delete from a large collection of files specified through wildcards. If you want DELQ to erase a file, simply respond with Y. Responding with N instructs DELQ not to erase a file.

As with the other delete facilities, you can use UNDELETE to restore the files.

EXAMPLE
The following instructs DELQ to ask you before deleting all the files in the current directory:

```
DELQ *.*
```

OF INTEREST
DEL, ERASE, DELWATCH, DELPURGE, XDEL, UNERASE

DELWATCH

SYNTAX

DELWATCH [/?|H] *x:* [*y:*] [B:*xxxxx*] [/D] [E:*ext*[+*ext*]] [/F:*xxxxx*] [/MU|ML] [/O:*ext*[*ext*]] [/S]

[/?|H]	Help screen for this command.
x: [*y:*]	The drive or drives for which DELWATCH will preserve deleted files.
[B:*xxxxx*]	The number of deleted files with the same name and from the same directory that DELWATCH will preserve. The range is 1 (the default value) to 65,535.
[/D]	Disables DELWATCH for the designated disk drives.
[E:*ext*[+*ext*]]	Ignores files with the designated file extension(s). You can designate up to 10 extensions. You can't use this with the /O parameter.
[/F:*xxxxx*]	Sets the maximum number of files to preserve. The default is 200 files for a hard drive and 20 files for a floppy disk. The range is 1 to 65,535.
[/MU|ML]	/MU loads DELWATCH into upper memory if it's available. /ML loads DELWATCH into lower memory.
[/O:*ext*[*ext*]]	Preserves only those files that match the designated extensions. You can designate up to 10 extensions. You can't use this with the /E parameter.
[/S]	Displays the status of DELWATCH.

CLASS

External: DELWATCH.EXE

FUNCTION

DELWATCH ensures successful recovery of deleted files. When it's active, files can be deleted but their space isn't reallocated for use until DELPURGE is used. DELWATCH has an extremely flexible set of parameters that allow you to limit the number of files and include or exclude certain types of files.

DELWATCH can be used on any or all drives or partitions. If you want to specify different parameters for different drives, you'll need to execute multiple DELWATCH commands.

SIDE EFFECTS

Like any TSR program, DELWATCH occupies memory. If upper memory is available, you can free base memory using the /MU parameter.

Because DELWATCH prevents erased files from being overwritten, erased files continue to occupy space on the disk. You may wish to limit the number of files DELWATCH will preserve and run DELPURGE fairly often.

DELWATCH can't be used with network drives.

DISKMAP provides an alternative method for assisting UNDELETE in recovering files (see the DISKMAP section in Appendix A). DISKMAP isn't quite as foolproof; however, it doesn't take up memory or prevent deleted file space from being reallocated.

EXAMPLES

The following sets DELWATCH to work with the B:, C:, and G: drives:

```
DELWATCH B: C: G:
```

This example sets DELWATCH to work with drive C:, ignore files with .BAK, $??, and .C00 extensions, and preserve no more than 150 files:

```
DELWATCH C: /E:BAK+$??+C00 /F:150
```

This example loads DELWATCH into upper memory and sets it to work with the D: drive:

```
DELWATCH D: /MU
```

OF INTEREST
DELPURGE, DISKMAP, UNDELETE

DIR

SYNTAX

DIR [/?|H] [*files*] [/2|W|L] [/D|S|A] [/C] [/N] [/P] [/R]

[/?|H]   [/?|H]

[*files*]   The designated files to display, including wildcards. The default is *.*.

[/2|W|L]   The format for the directory contents display. /2 displays in two-column format. /W displays in wide format (which omits file size and the date and time of the last change). /L is the default, single-column format including size, time, and date.

[/D|S|A]   /D displays only those files without the system attribute set (this is the default). /S displays only those files with the system attribute set. /A display files with and without the system attribute set.

[/C]   Copies the settings of the other parameters to the next DIR command.

[/N]   Stops DIR from pausing at each screenful of information.

[/P]   Causes DIR to pause at each screenful of information.

[/R]   Makes DIR remember the current parameter settings (except the file specification) and use these as defaults.

CLASS

Internal

FUNCTION

DIR lists the files matching the *files* designation. It also lists the drive, volume name, and path of the current directory as well as the number of files in the directory and the number of bytes available on the disk. It will also tell you if system files are present on the disk.

While DIR works with a robust set of parameters, it doesn't sort files as its cousin, XDIR, does. Also, it can't search subdirectories.

EXAMPLES

To list all system files in the current directory, type:

```
DIR /S
```

To list all *.DOC files in the current directory in a two-column format while pausing at each screen, type:

```
DIR *.DOC /2 /P
```

To list all files, including system files, on the A: drive, type:

```
DIR A: /A
```

OF INTEREST
XDIR, MORE, SORT

DISKCOMP

SYNTAX
DISKCOMP [/?|H] [x:] [y:] [/1] [/8] [/A] [/M] [/V]

[/?|H]   Help screen for this command.

[x:]   A floppy drive for comparison. If you don't include this, DISKCOMP assumes you want to use the current drive for comparisons.

[y:]   A second floppy drive for comparison against x:. If this is omitted, DISKCOMP will assume you mean the current drive.

[/1]   Compares only side one of a double-sided diskette.

[/8]   Compares only the first eight sectors of each track on a floppy diskette.

[/A]   Provides an audible prompt when DISKCOMP wants you to change diskettes or when it completes the process.

[/M]   Performs multiple comparisons of the same diskette. When each comparison is done, DISKCOMP will ask if you want to compare another diskette.

[/V]   Verifies that the entire diskette can be read.

CLASS
External: DISKCOMP.EXE

FUNCTION
DISKCOMP compares floppy diskettes to ensure they match. This is a useful check for critical diskettes created through DISKCOPY. DISKCOMP does a track-by-track check of sectors to make sure the diskettes are identical. If it finds a mismatch, DISKCOMP will alert you to the offending cylinder on the disk.

DR DOS 6 BY EXAMPLE

You can also compare a floppy diskette against an image file created through DISKCOPY. You can't, however, compare two image files.

SIDE EFFECTS

Because DISKCOMP compares track by track rather than file by file, you can't compare a 3.5-inch disk with a 5.25-inch disk (although they may contain the same files). The disks must match in size and density, and the copy must have been created using DISKCOPY. The only exception to this is a comparison between a floppy disk and an image file.

EXAMPLES

To compare the contents of two floppy disks, one in the A: drive and one in the B: drive, type:

```
DISKCOMP A: B:
```

Use the following command to compare two floppy disks but use the same physical disk drive for the comparison:

```
DISKCOMP A: A:
```

If you're logged onto drive A:, the following command has the same effect as the last:

```
DISKCOMP A:
```

This command compares the image file C:\STUFF\DISK.IMG created by DISKCOPY with the contents of the B: floppy:

```
DISKCOMP A: C:\STUFF\DISK.IMG
```

OF INTEREST

DISKCOPY, FC, COMP

DISKCOPY

SYNTAX

DISKCOPY [/?|H] [*source*] [*destination*] [/1] [/A] [/M]

[/?|H]	Help screen for this command.
[*source*]	The source floppy diskette drive.
[*destination*]	The destination floppy diskette drive or image file. If this is a floppy drive, it must match the source in size and density. If you omit the drive specification, DISKCOPY copies to the currently logged drive.
[/1]	Copies only the first side of the diskette.
[/A]	Sounds an audible alarm when you need to exchange diskettes or when the copy is complete.
[/M]	The multiple-copy parameter. This is useful for making many copies of a single disk or image file. After each copy is made, DISKCOPY will ask you if you want to make more copies. If you do, press Y; if you don't, press N.

CLASS

External: DISKCOPY.COM

FUNCTION

The DISKCOPY command provides a fast, efficient way to make exact duplicates of the contents of floppy diskettes. It won't copy 3.5-inch diskettes to 5.25-inch diskettes because it makes a track-by-track, sector-by-sector mirror image of the original diskette. If the destination diskette's format differs from that of the source (or is unformatted), DISKCOPY will format the destination diskette.

You can also use this command with a single disk drive. In this scenario, DISKCOPY copies as much as it can to memory and asks you to put the destination diskette into the drive. It will repeat this process as many times as necessary to copy the disk. If you have expanded or extended memory, DISKCOPY will use it (making the copying procedure more efficient). DISKCOPY can also use the temporary file designated through SET TEMP for temporary storage.

If you don't include a *destination* disk drive in the command, DISKCOPY will use the currently logged drive as the destination. If that's a hard drive and you haven't designated a destination file name for the image file, DISKCOPY will quit.

The /M parameter is a neat way to make multiple copies of a single disk. For the most efficient operation, first copy the contents of the disk to an image file on your hard drive (if you have one), then use the /M parameter to copy the image file to multiple floppies.

EXAMPLES

To copy the contents of the A: floppy drive to the B: floppy drive, type:

```
DISKCOPY A: B:
```

To copy the contents of the A: drive to another floppy that will be in the A: drive, type:

```
DISKCOPY A: A:
```

The following copies the contents of the A: drive to an image file called C:\STUFF\DISK.IMG:

```
DISKCOPY A: C:\STUFF\DISK.IMG
```

This command copies the contents of C:\STUFF\DISK.IMG to the A: drive, prompts for additional copies, and beeps when ready:

```
DISKCOPY C:\STUFF\DISK.IMG A: /A /M
```

OF INTEREST

XCOPY, DISKCOMP

DISKMAP

SYNTAX
DISKMAP [/?|H] [/D] *disk* [*disk*]

[/?|H]	Help screen for this command.
[/D]	Delete the existing DISKMAP file.
disk	The disk drive for which DISKMAP will create a file copy of the FAT.
[*disk*]	Additional disk drives (as many as you like) for which DISKMAP will create file copies of the FAT. It writes each copy to the appropriate drive.

CLASS
External: DISKMAP.EXE

FUNCTION
DISKMAP is an alternative to DELWATCH. While DELWATCH prevents deleted files from being overwritten, DISKMAP simply makes a map of where the files actually were. It does this by copying the FAT to a disk file that UNDELETE will look for. This disk file is called DISKMAP.DAT, and you'll find one of these in the root directory of each disk you map. The file is set to read-only.

DISKMAP has some advantages over DELWATCH. It really isn't a TSR and thus doesn't take up any memory. Also, it doesn't prevent DR DOS from reallocating the space taken up by deleted files like DELWATCH does.

But these advantages have drawbacks. Because DISKMAP doesn't protect the file space of deleted files, they can be overwritten and therefore may not be recoverable. Also, DISKMAP is a snapshot in time of what the FAT looked like. A DISKMAP file created several days ago won't be of much help because the FAT may have changed since then. It's best to run DISKMAP from the AUTOEXEC.BAT file to ensure that UNDELETE will have a reasonably recent FAT file to work with.

While DISKMAP isn't as effective as DELWATCH in recovering deleted files, it doesn't take up memory and is more effective than having UNDELETE attempt to recover files unaided.

SIDE EFFECTS

Because deleted files can be overwritten, using DISKMAP doesn't guarantee you'll be able to recover all deleted files.

You can't use DISKMAP to make a FAT file for a network drive (but then, you can't undelete files on a network drive anyway).

EXAMPLES

To tell DISKMAP to create FAT files for the C:, D:, and E: drives, type:

```
DISKMAP C: D: E:
```

To erase existing FAT files created by DISKMAP, enter:

```
DISKMAP /D
```

OF INTEREST

DELWATCH, DELPURGE, UNDELETE

DISKOPT

SYNTAX
DISKOPT [/?|H] [X:]

[/?|H]   Help screen for this command.

[X:]   The drive to be optimized. DISKOPT, being a menu-driven program, also allows you to change drives once DISKOPT is running.

CLASS
External: DISKOPT.EXE

FUNCTION
DISKOPT has two functions:

- To speed file access by rebuilding each file on the disk so that it uses consecutive sectors. This means DR DOS doesn't need to send the disk-drive head hither and yon to find each part of the file. Instead, the entire file is in neighboring sectors.

- To sort directories. When you use DIR, the files are sorted in the order you choose.

For ease of use, DISKOPT's commands are accessed via drop-down menus. Under the Optimize menu, you'll find the command to make all files contiguous. The Sort menu has directory-sorting options.

DISKOPT initially displays a map showing the location of used areas on the disk. If these are grouped together with few gaps, you don't need to do anything. If files are scattered all over the disk, however, it's best to optimize it.

While you can sort your directories, XDIR presents directories sorted in any manner you like.

SIDE EFFECTS

It's not a good idea to interrupt DISKOPT while it's running. Pressing the Escape key is a more graceful approach, but a power failure could be disastrous. Remember that DISKOPT is shuffling your files around on the disk and rebuilding the FAT to reflect these changes. Stopping DISKOPT in the midst of this process can result in corrupted files and a corrupted FAT.

Disk optimization is a tedious and time-consuming process. Before you attempt it, make sure you can get along without your computer for some time.

If you've made a DISKMAP file, optimizing the disk could radically change the FAT and make DISKMAP obsolete.

EXAMPLE

The easiest way to use the program is to run it and set everything from the menu commands. To do this, use the DISKOPT command.

OF INTEREST

DISKMAP, CHKDSK

DOSBOOK

SYNTAX
DOSBOOK [/?|H] [*command*] /B

[/?|H]   Help screen for this command.

[*command*]   Any DR DOS command. Entering a command name after DOSBOOK causes DOSBOOK to jump immediately to that entry in its documentation.

/B   Tells DOSBOOK to display its menus in black and white, which may make a laptop display more readable.

CLASS
External: DOSBOOK.EXE

FUNCTION
DOSBOOK is a reasonably detailed on-line reference guide for DR DOS commands. It has some rather nifty features, including multiple tables of contents, an electronic index, and the ability to backtrack.

The information in DOSBOOK is divided into three sections:

- DR DOS Basics. Covers the basics of using DR DOS.

- Commands and Utilities. Covers each of the commands and utility programs. It doesn't list device drivers and similar files.

- Troubleshooting. A guide to error messages.

DOSBOOK also has a set of keyboard commands:

- Enter. When the highlight bar is over an entry, press Enter to view that topic.

- Up Arrow/Page Up. Scrolls up through the reference text.

- Down Arrow/Page Down. Scrolls down through the reference text.

- Home. Moves the cursor to the top of the screen.
- End. Moves the cursor to the bottom of the screen.
- Control-Home. Moves to the top of a list.
- Control-End. Moves to the bottom of a list.

DOSBOOK is handy if you run it as a task in TaskMAX so that you can pop it up whenever you need it. It's covered in greater detail in Chapter 4.

EXAMPLES

This command runs DOSBOOK and adjusts the display parameters for black-and-white display only:

```
DOSBOOK /B
```

This command provides DOSBOOK reference entries about the ASSIGN command:

```
DOSBOOK ASSIGN
```

ERAQ

SYNTAX
ERAQ [/?|H] *files* [/S]

[/?|H]	Help screen for this command.
files	File specification; can include wildcards.
[/S]	Erase files with the system attribute set.

CLASS
Internal

FUNCTION
ERAQ and its pseudonym, DELQ, are similar to the DEL and ERA commands except they confirm before erasing files. They're handy for selecting files to delete from a large collection of files (using wildcards). If you want DELQ to erase a given file, simply respond with a Y. An N instructs ERAQ not to erase a file.

Like the other delete facilities, you can use UNDELETE to restore the files.

EXAMPLE
The following instructs DELQ to ask you about deleting all the files in the current directory:

```
ERAQ *.*
```

OF INTEREST
DEL, ERASE, DELWATCH, DELPURGE, XDEL, UNERASE

ERASE or ERA

SYNTAX

ERASE [/?|H] *files* [/C] [/S]

[/?|H] Help screen for this command.

files The file specification. ERASE accepts wildcards.

[/C] Tells ERASE to confirm that you want each file erased as it goes through the set of files designated by *files*.

[/S] Lets ERASE also delete files with the system attribute set.

CLASS
Internal

FUNCTION

ERASE, a pseudonym for the DEL command, removes a file or files from your disk. Actually, it marks the file as erased so DR DOS can use the sectors it occupied on the disk to store other files. This means that if you don't create or modify any files, you have an excellent chance of recovering an erased file with the UNDELETE command. As you create or modify existing files, however, your chances of successfully recovering the file diminish (DR DOS may overwrite data in the erased file with data from new or modified files).

If you use the DELWATCH command, you can recover as many erased files as DELWATCH is set to preserve. When DELWATCH is active, ERASE marks the files for deletion; however, DR DOS won't use their sector space until DELPURGE is issued.

If you try to erase all files in a directory, ERASE will ask you to confirm that you want to perform this task.

Keep in mind that XDEL is a more powerful command for deleting files, while QDEL is safer.

EXAMPLES

To delete the file JUNQUE.TXT, type:

    ERASE JUNQUE.TXT

To delete all files in C:\STUFF ending with .BAK, type:

    ERASE C:\STUFF*.BAK

To delete all files in the current directory, including system files, type:

    ERASE *.* /S

OF INTEREST

XDEL, DELWATCH, DELPURGE, UNDELETE, QDEL

EXE2BIN

SYNTAX

EXE2BIN [/?|H] *source[.ext] output[.ext]* [/S*hhhh*]

[/?|H]   Help screen for this command.

source[.ext]   The source file, including its complete path. If *.ext* is omitted, an .EXE extension is assumed.

output[.ext]   The destination file, including its complete path. If *.ext* is omitted, either a .BIN (image file) or .COM (command file) extension is assumed depending on the value in the Instruction Pointer field.

[/S*hhhh*]   The base segment, presented as a four-digit hexadecimal value.

CLASS
External: EXE2BIN.EXE

FUNCTION

This is a utility to convert a certain type of executable program file to either of two kinds of binary files. It is not of general interest. EXE2BIN can convert an .EXE file, created by a DR DOS linker, to either a command file or an image file. Every .EXE file has a header that informs DR DOS of the file memory requirements, the file size, the program entry point, and absolute segment address references. To be converted to a .BIN file, the .EXE file must meet these criteria:

- The initial instruction pointer must have a value of 0.
- The program cannot have a stack declared.
- The program entry point must have an absolute offset of 0.

To be converted to a .COM file, the .EXE file must meet these requirements:

- The initial instruction pointer must have a value of 100H.

- The program cannot have a stack declared.
- The program code and data, once loaded, cannot exceed 65,277 bytes.
- The program entry point must be 100H.
- The program cannot have absolute segment erase references that require segment fix-ups (these are stored in the .EXE file header).

Note that MS-DOS hasn't included EXE2BIN since version 3.2.

EXAMPLES

The following command converts the LOOPY.EXE program to LOOPY.COM:

```
EXE2BIN LOOPY
```

This variation converts LOOPY.EXE to LOOPY.COM but provides a base segment value of 1024H:

```
EXE2BIN LOOPY /S1024
```

EXIT

SYNTAX
EXIT [/?|H]

[/?|H]   Help screen for this command.

CLASS
Internal

FUNCTION
EXIT, as its name implies, allows you to exit from a secondary command processor (that is, an invocation of COMMAND.COM) and return to the original command processor or other calling program. For example, some programs, such as ViewMAX, let you temporarily exit to DR DOS by starting a second command processor. You exit from this DR DOS shell and return to the program by executing the EXIT command.

EXAMPLE
To exit from a secondary command processor, type EXIT.

OF INTEREST
COMMAND

FASTOPEN

SYNTAX
FASTOPEN [/?|H]

[/?|H]   Help screen for this command.

CLASS
External

FUNCTION
FASTOPEN is a statement added to the CONFIG.SYS file that speeds up disk accesses to commonly used files. It does this by keeping a memory-resident table of the most recently used files and their paths.

It takes a single argument in the CONFIG.SYS file: the size of the table. The syntax is

```
FASTOPEN = xxxxx
```

where *xxxxx* is any value between 128 and 32,768 bytes. The default, 512 bytes, is assumed if no value is entered. For more information, see Chapter 9.

DR DOS includes FASTOPEN.EXE for those programs that expect such a file. However, FASTOPEN.EXE has no real function. (MS-DOS has a functional FASTOPEN.EXE.)

FC

SYNTAX
FC [/?|H] [@]*files1* *files2* [/A] [/B] [/C] [/G*x*] [/L] [/M*x*] [/W]

- [/?|H]   Help screen for this command.

- [@]*files1*   The original files used in the comparison. This can be a single file or a set of files determined by wildcards. If sets of files are being compared, they must have matching file names.

  If "@" prefaces the file, FC assumes that *files1* is a single file containing a list of files for comparison.

- *files2*   A matching file name or set of files for the comparison.

- [/A]   ViewMAX output during ASCII file comparisons. Only the first and last lines of diverging sections of text are displayed.

- [/B]   Forces a binary comparison between the selected files. Normally, FC will do a binary comparison by default on files with extensions of .EXE, .COM, .BIN, .CMD, .LIB, and .OBJ.

- [/C]   Tells FC to ignore case during an ASCII file comparison.

- [/G*x*]   Changes the number of matching lines FC must find before it resynchronizes the ASCII files. The default value is 5.

- [/L]   Forces an ASCII file comparison.

- [/M*x*]   Allows you to set the number of mismatches FC will tolerate before giving up the comparison. The default value is 20. To set an unlimited number of mismatches, set this parameter to 0.

- [/W]   Limits mismatches to words; tabs and spaces are ignored. FC won't ignore carriage returns and line feeds.

CLASS
External: FC.EXE

FUNCTION

FC compares a pair of files, a set of files with matching names (specified by wildcards), or a set of files specified by a list file. FC has two comparison modes, ASCII and binary.

In ASCII mode, FC compares two text files line by line. It displays any discrepancy and resynchronizes the files after a certain number of matching lines. That number can be set using the /G parameter.

In binary mode, FC compares the files byte by byte. It displays each discrepancy and makes no attempt to resynchronize the files. By default, FC quits a binary comparison after 20 mismatches, although you can reset this value using the /M parameter.

FC is useful for checking changes to source code in programs you're developing and for finding changes between versions of text files. You can also use it to compare two binary files for changes (such files typically have .EXE, .OBJ, .COM, .LIB, .APP, .BIN, .OVL, and .LIB extensions). If you have a clean copy of COMMAND.COM for comparison, you can use FC to see if a computer virus has infected your working COMMAND.COM.

A good trick is to use file redirection to copy the output of FC to a file so you can compare the results at your leisure.

SIDE EFFECTS

Because most word processors don't generate pure ASCII files, FC often fails when comparing word processor files (typically when those files don't use standard carriage-return/line-feed pairs to mark line endings). In this case, FC will quit and display a message saying that the line exceeds 256 characters.

EXAMPLES

The following command check two copies of the ASCII source code, STUFF.C, and redirects the result of the comparison to the file CHECK.TXT:

```
FC STUFF.C C:\OLDCODE\STUFF.C > CHECK.TXT
```

To compare your COMMAND.COM with a copy of COMMAND.COM on a floppy diskette, type:

```
FC COMMAND.COM A:\COMMAND.COM
```

To compare all the .C files in the directory C:\D05 with their counterparts in the directory E:\WORKING, use this command:

```
FC C:\D05\*.C E:\WORKING\*.C
```

OF INTEREST
DISKCOMP

FDISK

SYNTAX
FDISK [/?|H] [/D]

[/?|H]   Help screen for this command.

[/D]   Delete a non-DR DOS partition.

CLASS
External: FDISK.COM

FUNCTION
FDISK is a utility that sets up a hard drive after that drive has been formatted by a low-level formatter. It divides a single physical drive into one or more partitions, which are contiguous areas of your drive that can be used for various purposes. A partition can be used by DR DOS or by other operating systems to hold files in a file system. The first partition is always C: and is called the *primary partition*. You can also have a single extended partition, which can be divided into several logical drives (starting with D:) of varying sizes. In DR DOS, the maximum size for a partition is 512 MB.

Non-DOS partitions are segments of the disk devoted to some other operating system, such as a version of UNIX. Some versions of UNIX provide a utility for reading MS-DOS compatible partitions.

You must run FDISK for a new hard drive, and before running FDISK you must perform a low-level format on the hard drive. See the literature that came with your hard drive or controller card for an explanation of how to do this.

A word of caution: FDISK erases files forever, so be sure this is what you want. For example, if you have a hard disk and decide to add an extended partition strictly for SuperStor's use, running FDISK will erase everything on your hard drive. Make a backup of your hard drive (using BACKUP or a third-party software package such as FastBack) before creating the extended partition.

Running FDISK is simple—type FDISK and press Enter. You'll be greeted with the menu shown in Figure A-1.

```
FDISK R1.60     Fixed Disk Maintenance Utility
Copyright (c) 1986,1988,1990 Digital Research Inc. All rights reserved.

Partitions on 1st hard disk (80.8 Mb, 812 cylinders):
No  Drive  Start  End    MB    Status  Type
 1   C:      0    606   60.4     A     DOS 3.31
 2   --    607    811   20.4     N     DOS EXT




Select options:
1) Create DOS partition
2) Delete DOS partition
3) Select bootable partition
4) Display logical drives in extended partition

Enter desired option: (ESC = exit) [?]
```

Figure A-1. FDISK main screen.

You'll see selection 4 of this menu only if you have an extended partition to display. If you have more than one hard disk installed, you'll see a fifth entry for selecting an alternative hard disk. If you want to leave without disturbing anything, just press the Escape key.

Notice that FDISK reports all sorts of interesting information about the current partitions:

No   Partitions are numbered in order. The primary partition is always 1, and the extended partition is always 2.

Drive   This is known as the partition or logical drive. For example, the boot partition (which can be your entire drive or some segment of it) is referred to as C:.

Start   The starting cylinder in the partition. The boot partition is 0; the extended partition can have any number.

End   The last cylinder in the partition.

MB   The number of megabytes in the partition.

Status   The bootable partition is marked *A* for active. Nonbootable partitions are marked *N*.

Type   The version of DOS used to create and format the partition. Notice that the figure says DOS 3.31, although it was created with DR DOS 6.0. DR DOS identifies itself to most programs as DOS 3.31, whereas MS-DOS identifies itself by the release number. DR DOS identifies itself properly if you use the VER command. Extended partitions are identified simply as Ext.

The FDISK menu offers you various choices:

1. Create a DOS partition.

   You usually create a DOS partition only if you're starting with a fresh hard drive, in which case you'll need to run FDISK from a DR DOS bootable floppy. Actually, FDISK would then be run automatically during the DR DOS installation process.

   You can also delete a partition and re-create it at some other size. Remember, partition deletion is forever. If you choose to create a DOS partition, FDISK will ask what type to create. Your options are to create a primary (bootable) partition, an extended partition (which you can create only if you already have a primary partition), or an additional logical drive in an existing extended partition. Enter the number corresponding to the option you've chosen.

   If you're creating a primary partition, FDISK will ask if you want to use the whole disk for it. For my 80-MB disk, it asked if I wanted to use cylinders 0 through 811. If I reply yes to this question, FDISK sets up the entire drive as a single active DR DOS partition. If I say no, I need to tell FDISK what cylinders to start and stop with. At a minimum, you must have 20 cylinders for DR DOS.

After setting the parameters, FDISK prepares the partition. It flags any bad sectors it encounters so you don't write data to these areas. If it finds bad sectors within the system area of the disk, it asks for another starting cylinder number. After it finishes, it asks you to enter a label for the partition. My C: partition is called Max, which is my nickname for the system. My extended partition, devoted to SuperStor, is called Attic; this is where I throw graphics files, clip art, and other such odds and ends.

If FDISK is run as part of the DR DOS installation process, DR DOS is installed in the bootable partition FDISK created. If FDISK is running alone, use SYS to put the core DR DOS files on the system and then COPY or XCOPY to copy the rest of the DR DOS files into a DR DOS directory.

2. Delete a DOS partition.

When you delete a partition, its contents are permanently destroyed. If you choose this option, FDISK will ask if you want to delete the DOS primary partition, the extended partition (if one exists), or a logical drive within an existing extended partition. If you want to delete an extended partition, you must first delete all the additional logical drives within it. If you choose to delete a partition, you must supply the partition number. You'll have one last chance to back out before the partition contents are irretrievably lost.

To delete a non-DOS partition, start FDISK with the /D parameter.

3. Select a bootable partition.

This option selects the active or boot partition. You can have only one active partition. This can be a DR DOS or non-DOS partition.

4. Display a logical drive in an extended partition.

This provides information on the size and type of all logical drives in the extended partition.

5. Select an alternate fixed disk.

   If you have more than one physical (not logical) hard disk drive, use this option to select the drive you want FDISK to work with.

SIDE EFFECTS

Be very careful with this command; FDISK can destroy all data in a partition or logical disk drive.

EXAMPLES

To start the program, use this command.

```
FDISK
```

To use FDISK to delete a non-DOS partition, use this variant:

```
FDISK /D
```

OF INTEREST

FORMAT

FIND

FIND [/?|H] [/B] [/C] [/F] [/N] [/S] [/U] [/V] *"find this"* [@]*files*

[/?|H]   Help screen for this command.

[/B]   Changes format, displaying the file names that contain the search string as headings, with the matches in each file shown below the headings.

[/C]   Lists each of the files specified by *files*, with the number of lines in each file that match the search string.

[/F]   Lists the names of the files that match *files* and contain the search string.

[/N]   Lists the names of the files and line numbers containing the search string.

[/S]   Scans subdirectories as well as the current directory.

[/U]   Means the search string must exactly match the specified case in the search string.

[/V]   Displays all lines in all files that don't match the search string.

"find this"   The search string.

[@]*files*   Additional files. Used when specifying a series of files to be searched.

CLASS
External: FIND.EXE

FUNCTION

FIND searches the files specified by name and extension in *files* for a specified string of text. This is a handy program for checking all the occurrences of such things as network addresses, particular functions or variables in program source code, or any other text you need to track down. While you can specify a range of files using wildcards, you can also search a series of specific files simply by listing them, separating the names with spaces.

If you don't specify file names, FIND waits to examine the input from the console (keyboard) or from a redirected file. You can stop this by pressing Ctrl-C.

Remember that the search string must be enclosed in double quotes. To search for double quotes themselves, you must put an extra set around the search string. For instance, to find, "Take that!" you would need to specify a search string of ""Take that!""

SIDE EFFECTS

While FIND will scan binary as well as text files, the results can be somewhat disappointing and noisy (due to frequent beeping from the computer).

EXAMPLES

To find the string "\\lobe\" in a series of files ending with the .BAT extension, type:

```
FIND "\\lobe\" *.BAT
```

To find the string "WeaselWord Version 5.3.11" in any .DOC file on the C: drive, type:

```
FIND "WeaselWord Version 5.3.11" *.DOC /S
```

The following command searches all .DOC files in the current directory for the string "Weaselword" and reports only those occurrences in which the second *w* is capitalized:

```
FIND "Weaselword" *.DOC /U
```

OF INTEREST

FC

FORMAT

SYNTAX

FORMAT [/?|H] *n:* [/T:*tt* /N:*ss]* [/F:*bytes*] [/1] [/4] [/8] [/A] [/S] [/U] [/V:*vollabel*] [/X]

[/?|H]	Help screen for this command.
n:	The disk-drive designation for the disk you want to format.
[/T:*tt* /N:*ss*]	Track and sector values. By defining the number of tracks and sectors properly, you can format any standard DOS disk or nonstandard disk. Standard DOS values are given in the following table.
[/F:*bytes*]	Specifies the size of the disk. The acceptable sizes are as follows:
[/1]	Formats only one side of the disk. This is useful if you're creating disks for a very early DOS machine, such as the Sanyo MBC 550 or the original IBM PC.
[/4]	Formats a 360-KB diskette in a high-density 1.2-MB drive. While this will create a 360-KB disk that can be read in a 360-KB drive, subsequently writing information to such a disk with a 360-KB drive can, due to hardware incompatibility, corrupt the disk.
[/8]	Uses eight sectors instead of nine. Use this if you're creating a disk for use in a computer running MS- or PC-DOS version 1.
[/A]	The computer will beep when it has finished formatting the disk.
[/S]	Places the DR DOS operating system files on the disk, making it "bootable." If DR DOS can't find the operating system files, it will ask you to put a disk in the drive that has the system files so it can copy them.

[/U]   DR DOS will do an unconditional format, which means it will ignore the opportunity to do a "safe" format and actually format the drive.

[/V:*vollabel*] Allows you to specify a volume label from the command line. Otherwise, DR DOS will prompt you for a volume label.

[/X]   Used to format a hard disk. DR DOS won't format a hard disk without this parameter, which helps guard against accidental formatting of the hard drive.

CLASS
External: FORMAT.COM

FUNCTION
FORMAT prepares a blank, unformatted disk to receive data or reformats a disk that contains data (restoring it to its original blank state).

If you place a previously formatted disk in the drive, and the specification you give FORMAT matches that of the previously formatted disk, DR DOS will perform a *safe format*. A safe format doesn't actually format the drive, but merely clears the directory and FAT so the disk appears empty to DR DOS. If you accidentally safe-format a disk with valuable information, you can use UNFORMAT to recover the disk contents. DR DOS can do this because it writes the directory information to an unused portion of the disk. If there isn't enough room on the disk for the directory information, DR DOS will warn you that it must destroy some data.

Safe formatting works only if the format specification and the floppy-disk format match. For example, if you place a previously formatted 1.2-MB disk in a 5.25-inch, high-density drive, DR DOS will perform a safe format. If you put a 360-KB disk in the same drive and don't use the command-line parameters to specify that a 360-KB disk is to be created, DR DOS will actually format the tracks and sectors of the disk. All previously stored information will be destroyed.

The following are the valid settings for the various FORMAT command-line parameters pertaining to floppy disks:

Diskette Type	Size [/F]	# of Tracks [T]	# of Sectors [/N]	# of Sides [/S]
5.25-inch	160	40	8	1
5.25-inch	180	40	9	1
5.25-inch	320	40	8	2
5.25-inch	360	80	9	2
5.25-inch	1.2	80	15	2
3.5-inch	720	80	9	2
3.5-inch	1.44	80	18	2
3.5-inch	2.88	80	36	2

The simplest way to specify the format for a disk is to use the /F parameter. Nonstandard hardware configurations may reject this parameter, however, in which case you'll need to use the /T and /N parameters together.

When you use the /X parameter to format a hard drive, be aware that all existing data on the hard drive will be lost. DR DOS will ask if you want to format the hard disk before it begins formatting.

SIDE EFFECTS

You can't format RAM disks; nor can you format network drives or those with assignments set by ASSIGN, SUBST, or JOIN. Once you complete an unconditional or actual format, all data originally residing on that disk is gone forever.

EXAMPLES

To format a diskette in the A: drive using the default format for the drive, type:

```
FORMAT A:
```

To format a 720-KB disk in a 1.44-MB drive (designated as B:), type:

```
FORMAT B: /F:720
```

or

    FORMAT B: /T:80 /N:9

To format a 360-KB disk in a 1.2-MB drive designated as the A: drive, use:

    FORMAT A: /4

or

    FORMAT A: /F:360

or

    FORMAT A: /T:40 /N:9

OF INTEREST
    UNFORMAT

GRAFTABL

SYNTAX
GRAFTABL [/?|H] [*xxx*] [/STATUS]

[/?|H]   Help screen for this command.

[*xxx*]   A three-digit number specifying the character set.

[/STATUS]   Displays the number of the current character set.

CLASS
External: GRAFTABL.COM

FUNCTION
GRAFTABL allows you to specify a code page for various language character sets. This command was designed to improve the display of such character sets with a CGA graphics adapter and isn't needed with an EGA or VGA graphics adapter. Once the code page is loaded, it remains resident until you reboot. You might find it more convenient to put this command in your AUTOEXEC.BAT file.

Valid code pages are shown in the following table:

Code Page Number	Definition
437	American English (the default if no other code page is loaded)
850	Multilingual
860	Portuguese
863	Canadian French
865	Norwegian

SIDE EFFECTS
Because this command remains in memory, it decreases the amount of memory available to applications. You can, however, use HILOAD to load GRAFTABL into upper memory.

EXAMPLES

To load the French Canadian code table, type:

```
GRAFTABL 863
```

To see which code page is loaded, type:

```
GRAFTABL /STATUS
```

OF INTEREST

NLSFUNC, CHCP, GRAPHICS, HILOAD, MODE

GRAPHICS

SYNTAX
GRAPHICS [/?|H] [COLOR] [/R]

[/?|H]   Help screen for this command.

[COLOR]   Activates color printers that support the IBM graphics command set. It allows eight colors to be output.

[/R]   Does not invert the display when printing. Normally, black is printed as white and white as black. If you use this parameter, black will print black and white will print white.

CLASS
External: GRAPHICS.COM

FUNCTION
Lets you send screen dumps to a printer that supports the IBM graphics command set. When you use the PrtSc key to send the screen contents to your printer, you can usually only print text. However, GRAPHICS allows you to print screen graphics as well. Check the manual for your printer to see if it supports the IBM graphics command set.

Once loaded, GRAPHICS remains in memory until you reboot. If you use this command, you might want to include it in your AUTOEXEC.BAT file.

SIDE EFFECTS
Because GRAPHICS remains in memory, it reduces the amount of memory available for applications. However, you can use HILOAD to load GRAPHICS into upper memory.

EXAMPLE

This command loads graphics and sets the output so that black and white aren't inverted:

```
GRAPHICS /R
```

OF INTEREST
　　GRAFTABL, HILOAD

HILOAD

SYNTAX
HILOAD [/?|H] *file*

[/?|H]   Help screen for this command.

file   The file specification, including the name and extension.

CLASS
Internal

FUNCTION
HILOAD loads a specified program into high memory instead of base memory, freeing the latter for use by applications. HILOAD is ideal for loading TSR programs such as the CURSOR, GRAFTABL, GRAPHICS, and JOIN commands. You can also load such programs as Borland SideKick and network drivers. You don't need to use HILOAD to load such DR DOS commands as KEYB, NLSFUNC, and SHARE.

To use HILOAD, you must have high memory available. If your computer is equipped with an 80386 processor, you must have already loaded EMM386.SYS. If you have an 80286-equipped computer, you must first load HIDOS.SYS. You can use the MEM command to determine whether high memory is present and how much is available. If you have insufficient high memory to load a program, it's loaded into conventional memory.

HILOAD and HIINSTALL are quite similar, though HILOAD is used after COMMAND.COM has been loaded. Experiment with HILOAD to determine which programs can be loaded into high memory, then use the command to load those programs from the AUTOEXEC.BAT file.

For more information on high memory and memory managers, see Chapter 5.

DR DOS COMMAND REFERENCE

SIDE EFFECTS

The presence of high memory can cause some programs to fail. Typically, these are file-decompression programs used when certain applications are installed. To head off this problem, DR DOS automatically appends the following line to your AUTOEXEC.BAT file when you use MemoryMAX to set up memory:

```
MEMMAX -U>NUL
```

This line disables high memory. You can either delete it from the AUTO-EXEC.BAT file or reenable high memory with the MEMMAX+U command.

If you're using a third-party memory manager such as QEMM, 386-to-the-MAX, or Move'em, you can't use HILOAD. However, these memory managers usually have an equivalent command.

EXAMPLE

To load the CURSOR utility, type:

```
HILOAD C:\DRDOS\CURSOR.EXE
```

JOIN

SYNTAX
JOIN [/?|H] [*disk1:*] [*disk2:\path*] [/D]

[/?|H]　　　　Help screen for this command.

[*disk1:*]　　　The original drive, which will become part of the specified directory in [*disk2:\path*].

[*disk2:\path*]　The reference drive and directory path. This must be an empty directory.

[/D]　　　　　Delete the JOIN between a drive and directory.

CLASS
External: JOIN.EXE

FUNCTION
JOIN allows DR DOS to reference a disk drive as if it were a directory of another drive. This command is usually used to trick older programs that don't work with hard drives or RAM drives. For example, you could make the C: drive a directory of the A: drive.

JOIN is tricky to use. You can't JOIN a drive to a subdirectory—it must be a directory from the root of the reference drive. The directory you use for JOINing must be empty. It can have subdirectories, but they'll be unavailable after the JOIN. The joined drive will also be unavailable except through the directory specified in the JOIN command.

After JOIN is done, remember to cancel it.

SIDE EFFECTS
JOIN can confuse programs (such as Ventura Publisher) that "remember" where files were. If the JOIN isn't active the next time the program runs, the program won't know where to access files of a program that's at risk with the JOIN command.

When JOIN is in use, don't use the following DR DOS commands on the JOINed drive:

- ASSIGN
- BACKUP
- CHKDSK
- DISKCOPY
- DISKCOMP
- FDISK
- FORMAT
- LABEL
- RESTORE
- SUBST

EXAMPLES

To JOIN the C: disk to the \HARD directory of the A: drive, type:

```
JOIN C: A:\HARD
```

To cancel the above JOIN, type:

```
JOIN C: /D
```

To check the status of any current JOINs, type:

```
JOIN
```

OF INTEREST

ASSIGN, SUBST

KEYB

SYNTAX

KEYB [/?|H] *aa*[+|-] [,*cpage*] [/ML|MH|MU]

[/?|H] Help screen for this command.

aa The country code.

[+|-] Typically, KEYB will automatically determine what type of keyboard is installed. If you find that the keys don't always match the characters they produce, you may need to set KEYB to force the correct keyboard type. Use a plus if you have an enhanced keyboard (type 101, 102, or 104) and a minus if you have an older keyboard (type 83 or 84).

[,*cpage*] The code page. If this isn't entered, the default code page for the country setting is used.

[/ML|MH|MU] Loads the KEYB program into a specified area of memory. /ML specifies that the program is to be loaded into conventional memory (loading KEYB here means that less memory is available for application programs). /MH loads the KEYB program into high memory, while /MU loads it into upper memory. Chapter 5 further describes upper and higher memory.

CLASS
External : KEYB.COM

FUNCTION

If you have a non-U.S. standard keyboard, this utility is for you. By specifying the country and keyboard, you ensure that the characters you see on the screen match those you expect from your keyboard. If you use KEYB, load it through the AUTOEXEC.BAT file to make sure it's always available.

For some keyboard settings, certain characters can only be entered using *dead keys*. These are actually combinations of keys, where you must press one key followed by another to create the character (such as an accented letter). The following are the acceptable country codes and their matching code pages.

Country Code	Code Page	Definition
BE	437, 850	Belgium
CF	863, 850	Canadian French
DK	865, 850	Denmark
SU	437, 850	Finland
FR	437. 850	France
GR	437, 850	Germany
HU	852, 850	Hungary
IT	437, 850	Italy
LA	437, 850	Latin America
NL	437, 850	Netherlands
NO	865, 850	Norway
PO	860, 850	Portugal
RU	866, 850	Russia
SP	437, 850	Spain
SV	437, 850	Sweden
SF	437, 850	Swiss French
SG	437, 850	Swiss German
TF, TQ	857, 850	Turkey
UK	437, 850	United Kingdom
US (the default)	437, 850	United States

A shortcut for switching between a country setting and the U.S. setting is to press Control and Alt together, then press F1 to switch to the U.S. setting. Press Control and Alt together and then F2 to switch back to the country setting. If you're using the Russian keyboard setting, use the right-hand Control key to toggle between the U.S. and Russian keyboards.

For more information about code pages, see Chapter 13.

EXAMPLES

To activate support for the Russian keyboard and code page 866, enter:

```
KEYB RU,866
```

To activate support for the French keyboard and code page 850 and force support for enhanced keyboards, type:

```
KEYB FR+,850
```

To display the current keyboard and code-page settings, enter:

```
KEYB
```

OF INTEREST

CHCP, NLSFUNC, MODE, GRAFTABL

LABEL

SYNTAX
LABEL [/?|H] [*disk:*] [*label*]

    [/?|H]   Help screen for this command.

    [*disk:*]   The disk-drive designation (such as A:). If you don't specify a drive, LABEL will assume you mean the current drive.

    [*label*]   The label you wish to assign to the disk. If you don't specify a label, you'll be prompted for one. If you don't reply with a label at that point, LABEL will ask if you want to delete the current label.

CLASS
External: LABEL.COM

FUNCTION
LABEL allows you to assign a volume label to a disk, edit an existing label, or simply delete a disk label altogether. The volume label is a good way to identify your disks. It's displayed whenever you use the DIR command to check the directory of the disk or use the VOL command to check the label.

A volume label can have up to 11 characters, including spaces. You can't use tabs or the following characters: <>{}[]()/\?*.:;,=+.

SIDE EFFECTS
You can't use LABEL on network drives or drives affected by the JOIN or SUBST command.

EXAMPLES
To change the label for the D: drive to MARTHA, type:

```
LABEL D: MARTHA
```

To delete the label in the A: drive, type:

```
LABEL A:
```

LABEL will then prompt you for a label, to which you reply by pressing the Enter key. LABEL will ask if you wish to delete the label, and you reply with Y.

OF INTEREST
  VOL

LOCK

SYNTAX
LOCK [/?|H] [*password*]

[/?|H] Help screen for this command.

[*password*] The password. If system security is active, LOCK will use this password by default. Otherwise, you must enter a password of up to 12 characters.

CLASS
External: LOCK.EXE

FUNCTION
LOCK lets you temporarily lock your system. You would normally use it if you had sensitive information and wanted to leave the computer momentarily. LOCK isn't easily bypassed and will take Ctrl-C, Ctrl-Break, and even Ctrl-Alt-Del in stride. For more information about DR DOS's security capabilities, see Chapter 10.

LOCK can be run from the command line. If you omit the password, it will use your system password. LOCK can also be run as a task in TaskMAX and won't allow task switching away from the LOCK screen. If you installed system security and TaskMAX with the INSTALL program, LOCK will automatically start as a task whenever you use TaskMAX.

If you're feeling adventurous, edit the LOCK screens to change their look. These screens are in the LOCK.TXT and LOCK.ERR files in the DR DOS directory.

SIDE EFFECTS
Once you specify a password for LOCK, you must use that password. Your system security password and master password won't work.

EXAMPLES

To lock the system and use the system security password, enter:

    LOCK

To run LOCK as a TaskMAX task and use the password TURNKEY, type:

    TASKMAX /C C:\DRDOS\LOCK.EXE TURNKEY

You can then switch to the LOCK task to lock the system. For more information about TaskMAX, see Chapter 6.

OF INTEREST
PASSWORD

MEM

SYNTAX
MEM [/?|H] [/A] [/B] [/D] [/M] [/P] [/S]

[/?|H]	Help screen for this command.
[/A]	A combination of the /B, /D, /M, and /S parameters. This parameter causes MEM to list information about system memory and its contents.
[/B]	Displays the memory areas used by the operating system and its component parts. This includes the BIOS, the memory control block (MCB), and device drivers.
[/D]	Displays the names and locations of all device drivers (both built-in and loadable).
[/M]	Graphically displays the locations of RAM, ROM, and EMS memory.
[/P]	Pauses scrolling at each screen of information. You'll want to use this in conjunction with the /A parameter.
[/S]	Displays the disk buffer chain (adjacent buffers are grouped together in the display).

CLASS
External: MEM.EXE

FUNCTION
MEM lets you see how much memory is available and what it contains. You'll find it useful when you need to know whether sufficient upper memory exists to load device drivers and TSR programs and when configuring EMM386. (For more information about using MEM to help configure your system, see Chapter 5.) The /B and /M parameters are the most useful. Figure A-2 shows typical results of the /M parameter.

DR DOS 6 BY EXAMPLE

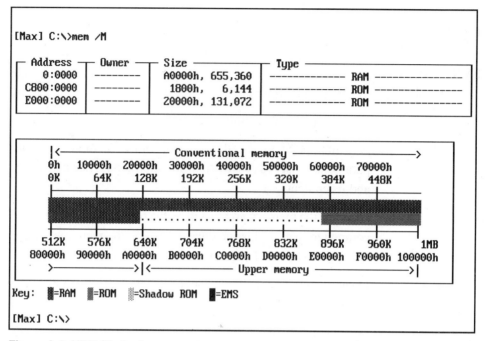

Figure A-2. MEM /M display.

If you issue the MEM command with no command-line parameters, you'll see a brief summary of the available conventional, high, extended, and expanded memory.

EXAMPLES

To see a simple summary of available memory, type:

```
MEM
```

To see everything pertaining to memory and its contents and pause the screen to study this information, type:

```
MEM /A /S
```

OF INTEREST
MEMMAX, HILOAD

MEMMAX

SYNTAX
MEMMAX [/?|H] [-|+L] [-|+U] [-|+V] [/L] [/U] [/V]

[/?|H] Help screen for this command.

[-|+L] The -L parameter disables access to lower memory, while +L reenables access. Use -L if you see the message "!Packed file is corrupt" when installing certain applications. After installation, use +L to reenable access to lower memory.

[-|+U] The -U parameter disables access to upper memory, while +U enables access to upper memory. The presence of upper memory can confuse certain applications.

[-|+V] The -V parameter disables video memory that the /VIDEO parameter used by EMM386 and HIDOS makes available. The +V parameter reenables access to this memory.

[/L] Shows the status of lower memory.

[/U] Shows the status of upper memory.

[/V] Shows the status of video memory made available by the /VIDEO parameter of EMM386 and HIDOS.

CLASS
External: MEMMAX.EXE

FUNCTION
MEMMAX can be used to disable or reenable access to lower memory (the first 64 KB of conventional memory), upper memory, or video memory or to check the status of such memory. You may need to disable these memory regions because the DR DOS memory managers can make more memory available than some programs will tolerate. For example, during the installation of certain programs, an error

message may appear as the program files are being decompressed. In fact, the DR DOS INSTALL program places the following in the AUTOEXEC.BAT file to prevent programs from running afoul of available upper memory:

```
MEMMAX -U >NUL
```

The / parameters let you examine the current status of memory regions. If you issue the MEMMAX command with no parameters, it reports on the status of upper, lower, and available video memory.

SIDE EFFECTS

You can't use the HILOAD program to load device drivers and TSR programs into upper memory until you either reenable upper memory with MEMMAX or remove the MEMMAX -U >NUL line from the AUTOEXEC.BAT file.

EXAMPLES

Use the following command to get a report on the status of lower memory:

```
MEMMAX /L
```

Use the following to disable access to lower memory:

```
MEMMAX -L
```

The following command enables access to upper memory:

```
MEMMAX +U
```

OF INTEREST
MEM, HILOAD

MKDIR or MD

SYNTAX
MKDIR|MD [/?|H] [*disk:*]*directory*

[/?|H]   Help screen for this command.

[*disk:*]   The disk-drive designator (such as A: or C:).

directory The directory name, including its complete path.

CLASS
Internal

FUNCTION
MKDIR and its short form, MD, are used to create directories that branch directly from the root directory of a disk or subdirectories that branch from any other valid directory.

Follow the rules for creating directories. Directories have the same naming restrictions as files: A directory name can comprise up to eight characters and, optionally, a three-letter extension preceded by a period. A directory path and name cannot exceed 63 characters. The directory can't have the same name as another directory branching from the same source, and it can't have the same name as a file in the source directory. If you have a directory called \TOM\FOOLERY, for example, you can't use that name again; if the \TOM directory contains a file called FOOLERY, you can't create a subdirectory of \TOM called \TOM\FOOLERY. You don't need to be logged on to a drive to create directories there.

If something goes wrong when you try to create a directory, MKDIR will display the following error message:

```
Unable to create directory
```

The problem can be caused by any of the following:

- The disk is full.
- A directory with that name already exists.
- A file with the same name as the directory already exists in the path.
- You specified a path for the directory that doesn't exist.

When you create a directory or subdirectory, DR DOS places in it two entries: ".." and ".". These entries are used by DR DOS and can't be deleted.

SIDE EFFECTS

It's not a particularly good idea to create directories and subdirectories on drives that are currently remapped by JOIN, SUBST, or ASSIGN. While it's possible to do, the new directories won't be where you thought they were when the JOIN, SUBST, or ASSIGN is cancelled.

EXAMPLES

This command creates a directory called STUFF that branches from the current directory:

```
MD \STUFF
```

This command creates the JUNQUE subdirectory, which branches from the newly created STUFF directory:

```
MD \STUFF\JUNQUE
```

This command creates a directory on the D: drive called MORESTUF.DOC:

```
MD D:\MORESTUF.DOC
```

OF INTEREST

CHDIR, DIR, XDIR, RENDIR

MODE

SYNTAX
MODE is the only command that performs multiple functions. Its syntax is listed by function.

CLASS
External: MODE.COM

Changing the display type:

SYNTAX
MODE [/?|H] *type* [*,lines*]

[/?|H]	Help screen for this command.
type	The display type.
[*,lines*]	The number of lines of text that can be displayed. Acceptable values are 25, 43, and 50.

You can use MODE to change the size and number of characters that can be displayed on your screen in text mode. If you have a monochrome and color monitor, you can use MODE to switch between them. The following table lists the valid settings for the *type* parameter. Note that not all parameters are supported by all display adapters. If you issue a MODE command that your adapter doesn't support, MODE will respond with this message:

```
Display adapter does not support requested mode
```

MODE

Parameter	Definition
CO40	Enables the color display adapter and sets the display to 40 characters per line.
40	Changes the currently enabled display to 40 characters per line.
BW40	Enables the color display adapter and sets the display mode to black and white with 40 characters per line.
CO80	Enables the color display adapter and sets the display to 80 characters per line.
80	Changes the currently enabled display to 80 characters per line.
BW80	Enables the color graphics adapter and sets the display mode to black and white with 80 characters per line.
MONO	Enables the monochrome display adapter (such as an original IBM MDA or Hercules-compatible monochrome graphics adapter). Such adapters have a fixed line width of 80 characters.

EXAMPLES

For a color adapter with a display of 80 characters per line and 43 lines per screen (this must be an EGA adapter or better), use this command:

```
MODE CO80,43
```

To change the currently enabled color display adapter from 80 characters per line to 40 characters per line:

```
MODE 40
```

To enable the MDA:

```
MODE MONO
```

Adjusting a color graphics adapter's alignment:

SYNTAX

MODE [*type*] ,*s* [,T]

[*type*]	The display adapter type (listed in the table in the previous section).
,*s*	The shift direction. Use ",R" to shift to the right and ",L" to shift to the left.
[,T]	Use this parameter to display the test line. MODE will ask if you can see the leftmost 0 or rightmost 9. If you answer no (N), it will continue to shift the display until you answer yes (Y).

MODE incorporates the capability to shift the display to the right or left to correct for misalignment, then display a row of numbers along the top of a CGA screen as a test pattern.

EXAMPLES

To shift the CGA display to the right, use:

```
MODE ,R
```

To change the CGA display to 40 columns, shift the display to left, and display the test line, use:

```
MODE CO40 ,L,T
```

Changing the number of rows and columns:

SYNTAX

MODE CON LINES=*ll* COLS=*cc*

CON   The console device.

LINES=*ll*   The number of lines displayed on the screen. Acceptable values are 25, 43, and 50.

COLS=*cc*   The number of columns displayed on the screen. Acceptable values are 40 and 80.

MODE offers an alternative method of changing the number of lines per screen (rows) and the number of characters per line (columns). This method uses MODE's ability to control the various input and output devices in the computer and changes the settings for the console (the display and keyboard). This applies only to the currently enabled graphics adapter and does not provide a way to switch between dual adapters.

EXAMPLES

To switch a VGA or better display adapter to 50 lines by 80 columns, use:

```
MODE CON LINES=50 COLS=80
```

To switch a color graphics adapter to 25 lines by 40 columns, use:

```
MODE CON LINES=25 COLS=40
```

Changing the typematic (repeat) rate:

SYNTAX

MODE CON RATE=*s* DELAY=*t*

CON   The console device.

RATE=*s*   The speed at which the key repeats. Acceptable values are 1 through 32, with 32 being the fastest.

DELAY=*t*   The time it takes for a key to respond to your keypress. Acceptable values are 1 through 4, with 4 being the longest delay.

The typematic rate defines how fast characters are repeated when you hold a key down and how much time elapses before the repeat action begins. You'll need to experiment to find the ideal settings.

EXAMPLE

The following command sets the typematic rate to the fastest possible speed and sets the longest delay before key repeating begins:

```
MODE CON RATE=32 DELAY=4
```

Configuring a printer:

SYNTAX

MODE LPT*n* [*c*] [,*lpi*] [,P]

LPT*n*	The printer port. This can be LPT1, LPT2, or LPT3.
[*c*]	The number of columns on the page, either 80 or 132. If you have a narrow-carriage printer, 80 is usually correct. If you have a wide-carriage printer, 132 is usually correct. If your printer accepts the IBM graphics printer command set, MODE will change the pitch of the printer automatically. This means that if you have a narrow-carriage printer and select 132, MODE will append the command to switch your printer to condensed print mode. The default setting is 80.
[,*lpi*]	The number of lines per inch. This can be set to either 6 or 8, with 8 being the default. If your printer understands the IBM graphics command set, MODE can switch your printer on demand.
[,P]	Loads MODE into memory. MODE can then see that DR DOS will continue attempting to send information to the designated port if the device is busy. If you want DR DOS to stop trying to send information under such circumstances, you can interrupt the printing operation by pressing Ctrl-Break. Reissuing the command without ",P" removes the continual-retry feature.

DR DOS 6 BY EXAMPLE

You can use MODE to configure your parallel printer port. This only affects information printed using DR DOS commands. Printer drivers within applications will control the printer directly and ignore these settings.

EXAMPLE

The following command configures DR DOS for a wide-carriage printer attached to the LPT2 parallel port:

```
MODE LPT2 132, 6, P
```

This sets the printer to six lines per inch and enables continuous retries if the printer is busy.

Configuring a serial port:

SYNTAX

MODE COM*n* *baud*, [*parity*] ,[*datalength*] ,[*stopbits*] [,P]

COM*n*	The serial port (COM1, COM2, or COM3)
baud	The transmission speed. Acceptable speeds are 110, 150, 300, 600, 1,200, 2,400, 4,800, 9,600, and, on some computers, 19,200 bps. You can abbreviate this value to the first two digits (9,600 becomes 96).
,[*parity*]	E for even parity (the default), O for odd parity, or N for no parity. If you're sending binary data, use N. (Parity is used for error detection.)
,[*datalength*]	The number of bits in the data. This can be either 7 (the default) or 8. Use 8 if you're sending binary data.
,[*stopbits*]	This can be 1 (the default) or 2. Stop bits are "extra bits" used to separate characters.

DR DOS COMMAND REFERENCE

[,P]   Loads MODE into memory so that DR DOS will continually retry transmission if a target device is busy. If you want DR DOS to stop trying to send information under such circumstances, interrupt the printing operation by pressing Ctrl-Break. Reissuing the command without ",P" removes the continual-retry feature.

MODE can also be used to set up a serial port. These settings are usually overridden by communications programs such as FileLink or CrossTalk.

EXAMPLES

To set COM1 to 2,400 baud, no parity, eight-bit data, and one stop bit, use:

```
MODE COM1 2400, N, 8, 1
```

To set COM3 to 9,600 baud, odd parity, seven-bit data, two stop bits, and continual retry on the port, use:

```
MODE COM3 9600, O, 7, 2, P
```

Redirecting the parallel port to the serial port:

SYNTAX

MODE LPT*n*=COM*n*

LPT*n*   Any of the three parallel ports: LPT1, LPT2, or LPT3.

COM*n*   Any of the three serial communications ports: COM1, COM2, or COM3.

Some older programs will only print to a parallel port. MODE gets around this problem by redirecting to a serial port the output that's normally sent to a parallel port. MODE loads itself into memory, slightly reducing the memory available for applications programs. To cancel redirection, run MODE with only the parallel port parameter.

Use MODE to set the parameters for the serial port.

EXAMPLES

To redirect the output for LPT1 to COM2, use:

```
MODE LPT1=COM2
```

To cancel redirection, use:

```
MODE LPT1
```

Preparing code pages:

SYNTAX

MODE *dev* CODEPAGE PREPARE = ((*list*) *charfile*)

dev   The DR DOS device—CON, LPT*n*, or PRN.

CODEPAGE   Can be abbreviated CP.

PREPARE =   Can be abbreviated PREP =.

((*list*) *charfile*) A list of code pages MODE is to prepare. If you're preparing more than one code page, separate their numbers with commas. Pay close attention to the parentheses. The entire statement must be enclosed, as does the list of code-page numbers. If you want to issue a second code page PREPARE command, you can leave any of the code pages in the original list unchanged simply by entering double commas in their place.

The following table lists the code pages MODE supports.

437	Belgium, Finland, France, Germany, Italy, Latin America, Spain, Sweden, Swiss French, Swiss German, United Kingdom, United States
850	ISO Multinational
852	Hungary
857	Turkey

860   Portugal

862   Israel

863   Canadian French

865   Denmark, Norway

866   Russia

charfile specifies the font file to be used. The EGA.CPI file provides screen fonts for EGA and VGA display adapters. The following are the printer support font files:

1050.CPI   Epson FX 850 or FX 1050

4201.CPI   IBM Proprinter or XL

4208.CPI   IBM Proprinter X24 or XL24

5202.CPI   IBM Quietwriter III printer

Code pages allow DR DOS to support international language character sets. You must prepare code pages before you can select or use them. This variation of the MODE command does just that. If you use code pages, you might want to put the MODE CP PREP statement in your AUTOEXEC.BAT file. For more information on code pages, see Chapter 13.

SIDE EFFECTS

If you're preparing code pages for a printer that isn't on-line, this command won't work. Worse, the error message may not appear immediately. Also, if you turn your printer off after preparing the code page, the code-page information will be lost. (See "Refreshing code pages" a little later in the MODE section.)

Code pages aren't supported for all video display adapters; you must have an EGA or VGA adapter.

EXAMPLES

The following command prepares three code pages—850, 863, and 437—for the console screen to use, then loads the EGA/VGA font files:

```
MODE CON CP PREP=((850,863,437)C:\DRDOS\EGA.CPI)
```

The following changes the set of prepared code pages (note that 850, the first code page on the list, is left intact because a comma was entered in its place):

```
MODE CON CP PREP ((,865,866)C:\DRDOS\EGA.CPI)
```

To prepare the list of code pages for an Epson FX 850 printer connected to LPT1, use:

```
MODE LPT1 CP PREP ((850,865,866)C:\DRDOS\1050.CPI
```

Selecting code pages:

SYNTAX

MODE *dev* CODEPAGE SELECT = *nnn*

dev	The DR DOS device, which can be LPT1, LPT2, LPT3, PRN, or CON.
CODEPAGE	Can be abbreviated CP.
SELECT =	Can be abbreviated SEL =.
nnn	The three-digit code-page number. See the preceding section, "Preparing code pages," for a table of acceptable code-page values.

After preparing code pages, you must select the active code page. Only one code page can be active on any given device.

SIDE EFFECTS

Make sure your printer is on-line if you're selecting a code page for it. Otherwise, nothing will be selected.

EXAMPLES

The following command selects code page 850 for the console (screen):

```
MODE CON CP SEL = 850
```

This command selects the same code page for the printer attached to parallel port LPT1 (you could also use PRN to specify this device):

```
MODE LPT1 CP SEL = 850
```

Refreshing code pages:

SYNTAX

MODE *dev* CODEPAGE REFRESH

dev   The DR DOS device, which can be LPT1, LPT2, LPT3, PRN, or CON.

CODEPAGE   Can be abbreviated CP.

REFRESH   Can be abbreviated REF.

If you turn off your printer after preparing and selecting a code page, you'll need to reload the code-page fonts into the printer. This version of the command reloads the selected fonts into the printer specified by the DR DOS device.

SIDE EFFECTS

Make sure your printer is on-line if you're selecting a code page for it. Otherwise, nothing will be selected.

EXAMPLE

To reload the code-page fonts into the printer on LPT2, type:

```
MODE LPT2 CP REF
```

Checking the status of code pages:

SYNTAX
    MODE *dev* CODEPAGE [/STATUS]

    dev   The DR DOS device, which can be LPT1, LPT2, LPT3, PRN, or CON.

    CODEPAGE   Can be abbreviated CP.

    [/STATUS]   The optional parameter for specifying a status request. It can be abbreviated /STA.

With all the possible code pages, you may need this command just to keep track of what's prepared and what's active for each device. This version of the command also reports on those code pages that are built into the computer (these are called *hardware code pages*).

EXAMPLE
    This command reports all available prepared code pages (including the hardware code page) for the CON device as well as the active code page:

```
MODE CON CP
```

OF INTEREST
    CHCP, NLSFUNC, KEYB, GRAFTABL

MORE

SYNTAX

MORE [/?|H]

[/?|H]   Help screen for this command.

CLASS

Internal

FUNCTION

A number of DR DOS commands, such as TYPE, DIR, and TREE, can produce more information than the screen can hold. This means the information you want to view at a readable pace will instead scroll right past you. MORE is a filter that takes the screen output of other commands and pauses at each screenful of information. It's used with the "|" piping symbol, which specifies that output is to be piped into MORE. (See Chapter 13 for a discussion of redirection and pipes.)

You can also use MORE by itself to redirect a file into it. This variation lets you use MORE in the same manner as TYPE except that it automatically pauses at each screen of information.

As MORE fills the screen, you'll see the following prompt:

```
Strike a key when ready . . .
```

To see the next screenful of information, press any key except Alt, Shift, or Control.

EXAMPLES

The following pipes the output of TREE into MORE:

```
TREE | MORE
```

To redirect the file README.DOC through MORE, use:

```
MORE < README.DOC
```

OF INTEREST
TYPE, DIR, TREE

MOVE

SYNTAX

MOVE [/?|H] [@]*files destpath* [/A] [/D:*date*] [/H] [/M] [/P] [/R] [/S] [/T] [/V] [/W]

[/?|H]	Help screen for this command.
[@] *files*	The files to be moved, specified by file name and type (wildcards are permitted). If the files aren't in the current directory, the drive designation and directory path must be included. *files* preceded by "@" specifies a single file that contains a list of files to be moved.
destpath	The complete path for the destination of the move. If the directory isn't on the current drive, the disk designation must be included.
[/A]	Moves files with the archive attribute bit set. MOVE won't change the attribute setting.
[/D:*date*]	Moves files that have been modified on or after the specified date. The date format is determined by the COUNTRY.SYS setting.
[/H]	Includes files with the hidden or system attribute bits set in the MOVE operation. If you don't use this parameter, such files will be ignored. MOVE doesn't alter the attribute bit setting. Note that this parameter is the same as that used for help; however, the help parameter always precedes any file names.
[/M]	Moves files with the archive attribute bit set and resets the bit for each moved file.
[/P]	Tells MOVE to prompt you about each file before actually moving it.
[/R]	Tells MOVE to overwrite read-only files at the destination.

[/S]	Includes all files in subdirectories in the MOVE. The subdirectory structure is copied during the MOVE; however, the original subdirectories remain.
[/T]	Includes all files in subdirectories and deletes the original subdirectory structure. The subdirectory structure is re-created at the destination. You can only use the /P, /V, and /W parameters in conjunction with the /T parameter.
[/V]	Verifies the files as they're moved before deleting the originals. If a mismatch occurs, MOVE aborts its operation.
[/W]	Waits for you to insert a diskette before beginning the MOVE.

CLASS

External: MOVE.EXE

FUNCTION

MOVE is similar to COPY except that it deletes the original files after making copies at the specified destination. It is also considerably faster than COPY if your move is to a different directory on the same drive.

SIDE EFFECTS

MOVE will overwrite matching files at the destination.

EXAMPLES

To move all files in the current directory to drive A:, use the following command:

```
MOVE *.* A:
```

The following moves all files in the LETTERS directory to the G:\ARCHIVE directory, including all files in subdirectories of LETTERS (where it reproduces the directory structure, then removes all empty subdirectories of LETTERS):

```
MOVE /LETTERS G:\ARCHIVE /T
```

To move all files created since January 1, 1991, in the MINUTES directory to the D:\ARCHIVE directory and verify each of the files for accurate duplication, use this command:

```
MOVE /MINUTES D:\ARCHIVE /D:01-01-91 /V
```

OF INTEREST
   COPY, XCOPY, REPLACE

NLSFUNC

SYNTAX

NLSFUNC [/?|H] *files* [/ML|MH|MU]

[/?|H]　　　　　Help screen for this command.

files　　　　　The COUNTRY.SYS file.

[/ML|MH|MU]　　Loads NLSFUNC into a specified memory area. /ML is base memory, /MH is higher memory, and /MU is upper memory.

CLASS
External: NLSFUNC.EXE

FUNCTION

NLSFUNC supports the extended country information by loading the keyboard translation table from the designated country information file (COUNTRY.SYS, specified by the COUNTRY= statement in your CONFIG.SYS file). After this is loaded, switch code pages using the CHCP command. You must run NLSFUNC before you can use CHCP.

You can only execute this file once before rebooting. For convenience, place it in your AUTOEXEC.BAT file.

For more information about code pages, see Chapter 13.

EXAMPLE

This command loads the extended country information:

```
NLSFUNC C:\DRDOS\COUNTRY.SYS
```

OF INTEREST
COUNTRY, CHCP, MODE, KEYB

DR DOS COMMAND REFERENCE

PASSWORD

SYNTAX
PASSWORD [/?|H] [[@]*spec*] [/D:*password*|/G:*password*|/P:*password*|/R:*password*|/W:*password*] [/N] [/NG] [/NP] [/S]

    [/?|H]   Help screen for this command.

    [[@]*spec*]   The password must be assigned to either a directory path or a file name (including its complete path, file name, and file extension), as specified by *spec*. Wildcards are allowed for file specifications. If the specification is preceded by "@" it refers to a file that contains a list of files to be protected.

[/D:*password*|/G:*password*|/P:*password*|/R:*password*|/W:*password*]

    The /D:*password* parameter pertains to files and means that the given password is required to delete the specified files. The password can have up to eight characters.

    The /G:*password* parameter issues a global password. You don't need a file or directory specification when you use this parameter. If many files and directories share the same password, this parameter lets you unlock all of them simultaneously. The password can be up to eight characters long.

    The /P:*password* parameter pertains to directories and prevents access to a directory or its files without the password. All subdirectories of the specified directory (and their contents) are also protected. Without the password, you cannot read, write, or delete files within the protected directory. The password can have up to eight characters.

    The /R:*password* parameter protects the specified files from being read, copied, modified, deleted, or renamed and from having their attributes changed without the password. The password can have up to eight characters.

The /W:*password* parameter protects the specified files from being deleted, renamed, or copied without the password. The password can have up to eight characters.

[/N] Removes password protection from the specified files. Before protection is removed, you'll be prompted to enter the password.

[/NG] Removes the global password previously set with the /G:*password* parameter, thereby locking all previously unlocked files and directories.

[/NP] Removes password protection from the specified directory. You'll be prompted to supply the password before protection is removed.

[/S] Extends protection to all matching files within subdirectories of the specified directory.

CLASS

External: PASSWORD.EXE

FUNCTION

PASSWORD is the second level of defense against the unauthorized use of files or directories (the first level is the system password). Because PASSWORD assigns or removes password protection from files or directories, you can use separate passwords to protect different types of information.

The global password parameter (/G) is useful for unlocking groups of files and directories with a single command. If you later issue the PASSWORD command with the /NG parameter, all such files will be relocked.

For more information on security, see Chapter 10.

SIDE EFFECTS

Don't forget your password! If you do, you'll need a sector editor such as the Mace MUSE program to recover the data.

You can't set a password for a file that resides on a network drive.

EXAMPLES

The following command sets the password WHODERE for the file C:\ACCOUNTS\PAYROLL.WKS and protects against unauthorized reading, writing, copying, or other modification of the file:

```
PASSWORD C:\ACCOUNTS\PAYROLL.WKS /R:WHODERE
```

This command assigns the password MOREDOCS to all files ending with a *.DOC extension in the D:\MANUALS directory and protects those files from deletion or modification:

```
PASSWORD D:\MANUALS\*.DOC /W:MOREDOCS
```

The command to assign the password DOLLARS to the subdirectory C:\INVEST and its subdirectories (the password is required to access, copy, or modify files in these directories) is:

```
PASSWORD C:\INVEST /P:DOLLARS
```

To set the global password IMIN to unlock all files protected by that password, use:

```
PASSWORD /G:IMIN
```

To relock all files previously unlocked with the global password, use:

```
PASSWORD /NG
```

OF INTEREST
ATTRIB, LOCK

PATH

SYNTAX
PATH [/?|H] [*drive*:][/*path*][;] . . .

[/?|H]   Help screen for this command.

[*drive*:]   The drive specification letter.

[/*path*]   The directory to be searched for executable files.

[;] . . .   Additional drive/directory specifications. These must be separated by a semicolon.

CLASS
Internal

FUNCTION
PATH defines a series of directories that DR DOS will search for executable files (those with .BAT, .COM, and .EXE extensions). Setting a PATH lets you access programs in the specified directories from any drive or directory. When you attempt to run a program, DR DOS searches the current directory for that program, then begins searching through all the directories listed in the PATH statement. If DR DOS can't find the requested program along the PATH, it will display the following error message:

```
Command or file name not recognized
```

The PATH statement is usually in the AUTOEXEC.BAT file, and many application programs modify it during installation. Because the information from the PATH statement is held in the DR DOS environment, you can check the current path by entering this environment command:

```
SET
```

SIDE EFFECTS

PATH defines a search path only for executable programs. You'll need APPEND to find other types of files.

EXAMPLES

To set a search path through various directories, type:

    PATH C:\WINDOWS;C:\WORD;D:\ARTLINE;C:\DRDOS

To clear the current search path, type:

    PATH;

OF INTEREST

APPEND

PRINT

SYNTAX

PRINT [/?|H] [*files*] [/D:*port*] [/B:*buffersize*] [/M:*maxtick*] [/S:*timeslice*] [/U:*busytick*] [/Q:*qsize*] [/C] [/T] [/P]

[/?|H]   Help screen for this command.

[*files*]   A file or files you want to put in the PRINT queue.

[/D:*port*]   The DR DOS device connected to your printer: PRN (the default), LPT1, LPT2, LPT3, COM1, COM2, or COM3.

[/B:*buffersize*]   Sets the size of the PRINT buffer in bytes. The default is 512. You can set this value only the first time you issue a PRINT command after boot-up. A larger print buffer usually improves PRINT performance; however, it also uses additional memory.

[/M:*maxtick*]   DR DOS divides a second into time slices (usually about 20, though this varies from computer to computer). PRINT and any other DR DOS commands you run must share the computer, and each is allocated a certain number of time slices. This parameter assigns the maximum number of time slices PRINT can use before returning control to DR DOS (the range is 1 to 255). Use it the first time you issue a PRINT command after boot-up. The /M parameter is used with the /U and /S parameters.

When the number of time slices is increased, PRINT runs faster; however, other tasks run more slowly.

[/S:*timeslice*]   Describes how often, in time slices, PRINT receives control of the computer. The default is 8, and the range is 1 to 255. This parameter can only be used the first time you issue a PRINT command after boot-up. Use this parameter with /M and /U.

[/U:*busytick*]   Specifies the number of time slices PRINT should wait if the printer is busy before returning control of the computer to DR

DOS. The default is 1, and the range is 1 to 255. This parameter can only be used the first time you issue a PRINT command after boot-up. Use it with the /S and /M parameters.

[/Q:*qsize*]   Sets the size of the print queue (or, more specifically, the number of files that can be in the queue). The default is 10 files, and the range is 4 to 32. This parameter can only be used the first time you issue a PRINT command after boot-up.

[/C]   Clears the specified file or files from the print queue. The file names can be placed before or after this parameter (actually, only one file name can precede the parameter; multiple file names can be placed after the parameter).

[/T]   Terminates all files in the queue.

[/P]   Adds the specified file or files to the print queue. As with the /C parameter, file names can be placed before or after this parameter.

CLASS

External: PRINT.COM

FUNCTION

The PRINT command provides a print queue for stacking multiple text files. These files print in the background while you run other programs. When you run PRINT for the first time after boot-up, part of it is loaded into memory. That's why you can only use some of the above parameters when PRINT is first run.

The default device is the PRN port (LPT1). If you don't specify a device, PRINT will ask you to verify that you want data sent to the PRN port.

SIDE EFFECTS

PRINT will stop running if you switch out of its task in TaskMAX or Microsoft Windows. It will resume operation when you reactivate its task.

EXAMPLES

To print all the .BAT files in the current directory to the PRN device, type:

```
PRINT *.BAT
```

The following command loads the memory-resident portion of PRINT with the device LPT2: port, a queue size of 20 files, a buffer size of 2,048 bytes, a maximum of 128 time slices for PRINT, a maximum of 20 busy time slices, and a time-slice setting of 4:

```
PRINT /D:LPT2 /Q:20 /B:2048 /M:128 /U:20 /S:4
```

When you enter the command with no arguments, it lists the current contents of the print queue:

```
PRINT
```

To clear the files ONE.TXT and TWO.TXT from the print queue, use:

```
PRINT /C ONE.TXT TWO.TXT
```

To clear the print queue, use:

```
PRINT /T
```

PROMPT

SYNTAX
PROMPT [/?|H] [*promptcodes*]

[/?|H] Help screen for this command.

[*promptcodes*] The series of codes (described in the table below), along with any text you would like to use, that make up your custom prompt.

CLASS
Internal

FUNCTION
PROMPT lets you modify the command-line prompt to include ASCII characters as well as any special characters listed in the table below. In fact, some ASCII characters must be entered as special characters. Such special characters must be preceded by a dollar sign ($). You can also use the prompt to execute commands and even change the screen colors if the ANSI.SYS drive is loaded.

The special PROMPT characters are:

Character	Definition
$	Must precede the following characters. If you want to display a dollar sign in your prompt, you'll need to use $$.
b	The "|" character.
d	The current date.
e	The escape character. This is useful for passing escape commands to the ANSI.SYS driver. These commands control screen-display attributes (blinking, reverse video, color, and so on). They require that ANSI.SYS be in your CONFIG.SYS file at start-up.
g	The ">" character.

h	A backspace. This is useful for erasing part of the results of another character (such as "t," which gives the current time to the nearest hundredth of a second).
l	The "<" character.
n	The currently logged drive letter.
p	The current directory, including its path.
q	The "=" character.
t	The current time.
v	The DR DOS version number and copyright statement.
x	Executes a program defined as PEXEC= in the DR DOS environment. To set this value, use SET PEXEC=*whatever*. This program runs each time you return to the command processor from an application program.
_	The underscore character; issues a carriage return and line feed, forcing the rest of the prompt to a new line.

DR DOS will install the following statement in your AUTOEXEC.BAT file to create the familiar C> prompt:

```
PROMPT [DR DOS] $P$G
```

EXAMPLES

To insert the time one line above the prompt (deleting all but the hours and minutes) and display the drive and directory on the prompt line, type:

```
PROMPT The current time is $t$h$h$h$h$h$h$_$p$g
```

The result would be something like this:

```
The current time is 2:43
C:\>
```

To run the program specified by PEXEC in the DR DOS environment (after returning to the command-line processor from an application) and display the current drive and directory, type:

```
PROMPT $X$P$G
```

RECOVER

SYNTAX
RECOVER [/?|H] *drive:filespec*

[/?|H]   Help screen for this command.

drive:filespec   The drive letter and file specification, including path, file name, and file extension.

CLASS
External : RECOVER.EXE

FUNCTION
RECOVER is a last resort if you discover that a text file has been corrupted. If you get a bad-sector error when attempting to read a file, the file has been corrupted. RECOVER rebuilds the file using only those sectors that are readable; whatever was in the bad sectors will be lost. It also marks any bad blocks it discovers in the FAT to prevent data from being written to those blocks.

You can also use RECOVER to rebuild corrupted data. However, you should only do this if you discover that the root directory of the disk is corrupted. When attempting to recover an entire disk, RECOVER destroys the old root directory and replaces it with a new one. All files rebuilt from lost cluster chains are placed in the root directory and named FILE*nnnn*.CHK (*nnnn* starts at 0000 and is increased by one for each additional recovered file). RECOVER could retrieve more of these files than the root directory can hold; if this happens, you'll need to copy the files to another drive, delete them from the disk undergoing surgery, and run RECOVER again. You'll also need a program such as EDITOR to find out the contents of these .CHK files.

SIDE EFFECTS
Use RECOVER to retrieve text information rather than binary program files. If you attempt to execute a binary file retrieved by RECOVER, it may fail or crash your

system because large sections of the program may be missing. Remember that RECOVER is a last resort; you probably won't need to use it if you back up your data frequently.

EXAMPLES

To retrieve all .DOC files in the D:\LETTERS directory, use the following command:

```
RECOVER D:\LETTERS\*.DOC
```

To retrieve all files on the A: drive, use:

```
RECOVER A:
```

OF INTEREST
BACKUP, RESTORE

RENAME or REN

SYNTAX

REN [/?|H] *oldname.oldext newname.newext*

[/?|H] Help screen for this command.

oldname.oldext The original file name and extension, including the complete path. The name can include wildcards.

newname.newext The new file name and extension, including the complete path. The name can include wildcards.

CLASS
Internal

FUNCTION
RENAME lets you change the name, extension, or both for a file or group of files. It can also be used to move a file from one directory to another. When you move a file this way, no copy remains in the original directory.

SIDE EFFECTS
You can't have two files with the same name in the same directory; therefore, you can't use RENAME to give a file an existing name.

EXAMPLES
To change the name AUTOEXEC.BAT to AUTOEXEC.WIN, use this command:

```
REN AUTOEXEC.BAT AUTOEXEC.WIN
```

To change all the files beginning with DRAFT and ending with .DOC to begin with ARC and end with .TXT, use:

```
REN DRAFT*.DOC ARC*.END
```

To move the file MYSTUFF.ARC to the G:\ATTIC directory, use:

```
REN MYSTUFF.ARC G:\ATTIC
```

OF INTEREST
COPY, MOVE, RENDIR

RENDIR

SYNTAX
RENDIR [/?|H] *originaldir newdir*

[/?|H]   Help screen for this command.

originaldir   The original directory name, including the complete path.

newdir   The new directory name, including the complete path.

FUNCTION
The RENDIR command lets you change the name of a directory much as RENAME lets you change a file name. If the directory doesn't branch from the current directory, enter the complete path for the directory in the original and new names.

SIDE EFFECTS
Remember that you can't have two directories with the same paths and the same names.

EXAMPLE
The following command renames the E:\ACCOUNTS\NEW directory to E:\ACCOUNTS\OLD:

```
RENDIR E:\ACCOUNTS\NEW E:\ACCOUNTS\OLD
```

OF INTEREST
RENAME, MKDIR

REPLACE

SYNTAX

REPLACE [/?|H] [@]*files path* [/A] [/H] [/M] [/N] [/P] [/R] [/S] [/U] [/W]

[/?|H]	Help screen for this command.
[@]*files*	The files you want to copy with REPLACE. This includes the drive designation, path, file name, and file extension. Wildcards may be used.
path	The destination, including the drive designation and complete path.
[/A]	Copies only those files that don't reside in the destination.
[/H]	Also copies files with the hidden or system attribute bit set.
[/M]	Copies only those files from the source that don't exist in the destination.
[/N]	Performs a dry run without copying any files, then reports on what it would copy during actual operation.
[/P]	Pauses and prompts you to verify that you want to copy each file.
[/R]	Allows REPLACE to overwrite destination files whose read-only attribute bit is set.
[/S]	Also checks subdirectories of the destination for files that match *files*.
[/U]	Copies only those files from the source that have older counterparts in the destination.
[/W]	Waits for you to change diskettes before looking for files on the source drive.

CLASS
External: REPLACE.EXE

FUNCTION
REPLACE is a specialized way of copying files. This utility was designed to help you update directories without disturbing existing files. It can also copy only those files that exist in the source but not in the destination.

EXAMPLES
To update the destination files in G:\SRCCODE with newer matching files from the source directory C:\DEVELOP, use this command:

```
REPLACE C:\DEVELOP\*.* G:\SRCCODE /u
```

To copy files with the *.ORD extension from the source D:\NEWSALES and that don't exist in the destination C:\ORDERS, use:

```
REPLACE D:\NEWSALES\*.ORD C:\ORDERS
```

OF INTEREST
COPY, XCOPY, MOVE, RENAME

RESTORE

SYNTAX
RESTORE [/?|H] *source destination* [*files*] [/S] [/P] [/A:*date*] [/B:*date*] [/E:*time*] [/L:*time*] [/M] [/N] [/R]

[/?|H]	Help screen for this command.
source	The source diskette.
destination	The destination disk drive.
[*files*]	The file or set of files you want to restore.
[/S]	Restores all the subdirectories branching from the current directory of the destination disk. If the directories no longer exist, RESTORE will re-create them.
[/P]	Tells RESTORE to ask you before overwriting files that have changed since the last backup or files with the read-only attribute set.
[/A:*date*]	Restores only those files that were created or changed on or after the date specified. The date format depends on the country setting.
[/B:*date*]	Restores only those files that were created or changed on or before the date specified. The date format depends on the country setting.
[/E:*time*]	Restores only those files that were created or changed at or before the time specified. The time format is hh-mm-ss.
[/L:*time*]	Restores only those files that were created or changed at or after the time specified. The time format is hh-mm-ss.
[/M]	Restores only those files that were changed or deleted since the last backup.

[/N]   Restores only those files that don't exist on the destination.

[/R]   Doesn't actually restore any files, but reports the files that would be restored.

CLASS

External: RESTORE.COM

FUNCTION

RESTORE complements BACKUP and lets you reload files from backup disks. It can retrieve all files, a specific set of files, or a single file. RESTORE will ask you to insert each backup disk, in order, in the source drive. Thus, you should number your disks clearly during the backup process.

The DR DOS 6.0 RESTORE utility can be used with BACKUP from any previous DOS version.

After completing its operation, RESTORE will set an ERRORLEVEL variable. If you're using RESTORE as part of a batch file, you can check the result of the restoration with an IF ERRORLEVEL statement. The possible values for ERRORLEVEL are:

Value	Definition
0	No problems encountered.
1	No files for restoration were found.
2	Some files were in use (a SHARE conflict) and could not be restored.
3	The RESTORE operation was terminated by a user-issued Ctrl-Break key sequence.
4	The RESTORE operation was aborted by a system error.

SIDE EFFECTS

Don't restore files to disks affected by SUBST, JOIN, or ASSIGN. This could damage the directory structure of the disk.

EXAMPLES

This command restores all files for all directories of the D: drive:

```
RESTORE A: D:\ /S
```

To restore all .DOC files in the C:\PROPOSAL directory, use:

```
RESTORE A: C:\PROPOSAL\*.DOC
```

OF INTEREST

BACKUP

RMDIR or RD

SYNTAX
RMDIR|RD [/?|H] [*drive:*]*directory*

[/?|H]   Help screen for this command

[*drive:*]*directory*   The disk drive and complete directory path of the directory you want to delete.

CLASS
Internal

FUNCTION
RMDIR removes directories. You can delete only one directory at a time, and that directory must be empty (it must not contain any files or subdirectories). You cannot remove either the current directory or the root directory of any drive.

SIDE EFFECTS
Don't try to remove a directory affected by the SUBST or JOIN command.

EXAMPLE
This command removes the \OLDSTUFF directory from the D: drive:

```
RD D:\OLDSTUFF
```

OF INTEREST
XDEL, RENDIR

SCRIPT

SYNTAX

SCRIPT [/?|H] [/U] *source destination* [/O=P|L] [/P=*pp*] [/T=*ss*] [/R]

[/?|H]   Help screen for this command.

[/U]   Removes SCRIPT from memory if you have installed it as a TSR program.

source   Can be a file or a DR DOS device. If you're running SCRIPT as a command-line utility, the source is a file, including the drive, path, name, and extension if it's not in the current directory. If you specify a device, such as PRN, LPT1, LPT2, LPT3, COM1, COM2, or COM3, SCRIPT is installed as a TSR program (you can also specify the CON console device for input but not for output). If running as a TSR, SCRIPT uses the output that would normally be sent to the device as its input.

destination   Again, this can be a file or a device. If you're loading SCRIPT as a TSR, this device becomes the redirected output device for the *source*. The source and destination devices can't be the same.

[/O=P|L]   Page orientation. /O=P specifies portrait mode, while /O=L specifies landscape mode. The default is portrait.

[/P=*pp*]   Point size. The default is 11 using the printer's default font (usually Courier).

[/T=*ss*]   Time-out. This is a bit tricky; most PostScript printers and network spoolers must wait a certain amount of time for additional data before determining that the job is done. If you have a very slow computer or a very short time-out, your job may not be completely transmitted when the spooler sends data or the printer gives up. Setting this value to less than the spooler or printer time-out will prevent such time-outs. The default is 10 seconds.

[/R]   Sends a software reset before sending data.

CLASS
External: SCRIPT.EXE

FUNCTION
SCRIPT lets you print text, using PRINT or COPY, on a PostScript printer. This is very handy for printing source-code listings and similar files. SCRIPT can translate all ASCII characters, including those in the Hewlett-Packard LaserJet II character set.

SCRIPT runs as a simple command-line utility to print the occasional text file on a PostScript printer or as a TSR that intercepts ASCII output destined for one port. It then translates that output into PostScript and sends the PostScript output to another port or to a file.

SIDE EFFECTS
If you have an application with a PostScript driver, such as a word processor, desktop publishing program, or graphics program, confirm that the application's PostScript output is not intercepted by SCRIPT and retranslated. The result will be a printout of the entire PostScript listing rather than the file itself.

EXAMPLES
The following command uses SCRIPT as a command-line utility and prints the file D:\SOURCE\HEADER.H on the PostScript printer attached to LPT2 (it also specifies 12-point type and sends a software reset before the print job):

```
SCRIPT D:\SOURCE\HEADER.H LPT2 /P=12 /R
```

To load SCRIPT as a TSR to intercept all output destined for LPT3, translate that output to PostScript, and send it out the LPT2 port, use:

```
SCRIPT LPT3 LPT2
```

OF INTEREST
PRINT, COPY

SET

SYNTAX

SET [/?|H] [*variable*=[*string*]]

[/?|H]　　　　　　　Help screen for this command.

[*variable*=[*string*]]　*variable* is a DR DOS environment variable, and *string* is whatever you set that variable equal to. This can be a path, a name, or a value. All lowercase letters are converted to uppercase. If *variable* exists in the DR DOS environment, the new setting overwrites the old value.

CLASS

Internal

FUNCTION

SET is a way to create and define variables in the DR DOS environment. Such variables are available to all programs, although they are usually set specifically for use by certain applications. The number of variables you can place in the DR DOS environment depends on the amount of environment space available. This is set with the /E: parameter in the SHELL statement in your CONFIG.SYS file. If you run out of environment space (you'll see an error message to that effect), increase the /E: value in the SHELL statement.

If you want to see which variables already exist in the environment, use the SET command with no parameters.

DR DOS uses a number of variables, some of which are listed in the following table:

Variable	Definition
COMSPEC	Set to the path and file name for the default command processor (usually C:\COMMAND.COM).
OS	Identifies the current operating system. It is set in the CONFIG.SYS file to DR DOS.

PATH   The current search path for executable files, defined by the PATH command. You can also set this through the SET PATH= statement.

TEMP   Set to a directory that holds temporary files. The default setting is C:\TEMP.

PEXEC   If this variable is used, and if the PROMPT string contains a $x statement, the program designated by PEXEC will run each time DR DOS returns to the command processor from an application program.

APPEND   The search path for nonexecutable files, set by the APPEND command. This only appears in the environment if APPEND was issued with the /E:ON parameter.

VER   The DR DOS version.

PROMPT   The prompt string, set by the PROMPT program. You can also set this with a SET PROMPT= statement.

You can test the contents of environment variables in a batch file. The syntax is *%variable%*.

EXAMPLE

To set the TEMP variable to point to the E:\RAMDRIVE directory, use this command:

```
SET TEMP=E:\RAMDRIVE
```

OF INTEREST

PATH, APPEND, PROMPT

SETUP

SYNTAX

SETUP [/?|H]

[/?|H]   Help screen for this command.

CLASS

External: SETUP.EXE

FUNCTION

Lets you configure DR DOS, MemoryMAX, ViewMAX, TaskMAX, and system security. See Chapter 2 for more information about SETUP.

SHARE

SYNTAX
SHARE [/?|H] [/L:*nnnn*] [/ML|MH|MU] [/X]

[/?|H] Help screen for this command.

[/L:*nnnn*] Specifies the number of file locks. The default is 20; the range is 20 to 1,024.

[/ML|MH|MU] Specifies where SHARE will be loaded. /ML specifies base or conventional memory, /MH specifies high memory (if it's available), and /MU specifies upper memory (if it's available).

[/X] Disables the SHARE operation.

CLASS
External: SHARE.EXE

FUNCTION
SHARE sets the maximum number of file locks. A file lock reserves a file, or a record within a file, for exclusive use by one program. This prevents multiple applications from accessing the same data or text file and perhaps corrupting that file. When locked, files can be accessed by only one program at a time. If you use SHARE, as you'll need to if you use TaskMAX, run it from the AUTOEXEC.BAT program.

SIDE EFFECTS
If you don't have enough locks, you'll occasionally witness strange goings-on while running TaskMAX. For example, certain programs will run out of file locks and report that the disk is full because they can't open another file.

EXAMPLES

To set the number of file locks to 60, type:

    SHARE /L:60

To cancel the SHARE operation, type:

    SHARE /X

SORT

SYNTAX
SORT [/?|H] [/R] [/+column]

[/?|H]   Help screen for this command.

[/R]   Reverses the sort order.

[/+column]   Starts the sort on the designated column number of the line. If you don't include this parameter, sorting starts at column 1.

CLASS
External: SORT.EXE

FUNCTION
Like MORE, SORT is a filter that transforms input. The SORT program does what its name implies: It sorts data files in either ascending or descending order. Because SORT is a filter, you can use the | piping command and the <> redirection commands.

SIDE EFFECTS
The SORT command is not case-sensitive and will consider *A* as *a*, *B* as *b*, and so on.

EXAMPLES

The following command sorts the output of the XDIR command in reverse order, starting at column 48 (the beginning column for file names if SuperStor is active), and redirects output to DIRFILE. The result is a file that's a reverse sort of the XDIR output.

```
XDIR | SORT /+48 /R > DIRFILE
```

This command sorts the file GLOSSARY.TXT and sends the output to the LPT2 port:

```
SORT <GLOSSARY.TXT > LPT2
```

SSTOR

SYNTAX
SSTOR [/?|H] [/B]

[/?|H]   Help screen for this command.

[/B]   Specifies a monochrome display adapter (or a color display adapter with a monochrome monitor).

CLASS
External: SSTOR.EXE

FUNCTION
SSTOR loads the SuperStor configuration program. This menu-driven program is covered in detail in Chapter 9.

EXAMPLE:
To run the SSTOR command and set the display for monochrome, type:

```
SSTOR /B
```

SUBST

SYNTAX
SUBST [/?|H] [*drive*: *drive:path*] | [[*drive*:] /D]

[/?|H]   Help screen for this command.

[*drive*: *drive:path*]   *drive*: is the new drive designation, while *drive:path* specifies the drive and path of the directory that will take on the new drive designation.

[[*drive*:] /D]   The /D parameter cancels all substitutions when entered alone. If /D is accompanied by *drive*:, only that specified drive substitution is cancelled.

CLASS
External: SUBST.EXE

FUNCTION
SUBST temporarily allows a specified directory (*drive:path*) to be addressed as if it were the specified drive (*drive*:). This command is often used to trick older programs, which may recognize only disk drives, into using subdirectories. It's also useful as a quick way of accessing a subdirectory at the end of a long path.

SIDE EFFECTS
SUBST won't work with network drives. Don't use the following commands on a drive created through SUBST: FORMAT, FDISK, DISKCOMP, DISKCOPY, BACKUP, RESTORE, RECOVER, CHKDSK, LABEL, or SYS.

EXAMPLES
To create a drive E: from the C:\OLDACCNT\DATA\PASTDUE directory, use this command:

```
SUBST E: C:\OLDACCNT\DATA\PASTDUE
```

To cancel that command, use:

```
SUBST E: /D
```

OF INTEREST
ASSIGN

SUPERPCK

SYNTAX

SUPERPCK [/?|H] [*parameters*]

[/?|H]   Help screen for this command.

[*parameters*] Super PC-Kwik has 23 separate parameters, all of which are explained in detail in Chapter 9.

CLASS

External: SUPERPCK.EXE

FUNCTION

SUPERPCK loads the Super PC-Kwik disk-caching software. Because it has a multitude of parameters that are best explained in the context of improving disk performance, refer to Chapter 9 for a discussion of this command.

SYS

SYNTAX
SYS [/?|H] *drive*:

[/?|H]   Help screen for this command.

drive: The target drive.

CLASS
External: SYS.COM

FUNCTION
The SYS command copies the DR DOS operating system files IBMBIO.COM and IBMDOS.COM (both system and hidden files), as well as the COMMAND.COM file, to a target disk. The computer can then start or boot from that disk.

EXAMPLE
To make the previously formatted disk in drive A: bootable, use this command:

```
SYS A:
```

OF INTEREST
FORMAT, VER

TASKMAX

SYNTAX
TASKMAX [/?|H] [/D:=*swapdir*] [/X[=*xxxx*]] [/E[=*eeee*]] [/L=*xxxx*] [/C *application*] [/K:*tt*] [/N[:*tt*] [*taskname*]]

[/?|H]	Help screen for this command.
[/D:=*swapdir*]	When TaskMAX runs out of memory for task swapping (or perhaps isn't set to swap to memory at all), it begins to swap tasks to disk. By default, tasks are swapped to disk in the C:\DRDOS\TMP directory. Use this parameter to specify a directory location for swap files. If you have a RAM disk or a disk partition with lots of space, you might want to select it as the location for swap files.
[/X[=*xxxx*]]	Use only when starting TaskMAX. The /X parameter specifies that tasks should be swapped first to expanded memory, and *xxxx* designates the number of KB of expanded memory dedicated to swapping. If the /X parameter is entered without a memory allocation value, all available expanded memory is used for swapping. Entering /X=0 prevents TaskMAX from accessing expanded memory and allocates such memory to application programs that might use it. If you enter a value for *xxxx* that's greater than the amount of expanded memory available, all expanded memory is dedicated to swapping.
[/E[=*eeee*]]	Use only when starting TaskMAX. The /E parameter specifies that tasks should be swapped to extended memory, and *eeee* designates the amount of extended memory in KB that is allocated to swapping. If the /E parameter is entered without a memory allocation value, all extended memory is dedicated to task swapping. If you enter /E=0, TaskMAX

won't use extended memory at all, leaving it available to applications. If you enter a value for *eeee* that is greater than the amount of extended memory available, then all extended memory is dedicated to swapping.

[/L=*xxxx*] TaskMAX must be active before you can use this parameter. The /L parameter allows you to limit the amount of expanded memory that can be used by each task. This value is universal and provides an expanded memory ceiling for all tasks.

[/C *application*] TaskMAX must be active before you can use this parameter. The /C parameter lets you start an application as a task directly from the DR DOS command line. You must specify the complete path, including drive and directory, when loading an application this way.

[/K:*tt*] TaskMAX must be active before you can use this parameter. The /K parameter immediately removes a task you designate with the task number *tt*.

[/N[:*tt*] [*taskname*]] TaskMAX must be active before you can use this parameter. This parameter specifies a name for a task. If you don't enter the task number *tt*, then the name is given to the current task. If you omit the name (*taskname*), the task returns to its original name.

CLASS

External: TASKMAX.EXE

FUNCTION

TaskMAX, the DR DOS task switcher, allows you to run multiple programs and switch between them. For detailed information about TaskMAX, see Chapter 6. That command reference details the command-line capabilities for running TaskMAX; however, you can run it in any of three ways:

- From the TaskMAX main menu, which you access by pressing the hot keys (set to Ctrl-Escape by default).

- From ViewMAX, where operation is controlled through the TaskMAX dialog boxes.

- From the command line.

When you switch tasks in TaskMAX, the background tasks are swapped out of conventional memory, allowing another task to run. The background task must be swapped to one of three places. If you have sufficient extended memory, the tasks can be swapped there. If you have enough expanded memory, tasks can be swapped there. Swapping to either extended or expanded memory provides the best performance. If you don't have enough extended or expanded memory or you want to allocate it to applications, TaskMAX will swap the background tasks to disk. If you specify that TaskMAX can use memory for swapping, it will continue to do so until it runs out of memory, at which point it swaps to disk.

Remember that TaskMAX defaults are set through the SETUP program, and these commands only override the default settings temporarily. The next time you activate TaskMAX, it will return to its default settings.

TaskMAX can only be removed from memory at the TaskMAX main menu or by rebooting your computer. You should avoid removing TaskMAX by rebooting because it will leave its rather large swap files on your disk.

EXAMPLES

This command sets the swap file directory to the root directory of the G: drive:

```
TASKMAX /D:=G:\
```

This command allocates 2,048 KB of expanded memory to task swapping:

```
TASKMAX /X=2048
```

DR DOS 6 BY EXAMPLE

This command limits the amount of expanded memory each program can access to 512 KB:

    TASKMAX /L=512

This command loads the ARTLINE.BAT application:

    TASKMAX /C C:\ARTLINE.BAT

TIME

SYNTAX

TIME [/?|H] [hh[:mm][:ss]]] [/C]

[/?|H]   Help screen for this command.

[hh[:mm][:ss]]]   The actual time, entered as the hour (*hh*), minutes (*mm*), and seconds (*ss*). The minutes and seconds entries are optional.

[/C]   This parameter provides a continual time display until you press a key.

CLASS

Internal

FUNCTION

TIME allows you to set the DR DOS internal clock. If you have a real-time clock in your computer (most computers do these days), the time is automatically loaded from it into the DR DOS clock at boot-up. If you have an older system without a real-time clock, put the TIME and DATE commands in your AUTOEXEC.BAT file so you're always reminded to enter the time and date at boot-up.

If you enter the TIME command with no parameters, it will display the current time setting and ask if you want to enter a different value. If you don't want to change the time, press Enter.

When entering time values, remember that TIME uses 24-hour, or military, time. In this system, 1:00 a.m. is 01:00 and 1:00 p.m. is 13:00.

SIDE EFFECTS

Note that setting the time doesn't affect the setting for a computer's real-time clock; it only affects the DR DOS software clock, which is activated after you boot your computer.

DR DOS 6 BY EXAMPLE

EXAMPLE

The following sets the DR DOS software clock to 5:34 p.m.:

```
TIME 17:34
```

OF INTEREST

DATE

TOUCH

SYNTAX

TOUCH [/?|H] [@]*files*[. . .] [/T:*hh*:*mm*:*ss*] [/D:*date*] [/F:E|J|U] [/P] [/R] [/S]

[/?|H] Help screen for this command.

[@]*files*[. . .] The file or files (including the file name and extension) you want to TOUCH, with the drive designation and complete path if the file or files aren't in the current directory. Wildcards can be used. If *files* is prefaced with "@," the specified file contains a list of files to be TOUCHed.

[/T:*hh*:*mm*:*ss*] Forces a time stamp of the file or files.

[/D:*date*] Forces a date stamp of the file or files.

[/F:E|J|U] Sets the date format to the European (/F:E), Japanese (/F:J), or U.S. (/F:U) standard. It overrides the country-code setting.

[/P] Causes TOUCH to verify that you want to TOUCH each file specified in the *files* argument.

[/R] Allows TOUCH to work with read-only files.

[/S] Extends the *files* argument to include all matching files in subdirectories of the specified directory.

CLASS
External: TOUCH.EXE

FUNCTION
TOUCH simply changes a file's time and date stamps. If you don't enter a specific time and date using the /T and /D parameters, TOUCH uses the current time and date.

EXAMPLE

To set the date for E:\PROGRAMS\DOSTUFF.EXE file to February 17, 1992, type:

```
TOUCH E:\PROGRAMS\DOSTUFF.EXE /D:02-17-92
```

TREE

SYNTAX
TREE [/?|H] [*drive:files*] [/B] [/F] [/G] [/P]

- [/?|H]　　　　Help screen for this command.

- [*drive:files*]　Causes TREE to search for files matching *files* on the specified drive. You can enter a file name and file type or specify a starting directory for the search. Wildcards are acceptable in the file specification.

- [/B]　　　　Tells TREE to omit the number of files in each directory in its display.

- [/F]　　　　Tells TREE to display the files that reside in the directories and subdirectories as it displays the directory structure.

- [/G]　　　　Displays the directory structure in a graphical format using lines to show the hierarchical directory structure.

- [/P]　　　　Pauses the display at each screenful of data and waits for you to press a key.

CLASS
External: TREE.COM

FUNCTION
TREE displays the directory structure of the disk, also known as the *directory tree*. It can do so in a simple text listing or in a graphical listing, using lines to show the relationship of the various directories and subdirectories. If you specify a disk or directory, it will begin its search there and show only the branches of the directory tree from that point. If you include a file specification, TREE will display all matching files in all subdirectories in its search path. If you include a file specification, you can't use the /G parameter.

DR DOS 6 BY EXAMPLE

EXAMPLES

This command displays the directory structure of the current disk, starting with the current directory:

    TREE

This command searches for all *.WKS files on the G: disk, starting with the \ACCOUNTS directory:

    TREE G:\ACCOUNTS*.WKS

This command provides a graphical display of the tree structure, starting with the C:\BOOK directory.

    TREE C:\BOOK /G

The resulting display is shown in Figure A-3.

```
[Max] C:\>tree C:\book /g
     bytes  files  path
    35,205     18  c:\book
   116,679      4  ├──winart
    32,563      3  ├──outline
 1,240,061     29  ├──chapters
   164,964     13  ├──vector
 1,097,869    130  └──bitmap
    13,067     40       └──icons
total files 237    total bytes 2,700,408

[Max] C:\>
```

Figure A-3. Typical TREE /B display.

OF INTEREST
DIR, XDIR

TYPE

SYNTAX

TYPE [/?|H] *files* [/P]

[/?|H]	Help screen for this command.
files	The file or files to be typed onscreen. The file name and type must be included; if the file is not in the current directory, the drive and path must also be included. Wildcards are permitted.
[/P]	This parameter pauses the display at each screen of information and waits for you to press a key before proceeding.

CLASS
Internal

FUNCTION

TYPE displays text files, allowing you to read their contents. If you use wildcards to specify multiple files, TYPE will precede each file listing with the name of the file. The /P parameter pauses output at each screen of information. This parameter is functionally equivalent to the TYPE *files* | MORE command.

TYPE responds to a number of control keys. Stop and start scrolling by pressing Ctrl-S. Start and stop printing by pressing Ctrl-P. Ctrl-C and Ctrl-Break stop TYPE altogether so you can stop scrolling through a very large text file.

EXAMPLE

The following command types the file README.DOC to the screen, pausing at each screenful of information:

```
TYPE README.DOC /P
```

OF INTEREST
MORE

UNDELETE

SYNTAX

UNDELETE [/?|H] [[*drive*:][*path*][*files*]] [/A] [/B] [/D:*date*| -*dd*] [/L] [/P] [/R:*type*] [/S] [/T:*time*]

[/?|H]	Help screen for this command.
[[*drive*:][*path*][*files*]]	The drive, directory path, and file specification for each file you want to recover.
[/A]	Undeletes all files matching the *files* specification in the specified path and drive without asking you to verify each undeletion.
[/B]	Sets the display for monochrome (not color); use it when executing UNDELETE from the main menu.
[/D:*date*| -*dd*]	Undeletes files by date. If the /D:*date* parameter is used, it undeletes all pending deletion files (created through DELWATCH) deleted on or before the specified date. The date entry format is specified by the country code. If the /D-*dd* parameter is used, all DELWATCH pending deletion files deleted over the past number of days specified by *dd* are purged.
[/L]	Lists all files that may be undeleted but doesn't undelete them.
[/P]	Pauses at each screen of information.
[/R:*type*]	Specifies the type of undeletion to use. The *type* argument can be DELWATCH, DISKMAP, or UNAIDED. If you use this parameter, UNDELETE will only attempt to recover those files for which it can use the specified type of recovery. For example, if you specify DISKMAP, pending deletion files created through DELWATCH won't be recovered.

DR DOS COMMAND REFERENCE

[/S]   Extends the search path for undeleting files to subdirectories of the specified drive and/or directory.

[/T:*time*]   Undeletes pending deletion files created with DELWATCH that were deleted at or after the specified time.

CLASS
External: UNDELETE.EXE

FUNCTION
UNDELETE recovers deleted files. Its success depends on the method you use to protect against unwanted deletions. If you're using DELWATCH, UNDELETE can recover the files. If you're using DISKMAP (and using it often), you have a very good chance of recovering your files unless you've written over their file space. If you aren't using an UNDELETE assistance method, UNDELETE still has a good chance of recovering the files. If it can't recover a file because its space has been reallocated to another file, it will display a "cannot recover" message.

UNDELETE runs either from the command line or from the main menu. To run UNDELETE in menu mode, issue the command with no parameters (except /B). Using UNDELETE from the main menu is discussed in detail in Chapter 9. If you know exactly what files you want to recover and what recovery method you want to use, running UNDELETE from the command line is more efficient.

Undeleting a file is a two-step process. First, examine the set of files you can undelete by appending the /L parameter to the UNDELETE command. After determining what you want to recover, use UNDELETE without the /L parameter to recover the files.

EXAMPLES
The following command lists files with a .DOC extension that can be recovered from the C:\LETTERS directory (the listing will pause at each screen of information, and the recovery type is DISKMAP):

```
UNDELETE C:\LETTERS\*.DOC /R:DISKMAP /L
```

This command undeletes these files:

```
UNDELETE C:\LETTERS\*.DOC /R:DISKMAP
```

To undelete all pending deletion files (from DELWATCH) on the C: drive and deleted after November 24, 1991, use:

```
UNDELETE C\*.* /D:11-24-91 /S
```

OF INTEREST
DELWATCH, DISKMAP

UNFORMAT

SYNTAX

UNFORMAT [/?|H] *drive*:

[/?|H]   Help screen for this command.

drive: The drive designation for the disk you want to unformat.

CLASS
External: UNFORMAT.COM

FUNCTION

When DR DOS formats a disk that already contains data, it writes a copy of the FAT for that disk to an unused disk area (if there's room). This is called a *safe format*. If you haven't overwritten the files on this disk, you can recover them with UNFORMAT. If you've written new files to the disk, UNFORMAT won't be able to retrieve all the original files. If the old FAT information itself has been overwritten, UNFORMAT will display the message stating that the UNFORMAT information has been overwritten.

EXAMPLE

The following command recovers files from the safe-formatted disk in the A: drive:

```
UNFORMAT A:
```

OF INTEREST
FORMAT, UNDELETE

UNINSTAL

SYNTAX
UNINSTAL [/?|H] [/C]

[/?|H]　　　　Help screen for this command.

[/C]　　　　　Removes old operating system files previously saved during INSTALL.

CLASS
External: UNINSTAL.EXE

FUNCTION
If you saved the old operating system during DR DOS installation, you can remove DR DOS and reload the old operating system using UNINSTAL. The /C parameter allows you to remove the old operating system files.

EXAMPLE
To remove DR DOS and reload the old operating system, type:

```
UNINSTAL
```

VER

SYNTAX
VER [/?|H]

[/?|H]   Help screen for this command.

CLASS
Internal

FUNCTION
VER reports the version of DR DOS.

SIDE EFFECTS
Programs that report the version of MS-DOS, such as the SI.EXE utility that comes with the Norton Utilities, won't report the correct DR DOS version; instead, they'll report DOS version 3.31.

EXAMPLE
To check the current DR DOS version, type:

```
VER
```

VERIFY

SYNTAX
VERIFY [/?|H] [ON|OFF]

[/?|H]   Help screen for this command.

[ON|OFF]   ON activates write verify, while OFF turns it off.

CLASS
Internal

FUNCTION
When VERIFY is active, DR DOS compares the file it has written with the data it should have written. This can eliminate problems with files written to bad disk sectors, but it also degrades disk performance. For maximum write speed, VERIFY is off by default.

To check the current status of write verification, enter the command with no parameters.

EXAMPLE
To turn disk verification on, type:

```
VERIFY ON
```

VOL

SYNTAX
VOL [/?|H] [*drive*:]

[/?|H]   Help screen for this command.

[*drive*:]   The drive specification.

CLASS
Internal

FUNCTION
VOL checks the volume label for the specified disk drive. The volume label is a title assigned to the disk during the FORMAT operation or with the LABEL command.

EXAMPLE
To display the volume label for the diskette in the B: drive, type:

```
VOL B:
```

OF INTEREST
FORMAT, LABEL

XCOPY

SYNTAX

XCOPY [/?|H] [@]*files* [*path*] [/A] [/D:*date*] [/E] [/H] [/L] [/M] [/P|C] [/S] [/V] [/W]

[/?|H]	Help screen for this command.
[@]*files*	The file specification, including the file name and file extension. Wildcards are permitted. If the files don't reside in the current directory, the disk-drive designation and directory path must be included. If the file specification is preceded by "@," the file specification is actually a file that contains a list of files to be copied.
[*path*]	The target directory for the files. If this directory isn't on the current drive, the disk designation must also be given. If you want to rename the files, you can specify a new file name and/or file extension as part of *path*.
[/A]	Copies only files with the archive attribute bit set. XCOPY won't change the attribute setting for the source files.
[/D:*date*]	Copies only files that have been modified on or after the specified date. The date format is set by the country-code setting.
[/E]	Causes XCOPY to create subdirectories in the destination directory, even if no files are ready to reside in them.
[/H]	Includes files with the hidden or system attribute bit set in the XCOPY operation. If you don't use this parameter, such files will be ignored. (Note that this parameter is the same as that used for help. However, the help parameter always precedes any file names.)
[/L]	Also copies the disk label.

[/M]	Copies only files with the archive attribute bit set and resets the archive bit for the source files.
[/P|C]	Confirms that you want each file copied.
[/S]	Also copies all files that match *files* in subdirectories of the specified source directory.
[/V]	Verifies each copied file against the original.
[/W]	Waits for you to insert a diskette before copying the files.

CLASS
External: XCOPY.EXE

FUNCTION

XCOPY uses memory more efficiently than COPY and therefore copies faster. It can be useful for reproducing a complete directory structure when you're copying files from one type of disk to another (where DISKCOPY couldn't be used). Copying an exact duplicate of the directory structure requires the /S and /E parameters.

XCOPY also sets a value for the ERRORLEVEL variable. You can check this value from within a batch file. The following are the possible values of the ERRORLEVEL variable:

ERRORLEVEL	Definition
0	No problems encountered.
1	No matching files found to copy.
2	XCOPY aborted by a user-issued Ctrl-C or Ctrl-Break.
4	XCOPY aborted due to lack of disk space at the destination, insufficient memory, an invalid drive designation, or initialization.
5	XCOPY aborted because of a disk write error at the destination.

EXAMPLES

To copy all *.DOC files from the C:\REPORTS directory to the G:\ARCHIVE directory, type:

    XCOPY C:\REPORTS*.DOC G:\ARCHIVE

This command copies only those .C files in the D:\SRC\V35 directory that have been modified (in other words, .C files with their archive bits set; the files are copied to the D:\RELEASE directory, and the archive bits in the source files are not reset):

    XCOPY C:\SRC\V35*.C D:\RELEASE /A

To copy the entire set of files and the directory structure from the A: disk to the C: disk, type:

    XCOPY A:*.* C:\ /E /S

OF INTEREST
COPY, MOVE, REPLACE, RENAME

XDEL

SYNTAX
XDEL [/?|H] [@]*files*[. . .] [/D] [/N] [/O] [/P] [/R] [/S]

[/?|H]   Help screen for this command.

[@]*files*[. . .]   The file specification, including the file name and file type. Wildcards can be used. If the files don't reside in the current directory or drive, add the complete path name and disk-drive identifier. If "@" precedes the file specification, the file contains a list of files to be deleted. If you want to specify more than one file without using wildcards, precede each file name with a single space.

[/D]   Deletes empty subdirectories if they're created or encountered. This is used in conjunction with the /S parameter.

[/N]   Deletes all specified files without prompting you to verify the operation.

[/O]   Overwrites the files in addition to deleting them. This provides a higher level of security than standard deletions because the latter can be recovered with UNDELETE or a disk-sector editing application (such as the Mace MUSE editor).

[/P]   Makes the delete operation a little safer. XDEL will ask for permission to delete each file before actually doing so.

[/R]   Allows XDEL to delete files with the read-only attribute set.

[/S]   Allows XDEL to extend the search for matching files to subdirectories of the specified directory.

CLASS
External: XDEL.EXE

FUNCTION

XDEL is an extended and handy form of the DELETE or ERASE command. Among its talents is the ability to sweep through an entire disk deleting backup files (such as those with the .BAK and .$?? extensions). You can also delete only those files you select by using the /P parameter.

SIDE EFFECTS

The /O option for XDEL is the only facility in DR DOS that can delete files in such a way that they can't be recovered. Use this option cautiously.

EXAMPLES

To delete all .BAK and $?? files from all directories and subdirectories on the C: drive, type:

```
XDEL C:\*.BAK C:\*.$?? /S
```

To delete selected files, type:

```
XDEL *.* /P
```

OF INTEREST

DEL, DELQ, UNDELETE

XDIR

SYNTAX

XDIR [/?|H] [+|-ADHRS] [*files*] [/B] [/C] [/L] [/N] [/P] [/R] [/S] [/T] [/W] [/X] [/Y] [/Z]

[/?|H]   Help screen for this command.

[+|-ADHRS]   Either displays (+) or doesn't display (-) files with particular attribute bits set. Usually, XDIR displays all files regardless of attributes. The attribute codes are A for archive, D for directory, H for hidden, R for read-only, and S for system.

[*files*]   The file specification, including the file name and type. Wildcards can be used. If the files don't reside in the current directory or current drive, you must add the complete path name and disk-drive identifier. If you omit the file specification, *.* is assumed.

[/B]   A brief version of the normal XDIR display showing only the files and paths.

[/C]   Tells XDIR to compute and display a checksum for each file that matches the file specification. This is useful for ensuring that two supposedly identical files are indeed identical (and is therefore helpful when checking for viruses).

[/L]   Produces the normal, verbose XDIR display.

[/N]   Specifies no alphabetical sorting.

[/P]   Tells XDIR to pause at each screen of information, waiting for you to press a key before it continues.

[/R]   Specifies reverse sort order, depending on other parameters. If no additional sorting parameters are given, the result is a reverse sort by file name. If the /X parameter is used, the result is a reverse sort by file extension. /T results in a reverse sort by time stamp. /Z produces a reverse sort by file size. Finally, using SuperStor with a /Y produces a reverse sort by compression ratio.

[/S]   Includes all subdirectories of the specified directory.

[/T]   Sorts the display by time stamp.

[/W]   Provides a wide display with only file and directory names.

[/X]   Sorts the display by file extension.

[/Y]   Sorts the directory by compression ratio. Use it if SuperStor is active.

[/Z]   Sorts the display by file size.

CLASS
External: XDIR.EXE

FUNCTION
The XDIR command is a marvelous extended directory utility. It allows you to find files anywhere on your computer.

EXAMPLES
To display all *.DBF files on all subdirectories of the C: drive, type:

```
XDIR C:\*.DBF /S
```

To display only the directories beginning with T on the D: drive, type:

```
XDIR +D D:\T*.*
```

To sort the current directory first by file extension and then by SuperStor compression ratio, type:

```
XDIR /X /Y
```

OF INTEREST
DIR, TREE

APPENDIX B

EDITOR Command Reference

The following is a complete list of EDITOR commands, presented in alphabetical order. Use this as your quick reference to EDITOR.

Backspace	Deletes the character to the left of the cursor. You can also use Ctrl-H.
Ctrl-A	Moves the cursor left by one word. You can also use Ctrl-left arrow.
Ctrl-C	Scrolls the screen down. You can also use PageUp.
Ctrl-D	Moves the cursor one character to the right.
Ctrl-E	Moves the cursor one line up.
Ctrl-F	Moves the cursor to the right by one word. You can also use Ctrl-right arrow.
Ctrl-G	Deletes the character beneath the cursor.
Ctrl-I	Equivalent to pressing Tab.
Ctrl-J	Calls up the help-screen sequence. You can also use the F1 key.
Ctrl-K-B	Sets the beginning of a block.
Ctrl-K-C	Inserts a copy of a block at the current cursor position.
Ctrl-K-D	Saves your file and returns to the EDITOR no-file (title) screen.

Ctrl-K-H	Hides a block.
Ctrl-K-K	Sets the end of a block.
Ctrl-K*n*	Sets a marker. *n* must be a number between 0 and 9.
Ctrl-K-S	Saves your file but does not exit.
Ctrl-K-V	Moves a block to the current cursor position.
Ctrl-K-W	Writes the contents of a block to a file.
Ctrl-K-X	Saves your file and exits from EDITOR to DR DOS.
Ctrl-K-Y	Deletes a block.
Ctrl-N	Forces everything to the right of the cursor to a new line.
Ctrl-P	Places the following control character into the file.
Ctrl-Q-B	Jumps to the beginning of the currently marked block.
Ctrl-Q-C	Jumps to the bottom of the file. You can also press the End key.
Ctrl-Q-D	Moves the cursor to the end of the line.
Ctrl-Q-K	Jumps to the end of the currently marked block.
Ctrl-Q*n*	Jumps to the preset marked position designated by a number from 0 through 9.
Ctrl-Q-N	Places a character into the file based on either the following decimal equivalent (just enter the number) or the hexadecimal equivalent (0x followed by the number in hexadecimal).
Ctrl-Q-R	Jumps to the top of the file. You can also press the Home key.
Ctrl-Q-S	Moves the cursor to the beginning of the line.
Ctrl-R	Scrolls the screen up. You can also use PageDown. (When you are in a file-name entry field, this reloads the last entry into a file-name field, such as at the no-file screen or when you use Ctrl-K-W).

APPENDIX B

Ctrl-S	Moves the cursor one character to the left.
Ctrl-T	Deletes all letters in a word to the right of the cursor.
Ctrl-U	Interrupts a command.
Ctrl-V	Toggles between inserting text and overtyping text. You can also use the Insert key.
Ctrl-W	Scrolls the screen one line down.
Ctrl-X	Moves the cursor one line down.
Ctrl-Y	Deletes the entire line.
Ctrl-Z	Scrolls the screen one line up.
Enter	Starts a new line.

APPENDIX C

The ViewMAX Command Reference

The following is a list of all ViewMAX commands. The listing is in the order that the commands appear, and the commands are listed in menu-by-menu order. I've also listed all of the keyboard shortcuts for the menu commands. These commands use the same general structure you might be familiar with from using Microsoft Windows or the X Window System. To pull down any of the menus, simultaneously press the Alt key and the first letter of the menu. For example, Alt-F pulls down the File menu. Once the menu is pulled down, you can run the highlight bar up and down with the up and down arrow keys or the mouse pointer. The highlight bar will only travel over currently active commands (those that aren't dimmed or grayed. Pressing Enter, or clicking with the mouse, activates the currently highlighted command.

You can also activate any command that isn't dimmed by pressing the highlighted letter in the command name. For example, you can pull down the File menu with Alt-F, then exit from DR DOS by pressing the X key (for exit). I find that it's easier to call up a commonly used command using the keyboard shortcut sequence.

For DR DOS 5.0 users, this list of commands covers DR DOS 6.0. As such, note that there are a few commands you don't have and that the commands are in a different order. However, the command descriptions are just as accurate for DR DOS version 5.0 as they are for version 6.0.

The File Menu

Access the File menu with Alt-F, and use the following letters to activate commands:

O for Open/run—This command runs an executable file (a program) or displays a directory in the window. *You must first select a file or directory folder before you can use this command.*

S for Show contents—For text files, this will create a window that allows you to read the file and scroll down through it. For binary files, you'll be able to view the file in both hexadecimal and ASCII text. *You must first select a single file.*

N for fiNd—This command allows you to search an entire drive for all files matching a file name or a wildcard mask. You can then click on a matching file and ViewMAX will display that file's directory.

C for Copy—This command copies objects from one window to another. Objects can be disks, files, or directory folders. *You must first select objects before you can use this command.*

D for Delete—This command deletes objects, including the entire contents of a floppy disk or a directory folder. *You must first select objects.*

I for Info/rename—This command tells you the size, creation time and date, and read/write status of an object, such as a disk, folder, or file. You can also use this command to rename a file or directory folder. *You must first select a single object.*

P for Password—This command attaches or removes a password from a file or directory folder. *You must first select a single file or directory folder.*

U for Undelete—This command calls the DR DOS UNDELETE utility. You can use this to recover deleted files and directories. For more information, see Chapter 14, Taking Charge of Your Disk.

APPENDIX C

F for Format disk—This command uses the default format for the type of floppy drive and formats floppy disks. You can't pass any arguments to this formatting command, so if you want to do anything fancy you need to use the DR DOS command-line FORMAT external command. *You must first select a floppy drive.*

X for Exit to DR DOS—This command is your way out of ViewMAX and back to the DR DOS command line.

The Options Menu

Use Alt-O to access the Options menu, and one of these letters to execute the option commands:

C for Configure application—Use this command to assign icons to application files (batch files, .EXE and .COM DR DOS executable files, and .APP GEM files). You can also assign icons to files associated with applications (which are called documents). *You must first select an application file.*

P for Preferences—This command accesses a dialog box that you can use to tailor how ViewMAX behaves. Things you can change include whether DR DOS will or won't warn you before deleting, copying, or overwriting files; mouse double-click speed; and using pull-down or drop-down menus.

G for Global password—Use this command to assign a global password, unlocking all files and directories protected with that password. You also use this command to remove a global password and lock the files and directories again.

O for cOlor schemes—This command enables you choose from a set of available color assignments for the various parts of ViewMAX, such as the background or window borders. It's like repainting your room, but much easier.

S for Save preferences—Use this command to save changes you've made through the Preferences command, configurations you've assigned to applications, and the current contents of the windows as the contents you'll see when you start DR DOS.

M for TaskMAX preferences—Use this command to select whether TaskMAX should be controlled by itself or by ViewMAX. You can also set the amount of expanded memory that's available to ViewMAX. *This is only available if TaskMAX is active.*

T for TaskMAX interface—This command is the equivalent of the TaskMAX main menu. You can start, delete, and switch tasks. *This is only available if TaskMAX is active and ViewMAX has control of TaskMAX.*

E for Enter DR DOS commands—Use this command to escape from ViewMAX to a DR DOS shell. Type EXIT and then press Enter to return to ViewMAX.

The View Menu

The View menu affects the way things appear in the active (highlighted) window. A few View menu commands have command keys that you can use to access them directly. All View menu commands can be accessed by first pressing Alt-V, followed one of these letters:

C for Close—This command closes the directory shown in the window and opens the next directory up in the directory tree. For example, if you close /JUNQUE/NONSENSE, you'll be left with /JUNQUE in the window. *You can also activate this command by simply pressing Alt-F4.*

Z for resiZe—This command zooms the active window or file/tree window pair to cover the whole screen or switches back to the top window/bottom window mode. *Pressing Alt-F5 will also activate this command.*

F for reFresh—This command redisplays the contents of the window. It also deselects all selected objects. *Just press F5 for a quicker way to use this command.*

APPENDIX C

T for show Tree—This command displays directory folders in the tree window in the same manner as the TREE command does from the DR DOS command line. This allows you to see the complete directory structure at a glance. *This command is only available when the tree window isn't active.*

H for Hide tree—This command removes the tree window from the active file window. This allows the file window to stretch out a bit, but you lose the ability to see the directory tree. *This command is only available when the tree window is active.*

X for show as teXt—Use this if you want to see text descriptions of the files instead of icons.

I for show as Icons—If you've previously chosen the Text command in this menu, this will display objects as icons instead of as text descriptions.

N for Name order—This command arranges the contents of the window in alphabetical order by file name, without regard to extension. Directory folders stay at the top.

Y for tYpe order—This command arranges objects in alphabetical order, first by file extension and then by file name. This is the default.

S for Size order—This command arranges objects in the active window by file size.

D for Date order—This command rearranges the folders and files into date order. Folders remain at the top of the window.

W for Wildcards—This command allows you to create a mask that filters what is shown in the window. For example, if you want to show only files beginning with IGN and with a file extension ending in SE, enter the following as the wildcard mask:

IGN*.?SE

The Help Menu

These commands bring up the brief help dialog boxes that explain the basic operation of ViewMAX. Press Alt-H (or F1) followed by one of these letters to reach the appropriate on-line help section.

W for Windows—This command calls the on-line help concerning how to use ViewMAX windows.

M for Menus—This command explains how ViewMAX menus work.

D for Dialogs—This command discusses the various controls within ViewMAX dialog boxes.

T for Trees—This command provides help for using the tree window.

The Information Menu

The Information menu enables you to access the desktop accessories and check the version of ViewMAX you're running. To access these commands, type one of the following letters:

A for cAlculator—This puts the four-function calculator onscreen.

C for Clock—You guessed it — this one puts the clock onscreen.

I for Information—Actually, you don't get much information at all — just the copyright date and the version of ViewMAX.

But I Don't Have a Mouse

I haven't emphasized using the keyboard as a mouse replacement because DR DOS is designed to be used with a mouse or other type of pointing device, such as a trackball. But maybe you don't have a mouse and you still want to play around with ViewMAX. That's more than fair, and Digital Research has designed ViewMAX to accommodate you. Just be prepared for a bit of awkwardness when attempting to mimic some mouse functions from the keyboard. However, certain commands will be easier to issue from the keyboard than from the mouse, so you may continue to use some keyboard techniques even after you get a mouse.

APPENDIX C

Navigating Without Benefit of Mouse

First, notice the gray rectangle in the active ViewMAX window. This rectangle takes the place of your mouse cursor. You can move it around the window with the arrow keys. If you want to switch windows, just press the Tab key. Scrolling up and down through the active window is done with the Pg Up and Pg Dn keys.

If you want to expand a window to full screen, press the Alt-F5 combination. Pressing that combination again returns to dual window mode. Finally, to close a directory and display that directory's parent in the window, press Alt-F4.

Now that you can navigate without a mouse, you need to know how to select an object. First, position the gray rectangle over the object. Next, press the space bar. If you want to deselect an object, press the space bar again. The Escape and F5 keys will both deselect all selected objects, not just the one in the gray rectangle.

Once you've selected an object, you can use any of the menu commands to manipulate that object. Take a look at the previous section for a list of all of the commands and access each command. For example, say you want to copy a couple of files:

1. First, use the arrow keys to place the gray rectangle over each object you want to copy. When the rectangle is in position over each, tap the space bar to select the object.

2. Next, press the Alt and F keys together to pull down the files menu. Press C to use the Copy command.

3. If the alert box telling you about the number of files to copy appears, press Enter to copy the files.

You can use this same technique to delete files, configure applications, check file contents, rename files, and perform other tasks. It should help you get by until you get a mouse.

Glossary

Application
: A program designed to accomplish or automate a specific real-world function, such as a database, spreadsheet, or word processor. By contrast, a system program or utility is more concerned with tasks specific to the computer system.

ASCII
: The American Standard Code for Information Interchange. This is the standard set of codes used to represent raw data, such as numbers, letters, and other characters in personal computers.

AUTOEXEC.BAT file
: One of two configuration files for personal computers running DR DOS or MS-DOS, the other being CONFIG.SYS. It executes each time you turn your computer on and is processed after the CONFIG.SYS file.

Batch file
: A type of executable file that contains a series of DR DOS commands. It must have a .BAT file extension.

Baud rate
: A measurement of communication speed for serial ports; roughly, the data transfer rate in bits per second.

Bit
: The smallest unit of data; an item of information that has one of two possible values (zero or one).

Buffer
   A memory area used as temporary storage during data transfer.

Byte
   Eight bits of data. A byte is required to represent a character.

Cluster
   An area on a disk comprising a group of contiguous sectors.

Code page
   A table defining the character set used by the computer.

Command
   A DR DOS utility program, either internal or external.

Command line
   The line you see, beginning with a prompt, when DR DOS is running. The commands you type on this line are interpreted, or *parsed*, when you press Enter.

Conditional execution
   In a batch or CONFIG.SYS file, a place where one or more commands may or may not be executed based on whether a condition is true or false.

CONFIG.SYS file
   One of two configuration files in DR DOS, CONFIG.SYS is processed before the AUTOEXEC.BAT file executes. Memory managers, general operating system options, and device drivers are loaded through this file.

Contiguous
   Without interruption. A set of sectors on a disk with no intervening blank sectors is said to be contiguous.

GLOSSARY

Conventional memory

The first 640 KB of memory, also known as *base memory*. Your applications, except for the rare protected-mode program, must run in this space.

Cursor

The blinking indicator on the screen that tells you where the next character you type will be displayed.

Cursor diamond

The cursor-control key layout pattern introduced in WordStar and used by EDITOR.

Data Communications Equipment

One of two types of serial communications equipment. Modems are usually DCE devices.

Data Terminal Equipment

One of two types of serial communications equipment. Personal computers are usually DTE devices.

Device

Hardware hooked into your computer. Examples are graphics adapters and mice.

Device driver

Programs that allow DR DOS to control and access hardware devices.

Directory

A way of organizing files. Directories are the computer equivalent of file drawers.

Disk cache

An area of memory that stores often-used disk data. Caching is a way of speeding the transfer of data to and from disk drives.

Disk drive
A device used to hold magnetic storage media, either fixed (hard drive) or removable (floppy drive). The disk drive reads data from or writes data to the storage medium.

Diskette
A floppy disk. Its format can be either 5.25- or 3.5-inch.

DOS
Short for Disk Operating System. DOS is a program that controls the operation of the computer and its devices.

Expanded memory manager
Also known as EMM; represents memory beyond 1,024 KB as LIM specification expanded memory.

Expanded memory specification
Also referred to as EMS (*see* Expanded memory manager).

Environment
In the case of DOS, a common set of definitions accessible by all applications. The PATH, APPEND, and SET variables are here, along with the prompt information.

Executable file
A program that can be run. This could be a DOS machine-code program (which will have an .EXE or .COM extension), a GEM machine-code program (one having an .APP extension), or a batch file (one having a .BAT extension).

Expanded memory
Memory located at an address greater than 640 KB; its use is defined by the LIM memory standard. This is "paged" memory and is useful only for data storage.

GLOSSARY

Extended memory

Memory above 1,024 KB on machines equipped with 16-bit (80286) or 32-bit (80386 or 80486) microprocessors.

External commands

DR DOS commands that run from executable files shipped with DR DOS. These files are stored in the \DRDOS directory.

File

A set of information stored on disk.

File allocation table

Also known as the FAT; a table that keeps track of free disk space and the space occupied by files.

File extension

The last three characters of a complete file name. These always follow a period and are generally used to signify the type of file.

File name

The first eight letters in a file specification, not including the extension.

Filters

Special DR DOS commands that can process the output of other commands as their own input.

Floppy disk

Removable magnetic media.

Formatting

The process of preparing a disk for data storage.

Graphical user interface

Also known as a GUI; an environment that replaces the command line with graphical objects. These objects allow you to control your computer and its applications. ViewMAX and Microsoft Windows are GUIs.

Handshaking

A method of controlling data flow between serial devices. Hardware handshaking uses specific lines in the RS-232 interface to signal when a device is alive, ready to send information, or ready to receive information.

Hard disk

A disk drive with nonremovable media. Hard disks are noted for their high speed and large data-storage capacity.

Hexadecimal

The base-16 numbering system used by programmers.

High memory

The first 64 KB of extended memory. The DR DOS memory managers can load part of the operating system into high memory, freeing additional conventional memory.

Hypertext

A method of organizing on-line help. Hypertext lets you jump easily from topic to topic.

Internal command

A DR DOS command executed from within the command processor without needing to access a file on disk.

Interrupt

A signal to the microprocessor that it must service some request.

GLOSSARY

Kilobyte
Also known as a KB; 1,024 bytes.

LIM
Lotus-Intel-Microsoft. This term is sometimes used to describe expanded memory.

Megabyte
Also known as an MB; 1,024 kilobytes.

Memory
The data-storage mechanism in your computer.

Microsoft Windows
The nearly standard multitasking, windowing graphical user interface for DOS-based personal computers.

Modem
Short for MOdulator/DEModulator. A device that allows computers to communicate via phone lines.

Multitasking
The ability of an environment or operating system to allow multiple applications to run simultaneously. On DOS personal computers, Microsoft Windows and Quarterdeck's DesqView are multitasking environments.

On-line help
Documentation about a command that is available directly through the computer.

Parallel port
A communications port that sends each bit of a byte in parallel over separate lines. This is the type of port normally used to connect to printers and is generally faster than communicating via a serial port.

Partition

A section of a hard disk set off by the FDISK utility. Each partition has its own drive letter and is treated by DR DOS as a separate hard disk (although it may be only one section of a hard disk).

Password

A set of characters required to gain access to a system, directory, or file when security is installed.

Path

Identifies where a file or subdirectory resides; lists its drive and parent directories.

Piping

Making the output of one command the input to another command.

PostScript

A popular page-description language for laser printers; a product of Adobe Systems.

Print queue

A list of files in memory that are waiting to be printed.

Print spooler

A utility that maintains a print queue.

Prompt

Information that identifies the DR DOS command line.

RAM

Random-access memory. This is memory that your computer can both write to and read from.

GLOSSARY

RAM disk
Memory made to look like a disk drive to DR DOS.

ROM
Read-only memory. This is memory that your computer can read from but can't modify. Your machine BIOS is stored in ROM.

Root directory
The top directory of a disk.

Serial port
A communication port that sends information one bit at a time across a single line.

Subdirectory
Any directory that branches from another directory.

Task switching
The ability of an operating system or environment to allow multiple tasks to be loaded into memory and then switch between these tasks. In a task-switching system, while multiple tasks can be loaded, only one task can be active. TaskMAX is a task-switching environment.

Terminate-and-stay-resident program
Also known as a TSR; a program that runs, loads itself into memory, and stays active but then returns you to the command line so you can run other programs. PRINT is a typical TSR.

Upper memory
The 384 KB of memory that spans the gap between conventional memory (the first 640 KB) and extended memory (memory above 1,024 KB).

Wildcards

Special characters used in DR DOS commands that allow for multiple matches. An asterisk (*) matches anything in that position and in all the following character places in either the file name or the extension. A question mark matches a single character in that position (also in either the file name or the extension).

Write-protect

The ability to prevent users from writing data to a floppy disk. For 5.25-inch diskettes, this requires tape over the notch; 3.5-inch diskettes have a sliding tab built into the case.

Index

:label
    and batch files, 195
    and CONFIG.SYS file, 97, 101
<, 313
>, 311
>>, 312
?, 87, 97, 100
@, 190, 194
|, 313
386-to-the-MAX, 85, 151

A

AMI BIOS, 96
ANSI.SYS, 92, 94, 132, 314
    installation, 44
    keyboard definition, 317
    screen colors, 315
    video modes, 316
APPEND, 331
    installation, 39
ASSIGN, 334
Atari ST, 244
ATTRIB, 65, 336
Attributes, 64
AUTOEXEC.BAT, 85, 96, 152
AUX device, 57

B

BACKUP, 72, 222, 338
Batch files, 187
    branching and looping, 191
    conditional testing, 193
    preventing echo, 190
    simple, 187
    SWITCH, 189
    variables, 188
BDOS, 86
Boot record, 6
BREAK, 112, 340
    installation, 34, 40
BUFFERS, 90, 112
    installation, 34, 41

C

CALL, 196
CD, see CHDR
CGA display adapter, 44
CHAIN, 97, 102
CHCP, 342
CHDIR, 343
CHKDSK, 74, 228, 346
CLS, 348
    and CONFIG.SYS, 97, 103
Code pages, 318
    CHCP, 324
    COUNTRY.SYS, 323
    dead keys, 318
    DISPLAY.SYS, 134
    installation, 31, 44
    KEYB, 323
    listing, 322
    manual installation, 323
    MODE, 323, 324
    NLSFUNC, 324
    PRINTER.SYS, 147, 323
    SETUP, 319, 850, 319
    steps to access, 319
Color settings
    during installation, 42
COM devices, 57
COMMAND, 349
Command line, 21, 47
    editing, 48-51
Commands, 48
    help for, 77
COMP, 351
CON device, 57
CONFIG.SYS, 85, 95, 98, 227
COPY, 60, 71, 299, 353
Country
    installation of, 38
COUNTRY.SYS, 114, 323
CPOS, 97, 104
CTTY, 357
CURSOR, 96, 359

D

Data, 3
Data compression, 12, 221
DATE, 361
dBASE III, 175
DCONFIG.SYS, 227
DEBUG, 26
DEL, 62, 363
DELPURGE, 365
DELQ, 62, 367
DELWATCH, 368
    installation, 33, 36
DESQview, 20, 44, 157
DEVICE, 94, 116
Device drivers, 93
Devices, 57
DEVSWAP.SYS, 133, 224, 227
DIR, 58, 226, 371
Directories, 4, 11
    disks and, 54
    making, 54
    removing, 56
    renaming, 57
    special symbols, 56
    tree structure, 12, 55
Directory table, 6
Disk Operating System, 3
    MS-DOS, 4
    PC-DOS, 4
    saving old system, 46
DISKCOMP, 373
DISKCOPY, 71, 375
    image files, 376
DISKMAP, 377
    installation, 33
DiskMAX, 33
    installation, 35
DISKOPT, 228, 379
    options, 229
Disks, 5
    bootable, 6
    formatting, 69
    repairing, 74
DISPLAY.SYS, 134
DOS, 3
DOSBOOK, 2, 77, 381
DPMI, 18
DRDOS directory, 32
DRIVER.SYS, 136
DRIVPARM, 117

E

ECHO, 97, 105, 190, 196
EDITOR, 2, 88, 175, 187
    block moves, 181
    command reference, 507
    control key sequences, 175
    creating files, 176
    cursor control, 178
    deleting text, 180
    embedding special characters, 185
    online help, 177
    place markers, 184
    repeating last entry, 185
    saving files, 181
    starting, 176
EMM386.SYS, 86, 138
EMMXMA.SYS, 87, 142
Environment size, 90
    installation, 40
Epson FX 850 and 1050
ERA, see ERASE
ERAQ, 383
ERASE, 384
ERRORLEVEL, 193
EXE2BIN, 386
EXIT, 388
    and CONFIG.SYS, 98, 106
External command, 48

F

FASTBACK, 222
FASTOPEN, 92, 119, 389
    installation, 34
FC, 390
FCBS, 90, 120
    installation, 41
FDISK, 28, 393
File allocation table (FAT), 6
File system, 11
FILELINK, 2, 17, 291, 304
    configuring, 306
    file transfers, 308
    moving to another computer, 305
    relocating itself, 304
    remote directories, 307
    slave mode, 304
    transmission speed, 306
FILES, 121
    and TaskMAX, 162
    installation, 34, 41
Files, 11, 51, 90
    attributes, 60

INDEX

examining text, 64
executable, 52
finding, 58
invalid characters, 52
moving, 60
names and extensions, 52
printing, 67
renaming, 53
searching for text, 66
segmented, 228
undeleting, 230
wildcards, 52
Filters, 313
FIND, 66, 398
Floppy disks, 5
    configuring, 117, 136
    copying, 71
    formatting, 69
    precautions with, 7
    tracks, 6
    unformatting, 70
    write-protecting, 8
FOR, 198
FORMAT, 69, 400
    quick-format, 70

G

GEM, 243
GEM Write, 175
Glossary, 519
GOSUB
    and batch files, 192, 199
    and CONFIG.SYS, 98, 107
GOTO
    and batch files, 200
    and CONFIG.SYS, 98, 108
GRAFTABL, 96, 404
    installation, 44
Graphical User Interface, 22, 243
GRAPHICS, 96, 406
Graphics mode applications, 166

H

Hard disks, 5, 9
    advantages of, 9
    backing-up, 72
    cylinders, 29
    low-level format
    parking, 10
    partitions, 10, 28
    restoring, 73
    types, 10

HIBUFFERS, 122
HIDEVICE, 94, 123
HIDOS.SYS, 86, 125, 143
HIINSTALL, 126
HILOAD, 96, 408
HISTORY, 90, 127
    installation, 34

I

IBM 4201 and 4202
IBM 4207 and 4208
IBM Quietwriter III
IF, 191, 193, 200
INSTALL, 128
Installation, 25
    code pages, 31
    main options, 30
    program control keys, 27
Internal command, 48

J

JOIN, 96, 410

K

KEYB, 323, 412
Keyboard
    selecting country configuration, 38

L

LABEL, 415
LASTDRIVE, 90, 129
    installation, 34, 40
LOCK, 21, 417
Lost chains, 74
LPT devices, 57

M

Mace MUSE, 233
Macintosh, 243
MD see MKDIR
MEM, 74, 92, 95-96, 419
MEMMAX, 421
Memory, 17
    checking available, 74
    conventional, 85
    expanded, 18, 85
    extended, 18, 85
    high, 86
    lower, 85
    manager, 85

random access, 17
tips for conserving, 97
upper, 85
used with TaskMAX, 35, 158
XMA, 86
Memory manager, 85
MemoryMAX, 25
Microsoft Windows, 23, 44, 154, 157, 158, 160
MKDIR, 54, 423
MODE, 57, 425
    code pages, 323
    controlling parallel ports, 294
    controlling serial ports, 298
Monitor, 13
MORE, 437
MOUSE.SYS, 95
MOVE, 60, 439
MS-DOS, 4
    DOS SHELL, 21, 33
Multitasking, 157

N

Networks, 94
    Novell, 155
    PC/NFS, 88, 156, 223
NLSFUNC, 442
NUL device, 57

O

Online help, 77

P

Page frame, 86
Parallel ports, 13
    connectors, 293
    controlling with MODE, 294
    how they work, 291
    troubleshooting, 302
    wiring distances, 293
Parking, 10
Partitions, 10, 28
PASSWORD, 236, 238, 443
PATH, 48, 446
    installation, 39
PAUSE, 190, 203
PC, 18
PC-AT, 18
PC-DOS, 4
PC-Kwik, 13, 26, 209
    advanced parameters, 217
    and Microsoft Windows, 154, 210, 213

and TaskMAX, 220
Bernoulli drives
    configuration, 210
    disabling, 214
    expanded memory, 210
    extended memory, 210, 213
    installation, 33, 36
    parameters, 214
    run-time parameters, 216
PC-XT, 18
PCKWIN.SYS, 210
Piping, 311
PostScript, 68, 299, 300
PRINT, 67, 299, 448
Print spooler, 299
PRINTER.SYS, 147, 323
PROMPT, 451
Prompt, 47
    installation, 42
Protected mode, 18
PS/2, 86

Q

QEMM, 85, 151
Quick format, 70

R

RAMDRIVE.SYS, 95, 154
RD, see RMDIR
RECOVER, 454
Redirection, 189, 311
REM, 130, 204
REN, see RENAME
RENAME, 52, 456
RENDIR, 57, 458
REPLACE, 60, 459
RESTORE, 73, 461
RETURN
    and batch files, 205
    and CONFIG.SYS, 109
RMDIR, 56, 464

S

SCRIPT, 68, 300, 465
Security, 20
    directory, 236
    file, 238
    global password, 237, 240
    installation, 34, 45
    master password, 234
    PASSWORD, 236, 238

INDEX

removing, 241
screen lock, 240
system, 234
types, 233
user password, 234
Segmented files, 228
Serial ports, 13
    connectors, 297
    controlling with MODE, 298
    how they work, 295
    null modem, 303
    troubleshooting, 303
    wiring distances, 14
SET, 467
SETUP, 88, 469
SHARE, 92, 470
    installation, 34, 44
SHELL, 131
SHIFT, 206
SID, 26, 325
    command summary, 326
    starting, 325
SMARTDRV.SYS, 95, 154
SORT, 472
SSTOR, 224, 474
SSTORDRV.SYS, 148, 224, 227
SUBST, 475
SUPERPCK, 477
SuperStor, 12, 133
    and Microsoft Windows, 154, 222
    compressed drives, 227
    compression statistics, 227
    installation, 33, 223, 225
    installation considerations, 222, 224
    memory requirements, 26, 221
    partition, 28
SWITCH
    and batch files, 189, 208
    and CONFIG.SYS file, 98, 110
Syntax conventions, 24
SYS, 478
SYSEDIT, 88

T

Task switching, 19, 157
TaskMAX, 2, 18, 157, 479
    adding tasks, 165, 172
    and DISKOPT, 174
    and FILES, 162, 174
    and Microsoft Windows, 154, 160
    and SHARE, 44, 162
    changing swap directory, 172
    changing task names, 173

    checking status, 164
    configuration, 158, 174
    cut-and-paste, 166
    deleting tasks, 166, 173
    expanded memory, 161, 170-171
    extended memory, 161, 170
    hot keys, 160
    installation, 33-35
    running, 163
    sector editors, 174
    shift keys, 159
    switching tasks, 165
    temporary files, 174
Text mode applications, 166
TIME, 483
TIMEOUT, 98, 111
TOUCH, 485
Touch-Up, 244
TREE, 55, 487
TYPE, 64, 489

U

UNDELETE, 230, 490
    and DELWATCH, 230
    and DISKMAP
    options, 232
    unaided, 231
UNFORMAT, 70, 493
UNINSTAL, 494

V

VCPI, 18
VDISK.SYS, 95, 149
Ventura Publisher, 87, 162, 244
VERIFY, 496
    installation, 40
Video mode, 13
ViewMAX, 1, 22, 243
    active window, 248
    close box, 251
    command reference, 511
    desk accessories, 271
    dialog box, 254
    disk formatting, 267
    escaping to DR DOS, 284
    examining objects, 262
    file configuring, 273
    file copying, 258
    file deleting, 261
    file finding, 269
    file icons, 276
    file menu, 512

file viewing, 264
  folder, 248, 251
  GEM accessories, 273
  GEM applications, 283
  help menu, 516
  information menu, 516
  installation, 33, 37
  menu bar, 254
  mouse control, 245
  online help, 271
  options menu, 513
  preferences, 256
  resizing box, 251
  running, 246
  scroll bar, 249
  security, 265
  TaskMAX, 284
  title bar, 254
  tree window, 248, 252
  undeleting files and folders, 270
  using ViewMAX without a mouse, 516
  view menu, 514
  windows, 245
Virtual disks, 5, 10
VOL, 497

W

Wildcards, 52
WordStar, 175

X

XCOPY, 60, 71, 498
XDEL, 56, 62, 501
XDIR, 59, 65, 226, 503

M&T BOOKS

A Library of Technical References from M&T Books

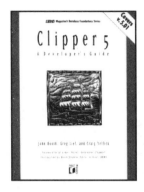

Clipper 5: A Developer's Guide
by Joseph D. Booth, Greg Lief, and Craig Yellick

An invaluable guide for all database programmers developing applications for Clipper® 5. Provides a quick introduction to Clipper 5 basics and discusses common programming needs such as designing data files, user interfaces, reports, and more. Advanced topics include networking, debugging, and pop-up programming. Code examples are used throughout the text, providing useful functions that can be applied immediately. All source code is available on disk in MS/PC-DOS format. 1300 pp. approx.

Book & Disk (MS-DOS)	Item #242-X	$44.95
Book only	Item #240-3	$34.95

DOS 5 User's Guide
A Comprehensive Guide for Every PC User
by Dan Gookin

Take control of the MS-DOS® operating system with this complete guide to using the world's most popular operating system. *DOS 5 User's Guide* contains clear, concise explanations of every feature, function, and command of DOS 5.0. Novice PC users will gain a quick start on using DOS, while advanced users will learn savvy tricks and techniques to maneuver their way quickly and easily through the system. Practical discussions and helpful examples teach readers how to edit text files, use directories, create batch files, and much more. Advanced topics include using EDLIN, the DOS text editor; configuring the system; and using the DOS shell. 771 pp.

Book only	Item #188-1	$24.95

1-800-533-4372 (in CA 1-800-356-2002)

M&T BOOKS

A Library of Technical References from M&T Books

**Internetworking
A Guide to Network Communications
LAN to LAN; LAN to WAN
by Mark A. Miller, P.E.**

This book addresses all aspects of LAN and WAN (wide-area network) integrations, detailing the hardware, software, and communication products available. In-depth discussions describe the functions, design, and performance of repeaters, bridges, routers, and gateways. Communication facilities such as leased lines, T-1 circuits and access to packed switched public data networks (PSPDNs) are compared, helping LAN managers decide which is most viable for their internetwork. Also examined are the X.25, TCP/IP, and XNS protocols, as well as the internetworking capabilities and interoperability constraints of the most popular networks, including NetWare, LAN Server, 3+Open™, VINES®, and AppleTalk. 425 pp.

Book only   **Item #143-1**   **$34.95**

**LAN Primer
An Introduction to Local Area Networks
by Greg Nunemacher**

A complete introduction to local area networks (LANs), this book is a must for anyone who needs to know basic LAN principles. It includes a complete overview of LANs, clearly defining what a LAN is, the functions of a LAN, and how LANs fit into the field of telecommunications. The author discusses the specifics of building a LAN, including the required hardware and software, an overview of the types of products available, deciding what products to purchase, and assembling the pieces into a working LAN system. *LAN Primer* also includes case studies that illustrate how LAN principles work. Particular focus is given to Ethernet and Token-Ring. 221 pp.

Book only   **Item #127-X**   **$24.95**

1-800-533-4372 (in CA 1-800-356-2002)

M&T BOOKS

A Library of Technical References from M&T Books

Delivering cc:Mail
Installing, Maintaining, and Troubleshooting a cc:Mail System
by Eric Arnum

Delivering cc:Mail teaches administrators how to install, troubleshoot, and maintain cc:Mail, one of the most popular E-mail applications for the PC. In-depth discussions and practical examples show administrators how to establish and maintain the program and database files; how to create and modify the bulletin boards, mail directory, and public mailing lists; and how to diagnose and repair potential problems. Information on using the management tools included with the package plus tips and techniques for creating efficient batch files are also included. All source code is available on disk in MS/PC-DOS format. 450 pp.

Book & Disk	Item #187-3	$39.95
Book only	Item #185-7	$29.95

The Complete Memory Manager
Every PC User's Guide to Faster, More Efficient Computing
by Phillip Robinson

Readers will learn why memory is important, how and when to install more, and how to wring the most out of their memory. Clear, concise instructions teach users how to manage their computer's memory to multiply its speed and ability to run programs simultaneously. Tips and techniques also show users how to conserve memory when working with popular software programs. 437 pp.

Book	Item #102-4	$24.95

1-800-533-4372 (in CA 1-800-356-2002)

M&T BOOKS
A Library of Technical References from M&T Books

Advanced Graphics Programming in C and C++
by Roger T. Stevens and Christopher D. Watkins

This book is for all C and C++ programmers who want to create impressive graphic designs on their IBM PCs or compatibles. Through in-depth discussions and numerous sample programs, readers will learn how to create advanced 3-D shapes, wireframe graphics, solid images, and more. All source code is available on disk in MS/PC-DOS format. Contains 16 pages of full-color graphics. 500 pp. approx.

Book/Disk (MS-DOS)	Item #173-3	$39.95
Book only	Item #171-7	$29.95

Graphics Programming with Microsoft C 6
by Mark Mallett

Written for all C programmers, this book explores graphics programming with Microsoft C 6.0, including full coverage of Microsoft C's built-in graphics libraries. Sample programs will help readers learn the techniques needed to create spectacular graphic designs, including 3-D figures, solid images, and more. All source code in the book is available on disk in MS/PC-DOS format. Includes 16 pages of full-color graphics. 500 pp. approx.

Book/Disk (MS-DOS)	Item #167-9	$39.95
Book only	Item #165-2	$29.95

The Verbum Book of PostScript Illustration
by Michael Gosney, Linnea Dayton, and Janet Ashford

This is the premier instruction book for designers, illustrators, and desktop publishers using Postscript. Each chapter highlights the talents of top illustrators who demonstrate the electronic artmaking process. The narrative keys readers in to the artist's conceptual vision, providing valuable insight into the creative thought processes that go into a real-world PostScript illustration project. 213 pp.

Book only	Item #089-3	$29.95

1-800-533-4372 (in CA 1-800-356-2002)

M&T BOOKS

A Library of Technical References from M&T Books

Advanced Fractal Programming in C
by Roger T. Stevens

Programmers who enjoyed our best-selling *Fractal Programming in C* can move on to the next level of fractal programming with this book. Included are how-to instructions for creating many different types of fractal curves, including source code. Contains 16 pages of full-color fractals. All the source code to generate the fractals is available on an optional disk in MS/PC-DOS format. 305 pp.

Book/Disk (MS-DOS)	Item #097-4	$39.95
Book only	Item #096-6	$29.95

Advanced Graphics Programming in Turbo Pascal
by Roger T. Stevens and Christopher D. Watkins

This new book is must reading for Turbo Pascal programmers who want to create impressive graphic designs on IBM PCs and compatibles. There are 32 pages of full-color graphic displays along with the source code to create these dramatic pictures. Complete explanations are provided on how to tailor the graphics to suit the programmer's needs. Covered are algorithms for creating complex 2-D shapes, including lines, circles and squares; how to create advanced 3-D shapes, wire-frame graphics, and solid images; numerous tips and techniques for varying pixel intensities to give the appearance of roundness to an object; and more. 540 pp.

Book/Disk (MS-DOS)	Item #132-6	$39.95
Book only	Item #131-8	$29.95

M&T BOOKS

A Library of Technical References from M&T Books

Using QuarkXPress 3.0
by Tim Meehan

Written in an enjoyable, easy-to-read style, this book addresses the needs of both beginning and intermediate users. It includes numerous illustrations and screen shots that guide readers through comprehensive explanations of QuarkXPress, its potential and real-world applications. *Using QuarkXPress* contains comprehensive explanations of the concepts, practices, and uses of QuarkXPress, with sample assignments of increasing complexity that give readers actual hands-on experience using the program. 340 pp.

Book/Disk	Item #129-6	$34.95
Book only	Item #128-8	$24.95

An OPEN LOOK at UNIX
A Developer's Guide to X
by John David Miller

This is the book that explores the look and feel of the OPEN LOOK graphical user interface, discussing its basic philosophy, environment, and user-interface elements. It includes a detailed summary of the X Window System, introduces readers to object-oriented programming, and shows how to develop commercial-grade X applications. Dozens of OPEN LOOK program examples are presented, along with nearly 13,000 lines of C code. All source code is available on disk in 1.2 MB UNIX cpio format. 482 pp.

Book/Disk	Item #058-3	$39.95
Book only	Item #057-5	$29.95

Turbo C++ by Example
by Alex Lane

Turbo C++ by Example includes numerous code examples that teach C programmers new to C++ how to program skillfully with Borland's powerful Turbo C++. Detailed are key features of Turbo C++ with code examples. Covers both Turbo Debugger and Tools 2.0 — a collection of tools used to design and debug Turbo C++ programs — and Turbo Profiler. All listings available on disk in MS/PC-DOS format. 423 pp.

Book/Disk (MS-DOS)	Item #141-5	$36.95
Book only	Item #123-7	$26.95

1-800-533-4372 (in CA 1-800-356-2002)

M&T BOOKS

ORDER FORM

To Order: Return this form with your payment to M&T books, 501 Galveston Drive, Redwood City, CA 94063 or **call toll-free 1-800-533-4372 (in California, call 1-800-356-2002).**

ITEM #	DESCRIPTION	DISK	PRICE

Subtotal

CA residents add sales tax ____%

Add $3.75 per item for shipping and handling

TOTAL

NOTE: **FREE SHIPPING** ON ORDERS OF THREE OR MORE BOOKS.

Charge my:
- ☐ **Visa**
- ☐ **MasterCard**
- ☐ **AmExpress**

- ☐ **Check enclosed, payable to M&T Books.**

CARD NO. _____

SIGNATURE _____ EXP. DATE _____

NAME _____

ADDRESS _____

CITY _____

STATE _____ ZIP _____

M&T GUARANTEE: If your are not satisfied with your order for any reason, return it to us within 25 days of receipt for a full refund. Note: Refunds on disks apply only when returned with book within guarantee period. Disks damaged in transit or defective will be promptly replaced, but cannot be exchanged for a disk from a different title.

1-800-533-4372 (in CA 1-800-356-2002)

 Digital Research ®

Get the Best Thing that Ever Happened to DOS for a Special Price

DR DOS ™ 6.0 ORDER FORM

YES, I've read all about DR DOS 6.0 and now I want it! Please rush me one copy of the full DR DOS 6.0 product, direct from Digital Research Inc., at the special discount price of $49*, that's a **$50 savings** off the $99 Suggested Retail Price.

I understand that DR DOS 6.0 is the most advanced, fully DOS-compatible operating system available and will help me get more out of my PC's processor, memory, and hard disk. I realize that I can return DR DOS 6.0 within 60 days of receipt for a full refund if I'm not completely satisfied. (Offer valid through June 30, 1992 - Includes Software User's Guide, and Quick Reference Guide)

DR DOS 6.0	$ 49
Shipping and handling	$ 9.95
Plus applicable sales tax in following states	$.
MA 5%, TX 7.75%, CA 7.75%, IL 6.25%, VT 5%	
Total enclosed:	

I prefer to pay as follows:

☐ Check or money order enclosed
☐ MasterCard   ☐ VISA   ☐ AmEx

Card No.:_____ Exp. Date:_____

Card Holder Name _____

Signature _____
(all orders must be signed)

Ship to: _____
Company Name: _____
Street:_____
City_____ State_____ Zip_____
Daytime Phone:_____ FAX _____

ORDER NOW! Complete this coupon and fax to: (408) 649-8209
Or send to: Digital Research • Box DRI • Monterey, CA 93942 • (408) 647-6675 *(orders are subject to acceptance)* ***plus shipping & handling***

Digital Research is a registered trademark, and the Digital Research logo and DR DOS are trademarks of Digital Research Inc. Copyright © 1991, Digital Research Inc.